D1490774

# LOWELL THOMAS,

14858

when he was a young man, worked in the Cripple Creek area of the West as a gold miner, as a range rider, and eventually as a reporter. On a hunch, he joined Lawrence of Arabia in 1917 in the Near East and was able to get motion pictures of the war against the Turks. This resulted in Mr. Thomas's first lecture tour, which was a stupendous success. Other tours followed, and in 1925 Mr. Thomas began his radio career in Pittsburgh. In 1930 he was chosen to replace Floyd Gibbons on a network daily news program. Since that time, broadcasting twice nightly five nights a week, Lowell Thomas has been heard by more people than any other man in history.

The recipient of many honorary degrees, Mr. Thomas is also a director of the Explorers Club and one of the discoverers and promoters of "Cinerama," as well as the author of innumerable articles and over forty books. He and his wife live in Pawling, New York.

WITHDRAWN
FROM LIBRARY

# HISTORY AS YOU HEARD IT

# HISTORY AS YOU HEARD IT

by

LOWELL THOMAS

Garden City, N. Y.

DOUBLEDAY & COMPANY, INC.

14858

909.82
T36h

LIBRARY OF CONGRESS CATALOG CARD NUMBER 57-5523
COPYRIGHT © 1957 BY LOWELL THOMAS
ALL RIGHTS RESERVED
PRINTED IN THE UNITED STATES OF AMERICA

8-1962

Don. by Mrs. John d. Stang

# FOREWORD

The year 1930 is not one that many people remember with pleasure. Few reputations were made in that year; it was a time when many things were ending and very few were beginning. And so it is a pleasure for me to remember that something important *did* begin in that year and that I had a hand in it.

To many it may seem incredible that as recently as 1930 there was only one daily network newscast. And it had been on the air for only seven months. But in that time it had brought further fame to a picturesque war correspondent named Floyd Gibbons. His popularity was no doubt enhanced by the fact that his program preceded Amos n' Andy, and also because he gave the impression of having developed a faster tempo as a talker than anyone who had faced the microphone up to then. His broadcasts were made over what, in this business, we call "another network." With his staccato, machine-gun delivery, he reeled off fifteen minutes of news each evening on behalf of *The Literary Digest*, and his public, as well as his sponsor, held him in high regard. His picture, with the famous eye patch, which was the badge of a wound he received while a correspondent during World War I, was familiar everywhere.

In the summer of that year came a bombshell: Floyd Gibbons would no longer be on the program. He and his sponsor had reached a parting of the ways. This appeared to leave the field open for our network, if we could only find a successor whom the sponsor would be willing to accept. Whereupon followed a contest between the "other network" and ourselves, with endless auditions. Columnists, personalities from the platform, war correspondents, and editors were given a tryout. None satisfied the *Digest* hierarchy, who had become accustomed to Floyd Gibbons and his skill as a fast talker. They had virtually decided to give up radio, when one of my associates had an inspiration. He said he knew just the man, a young American whom he had heard at Covent Garden Royal Opera House in London. And that was how I first learned about Lowell Thomas, who also had been a war correspondent in World War I and had been building up quite a world-wide reputation for himself on the platform with his exclusive eyewitness story of the Palestine campaign. He had been the only American to bring back an account of Allenby's capture of Jerusalem.

And he had also been the only observer with the Arabian army. As the so-called "discoverer" of Lawrence of Arabia, Walter Duranty, New York *Times* ace correspondent, later acclaimed him as having made the number-one scoop of World War I. Millions had heard him tell that story on the platform, and his book, *With Lawrence in Arabia,* had added to his fame.

Despite the fact that he had written other books and had an almost unique background as a speaker, I wondered whether he would fit into the new medium, whether he might be acceptable as a successor to Floyd Gibbons, where so many others had failed.

At any rate, we invited him to New York, and without telling him what the objective was, I persuaded him to face a microphone and "just talk about anything for fifteen minutes." This he did, while I concealed from him that a prospective sponsor was listening to his voice, piped from the studio to another part of the building.

The *Digest* editors for once showed enthusiasm. But they wanted another test. Would he come back a few nights later and talk about that day's news? They would listen to him at six o'clock and then a half hour later would listen to Floyd Gibbons, whose contract still had several weeks to run.

As to what happened next, I remember part of it, but Lowell himself tells the story as follows:

"Bill Paley saw what appeared to be a real chance to land *The Literary Digest* contract. He said to me, 'We must not fail. This tryout news broadcast must be a masterpiece. Columbia will loan you its best brains to prepare it!' This gave me quite a jolt. Here I had been involved in public speaking almost all my life, and also had been a newsman for some twenty years. I didn't quite understand how Columbia's 'best brains' could help me prepare a fifteen-minute talk. But I replied, 'Okay. If you are going to loan me your finest brains, why, I'll round up all the best brains I can think of and we'll really make it an event!'

"Three days later, here's what happened: I rented the penthouse at the Princeton Club in New York for an all-day session. Mr. Paley sent his 'best brains' and I brought mine. That is, I called up my publisher at Garden City, Long Island, and said, 'Mr. Doubleday, have you any brains out there?' When I explained, he told me that he would send in several of their 'brightest young men.' So when we sat down at the Princeton Club at 9 A.M. that morning to discuss how to prepare a radio news broadcast and what to include, our group was made up of the following geniuses and near geniuses: from CBS,

Jesse Butcher, director of public relations (which some months later became the first radio news department). Butcher was a veteran newsman from the New York *Times*. Also, Nick Dawson, whom I was told was able to do 'almost anything in radio.' He had been an actor, a circus man, and had many talents. And for his third man Mr. Paley sent Paul Kesten, one of their young executives, who later demonstrated so much ability that he became chairman of the Board of CBS. Doubleday loaned me George Elliman and a young manuscript reader who spent his spare time writing verses, for which he later became famous. His name, Ogden Nash.

"I also brought along Prosper Buranelli, who had been a star feature writer on the New York *World*, and an old personal friend who had managed several road companies of my Allenby-Lawrence show, and who likewise later became famous. His name, Dale Carnegie.

"This was in the Prohibition era, and knowing something about the habits of newspapermen, I brought a flagon of something that might refresh them from our farm in Dutchess County, a region famous for its apples. Nick Dawson and Dale Carnegie got into an argument as to how you should start a news broadcast. At the end of the day they still hadn't come to an agreement. Never was there a stormier debate than went around that penthouse table. We never did get down to the business of writing a script, except for a few paragraphs turned out by Ogden Nash.

"Late in the afternoon, seeing that we were getting nowhere, Prosper Buranelli and I quietly disappeared, the others not even missing us. We hurriedly put together some notes, and with these I went up to CBS and went on the air at six o'clock."

And that's the story of the beginning of the longest continuous run of any daily sponsored program in the history of radio. On September 29, 1930, there began an association between Lowell Thomas and radio that has lasted for twenty-six years. No wonder our CBS radio president, Arthur Hall Hayes, recently introduced him to a banquet audience as "Mr. Radio." For it is an unofficial title which no one can contest.

How many million words Lowell has poured into microphones since that time, no one could possibly say. But these broadcasts, beginning at a time of national depression and confusion, continuing through the eventual upsurge of recovery, entering and following through the momentous days during which World War II devastated and transformed the world, and continuing into our exciting present, will give the reader a fascinating panorama of changing times and history on the march.

We are looking forward to many more years of news broadcasts by Lowell Thomas, with the knowledge that at a future date they will make another vivid and kaleidoscopic book. At any rate, I have written this foreword in the hope that it may give you a little of the background of how I helped launch radio's most durable career.

WILLIAM S. PALEY

# CONTENTS

CHAPTER I — 1930                                                              1

This was an ominous year for the world in the full meaning of the word
—a year of omens, portents of terrible things to come. The broadcasts cover
only the last three months, and yet many of the great names of our time already appear in the news. Hitler apes Mussolini and threatens to seize power
and conquer Russia. Stalin collectivizes the land of the Soviet Union with an
iron hand and starts the purge trials which will end with the judicial murder
of his opponents. In Spain, criticism of the monarchy becomes louder and
talk of revolution increases. In India, Mahatma Gandhi shakes the British
Empire with his policy of non-violent resistance.

At home, the great issue is the depression, with a slumping stock market.
Franklin D. Roosevelt is re-elected governor of New York and begins to look
like possible presidential timber for 1932.

CHAPTER II — 1931                                                            5

The most important international event of this year is the beginning of full-
scale Japanese military action in Manchuria. China appeals to the League of
Nations—the first of the major challenges that the League is unable to handle
and that eventually destroy it. In Europe, tension increases. Alfonso XIII
abdicates the throne of Spain, and his opponents begin to jockey for position
in the race for power. Hitler's Nazis defy and disrupt the German Reichstag.
Stalin's massacre of the kulaks—peasants trying to avoid the collectivization
of the land—is stepped up.

At home, President Hoover declares a moratorium on Germany's World
War I debts. Jimmy Walker's conduct as mayor of New York comes under
fire, with demands for an investigation. The law finally catches up with Al
Capone—for not paying income taxes.

CHAPTER III — 1932                                                          17

The two biggest stories of the year are both American. Franklin D.
Roosevelt is elected President of the United States, the first of his four victories. The Lindbergh baby is kidnaped, the beginning of one of the most
tragic episodes in the history of crime.

The bonus army marches on Washington, to be dispersed by troops under
the command of General Douglas MacArthur—an incident his enemies will
never forget, not even when he becomes the hero of the Pacific war a decade
later. Jimmy Walker resigns as mayor of New York, preferring not to be exposed by his investigation.

Abroad, the Japanese complete their conquest of Manchuria by setting up

Henry Pu-yi as their puppet Emperor. Hitler polls eleven million votes in the German election. Stalin ousts his former allies, Kamenev and Zinoviev, and strengthens his position as dictator.

CHAPTER IV — 1933                                                        31

Hitler becomes Chancellor of Germany, stages the Reichstag fire, takes his Reich out of the League of Nations, and foments anti-Semitism in Germany and Nazi conspiracy in Austria. Japan also walks out of the League, which becomes more and more feeble as international animosities increase. The British Empire is flouted by Gandhi, who fasts and goes to jail, and by De Valera, who gets Southern Ireland's oath of allegiance to the Crown abolished. President Roosevelt recognizes the Soviet Union officially.

At home, President Roosevelt closes the banks temporarily to prevent financial panic, takes America off the gold standard, and receives from Congress the authority to establish the New Deal. Prohibition ends with a popular vote against the Eighteenth Amendment. La Guardia becomes mayor of New York.

CHAPTER V — 1934                                                         49

Hitler's power grows with giant steps. He has the leaders of the storm troopers executed in a savage purge and causes Chancellor Dollfuss of Austria to be murdered by local Nazis. He signs a ten-year non-aggression pact with Poland. He holds the first of his spectacular meetings with Mussolini. He insists that the Germans believe in themselves as a super-race. The names of his henchmen begin to have a sinister sound—Goering, Goebbels, Himmler. We will hear much more of them as time passes.

In Russia, mass murder follows the assassination of Stalin's lieutenant in Leningrad. In Spain, Red atrocities become common in many places. In France, the Stavisky scandal touches off a heated quarrel that threatens to disrupt the national life.

At home, President Roosevelt presses forward with his schemes for social reform. Drought scourges a wide belt in the Southwest. Bruno Richard Hauptmann is captured and accused of kidnaping the Lindbergh baby. Dillinger is shot down outside a movie house, following one of the biggest man hunts on record.

CHAPTER VI — 1935                                                        61

Mussolini starts the downfall of the League of Nations by invading Ethiopia in spite of its warnings. The world becomes more than ever split between the democracies and the Fascist powers. The Saar votes for union with Germany. Hitler attacks all religious bodies. In Russia, Stalin puts two old Bolsheviks and colleagues of Lenin, Kamenev and Zinoviev, on trial for their lives.

At home, the Supreme Court declares the NRA unconstitutional.

Hauptmann is sentenced to die for the Lindbergh kidnaping. Will Rogers and Wiley Post crash to their death in the Arctic waste. Huey Long is assassinated.

## CHAPTER VII — 1936        73

The Spanish Civil War erupts into an inferno of fire and steel, of violent battles, mass murder, and unspeakable atrocities. The rebels under Franco drive steadily forward, wreaking terrible revenge for the bloodstained orgies of the Communist-dominated Loyalists. Russia, too, sees more bloodshed —Stalin executing his opponents, including Kamenev and Zinoviev, after a repulsive mock trial in which the victims confessed everything, groveled, and begged for mercy. Hitler tears up the Versailles Treaty, remilitarizes Germany, and marches into the Rhineland. But he suffers humiliation in the Olympic Games when America wins mainly because of her Negro athletes, led by the great Jesse Owens. Mussolini continues his conquest of Ethiopia.

The news from abroad carries one of the great love stories of all time. Edward VIII abdicates the British throne in order to marry Mrs. Simpson, and the two are known from then on as the Duke and Duchess of Windsor.

At home, President Roosevelt wins an overwhelming victory in his campaign for re-election. Landon carries only Maine and Vermont out of the forty-eight states. Social security begins, but in New Deal circles there is much talk of curbing the Supreme Court because it has balked Roosevelt policies by declaring them unconstitutional. Bruno Richard Hauptmann is executed for the kidnap-death of the Lindbergh baby. Cardinal Pacelli visits the United States.

## CHAPTER VIII — 1937        87

The Spanish Civil War continues amid scenes of death and destruction. War in China flares up again. Japan seizes Shanghai and deliberately bombs the American gunboat *Panay*. Japan, Germany, and Italy sign the anti-Comintern Pact aimed at Russia. Meanwhile Stalin's fury is turned against his internal enemies—a holocaust of executions, including the leader of the Red Army, Marshal Tukhachevsky. A terrorist vendetta between Jews and Arabs breaks out in Palestine.

At home, controversy over the possible packing of the Supreme Court goes on. However, President Roosevelt raises a storm when he appoints Justice Black in the normal way, for the new Justice is criticized as a former member of the Ku Klux Klan. The greatest disaster on the American scene is the burning of the German dirigible Hindenburg at Lakehurst, New Jersey. The death of John D. Rockefeller removes one of the powerful labor barons of a previous era, the wizard who founded Standard Oil and made a legendary fortune out of it.

## CHAPTER IX — 1938 99

This is a year of colossal diplomatic victories for Hitler. He seizes Austria, demands the Czech Sudetenland, gives all of Europe a bad case of war jitters, and compels Chamberlain and Daladier to come to Munich and bow to his demands. Chamberlain returns to London, where, in one of the most ironic speeches in the history of European international relations, he declares that Britain and Germany will never go to war with one another again. But Winston Churchill criticizes the Munich agreement as a fearful defeat. Meanwhile, Anthony Eden has resigned from the Chamberlain Cabinet, claiming that the Prime Minister is endangering the democracies with his appeasement of Hitler and Mussolini.

In Russia, Stalin continues to claw to death the remnants of opposition to his monstrous tyranny. In Siberia his generals defeat the Japanese in undeclared warfare along the border of Manchuria. There is more fighting in China, more terrorism in Palestine.

At home, there is resentment among the oil companies whose holdings in Mexico have been seized by the Mexican Government. Richard Whitney, five times president of the New York Stock Exchange, goes to jail for misusing securities in his care.

## CHAPTER X — 1939 115

This is the year of war. Hitler's continuing aggressions leave Britain and France no alternative. He seizes all of Czechoslovakia. He demands the Polish Corridor and forces the Allies to guarantee the integrity of Poland. He signs an agreement with Stalin, crushes Poland in a lightning campaign featuring a co-ordination of tanks and planes that foreshadows gigantic battles to come, and divides the spoils with his partner in crime from Moscow. Britain and France declare war, but after the German conquest of Poland hostilities subside into the lull of the "phony war." Hitler opens his peace offensive. His opponents fail in their attempt to assassinate him at the Munich beer hall where the Nazi movement began.

Stalin attacks Finland, and the world is startled by the Finns' heroic defense of their soil. In Siberia, the Manchurian border fighting goes on. Violence in Palestine increases after the publication of the British White Paper, which satisfies neither Jews nor Arabs. In Spain, the Civil War finally ends, but its toll will shortly become pale in the shadow of World War II. In Rome, Cardinal Pacelli becomes Pope under the title of Pius XII.

At home, President Roosevelt signs the Neutrality Act but warns that we cannot remain indifferent to what is happening abroad.

## CHAPTER XI — 1940 131

The year's news is headed by the list of Hitler's victims—Denmark, Norway, Holland, Belgium, France—all knocked over like ninepins as the Nazi tyrant turns the "phony war" into total war. He occupies a ring of territory facing Britain along a tremendous arc from the Norwegian Arctic to the Pyrenees. But Britain, now led by Winston Churchill, fights back against the blitz from the sky and all-out submarine warfare. Most of the British Army on the continent is saved at Dunkirk, and Churchill pledges a fight to the end, whipping up the spirits of his countrymen with the most stirring eloquence of the war.

Meanwhile Mussolini joins Hitler and attacks Greece, only to be defeated. The Finnish war ends with the imposition of harsh Soviet terms. In Mexico, Stalin's old antagonist, Trotsky, is assassinated, apparently at the Red tyrant's orders.

At home, President Roosevelt smashes the old precedent by winning a third term over Wendell Willkie. He repeats that our troops will not go to war. But he puts an embargo on scrap iron for Japan and leases British bases. The first American boys are drafted for service in the armed forces. John L. Lewis resigns as head of the C.I.O. and is succeeded by Philip Murray.

## CHAPTER XII — 1941                                          159

Pearl Harbor. For Americans this is the event of the year—the Japanese striking savagely at our naval base in Hawaii even as their emissaries are talking peace in Washington. The troops of the Mikado hit strategic points throughout the western Pacific area. Wake, Guam, and Hong Kong quickly fall. Battles rage in the Philippines and in Malaya, where Singapore is the prize. General MacArthur commands our defense, but it is evident that he is pitifully undermanned.

The second greatest event of the year is the German-Russian war—Hitler turning ferociously on his partner, sending his armies hurtling into the Soviet Union. He wins titanic victories in the South and sweeps into the Ukraine. But the Russians fight back fiercely, scorch their earth, and hold both Moscow and Leningrad. The British help the Russians by pounding Hitler's Reich from the air. Resistance in the occupied territories grows, so does the execution of hostages. But the Germans have a strong foothold in the Mediterranean since their conquest of Greece and Crete while bailing Mussolini out. And their panzer divisions are already operating against the British in North Africa.

The strangest story of the year concerns Rudolf Hess, a prisoner of the British after hopefully flying to Scotland with a proposal for a common front against Russia.

At home, President Roosevelt signs the Lend-Lease Bill and the repeal of the Neutrality Act. In a dramatic meeting at sea he confers with Winston Churchill. All of this becomes of secondary importance when the bombs begin to fall on Pearl Harbor.

## CHAPTER XIII — 1942                                          187

This year is a complicated one, with a tangle of military events all around the world. The Japanese continue their rapid drive in the Pacific all the way from Burma to New Guinea. For the British, the saddest moment is the fall of Singapore; for Americans, the fall of the Philippines, after the heroic defense of Bataan and Corregidor, and the Bataan death march.

But our counteroffensive gets under way too. General Doolittle leads his planes in a bombing attack on Tokyo. Our Navy wins the battles of the Coral Sea and Midway Island. And our Marines begin the long road back when they land on Guadalcanal, where a hideous battle in the jungle quickly develops.

In Russia the Germans push their invasion onward into the death-trap of Stalingrad. In North Africa, Marshal Rommel becomes famous as the Desert Fox—until he is caught between the British under General Bernard Montgomery and the American landings under General Dwight D. Eisenhower. Most of North Africa is quickly seized, with Rommel pushed back into Tunisia.

Hitler retaliates by occupying all of France, but he loses the French fleet when it is deliberately scuttled by the crews. He faces more unrest among the captive peoples, especially in Yugoslavia, where General Mikhailovitch and his Chetniks are now waging a real war. All the while the British are smashing the Nazi homeland from the air. They are cheered by the arrival of the first American soldiers.

## Chapter XIV — 1943                                            217

The tide has turned irrevocably against the Rome-Berlin Axis. The Germans lose their Sixth Army at Stalingrad and begin a big-scale retreat in Russia. They are swept out of North Africa, Sicily is taken from them, the battle of Italy begins—and their Fascist partner collapses. Mussolini falls, and Italy surrenders.

The big political development of the year is the Teheran Conference—the first meeting of Roosevelt, Churchill, and Stalin. The second front in Europe is decided on; command of it goes to General Eisenhower.

But there are sinister signs of Soviet hostility. Moscow claims that the part of Poland occupied by the Russians in 1939 belongs to Russia. Stalin indicates that he intends to have a Communist Poland after the war.

In the Pacific there are more American victories—Bougainville, Tarawa, the Bismarck Sea, and others. The rollback of the Japanese line across the Pacific is gathering momentum.

## Chapter XV — 1944                                             243

Hitler's power begins to crumble, and there is a second unsuccessful attempt to assassinate him. General Eisenhower hurls his men into France, where they advance at breakneck speed—suffering only one real defeat, the Battle of the Bulge. Otherwise, it is a race to get to Germany first. General de Gaulle assumes political power in France.

At the same time the Russians are driving forward at the other end. Marshal Zhukov commands the center and batters his way into East Prussia as other Soviet armies begin to swamp the nations of Eastern Europe. In Italy the slow, dogged advance under General Clark continues.

In Greece the British return only to find a Communist rising on their hands. In Yugoslavia there is civil war between Mikhailovitch's Chetniks and Tito's Red partisans. Communist conspiracy begins to look uglier in the liberated nations.

In the Pacific it is a year of great and costly American victories—Eniwetok, Saipan, Guam. MacArthur keeps his promise and returns to the Philippines.

At home President Roosevelt wins a fourth term. Senator Harry Truman of Missouri is the new Vice-President. Former Vice-President Henry Wallace begins to demand a more pro-Soviet foreign policy.

CHAPTER XVI — 1945                                              279

This is a year of great events in quick succession. Germany and Japan both surrender unconditionally. Hitler commits suicide in his Berlin bunker as Marshal Zhukov's troops storm through the wreckage of the city. Mussolini is captured and executed by Italian Communists. MacArthur assumes control of Japan and begins a process of democratization.

President Roosevelt dies, and is succeeded by Vice-President Truman. In England, Winston Churchill suffers a staggering defeat in the elections. He is succeeded by Socialist Clement Attlee, who starts to nationalize British industry.

As the year ends, two great problems are formidable—one caused by science, the other by politics. The atom bomb has knocked Japan out of the war, but it also raises the fear of a new and more horrible kind of conflict. Men and women everywhere begin to be tormented by the question of whether this new destructive force can be controlled and harnessed for peace instead of war.

The political problem follows from the Yalta Conference between Roosevelt, Churchill, and Stalin. Roosevelt tells the country that peace and freedom have now been secured, but some critics question the wisdom of trusting Stalin, a feeling that will become general as he breaks his promises, foments civil war in China, imposes Communist tyranny on the nations of Eastern Europe, and shows the first signs of disrupting the new United Nations.

CHAPTER XVII — 1946                                             305

The war is over, but there isn't much peace. The Russians are stirring up trouble wherever they can, with their greatest success in China. In the United Nations they use the veto to hamstring the organization. They turn down the Baruch Plan for controlling atomic energy. In Moscow, Stalin unleashes a cultural purge against writers, artists, and scientists. In Fulton, Missouri, Churchill describes the dividing line between the Communist countries and the democracies as an "iron curtain"—a phrase that quickly becomes famous.

Violence breaks out in many places. India, as independence nears, sees Moslems fighting Hindus. In Yugoslavia, Tito executes Mikhailovitch, and claims Trieste. In Argentina, Colonel Perón seizes power. In Italy the house of Savoy falls before the new republic. In Palestine more terrorism as the Jews fight both the Arabs and the British.

At home President Truman ousts Henry Wallace as Secretary of Commerce for an unauthorized speech calling for a new pro-Soviet policy.

CHAPTER XVIII — 1947                                                  319

By now it is clear that Stalin doesn't want a settlement of the international situation. His henchmen—Vishinsky, Gromyko, Molotov—continue to use the veto at the U.N. and stymie every Big Four meeting on peace treaties for Germany and Austria. The Communist grip on Eastern Europe grows tighter. Stalin sets up a new Communist organ—the Cominform—to coordinate conspiracy throughout the world.

But the West answers with the Marshall Plan. And America states at the U.N. that our atomic bombs will not be destroyed.

The British withdraw from the subcontinent of Hindustan—leaving it to be partitioned between India and Pakistan. In Palestine, Jews and Arabs gird for war over the coming partition. There is fighting in Indonesia, Greece, Trieste. Britain plunges into austerity under the impact of the dollar crisis —cheered only by the gaiety surrounding the wedding of Princess Elizabeth and the Duke of Edinburgh.

At home Henry Wallace says he will head a third party in revolt against the anti-Communist policy of President Truman. Congress passes the Taft-Hartley law over the President's veto. John L. Lewis withdraws from the A.F. of L. Henry Ford dies—the genius who transformed daily life by means of the mass production of automobiles.

CHAPTER XIX — 1948                                                   335

For Americans, the story of the year is the election—President Truman winning in spite of the Dixiecrat revolt, the Wallace Progressive party movement, and the almost universal prediction of a Dewey victory by the pollsters.

Abroad the big story is the establishment of the Jewish state of Israel—the re-emergence of a people whose national life had been submerged for two millennia. The Jewish-Arab conflict develops into war.

In India, more violence, and the assassination of Gandhi. Communist conspiracy goes on. There is war in China and Indochina and Greece, a Red coup in Czechoslovakia, the arrest of Cardinal Mindszenty in Hungary. In Yugoslavia, Marshal Tito rebels successfully against Soviet domination—the first big split in the Communist ranks. In Germany, Stalin throws a blockade around Berlin, only to be beaten by the Allied airlift.

America is horrified by the revelation of Red espionage in Washington, with emphasis on the accusations against Alger Hiss. Scientists are amused and then outraged by the theories of Stalin's pet biologist, Lysenko.

At home there is mourning for the passing of three famous Americans— General Pershing, Charles Evans Hughes, and Babe Ruth.

CHAPTER XX — 1949                                              357

This is the year in which the balance of power between East and West becomes generally stabilized. China falls to the Communists and East Germany becomes a new Soviet satellite. But the North Atlantic Treaty Organization is formed to protect Europe, and the West German Federal Republic gains its independence. One hopeful sign is the widening split between Tito and the other Communist countries.

The tide turns against the Greek Reds, their rebellion is a failure. Peace comes to Indonesia and the Middle East.

At home Shostakovitch stars at the Waldorf "peace conference" of Reds and their dupes. Our top Communists are convicted of conspiracy. In Washington the "revolt of the Admirals" fails with the dismissal of Admiral Denfeld.

CHAPTER XXI — 1950                                              371

North Korean troops invade South Korea in the most brazen Communist aggression of the post-war period. At first successful, they drive all the way to the Pusan perimeter, only to be hurled back by MacArthur's Inchon landing. Then the Chinese Reds enter the fighting, helped by the fact that MacArthur is forbidden to attack their "Manchurian sanctuary." The result is stalemate roughly along the line of the 38th parallel.

For once the United Nations have been helped by Soviet tactics—the Security Council acting promptly to deal with the Korean crisis because the Russian delegate is boycotting it.

The new outbreak of fighting emphasizes President Truman's decision to push work on the hydrogen bomb. It also aids Senator McCarthy in his charges of Communist activity in America. The magnitude of Soviet espionage becomes clearer with the conviction of Alger Hiss.

Abroad, two old men pass from the scene where they have long been central figures—Jan Christiaan Smuts and George Bernard Shaw.

CHAPTER XXII — 1951                                             389

The most dramatic moment of the year is President Truman's dismissal of General MacArthur.

In Korea truce talks begin amid a barrage of abuse, accusations, and propaganda from the Communist side of the tent. In Hungary an anti-Semitic purge of the Communist party begins. In Iran, Premier Mossadegh nationalizes the Abadan oil refinery and starts his country down the road to bankruptcy. In the Suez Canal zone, anti-British rioting. In Britain two top diplomats suddenly disappear.

There are hopeful developments in Europe. The Schuman Plan for an international pool of coal and steel is established; Winston Churchill returns to power.

At home unpleasant things demand attention. The Rosenbergs are caught and convicted. A scandal involving influence peddlers and five-percenters breaks out in Washington. The televised crime investigations keep the public spellbound—and make Senator Kefauver of Tennessee a power in national politics.

CHAPTER XXIII — 1952                     411

General Eisenhower becomes President of the United States after a landslide victory over Adlai Stevenson.

In Korea the truce talks go on, the big problem being what to do with the prisoners who refuse to go back to Communism.

France begins to have trouble with the empire. Rebellion flares in North Africa. In Indochina, French troops are forced to retreat before the Communist hordes.

In the Suez Canal zone there is anti-British rioting. King Farouk falls after a violent outburst in Cairo, and is replaced by a military junta. In South Africa new segregation laws cause unrest among the colored people of the Cape.

The year sees four important deaths: King George VI of Britain (who is succeeded by his daughter, Elizabeth II); William Green, long-time head of the A.F. of L.; Chaim Weizmann, first President of Israel; and Eva Perón, wife of the Argentine dictator and one of the world's most scintillating and powerful women.

CHAPTER XXIV — 1953                     433

This year is memorable for the disappearance of one of the most repulsive tyrants of all time—Joseph Stalin. His death touches off a brutal struggle for power inside the Kremlin, and Beria loses out to Malenkov. Beria's execution is followed by a purge of his henchmen throughout the Communist apparatus.

In Korea the exchange of prisoners gets under way, and America is shocked when twenty-three brain-washed G.I.s decide to stay with Communism. In Iran, Mossadegh falls in time for Iran to avoid bankruptcy. Trouble continues in Indochina, in the Suez Canal zone, and in Kenya, where the Mau Maus are becoming a deadly menace. In East Germany there is rioting against Communist control.

At home President Eisenhower signs the tidelands oil bill. The Communist issue is still important, with the Rosenbergs executed, the late Harry Dexter White accused, and Fort Monmouth under investigation. The death of Senator Taft removes the man who for years has been known as "Mr. Republican."

The pleasantest story of the year comes from Britain, where young Queen Elizabeth is solemnly crowned with all the pomp and ceremony of age-old tradition. Across the world Hillary and Tensing reach the top of Mount Everest just in time to present their achievement to the Queen as a coronation gift.

CHAPTER XXV — 1954                                    451

Another television extravaganza for Americans—the army-McCarthy hearings, when we hear about Private Schine and the favors that Roy Cohn tried to get for him. Later come the censure of McCarthy by the Senate and the senator's attack on President Eisenhower for expressing approval of it.

Abroad, West Germany gets the right to rearm. Disputes end in Trieste and the Suez Canal zone. A crypto-Communist regime is overthrown in Guatemala.

Against this is the tragic name of Dienbienphu in Indochina, where the French are overwhelmed by the Reds. In Paris, Mendes-France becomes Premier, and arranges a truce.

Two unusual stories come from Britain. Roger Bannister wins the four-minute mile. And a Roman sanctuary to the sun god Mithras is discovered.

CHAPTER XXVI — 1955                                    471

Khrushchev and Bulganin take over from Malenkov before the year is five weeks old. The Soviet "new look" startles the world, with apparent amiability replacing the old Stalinist scowl. The new Soviet leaders attract attention —first at the Big Four Geneva meeting, and then when they go to Yugoslavia to apologize to Tito.

There is trouble in Goa, Cyprus, North Africa, Indochina. There is a threat of war over the islands in the Formosa Strait. The nations of Asia and Africa meet at Bandung to discuss their problems. In Britain, Churchill retires. In Argentina, Perón falls. Austria becomes free.

At home the main concern is for President Eisenhower, who suffers a heart attack that leaves his political future in doubt. The nation is divided by controversy over the Dixon-Yates contract and the publication of the Yalta documents. Ford approves a guaranteed wage for its employees, and starts a trend. The Salk polio vaccine proves effective. President Eisenhower announces that we intend to put a man-made moon into the sky. Albert Einstein dies—the greatest mathematical physicist of his time.

# HISTORY AS YOU HEARD IT

# 1930

---

*This was an ominous year for the world in the full meaning of the word—a year of omens, portents of terrible things to come. The broadcasts cover only the last three months, and yet many of the great names of our time already appear in the news. Hitler apes Mussolini and threatens to seize power and conquer Russia. Stalin collectivizes the land of the Soviet Union with an iron hand and starts the purge trials which will end with the judicial murder of his opponents. In Spain, criticism of the monarchy becomes louder and talk of revolution increases. In India, Mahatma Gandhi shakes the British Empire with his policy of non-violent resistance.*

*At home, the great issue is the depression, with a slumping stock market. Franklin D. Roosevelt is re-elected governor of New York and begins to look like possible presidential timber for 1932.*

---

*September 29, 1930*—Adolf Hitler, the German Fascist chief, is snorting fire. There are now two Mussolinis in the world, which seems to promise a rousing time. Adolf has written a book called the German Fascist Bible. In it this belligerent gentleman states that a cardinal policy of his now powerful German party is the conquest of Russia. That's a tall assignment, Adolf. You just ask Napoleon.

*September 30, 1930*—Roosevelt has been nominated. I suppose you all know that by now.

Al Smith and Franklin Roosevelt are the Alphonse and Gaston of modern politics. Franklin Roosevelt twice nominated Al for the presidency, and today the tables were turned when Al nominated Roosevelt for governor of New York for a second term.

Was Al Smith's speech wet? I'll say it was!

*October 1, 1930*—In London the British Imperial Conference opened today. It is expected to have a large bearing on the future of the British Empire. Is the British Empire gradually and quietly breaking up?

Detroit says that twenty-one of the city's millionaires—including Ford, Chrysler, and Fisher—have agreed on a program to create twenty-five thousand new jobs for the unemployed out there.

*October 3, 1930*—The President is back in Washington. His address yesterday in Cleveland, as you know, dealt largely with present business conditions, and Mr. Hoover denounced any idea of reduction of American standards of living.

*October 8, 1930*—In London, where the Imperial Conference is being held, the British Dominions have said "no" to the proposal of Empire Free Trade.

Canada and South Africa led the opposition. Old John Bull doesn't seem able to order his children around any more.

*October 9, 1930*—A bad day in the stock market. This is the first time that all important industrial shares have fallen below the level of the panic of last November.

*October 13, 1930*—One hundred and seven followers of Adolf Hitler, the Fascist leader, the man who would imitate Mussolini, took their seats in the Reichstag. They defied a parliamentary rule by coming in full Fascist uniform—black military boots, brown shirts and trousers.

*October 17, 1930*—The Democrats are getting more and more optimistic about their chances in the approaching election. The New York *Evening Post* is an independent Republican paper, but it admits there is unusual pessimism in Republican quarters.

*October 20, 1930*—Half the headlines in today's papers concern politics. That's natural, for Election Day is only two weeks off.

In Pennsylvania, says the New York *Evening World*, the dry issue is cutting through both parties.

*October 21, 1930*—The Jews in England and America are up in arms today, protesting bitterly against the statement of policy issued yesterday by the British Government. Prime Minister MacDonald gave out word that Palestine was to remain the Jewish homeland but that no more Jews were to move there for the present because the country could not absorb any more population.

*October 23, 1930*—The President of China has become a Christian. General Chiang Kai-shek is the strong man of China, the war lord. And now he has been baptized a Methodist.

*October 24, 1930*—About that important event when the President of China was baptized a Christian. The Shanghai correspondent of the New York *Times* points out that the wife of President Chiang Kai-shek was educated in America and is a Christian, and that she married Chiang in a semi-Christian ceremony.

*October 25, 1930*—President Hoover has authorized the Post Office Department to take on two hundred thousand additional postal employees for the two weeks before Christmas.

*October 31, 1930*—The best-known traveling salesman in the world is going on the road again. I mean that popular young man, the Prince of Wales, who sets forth periodically to peddle British good will. He is planning a trip to Latin America in a month or two.

*November 5, 1930*—The Nobel Prize for Literature this year has come drifting across the Atlantic. It has been awarded to Sinclair Lewis, author of *Main Street* and *Babbitt.*

*November 7, 1930*—This is Soviet Russia's thirteenth birthday. Many thought the Soviet Government wouldn't last so very long. But it's still there and they are celebrating their thirteenth birthday in a big way.

Stalin and other Communist moguls reviewed the parade in Red Square before the walls of the Kremlin.

Governor Roosevelt of New York issued a statement this afternoon denying that he is in any way interested in a Roosevelt-for-President boom.

*November 11, 1930*—A sensational report comes from Russia. The Soviet Government has let out a roar about a gigantic international plot to overthrow the Bolsheviks. Eight prominent Russian professors and engineers have been arrested as ringleaders. Curiously enough, the mysterious Lawrence of Arabia is dragged in. The Bolsheviks say that Lawrence has a prominent part in the plot.

*November 14, 1930*—The Bolsheviks are fighting peasants who don't want their land collectivized; that is, they don't want it taken over by the government. The Reds are seizing the peasants' crops.

*November 17, 1930*—Uncle Sam's regulars are going to have a new chief. The Army, I mean. Major General Douglas MacArthur. That's his name. Yes, and he is going to be the youngest Chief of Staff that our Army has had since the World War.

*November 20, 1930*—Out in India there's a man in jail, a little brown man who wears a loincloth. They call him Mahatma Gandhi. He's the leader of India's resistance to British rule.

*November 26, 1930*—In a Moscow courtroom today a man read what was virtually his own sentence of death. He is Professor Ramzin, one of those eight engineers and professors who are on trial for their lives before a Bolshevik judge.

He made a full confession charging that he and his companions had conspired with French and British high officials to overthrow the Soviet Government.

*November 27, 1930*—The reporters at that dramatic trial over in Moscow are describing the setting in the courtroom as being like a Russian film tragedy. Six of the eight professors who have testified all told the same story, how they were secretly working against the Bolsheviks.

*December 2, 1930*—The big news is President Hoover's message to Congress.

The President discussed the economic situation of the country and declared there was no cause for pessimism. I'm sure we are all glad to hear that.

*December 8, 1930*—That weird trial over in Moscow has come to an end. Of the eight professors and engineers on trial, five were sentenced to death and three were ordered to prison. Then came a flash saying that the death sentences have been commuted to imprisonment.

*December 12, 1930*—It looks as though a revolution of major proportions has broken out in Spain.

The Democrats rose in their wrath over the President's suggestion that Congress was playing politics with human misery. Then the Republican insurgents trained their guns on the White House too.

*December 15, 1930*—Over in Spain martial law was declared late this afternoon. Revolution seems to be springing up everywhere.

The revolt is said to be directed against the King. The rebels are demanding a republic.

*December 17, 1930*—Today's Einstein note is about a meeting of an American Legion post out in California. A motion was introduced declaring that the famous German scientist should not be permitted in California. What they don't like is his pacifism—the way he says that there shouldn't be any more preparation for war.

*December 22, 1930*—President Hoover won his unemployment relief fight. The bills he proposed for spending money to provide jobs for the jobless passed both Houses.

*December 31, 1930*—The widow of Lenin, the founder of Bolshevism in Russia, has withdrawn from all political activity. She doesn't like the way Stalin threw out the moderate Communist leader Rykov.

# 1931

The most important international event of this year is the beginning of full-scale Japanese military action in Manchuria. China appeals to the League of Nations—the first of the major challenges that the League is unable to handle and that eventually destroy it. In Europe, tension increases. Alfonso XIII abdicates the throne of Spain, and his opponents begin to jockey for position in the race for power. Hitler's Nazis defy and disrupt the German Reichstag. Stalin's massacre of the kulaks—peasants trying to avoid the collectivization of the land—is stepped up.

At home, President Hoover declares a moratorium on Germany's World War I debts. Jimmy Walker's conduct as mayor of New York comes under fire, with demands for an investigation. The law finally catches up with Al Capone—for not paying income taxes.

January 2, 1931—The old stock market must have made a good New Year's resolution.

When trading began this morning, after the holiday, prices rose steadily, which is the way we hope the market will keep going all through the new year.

January 3, 1931—France is in mourning. For Marshal Joffre is dead.
There will be a solemn funeral, and after that the hero of the Marne will pass into history.

January 5, 1931—The House of Representatives passed a bill today authorizing the President to distribute forty-five million dollars to the farmers for drought relief.

January 7, 1931—Well, the new year may have marked the turning point. The year 1931 is just a week old today, and sixty thousand of the jobless have already gone back to work.

There seem to be many people who think this country ought to adopt a scheme of unemployment insurance.

*January 10, 1931*—The Eastern Air Transport Line has gone in for this latest gadget of aviation—the flying hostess. Five snappy girls are already on duty, flying in the big planes between New York and Washington.

*January 13, 1931*—The British Government is offering a kind of dominion status to India which would put India practically on the same footing as Canada and Australia and the other British dominions.

*January 15, 1931*—President Hoover tonight signed the drought-relief bill.

*January 17, 1931*—From Washington there comes a blast against the Communists. The Hamilton Fish Committee claims that the Communist party over here is trying to foment Red revolution and that it is just a tool of the Bolsheviks in Moscow.

*January 22, 1931*—It is reported out in India that the British Government will soon declare a general amnesty for political prisoners. Fifty thousand people are in jail in India as a result of the non-violent rebellion which Gandhi started. The most important prisoner of all, of course, is Mahatma Gandhi himself.

*January 23, 1931*—Here comes the old story—Germany doesn't want to pay that huge reparations bill.

One of the biggest steel mills in the world is being built near Magnet Mountain in remote Siberia.

The work is being done under the direction of American engineers.

*January 24, 1931*—Word from Russia tells of another big move to end private ownership of land over there. A statement signed by Stalin, the Red dictator, announces the beginning of what it calls a decisive final drive to eliminate the kulaks. The kulaks are the well-to-do peasants who cling to their land.

The idea is to force private owners to the wall.

*January 26, 1931*—Well, I see where the American Legion has come out with an official declaration about the cash payment of the bonuses.

Thousands of ex-servicemen who have payments coming from the government during the next few years want the money put on the line right away.

A little brown man in a loincloth was released today from prison at

Poona out in India. With him may rest the future of the British Empire, Mahatma Gandhi, leader of the Nationalist movement in India.

Papers everywhere are carrying a story today about thirteen thousand men from various countries getting jobs in Russia. They are engineers and technicians.

And a large percentage of them will be Americans. A still larger percentage will be Germans.

*January 27, 1931*—The new French Government was sworn in today. The new Premier is Senator Laval.

*February 5, 1931*—Stalin, the Red dictator, made a threatening speech.

"Let us fan the flames of world revolution," he shouted, "and we will overturn the whole world!"

*February 7, 1931*—President Hoover has accepted the compromise offered by the leaders in Congress.

He has okayed an addition of twenty million dollars to be added to the twenty-five million already appropriated for drought relief.

The farmers in the Middle West and Southwest have been just about desperate because of the lack of moisture. But today the floodgates of the heavens opened and down came a good, hard, soaking rain.

*February 9, 1931*—The newest decree of the Soviet Government is that hundreds of thousands of women are to be put to work in factories. Their children will be placed in the care of government nurses.

*February 10, 1931*—Early in the day's session all the Nazi deputies walked out and seceded from the Reichstag. Hitler's men raised their arms in a Fascist salute.

*February 11, 1931*—I doubt whether there's any problem which is being argued so widely and sharply at present as the soldiers' bonus.

Secretary of the Treasury Mellon is against the idea of immediately paying the money still due the soldiers.

*February 16, 1931*—The soldiers' Bonus Bill has passed the House of Representatives.

It looks this evening as if King Alfonso over in Spain may lose his crown.

*February 17, 1931*—King Alfonso declared he would step down from his throne and leave Spain if he thought it for the good of the country.

Lord Irwin, Viceroy of India and Mahatma Gandhi, the emaciated saint, talked for four hours.

When Gandhi emerged from the conference he had a smile on his thin, careworn face. "I am satisfied, even optimistic!" he exclaimed.

Winston Churchill, one of the leading figures in the Conservative party, has broken with his colleagues—over the question of India. He's playing a lone hand now, and that gives him a bit of leisure. So he's going to use that leisure for a favorite amusement of English notables—coming to America for a lecture tour.

*February 18, 1931*—A cabinet government has been formed in Spain. But it doesn't consist of the liberal elements whose support King Alfonso wanted to gain.

The King finally had to fall back on his loyal friends, the Conservatives.

*February 19, 1931*—Professor Hermann Oberth believes he can construct a rocket that will fly from Vienna to New York in twenty minutes!

The Bonus Bill has passed the Senate.

There has been rain all over the country, and that's a mighty good thing. It looks as if that drought might be over.

*February 20, 1931*—Gandhi, in his conversations with Lord Irwin, demanded that Great Britain forget about that Round Table Conference which met in London a few weeks ago. He wants the British Government to make terms directly with him and with his Indian Nationalist party.

*February 21, 1931*—King Alfonso has definitely staked his crown on the issue of the coming elections in Spain.

*February 25, 1931*—A big scene was put on today in a courtroom out in Chicago. Al Capone, the big shot of big shots, was taken under arrest before a Federal judge to answer a charge of contempt of court.

Scarface Al was guarded by three squads of picked Chicago detectives, a sort of royal escort—and crowds gathered to get a look at him.

*February 26, 1931*—The House of Representatives has just passed the Bonus Bill over President Hoover's veto.

*February 27, 1931*—The Bonus Bill is a part of the law of the land. The Senate passed it today over President Hoover's veto.

*March 4, 1931*—Mahatma Gandhi, the Indian Nationalist leader, and

Lord Irwin, the British Viceroy, signed an agreement which puts an end to the rebellion in India.

And thus comes to a close that strange campaign of non-violent revolt and civil disobedience.

*March 6, 1931*—In an interview today Gandhi told a group of newspapermen that he expected to accomplish the complete independence of India. But that, he explained, doesn't mean separation from the British Empire. He wants India to remain within the British Commonwealth of Nations as an equal partner.

*March 7, 1931*—Five bishops of the Catholic Church in Germany have come out with a statement forbidding Catholics to belong to Hitler's fire-eating Fascist organization. The bishops say that Hitler is teaching a doctrine of hatred which is unchristian.

*March 11, 1931*—All the New York newspapers this afternoon carried headlines about the big attack that is being made on Mayor Walker. Various civic organizations and religious bodies demand that the mayor's administration be investigated. Some think he ought to be removed.

*March 13, 1931*—And now comes what is said to be the first successful scientific experiment with a rocket. A German named Poggensee got up a contraption containing photographic apparatus which is shot into the air.

The rocket went sailing to a height of fifteen hundred feet and snapped its pictures.

*March 18, 1931*—Governor Roosevelt made public the charges that have been filed with him by the City Affairs Committee of New York.

Mayor Walker's conduct, says the complaint, has been incompetent, inefficient, and futile—and has brought the city into disrepute.

*March 27, 1931*—The most popular clown in the world today received the Legion of Honor in Paris. I mean Charlie Chaplin, of course.

*March 28, 1931*—The Indian Nationalist Congress voted to support Mahatma Gandhi and his plan for making peace with the British authorities.

*April 9, 1931*—The official Communist newspaper, *Pravda*, charges that President Hoover was one of the plotters who formed the supposed big international conspiracy against the Soviet Government.

*April 13, 1931*—The elections in Spain went heavily against the King.

*April 14, 1931*—King Alfonso XIII signed his name to a document which brings to an end the old and historic monarchy. The Republicans threatened to start a revolution right away. Then the King offered to abdicate in favor of his son, the Crown Prince. Again the Republicans said "no." Then finally Alfonso had to choose between renunciation of the throne and violent revolution.

*April 22, 1931*—Uncle Sam has recognized the new Republic of Spain.

*April 27, 1931*—Over in Palestine they are trying to negotiate a settlement of the long-standing dispute between the Zionists and the Arabs. The Arab Executive Commission has been invited to talk the situation over with Sir John Chancellor, British High Commissioner in the Holy Land.
The Arabs have refused.

*April 28, 1931*—Governor Roosevelt has dismissed the charges against Mayor Walker.
He issued a statement that he found no sufficient justification for removing the mayor from office.

A traveling salesman is supposed to bring home orders, and they say that H.R.H. the Prince of Wales has done just that. He has brought back from South America orders to the tune of about fifty million dollars.

*May 2, 1931*—The government at Washington has not changed its attitude on the subject of foreign debts. President Hoover's administration has made it clear that foreign countries that owe the United States money will be expected to pay.

*May 11, 1931*—All day in Madrid mobs rioted in the streets. Their anger was turned principally against churches and religious institutions.

*May 12, 1931*—Conditions in Madrid this afternoon were back to normal, or nearly so. But while the government was restoring order in the capital, the anti-clerical wave swept to other cities.
An immense treasure in the form of works of art has been destroyed in blazing churches and in bonfires built by the radical mobs in the streets.

*May 13, 1931*—The government has suppressed the disorders in Madrid and in some of the other large cities with a strong hand. But there was more ugly mob fighting today.

*May 15, 1931*—Toscanini was struck by an angry Fascist.

The maestro was to conduct a concert at Bologna. A delegation of Fascists asked him to play the Fascist anthem, "Giovinezza."

Toscanini refused.

The argument there in Bologna waxed hot and furious, and finally one of the Fascists struck the maestro. Local Fascist officials called upon him and ordered him to leave town.

Today a papal encyclical, or at least a summary of one, was announced to the world over the radio.

"It is therefore absolutely necessary," declared Pope Pius, "to reconstruct the whole economic structure to bring it back to the requirements of social justice."

*May 23, 1931*—All of Spain is getting ready for general elections.

*May 26, 1931*—President Chiang Kai-shek, head of the Nationalist government, states that the discontented elements of southern China are Communists. He declares that he has been compelled to choose between communism and war, which means that he will choose war.

*June 8, 1931*—They say that the Fascist government is willing to put the O.K. on Catholic societies in Italy so long as these societies are run locally by the parish priests and the bishops, and not by leaders whom the Fascists might consider as being mixed up in politics.

*June 20, 1931*—President Hoover has declared that the United States Government intends to do something to help Germany in her present economic plight. He proposes a one-year suspension of both payments on reparations and payments on war debts—a one-year breathing spell for everybody.

*June 29, 1931*—The results of the Spanish elections are what everybody expected. Monarchist supporters of ex-King Alfonso were decisively beaten by the Republicans.

*June 30, 1931*—The Italian Government announced today that it intends to put the Hoover Plan into effect at once.

So far as reparations go, the Italian Government will not ask Germany to make the payments which are due this year. Fritz will not have to shell out one pfennig to the Duce.

*July 6, 1931*—President Hoover has just given out word that an agreement has finally been reached between the United States and France on the subject of the Hoover Plan. Germany will be required to pay some money to France. But this money will be immediately loaned right back to Germany.

Stalin declares the Soviets will have to get away from the idea of paying a man according to what he needs instead of what he earns. And he wants to inaugurate a new system of paying skilled workers more than common labor.

*August 1, 1931*—A Red radical blast echoes booming as George Bernard Shaw and Lady Astor come tripping gaily out of Russia after their visit to the land of the Soviets.

The white-bearded Irish dramatist says he is redder now than ever, that he was a Communist before Lenin.

Lady Astor delivered herself of the opinion that Russia is the best-run country in the world.

*August 20, 1931*—Stalin, in a remarkable speech, declared that the present economic crisis is no time for nations to display petty envy and stupid rivalry. He believes that the interests of the workingmen all over the world are vitally involved, and he declares that Soviet Russia is willing to co-operate with the capitalistic governments in any honest way.

*August 28, 1931*—In New York, Governor Franklin D. Roosevelt handed the legislature a proposal to raise twenty million dollars for unemployment relief. He wants to use the money to finance public works, which would provide employment for from six hundred thousand to a million workers.

*August 29, 1931*—Gandhi has sailed, amid a scene of wild demonstrations, on his way to London to attend the conference which it is hoped will definitely decide the fate of India.

*August 31, 1931*—The Vatican and the Fascist government have effected a compromise, according to which Mussolini withdraws his opposition to Catholic clubs and the Pope guarantees that these organizations will keep strictly off the subject of politics.

*September 3, 1931*—We hear a swan song tonight. Yes, it's a swan song of the *Anschluss*. Both Austria and Germany announce the abandonment of the proposed customs union between Germany and Austria.

*September 12, 1931*—It seems to be a game of hide-and-seek over in London—that is, the crowds are doing the seeking and Mahatma Gandhi is doing the hiding.

*September 15, 1931*—Gandhi made his plea today. He spoke soft pleading words. "If I want freedom for India," he declared, "it is for India as a valued partner of Great Britain, not held by force, but by the silken cord of love."

However, the Mahatma is not such a visionary but that he knows what it's all about. Speaking of the freedom of India, he said to the British, "It might be of considerable interest to you in balancing your budget."

*September 19, 1931*—Tonight the Army of Japan is in strategic control of all of southern Manchuria. The Japanese have seized every point of military importance. The Mikado's troops have even invaded the Chinese province of Shantung.

The most spectacular incident in the sudden flare-up was the capture of Mukden, the capital of Manchuria. There was a savage battle before the city was captured and before the Chinese garrison was disarmed.

The immediate cause for the demonstration of military power by Japan was the cutting of the Manchurian railroad. Part of the line was raided and destroyed by the Chinese. Japan is in control of the Manchurian railroad and is required to protect it.

The Chinese, on their part, claim that the cutting of the Manchurian railroad is just an excuse.

*September 23, 1931*—Today was "Humiliation Day" in China. All over the country the Chinese staged ceremonies to protest against the way the Japanese have acted. Mass meetings were held and the Chinese people were urged not to buy any Japanese goods.

*September 24, 1931*—At Geneva today China presented to the League of Nations a complete acceptance of the League's proposal that both China and Japan put a stop to the use of military force in that quarrel about Manchuria. The Chinese want the League to arbitrate the dispute.

*September 30, 1931*—An independence movement is under way in that northern province where the Chinese and Japanese have been fighting. The idea is to make Manchuria a country all by itself.

The Chinese claim that this Manchurian demand for independence has been inspired and instigated by Japan. They say that the Japanese have cooked up the whole agitation simply as a means for getting Manchuria under their own control.

*October 5, 1931*—The broad Pacific has been flown at last. And that fact is a great milestone in the history of aviation. Hugh Herndon and Clyde Pangborn did it.

*October 10, 1931*—Well, at last the United States Army prefers monoplanes. The War Department has just issued nearly two million dollars' worth of contracts for new airplane equipment. And nearly all of the money is to be spent for new military monoplanes.

Uncle Sam for a long time remained faithful to the old biplane type.

*October 16, 1931*—For the first time a Chinese Army commander has been ordered to resist the Japanese. Heretofore, while there has been ugly fighting, the Chinese military forces have made no organized resistance. They have retreated and evacuated sections of Manchuria in the face of the advancing Japanese regiments.

*October 19, 1931*—The jury found Capone guilty of income tax violations, and the big shot is liable to get anything up to seventeen years in prison and fifty thousand dollars by way of fine.

There seems to be something inevitable and tranquil about the passing of the world's greatest inventor. Edison himself felt that way. He told his family gathered at his bedside that his work was done. He had completed what he had been called upon to do. He couldn't do anything more. And so he was well content to go.

Yes, the almost legendary Edison died in a great fullness of years and renown.

*October 20, 1931*—Well, Major Jimmy Doolittle made another amazing flight tonight. He flew from Ottawa, Canada, to Mexico City in twelve hours and thirty-five minutes.

*October 24, 1931*—The news has been flashed far and wide that they opened the biggest bridge in the world today. There was an imposing ceremony and the great George Washington Bridge across the Hudson River was formally turned over to traffic.

His honor the judge uttered some stern words in Chicago this afternoon. He said, "Eleven years in prison and a fifty-thousand-dollar fine." That's the sentence, stiff music, that Scarface Al Capone has to face.

Here's what the League of Nations said today, "Now listen, Japan, what we want you to do is take your soldiers out of Manchuria on a specified date."

And here's Japan's reply to that. It's very short—it's just a two-letter word. Japan says, "No."

*November 3, 1931*—A dramatic but not unexpected move in British politics comes in the resignation of Lloyd George from the leadership of the Liberal party.

He split his party right in two during the recent election campaign in England.

*November 5, 1931*—The biggest battle of all this recent trouble is going on in Manchuria.

*November 6, 1931*—The Chinese military forces opposing the Japanese have been crushed after a three-day battle.

*November 9, 1931*—The League of Nations today received a note from Japan which indicates that the Japanese intend to prolong their occupation of Manchuria indefinitely.

*November 16, 1931*—Heavy fighting is reported again in Manchuria. Another battle is on at Tokyo, a different kind of battle—the struggle for control between the peace party and the war party in the Japanese Government.

*November 25, 1931*—Mahatma Gandhi today rejected the terms that the British Government has offered to India.

*November 30, 1931*—The British Indian Government has decreed rigorous measures to stamp out terrorism in Bengal.

*December 1, 1931*—Over in London the Round Table Conference on India came to an end today. The conference died a gloomy death, with open admissions of flat failure.

Gandhi declared that he and the British Government had finally reached a parting of the ways.

*December 2, 1931*—In the House of Commons, Prime Minister Ramsay MacDonald declared that the British Government had no idea of granting independence to India. He explained that the Indian people themselves do not want it.

*December 7, 1931*—The Seventy-second Congress went into session today.

In the Lower House the expected took place. The Democrats had everything their way and elected John N. Garner of Texas as Speaker.

*December 11, 1931*—Today Winston Churchill of England landed in the United States for a lecture tour. He, of course, is well known as one of the most interesting and provocative persons in British public life.

*December 16, 1931*—Senator Borah came out today with a blast in favor of Soviet Russia. The senator has introduced a resolution calling upon Uncle Sam to establish diplomatic relations with the Red regime at Moscow.

Out in India the police have made a raid on the headquarters of the leader of what is called the "No-Rent Campaign." He is Pandit Jawaharlal Nehru.

*December 18, 1931*—Jack "Legs" Diamond was killed as the result of a well-laid plot. The killers trailed the notorious underworld leader patiently. They followed him in a big sedan.

Apparently he was asleep in bed when the killers entered the house, pushed their way into Diamond's room, and shot him three times as he lay in bed.

*December 21, 1931*—Winston Churchill came to the United States a week or so ago to deliver a series of lectures, and right off the bat he was hit by an automobile. He was crossing the street in New York when a car coming along clipped him.

Churchill took all the blame for the accident. He says he was confused by the fact that in this country cars drive on the right side of the road while in England they keep to the left.

*December 28, 1931*—Mahatma Gandhi returned home today. He landed on Indian soil and received a turbulent welcome. In his first speech Gandhi said that he would not flinch in sacrificing the lives of a million people if necessary to purchase the liberty of India.

*December 29, 1931*—At Peiping today Marshal Chiang, the former war lord of Manchuria, announced that he had ordered the Chinese troops withdrawn from Chinchow. And, furthermore, he has ordered them to retire southward inside the Great Wall. This meets the Japanese demand that the Chinese take their armies out of Manchuria.

# 1932

*The two biggest stories of the year are both American. Franklin D. Roosevelt is elected President of the United States, the first of his four victories. The Lindbergh baby is kidnaped, the beginning of one of the most tragic episodes in the history of crime.*

*The bonus army marches on Washington, to be dispersed by troops under the command of General Douglas MacArthur—an incident his enemies will never forget, not even when he becomes the hero of the Pacific war a decade later. Jimmy Walker resigns as mayor of New York, preferring not to be exposed by his investigation.*

*Abroad, the Japanese complete their conquest of Manchuria by setting up Henry Pu-yi as their puppet Emperor. Hitler polls eleven million votes in the German election. Stalin ousts his former allies, Kamenev and Zinoviev, and strengthens his position as dictator.*

*January 4, 1932*—Mahatma Gandhi, India's little holy man, was arrested in the early hours this morning during his weekly period of silence. He preserved his silence when the police told him that he must come away to jail.

*January 5, 1932*—Tonight the Japanese Army in Manchuria is marching southward toward the Great Wall of China.

*January 6, 1932*—Governor Roosevelt attacked President Hoover's administration in Washington and called for a change. The public, proclaims the governor, asks that they be given a new leadership.

I think we can summarize Governor Roosevelt's message to the legislature by saying that it sounded suspiciously presidential.

*January 12, 1932*—Today a familiar figure makes his departure from the scene of public affairs. He is the patriarch of the American bench, Justice Oliver Wendell Holmes of the United States Supreme Court.

Justice Holmes is ninety years old. He explains that his health is not too good. In a letter to the President he writes, "The time has come, and I bow to the inevitable," and so saying, the veteran Justice hands the President his resignation from the Supreme Court.

*January 28, 1932*—The armed forces of the Mikado seized Shanghai today. Bitter fighting has been going on, a battle with machine guns in a crooked, crowded quarters. And there were bombs from the sky.

*February 3, 1932*—Shanghai—heavy fighting raged all day. The turmoil of battle was unceasing; the big guns of warships; the boom of cannon from Chinese forts; the crash of field artillery amid ruins; the rattle of machine guns and rifle fire; the charge and countercharge of fighting men.

*February 8, 1932*—Ex-Governor Alfred E. Smith dropped in to see Governor Franklin D. Roosevelt. They had a friendly chat. Apparently they didn't talk about the statement given out by ex-Governor Smith yesterday.

Ex-Governor Smith's explanation of his position doesn't do his old friend Governor Roosevelt any good. He says that if the Democratic convention calls upon him to run for the presidency he won't refuse.

*February 12, 1932*—A gathering of Democratic leaders, who represent an overwhelming majority of the New York State delegates to the national convention, decided that the New York State delegation will go to the convention unpledged to either Governor Roosevelt or former Governor Smith.

*February 16, 1932*—The great Japanese offensive at Shanghai seems to be under way. All day the Japanese heavy guns have been shelling the Chinese positions. The detonations were so heavy that throughout the International Settlement windows shook and rattled.

*February 18, 1932*—Here are the first state-by-state returns in the *Literary Digest* prohibition poll. Five thousand two hundred fifty-two votes have rolled up from Georgia; 1,664 of them are in favor of, and 3,588 are against the Eighteenth Amendment.

Tonight's returns on Illinois show that out of 3,454 votes, 493 are for prohibition, 2,961 go the other way.

The most populous state in the Union comes through with a total counted ballot of 257,215—32,338 of which favor the Eighteenth Amendment, 224,877 are against. Seven to one wet, says New York State.

*February 23, 1932*—The Japanese are trying desperately to force the

Chinese out of the peninsula on which Shanghai is situated. The Chinese troops held on grimly, and when the smoke of battle had blown away they were still holding onto their positions.

*March 1, 1932*—Massachusetts was turned into a battleground today. Former Governor Alfred E. Smith said yes. He made his formal entry into the Massachusetts primaries as a candidate for the Democratic presidential nomination.

A battle raged fiercely at Shanghai all day. And the Mikado's generals claim a victory all along the line.

*March 2, 1932*—I am sorry to say tonight that there is no favorable news about the Lindbergh baby.

A frantic search is on. Airplanes have been out hunting, the police have been searching over a wide area.

The Lindbergh home near Hopewell, New Jersey, is an isolated house in the country. Last night at seven-thirty the baby was put to bed by his mother and his nurse. At ten o'clock the nurse discovered the child was missing. Sometime between seven-thirty and ten a man stole up to the house and put a ladder to the window of the child's room. His footprints were later found on the soft ground. He took the child and carried him down the ladder.

The world's most famous baby has been kidnaped, and the attention of literally the whole world has been aroused.

*March 3, 1932*—Tonight there is a flood of clues, just clues. Some may mean something. Most are sheer nonsense. The main fact is that the baby is still missing. After two days of the most intense searching that this country has ever known, nobody seems to have picked up the real trail of the kidnapers.

Today's *Literary Digest* list gives us 24 states, and they are represented by a total of 1,323,284 votes. The dry cause is supported by 299,207, while the vote against prohibition is 1,024,077.

*March 4, 1932*—Thus far the frantic hunt for the missing child has resulted in little more than a wild haze of rumors. There seems to be some doubt as to whether or not Colonel Lindbergh has been in communication with the kidnapers.

The League of Nations today adopted a resolution saying the fighting at Shanghai must stop and demanding that Japan withdraw her troops.

*March 8, 1932*—In Manchuria today a man whom they call Henry

Pu-yi was received with honors and greeted as the ruler of the northern province. Well, Henry Pu-yi is the former boy emperor of China who was deposed by the revolution which started the Chinese Republic on its way. He's been living in retirement since. Now he is to be inaugurated as the head of the government which is being set up in the northern province under the protection of Japan.

*March 9, 1932*—Governor Roosevelt swept New Hampshire in yesterday's primary. He was opposed by ex-Governor Smith but won by a two-to-one vote.

The Irish Free State has a new president tonight. Yes, he is Eamon De Valera.

*March 14, 1932*—The German election looks like a tremendous personal tribute to the former war leader. Von Hindenburg polled more than 18,500,000 votes. When he was elected President in 1925 his total was about 14,500,000.

Hitler polled more than 11,300,000 votes. Two years ago in a national election Hitler polled a total of only 6,400,000—so that yesterday he made a gain of nearly five million ballots.

Next come the Communists with nearly five million votes.

*March 16, 1932*—Governor Franklin D. Roosevelt of New York is running ahead in the North Dakota primary election.

Well, well, the Babe has signed up. Let the bells ring out. Down in Florida today Babe Ruth put his signature on a contract for one year. The Bambino had quite an argument with Colonel Jake Ruppert, owner of the New York Yankees, before they finally came to terms. But now they have split the difference and compromised for seventy-five thousand berries.

*March 22, 1932*—The De Valera government at Dublin announces that it intends to abolish the oath of allegiance to the King.

*March 24, 1932*—Governor Roosevelt of New York scored in the Georgia presidential primaries yesterday. The Georgians gave Roosevelt a ten-to-one majority over Garner.

*March 29, 1932*—President Hoover today came out with a definite statement that he is opposed to any immediate soldiers' bonus payments.

*March 31, 1932*—Once more we hear of a search of the country in the neighborhood of the Lindbergh home.

Agents of the Federal government have been going over every inch of the ground among the hills.

*April 4, 1932*—The House of Representatives this afternoon passed the Philippine Independence Bill.

*April 8, 1932*—A thousand members of the American Legion and of the Veterans of Foreign Wars paraded through the streets and assembled at the steps of the Capitol.

They presented a petition signed by more than 2,400,000 names demanding the payment of the bonus.

*April 11, 1932*—Colonel Lindbergh paid fifty thousand dollars to men who he was convinced had stolen the child.

The Lindberghs are certain that they were dealing with the kidnapers. Professor John F. Condon, who inserted mysterious advertisements in the newspapers, is said to have been the intermediary through whom Colonel Lindbergh contacted the kidnapers.

*April 13, 1932*—News is definite tonight that some of the bank notes in the Lindbergh case are in circulation.

*April 14, 1932*—Handwriting experts have gone over the notes delivered to Dr. Condon and compared them with the notes left in the baby's cradle. These experts declare that the handwriting is the same. They are sure that the man who wrote to Dr. Condon and later got the fifty thousand dollars ransom from Colonel Lindbergh is the same as the one who wrote the notes left by the kidnaper.

*April 18, 1932*—The match king who killed himself in Paris now appears in the light of a colossal swindler. From the report of a committee that has been investigating in Stockholm, it would indeed appear that Ivar Kreuger must be rated as the greatest crook in history—that is, greatest so far as the magnitude of his devious projects is concerned.

Giant utilities corporations have gone into the hands of receivers, great industrial enterprises built up by Samuel Insull, financier and industrialist and patron of the arts.

*April 19, 1932*—The New York governor comes forward with the emphatic statement that he is not trying to set class against class, as ex-Governor Smith charged. In a former speech Franklin Roosevelt declared that the Hoover administration was helping the rich and ignoring the little fellows.

*April 20, 1932*—President De Valera stood before the lawmakers of Erin and read his bill for the abolition of the oath of allegiance to King George. The bill was promptly passed by the Irish parliament.

*April 25, 1932*—Jimmy Walker was again made a target by Judge Samuel Seabury today. In the investigations before the Hofstadter Committee, Seabury has been trying to get something on Jimmy for months.

*April 28, 1932*—And now here is something that we have all been waiting for—the final totals that show the way the country has divided on prohibition in this immense *Literary Digest* poll. The final dry vote is 1,236,660. The complete total for the wet side of the question is 3,431,877. That represents a majority of a trifle less than three to one against the Eighteenth Amendment.

*May 3, 1932*—Well, Al Capone is on his way to Leavenworth, where he'll occupy a cell for the next seven and one half years; that is, with time out for good behavior.

"It's a dirty deal," he cried, "a bum rap. The Supreme Court didn't treat me fair. I'm a good citizen. I did lots of good."

*May 5, 1932*—That peace pact was signed at Shanghai.

*May 11, 1932*—The Japanese Government has ordered all its land forces brought home from Shanghai within a month.

*May 13, 1932*—The whole country, in fact the whole world, seems to be staggering today under the shock of the tragic news from Hopewell, New Jersey. The baby's body was found in a patch of woods not far from the Lindbergh home.

*May 16, 1932*—The assassination of Premier Inukai of Japan may have serious consequences.

The moving spirits are a crowd of war-hungry young officers who resent the withdrawal from Shanghai.

The police believe the gang became frightened and killed the Lindbergh child to make sure of their escape.

*May 18, 1932*—The leaders of the Japanese Army are making a determined effort to control the Cabinet. This comes as an aftermath to the assassination of Premier Inukai.

*May 20, 1932*—Dr. Condon, the much-publicized "Jafsie," was before the Bronx County Grand Jury this morning for two and a half hours. The aged schoolteacher told a detailed story of the fantastic negotiations which culminated in his throwing Colonel Lindbergh's fifty thousand dollars over a cemetery wall.

*May 25, 1932*—The march of the bonus army on Washington, D.C., becomes more promising of excitement every day. It looks as though before it's over it will rival the historic march of Coxey's Army.

*May 26, 1932*—They had it hot and heavy today again in the Seabury-Walker show. The most dramatic moment occurred when Mayor Walker burst out:

"I am supposed to be a witness here at an inquiry, but it looks as if somebody wants my life."

As for the $246,000 which the mayor received as the result of an account in a stockbroker's office which he shared with Paul Block, the mayor admitted that he had not put up a cent of margin. The transaction, he explained, was simply a question of the kindness of Mr. Block, who is a rich and notoriously good-natured newspaper publisher.

*May 31, 1932*—President von Hindenburg late this afternoon commissioned Franz von Papen to form a temporary government replacing that of the retiring Chancellor Bruening.

*June 2, 1932*—At least eight of these bonus armies are marching on Washington, more than three thousand war veterans.

*June 7, 1932*—The new government of Franz von Papen has sounded the death knell of democracy in Germany. The new Cabinet of soldiers and aristocrats pointedly denounces parliamentary government as a failure.

*June 8, 1932*—The bonus army in Washington, after its successful parade, settled down today for a grim siege of Congress.

*June 10, 1932*—A maid connected with the Lindbergh family died today. What makes it startling is that she died of a quick and deadly poison. In fact, the county prosecutor's office is convinced she committed suicide.

The head of the New Jersey State Police admitted that Violet Sharp had been under suspicion.

*June 14, 1932*—Well, I've had a thrill such as comes once in a lifetime: my first sight of a national political convention. Republicans gathered in Chicago to select a candidate.

*June 16, 1932*—The Hoover demonstration in Chicago today was an emotional affair. But I can't say it was really exciting. Everybody knew that it was all "in the bag."

*June 27, 1932*—This Democratic convention is more colorful than the show staged by the Republicans here two weeks ago. There is something like the spirit of a carnival throughout Chicago.

*June 29, 1932*—The wets captured control of the Democratic Platform Committee. They forced through an out-and-out repeal plank by a vote of two to one.

*July 1, 1932*—After those three ballots which showed Governor Roosevelt far in the lead, the situation is unchanged. Mr. Roosevelt had 682 and a fraction on the third. Al Smith had 201¾ on the first, then lost a few on the third ballot.

Once again Helen Wills Moody has won the tennis championship of England. This is the fifth time the mighty Helen has won this title.

During that all-night session Al Smith displayed the coolness of the veteran campaigner. Talking about the convention? Not at all. He was telling us stories.

*July 4, 1932*—The furor created by the nomination of Governor Roosevelt and Speaker Garner has not subsided yet.
The followers of Alfred E. Smith are sore.

*July 5, 1932*—The bonus expeditionary forces marched up Capitol Hill in Washington today and then marched right down again. They made a brief demonstration on the Senate steps with songs and speeches and boos for President Hoover.

*July 7, 1932*—Uncle Sam was preparing today to give the bonus army in Washington train tickets home. But the bonus veterans reply, We want meal tickets, not train tickets.

*July 22, 1932*—President Hoover's signed the two-billion-dollar relief bill passed by Congress.

The commissioners of the District of Columbia have given the veterans until midnight tonight to evacuate the dilapidated government buildings in which eighteen hundred of them have been billeted.

*July 25, 1932*—A treaty of non-aggression between Soviet Russia and

Poland was signed today. This protects Poland's eastern border from Russia.

*July 28, 1932*—Military force was used against the bonus army today. Cavalry, infantry, and several field tanks were in action. The veterans were driven by tear gas and fixed bayonets.

*July 29, 1932*—The bonus expeditionary force in Washington was a tragic spectacle today. There was another military offensive against them this afternoon. The squatters were warned to leave or the soldiers would put them out—with tear-gas bombs and fixed bayonets.

So today it is a disheveled and dejected army that is moving over the borders of the District of Columbia into the adjoining states.

General Douglas MacArthur, Chief of Staff of the United States Army, said that military action against the bonus army had become inevitable. "In fact," said the general, "if it had been delayed it might have led to insurgency and insurrection."

*August 1, 1932*—Adolf Hitler, after prophesying for two years that the voice of the German people would make him dictator, received in yesterday's election only 37½ per cent of the total vote cast.

*August 4, 1932*—What with Bill Miller of Stanford carrying off the crown in the pole vault, John Anderson of the New York Athletic Club winning the discus throw, and George Sailing of Iowa romping home first in the 110-meter hurdles, Uncle Sam won four out of five first places in yesterday's Olympic events at Los Angeles. The Stars and Stripes flies at the head of the mast to the tune of some 208½ points.

*August 9, 1932*—Early this morning the followers of King Alfonso staged a counterrevolution. The Spanish Republic is only sixteen months old, and this is the first serious attempt to upset it.

Seville is in the hands of the rebels.

*August 11, 1932*—When New York's Mayor Walker arrived in Albany, it looked more as if he had come on a triumphal procession rather than a journey to defend his official existence. Crowds cheered him in the streets, some of them acclaiming him as the next governor of New York State.

The monarchist rebellion in Spain seems to have turned into what theatrical people call one big flop. The Republican forces have gained the upper hand everywhere today.

*August 16, 1932*—Drama of a powerful and romantic kind broke out at the trial of Mayor Jimmy Walker of New York City in Albany today. The name of a well-known Broadway actress and a friend of Mayor Jimmy was openly mentioned. Governor Roosevelt took all precautions to keep her name off the record. It was the mayor himself who mentioned her to a reporter in the corridor. She's Betty Compton.

*August 26, 1932*—The crisis, the major financial crisis of the depression, is definitely at an end. So says President Hoover.

*August 29, 1932*—Hitler had lunch with Chancellor von Papen and General von Schleicher, the real power behind the throne in the Von Papen Cabinet.

The purpose of the luncheon party was to persuade Hitler to accept the position of Vice-Chancellor of the German Republic.

This offer Hitler refused. He still insists on becoming Chancellor.

*August 31, 1932*—Jimmy Doolittle no sooner loses one airplane speed record than he creates another. At the airport at Cleveland today he set a new high mark of 292½ miles an hour.

*September 2, 1932*—Jimmy Walker's resignation wasn't exactly a surprise, but people were startled when they saw the front pages of this morning's newspapers.

Jimmy Walker quits as mayor of New York rather than face the rest of the hearing before Governor Roosevelt.

*September 15, 1932*—Emperor Hirohito formally recognized the government of Manchukuo—which used to be Manchuria—as an independent state separated from China. Henry Pu-yi, former boy emperor of China, officially recognized as President of this new state.

*September 16, 1932*—Huey Long, the Kingfish, comes out today with a remedy to save the poor old United States. He's going to start a nation-wide campaign to rid America of its multimillionaires.

*September 19, 1932*—Governor Roosevelt's stumping tour has taken him now as far as Montana. He told the miners of Butte today that if he were elected President he would call a conference to make an attempt to stabilize the price of silver.

*September 21, 1932*—For the first time in thirty-two years the regular Republicans wrenched the control of Wisconsin away from the La Follette family. The nomination for the governorship was won away from Governor Philip La Follette, younger son of the late Senator Fighting Bob. His successful rival is then Walter Kohler, the bathtub king.

*September 22, 1932*—The Soviet Government of Russia has agreed to recognize the state of Manchukuo, which Japan erected in place of what used to be the Chinese territory of Manchuria.

*September 26, 1932*—The Mahatma today broke the fast unto death which he undertook as a protest against the proposed settlement of the Indian voting problem.

Mr. Gandhi read the government's statement announcing an agreement. Then he smiled and whispered, "Passive resistance has triumphed."

*October 3, 1932*—In all the capitals of the world the principal topic of discussion today was the report of the Lytton Commission of the League of Nations condemning the behavior of Japan in Manchuria.

The attitude of Japan is defiant.

*October 5, 1932*—Reports from President Hoover's special train say that he was so encouraged by his reception at Des Moines last night that he's going to continue his campaign.

The Democrats are all excited over that reunion last night between Governor Franklin D. Roosevelt and ex-Governor Alfred E. Smith. Al walked across the platform in Albany, grabbed Mr. Roosevelt's hand, and exclaimed, "How are you, you old potato?"

This is the greeting that Al reserves for his real old friends.

*October 11, 1932*—There has been an upheaval in the Soviet Government of Russia. Gregory Zinoviev, former president of the Communist International, has been kicked out of the Communist party.

Leo Kamenev, former Ambassador to Italy, was also expelled from the party, together with twenty-two other prominent leaders of the Soviet.

*October 12, 1932*—Today we are beginning to find out why the Communist party in Moscow expelled Gregory Zinoviev and other prominent Communists. It was because of a plot to overthrow the leadership of Stalin. Communists kicked out of the party were former followers of Trotsky.

*October 14, 1932*—Samuel Insull appears to be safe in Greece, safe for thirty days, at any rate. The Foreign Office at Athens today announced that it will neither let him be extradited nor deport him.

*October 17, 1932*—There's a rumor in Moscow that another prominent Communist has been placed under guard by the authorities, Bukharin, former secretary of the Communist International.

*October 20, 1932*—The *Literary Digest* editors tell me that the ballots in their big presidential poll are piling up, mountains of them. Marion, Ohio, the old home of President Harding, goes for Roosevelt: Hoover, 405; and Roosevelt, 659.

Then there's Davenport, Iowa, which hits close to President Hoover's birthplace. It also goes for Roosevelt. Hoover, 760; Roosevelt, 1,041.

On the other hand, the New England states continue to show solid Hoover majorities.

*October 31, 1932*—A hunger march swooped down today on the famous Loop district of Chicago, a boisterous parade of fifteen thousand men, women, and children who carried red banners and shook their fists at City Hall. They were protesting against the reduction of relief for the unemployed.

*November 1, 1932*—In Reno, Nevada, today the acting governor of the state proclaimed a two-week bank holiday. As a result thirteen of the twenty-five banks in Nevada have temporarily closed down.

You can get three hundred thousand dollars at three to one that Roosevelt will be elected. You can get even money that Roosevelt will carry California by a 175,000 majority. You can get even money that F.D. will carry New York by twenty thousand.

*November 2, 1932*—President Hoover will leave Washington at four o'clock tomorrow afternoon for his fifth trip to the Middle West during this campaign.

*November 4, 1932*—The long-expected arrest of Samuel Insull took place today. The Athens police, at the request of Uncle Sam, took the former utilities baron of Chicago into custody.

*November 7, 1932*—The candidates are going to be talking up to the last possible moment. President Hoover, on his way to his home in California, will be speechmaking tonight in Elko, Nevada. Governor Roosevelt has been visiting his home territory in the Hudson River Valley, winding up with an important address next door to me at Poughkeepsie. Norman Thomas is speaking in Milwaukee.

Although Adolf Hitler was the chief loser in the German election yesterday, he declared that he would not abandon his fight but would carry on to the bitter end. The Hitlerites lost thirty-five seats in the German parliament. Hitler himself in a veiled way, and his followers openly, are threatening what the Germans call a *Putsch*.

The Supreme Court today ordered new trials for seven Negro boys. The Supreme Court's opinion caustically criticized the conduct of the trial at Scottsboro, Alabama, and also the decision of the Alabama Supreme Court upholding that trial.

*November 9, 1932*—As the returns keep coming in, that Democratic victory grows more and more stupendous.

Latest reports show that Mr. Roosevelt captured forty-two out of forty-eight states. These give him 472 electoral votes.

It seems definite that the new Congress will be wet.

Mr. Hoover intends to return to private life and try to recoup his personal fortune, which has suffered severely in the last few years, and he intends to make his permanent residence in Palo Alto, for which he has always had a strong preference.

*November 10, 1932*—Italy is going right on with those plans to send that squadron of twenty-four seaplanes across the ocean to Chicago for the exposition in March 1933. They will span the Atlantic led by no less a celebrity than General Balbo, Mussolini's Air Minister.

*November 15, 1932*—Trotsky has been permitted to move. In fact, he is already on his way—bound for Denmark.

*November 21, 1932*—Hindenburg and Hitler met today. And the aged President gave the Nazi chief the opportunity to become Chancellor—if he could arrange a cabinet with a workable majority in the Reichstag to back it up. Hitler has written Von Hindenburg what is believed to be a refusal.

Some observers insist that Hitler will not become Chancellor and that he is headed for his final downfall.

The first regular business session of the Third India Round Table Conference was held in London today in the House of Lords. Only the Indian extremists are absent. And, of course, Mahatma Gandhi is in jail.

*November 22, 1932*—For the first time a President and President-elect of the United States have held a conference at the White House. The eyes of the world have been upon that meeting this afternoon, for it concerned the gigantic sum of eleven billion dollars, the war debts owed by the nations of Europe to Uncle Sam.

*November 23, 1932*—Hitler reported to President von Hindenburg that he was unable to collect around him any government that could be sure of a majority in the German parliament.

*November 28, 1932*—President von Hindenburg probably will invite General von Schleicher, who was the power behind the throne in the Von Papen government, to form the new Cabinet.

Schleicher probably will not accept unless he is able to enlist the support of Adolf Hitler and his party.

*November 29, 1932*—An army of hunger marchers is converging on Washington, D.C.

*December 2, 1932*—President von Hindenburg today named General von Schleicher Chancellor of the German Republic, and the general accepted.

*December 7, 1932*—Fists swung, chair legs were brandished, inkwells and books flew all over the chamber of the Reichstag.

The Hitlerites and the Communists, finding words too feeble to express their feelings, took off their coats and just let themselves go.

*December 13, 1932*—A survey of the United States shows that in several communities fiat money is being used. Teachers and others are being paid in scrip at Bloomington, Illinois. City employees of Philadelphia are getting credit from merchants on city warrants.

Furthermore, the barter idea is spreading.

*December 14, 1932*—There was tremendous indignation in Washington today over the decision of the French Government to default on its war-debt installment.

*December 15, 1932*—Six nations today paid installments to the U.S.A. John Bull was the first with his $95,500,000. Then Italy with $1,245,437.

The defaulting nations are France, Belgium, Poland, Estonia, Greece, and Hungary.

*December 26, 1932*—Washington is like the scene of a gold rush. The largest and most ravenous horde of political job seekers ever seen in the history of the country has begun to invade the capital.

# 1933

*Hitler becomes Chancellor of Germany, stages the Reichstag fire, takes his Reich out of the League of Nations, and foments anti-Semitism in Germany and Nazi conspiracy in Austria. Japan also walks out of the League, which becomes more and more feeble as international animosities increase. The British Empire is flouted by Gandhi, who fasts and goes to jail, and by De Valera, who gets Southern Ireland's oath of allegiance to the Crown abolished. President Roosevelt recognizes the Soviet Union officially.*

*At home, President Roosevelt closes the banks temporarily to prevent financial panic, takes America off the gold standard, and receives from Congress the authority to establish the New Deal. Prohibition ends with a popular vote against the Eighteenth Amendment. La Guardia becomes mayor of New York.*

*January 1, 1933*—In New York, Governor Lehman and Mayor O'Brien were sworn in, together with a whole string of other victors at the last election.

Nineteen thirty-two will not be considered a joyous era of cheer and abundance, especially for the Republicans.

*January 5, 1933*—Mrs. Coolidge went upstairs to the former President's room in the Beeches, the estate at Northampton which the Coolidges recently bought. There she found the body of her husband on the bed. Former President Calvin Coolidge, victim of a sudden stroke of heart disease.

*January 10, 1933*—A terrific battle is being waged along the Great Wall of China.

*January 11, 1933*—The Chinese defenders of the Great Wall have been put to flight.

*January 13, 1933*—President Hoover today handed down an unequivocal, emphatic veto of the Philippine Independence Bill.

*January 17, 1933*—The Filipinos can have their independence. The Senate this afternoon followed the example of the House of Representatives and overrode President Hoover's veto of the measure, which gives independence to the islands in anywhere from ten to thirteen years.

President-elect Roosevelt gives unequivocal support to President Hoover's foreign policy in the Far East. Mr. Roosevelt stands behind Mr. Hoover in refusing, among other things, to recognize the state of Manchukuo, which Japan has erected upon the territory of what once was Manchuria.

*January 19, 1933*—The entire population of three Cossack communities in the south of Russia has been banished to the frozen north. They failed to co-operate with the Soviet agricultural program.

*January 23, 1933*—The Twentieth Amendment was added to the Constitution of the United States when the legislature of Missouri ratified. The amendment eliminates the Lame Duck Session of Congress and advances the date for the inauguration of presidents.

*January 24, 1933*—One of the bloodiest battles in South American history has been raging in the Gran Chaco territory. The battle now is in its fifth day.

This conflict between Bolivia and Paraguay is another of these undeclared wars that are the fashion today.

*January 27, 1933*—From Warm Springs, Georgia, word that President-elect Roosevelt aims to extend the activities of the Federal government *beyond anything that has been known up to now*. Industries which heretofore have escaped the slightest touch of government control will in the next administration feel the hand of Washington.

*January 29, 1933*—The Von Schleicher Cabinet in Berlin has resigned.

*January 30, 1933*—About eleven o'clock this morning the world was startled by the news that Adolf Hitler, the forty-three-year-old son of an obscure government official in Austria, had been made Chancellor of the German Republic.

Japan has informed the League of Nations that, unless its report on the

Manchurian issue is favorable to Japan, that country will withdraw from the League.

*February 2, 1933*—A project which will affect the welfare of ten states was announced today by President-elect Roosevelt, a plan to develop the entire valley of the Tennessee River.

*February 8, 1933*—Old Erin, the once distressful isle, has advanced one step nearer to the status of a republic. That's the interpretation put upon the re-election of Mr. Eamon De Valera to the presidency of the Irish Free State.

*February 10, 1933*—They are saying in Washington today that the powers which Congress is being asked to give to President-elect Roosevelt after his inauguration have in many respects the aspect of a dictatorship.

*February 12, 1933*—The world's first station for radio communication by ultra-short wave was inaugurated at the Vatican, the venerable and splendid palace of the popes.

Pope Pius XI made an address into the microphone, and so did Marconi, the inventor of wireless telegraphy.

*February 16, 1933*—The principal thing the whole world is talking about today is the attempted assassination of Mr. Roosevelt. Mayor Cermak of Chicago was struck by one of the bullets intended for our next President.

Mrs. W. L. Cross of Miami grabbed the would-be assassin's wrist while he was firing. She it was who deflected the bullets from the President-elect. The gunman is a bricklayer known in Paterson and Hackensack, New Jersey, as a hater of the rich and powerful, a lone-wolf soapbox orator.

The Miami police and Mr. Roosevelt's bodyguard had a hard time rescuing Zangara from the mob.

*February 19, 1933*—The report of the examining physicians is that Zangara, the would-be assassin, is a psychopathic personality: intelligent and fairly well educated, but a crank "whose pet schemes and morbid emotions run in conflict with the established order of society."

*February 20, 1933*—The House of Representatives voted on the repeal resolution adopted by the Senate last week. And the Blaine resolution went over by a vote of 289 to 121.

This means that the repeal of the Eighteenth Amendment is put up to conventions in the various states.

*February 24, 1933*—A historic and dramatic scene took place today in Geneva. The Assembly of the League of Nations took up the report of its Committee of Nineteen, that report which condemns the action of Japan in Manchuria.

The report was adopted by a vote of forty-two to one, Japan's being the only voice that said no.

When the vote was announced, the Japanese delegation—headed by its grim-looking chief, Yosuke Matsuoka—rose and walked out.

*February 28, 1933*—Following the fire in the Reichstag—the parliament building in Berlin—the Hitler Cabinet issued an edict suspending civil rights throughout Germany.

They called the burning of the parliament building the first step of a Communist revolution and ordered the arrest of all Communist members of the German parliament and all other leaders of the Reds.

Pennsylvania, Indiana, Arkansas, Maryland, Delaware, and Ohio are passing measures to protect the banks and their depositors.

*March 1, 1933*—The Dail, the Irish parliament, passed a bill abolishing the oath of allegiance to the British Crown. Another step toward the establishment of an Irish republic in place of the present free state.

*March 3, 1933*—Thirty states of the Union have now taken measures to protect bank deposits.

*March 5, 1933*—President Roosevelt assumed office yesterday in a moment of national crisis. The front pages of the newspapers told of the two-day suspension of bank payments in New York, the center of the nation's finances, and in Illinois too, and in other states. And now there's a bank moratorium in every state in the Union.

The inaugural address promises action, action swift and decisive. The new President declares that if it is necessary in the present crisis he will call upon Congress to grant him those immense powers that are commonly given to a President in time of war.

*March 6, 1933*—President Roosevelt has ordered the closing of all the nation's banks.

The victory of Chancellor Hitler and the Nazis was even more sweeping than this morning's news indicated. According to late figures today, the total of the Nazi vote approached twenty million.

Mayor Tony Cermak passed away early this morning in the Jacksonville Memorial Hospital in Miami. He died as a result of a bullet which was intended for President Roosevelt.

*March 7, 1933*—The outstanding feature of the second day of the national bank holiday proclaimed by the new President was the feeling of cheerfulness, even of levity, that prevailed everywhere.

The situation, as it stands now, is that banks may cash checks for pay rolls and necessities of life.

Perhaps the most striking outcome of the banking crisis is the amazing prestige that President Roosevelt has won for himself.

*March 8, 1933*—Most commercial banks were opened today for the limited service permitted by the Treasury.

*March 9, 1933*—The Seventy-third Congress assembled in extraordinary session amid scenes of excitement. President Roosevelt's first message to Congress had an instantaneous and electric effect on the country at large. Everybody was struck with its terseness. It was only five hundred words long. For one thing he said, "Our task is to reopen all sound banks."

*March 10, 1933*—Late this afternoon President Roosevelt issued an executive order empowering the Secretary of the Treasury to open some banks immediately for emergency business.

Mr. Roosevelt's second message was marked by terseness, clarity, and force. The big thing in it was his request to the Congress to give him virtually the powers of a dictator so that he can make the most sweeping reduction in Uncle Sam's expenses.

The reductions he wants to make will, it is estimated, save in the neighborhood of $614,000,000 a year.

*March 12, 1933*—The President's proclamation declares that tomorrow banks that are members of the Federal Reserve System will reopen in twelve Federal Reserve cities.

On succeeding days other banks will reopen—that is, if they are in sound condition.

*March 13, 1933*—Today the President sent another one of those brief messages for which he is becoming famous, and in it he asked Congress to make beer legal immediately.

In all the twelve key cities of the U.S.A., the Federal Reserve cities, both national and state banks threw open their doors.

The stock exchanges are still closed and likely to remain so for a few days.

*March 14, 1933*—The new President is planning to speak to the people of the United States over the radio regularly.

Hundreds more banks opened their doors this morning.

The New York Stock Exchange will open for trading tomorrow at ten o'clock.

*March 16, 1933*—The Roosevelt Economy Bill, which the Senate passed last night, went to the House today, and the representatives passed it in jig time.

*March 19, 1933*—The Oxford Union, one of England's most hallowed scholastic institutions, met in solemn conclave and passed the following almost incredible resolution—"That this house will in no circumstances fight for King and country."

*March 20, 1933*—Most of the Nazi outrages are perpetrated on people of Jewish faith, name, and origin.

Germany has been overwhelmed by a wave of brown-shirt hoodlumism.

Giuseppe Zangara, the man who tried to assassinate President Roosevelt and killed Mayor Tony Cermak of Chicago, was executed today in the electric chair at the state prison in Raiford, Florida.

*March 21, 1933*—President Roosevelt today sent to Congress his communication on unemployment relief.

It calls for a broad public works program to create employment.

The House of Representatives today passed the Cullen Act, making it legal to brew, sell, and drink beer of 3.2 per cent strength. The Senate passed it yesterday.

*March 22, 1933*—Jewish organizations in America are retaliating as far as they can by boycotting both German goods and ships.

*March 27, 1933*—The Mikado's government today issued a proclamation giving formal notice of its withdrawal from the League of Nations.

*April 2, 1933*—The Prussian Academy of Science has accepted Einstein's resignation from its membership. Their statement declares that they accept the great mathematician's resignation without regret.

In New York prominent musicians have sent a round-robin letter to Hitler protesting the treatment of prominent Jewish musicians in Germany. First on the list of signatures is that of Toscanini.

*April 4, 1933*—In the Michigan election to select delegates for the convention to consider the repeal of the Eighteenth Amendment, the anti-prohibitionists were victorious, three to one.

*April 5, 1933*—Wisconsin followed the example of Michigan in voting overwhelmingly for the repeal of the Eighteenth Amendment.

President Roosevelt today issued an executive order that all private individuals who have more than a hundred dollars' worth of gold must hand it over to the Federal Reserve Bank before May 1.

*April 6, 1933*—The principal excitement for millions of Americans tonight is the reapproach of the amber-colored liquid.

In nineteen states midnight will be the zero hour for the 3.2 per cent stuff.

*April 10, 1933*—President Roosevelt asks Congress to create a Tennessee Valley Authority to develop electric power and provide for flood control.

*April 13, 1933*—President Roosevelt sent a message to Congress asking for legislation to ease the mortgage burdens on the little fellows. He asks Congress to erect what will be called the Home Owners Loan Corporation.

*April 20, 1933*—In foreign countries Uncle Sam's stepping off the gold standard caused nothing short of dismay.

*April 21, 1933*—Ramsay MacDonald, Prime Minister of Great Britain, arrived in New York this morning and went straight to Washington for the conference to which President Roosevelt invited him.

*April 23, 1933*—In Washington the conference between President Roosevelt and Prime Minister MacDonald of Great Britain has started an effort for world-wide action on economic subjects.

The French delegation, headed by former Premier Herriot, arrived in America today.

*April 24, 1933*—Observers are pointing out the extraordinary number of aggressive steps that Mr. Roosevelt has initiated since he became President. He has set on foot more important policies in seven weeks than most presidents are responsible for in four years of office.

*April 26, 1933*—The Prime Minister and the President have agreed that steps must be taken to re-establish an international standard of money.

As soon as Mr. MacDonald left Washington, the President resumed his conversations with former Premier Herriot of France, likewise Prime Minister Bennett of Canada.

*April 27, 1933*—This is the first time I've been literally up in the air while broadcasting. And it's the first news broadcast ever to be made from an airplane—so the NBC people tell me.

*May 3, 1933*—The measure creating the Tennessee Valley Authority, commonly known as the Muscle Shoals Bill, was passed by the Senate by a vote of sixty-two to twenty.

*May 8, 1933*—Ideas expressed by Mr. Roosevelt over the air last night are being put into actual form today. That is, legislation for a partnership of planning between the government and farming, the government and industry, and the government and transportation.

*May 18, 1933*—Congress is busy considering the administration's Industrial Recovery Bill—the bill to authorize that gigantic and comprehensive program involving the expenditure of $3,300,000,000.

*May 23, 1933*—Since Mr. Roosevelt went into office we have been hearing much about his so-called "Brain Trust." Among the most conspicious of these gentlemen of the Brain Trust are Professor Raymond Moley, who is now an Assistant Secretary of State, Professor Rexford G. Tugwell, Assistant Secretary of Agriculture, and Adolph Augustus Berle.

At this moment the Japanese Army is at the gates of Peiping, old Peking, when the Japanese seem to be in control of not only Manchuria and much of northern China.

*May 24, 1933*—The House of Representatives today passed the Bank Bill presented by Congressman Steagall of Alabama. This is the bill which provides that Uncle Sam will guarantee your deposit in the bank.

*May 25, 1933*—The Japanese delegate to the Disarmament Conference at Geneva precipitated a dramatic surprise today. He came before the other delegates, demanding not a decrease but an increase of the Japanese Navy.

*May 29, 1933*—Mahatma Gandhi, sage and holy man of India, ended his twenty-one-day fast today. Many thought he would never survive.

*June 1, 1933*—A wily circus press agent made some capital out of the bank inquiry of the Senate Committee on Banking and Currency.

A female midget about thirty inches tall was brought into the committee room and introduced to the Morgan partners, including the great J.P. himself. Mr. Morgan, a punctilious man, rose to greet the miniature woman and had to bend almost double to shake hands. Then he sat down. The press agent of the circus picked the midget up and plunked her down on the lap of J. P. Morgan. The next thing the bystanders knew a cameraman, conveniently located, flashed his bulb and, lo, there was a picture of J. P. Morgan with a female midget on his knee.

*June 5, 1933*—The U. S. Senate today passed the resolution repealing the gold clause, the clause which specifies that Uncle Sam's public debts must be paid in gold.

The Senate today passed the Home Owners Relief Act, which provides direct loans to home owners.

*June 7, 1933*—The Four-Power Pact has just been signed in London. Great Britain, Italy, France, and Germany have initialed the pact whereby they agree not to participate in any wars for a period of ten years.

When the former bone-dry state of Indiana went two to one for repeal, the wet forces considered it a signal victory.

*June 13, 1933*—When it comes to world's fairs, you can't beat Chicago, with its "Century of Progress" Exposition. It was announced today that in the first seventeen days more than a million people have passed through the turnstiles.

*June 15, 1933*—England is paying 10 per cent of her June 15 war-debt installment as a token. Italy, approximately one million of the thirteen million due. France will default on her June war-debt installment—default entirely, just as she did in December. The one country to pay in full is Finland.

*June 16, 1933*—Shortly before sunrise this morning the Seventy-third Congress folded up its tents and prepared to go back home and attend to the important job known as mending fences—political fences, of course.

Thus ends one of the most extraordinary sessions of our national legislature in our national history. It left more power in the hands of a President than has ever been handed over before.

The President issued a statement: "History probably will regard the National Industrial Recovery Act as the most important and far-reaching legislation ever enacted by the American Congress."

*June 22, 1933*—Let's start tonight with an important announcement by the U.S. delegation to the World Economic Conference in London. They have informed the conference that Washington considers any temporary pegging of the dollar as inopportune at the present moment. The reason is that the principal objective of the administration just now is to raise prices.

The Hitlerites are trying to reorganize religion. They want to abolish the use of the Old Testament in the churches and the schools.

The grounds for the objections of the German Christians to the Old Testament is that it is a Jewish book written to glorify the Jewish race.

*June 28, 1933*—At noon yesterday our paper dollar was worth eighty gold cents; that is, based on the quotation for French francs. Today the dollar went down to seventy-six and a half cents in gold.

The Soviet Government has just finished building what must be the longest canal in the world. It extends over 152 miles and connects the Baltic with the White Sea.

*June 30, 1933*—The administration wants to lose no time putting in force the National Recovery Act. General Hugh Johnson, the administrator, issued a statement today calling for speed. He urged the various industries of the country to get a move on and perfect their codes.

*July 3, 1933*—President Roosevelt threw a bombshell into the midst of that World Economic Conference, and today practically everybody is saying the conference is as good as finished. In a cablegram the President uttered a palpable rebuke to the gold-standard nations, especially France, for the attempts to cajole Uncle Sam into a temporary stabilization of the currency.

The reports concerning the bust-up of the marriage of Douglas Fairbanks and Mary Pickford are true.

*July 5, 1933*—Trade relations between Uncle Sam and Soviet Russia became a reality today. We have sold eighty thousand bales of cotton to Comrade Stalin by means of loans made to the Soviet Government by the RFC.

This is interpreted as meaning that full recognition of the Soviet by Uncle Sam is inevitable.

General Balbo and his fleet of twenty-four of Premier Mussolini's best seaplanes are safe in Reykjavik, the capital of Iceland.

*July 10, 1933*—General Johnson, administrator of the NIRA, as the Recovery Act is now called, has the President's O.K. on the code of fair practices formulated by the textile industry.

*July 12, 1933*—General Balbo—beard, armada, and all—is on North American soil. They've jumped the Atlantic. They took off from the harbor of Reykjavik, Iceland, and alighted on the water outside Cartwright, Labrador.

More news from NIRA. The shipbuilding and ship-repairing industry has prepared its code of fair competition and submitted it to Administrator General Johnson.

*July 17, 1933*—The provisions of NIRA, the National Industrial Recovery Act, went into effect today.

*July 20, 1933*—Wiley Post, this morning, was somewhere over the Pacific Ocean speeding for Alaska. Once he's done that, he will have crossed two oceans and accomplished the most difficult and dangerous part of his whirl around the globe.

*July 21, 1933*—General Balbo and his merry men learned today what it means to receive an official welcome from New York City.

For a while it seemed probable that Tennessee would go dry.
But the final complete returns indicate how closely accurate that *Literary Digest* poll was. The repeal forces won by the bare majority of some nine thousand votes.

Chicago is certainly doing herself proud entertaining General Balbo, Italy's colorful Air Minister, and the crews of his twenty-four seaplanes.

*July 25, 1933*—General Balbo, with his noble black beard and his noble squadron, is on the return lap of his historic voyage. The planes rose from the waters of Jamaica Bay, New York, about ten o'clock this morning.

*July 27, 1933*—That World Economic Conference died in London today.
Neville Chamberlain, British Chancellor of the Exchequer, put the blame on the American decision rejecting currency stabilization.

*July 31, 1933*—The NIRA program is still going ahead full speed.

*August 1, 1933*—India is in a turmoil again. First of all, Gandhi is in jail once more with thirty-two of his principal supporters. They were arrested as they started a civil disobedience march.

*August 4, 1933*—New York City Fusionists have finally found a candidate. The elements opposing Tammany Hall have selected Major Fiorello La Guardia, the fiery little Italian who has long been a familiar figure in New York political campaigns and the House of Representatives at Washington.

That girl NIRA certainly has a lot of fancy beaus. Today she was dated up by J. P. Morgan. The news from Wall Street is that the plutocratic and historic house of Morgan has signed the code.

*August 10, 1933*—The government of Austria is planning drastic measures to suppress the terrorism created by the agitations of the Nazis.

*August 11, 1933*—General Johnson, administrator of NIRA, says that numerous complaints have come to him about "chiselers"—people who have signed NIRA pledges and then ignored them.

*August 16, 1933*—A big political trial started in Germany today, the trial of the men whom the Hitler government accuses of having set fire to the Reichstag, Germany's house of parliament in Berlin.

*August 17, 1933*—General Johnson made the flat statement that if the steel industry does not adopt a code the NRA officials will write one for it.

*August 28, 1933*—Professor Raymond Moley, so-called head of President Roosevelt's brain trust, has resigned as Assistant Secretary of State.

*August 29, 1933*—"Who socked Huey Long?"
That incident on Saturday night at the Sands Point Beach Club on Long Island is engaging the attention of the entire country. The Louisiana senator himself says that he was "ganged," as he puts it, by four men in the washroom of the club.

A story I got from one reliable source is that Huey walked into the washroom and shoved someone. The man he pushed promptly swung on the senatorial eye.

Secretary of the Interior Ickes has been appointed the czar of the oil industry in the U.S.A. Mr. Ickes will administer the oil code recently drawn up under the National Recovery Act.

Uncle Sam won the first round in his attempt to bring Samuel Insull home. The Court of Appeals of Greece has approved the application of the American Legation for the formal arrest of the Chicago utilities king.

*August 30, 1933*—Henry Ford has announced that wages and working hours in his plant are far above the requirements of the code. He also intimates that he is therefore going to do nothing about NRA.

Administrator Johnson declared today that Uncle Sam will buy no more cars from the Ford plants until Henry signs. Uncle Sam is a good customer for cars.

A gang of Nazis broke into the Austrian prison at Innsbruck, overpowered two wardens, and rescued Nazi leader Franz Hofer, who had been in prison for his Nazi propaganda work in Austria.

*September 5, 1933*—Cuba's new President was on the job just twenty-two days. An army sergeant named Batista, who has no official position, is the actual ruler of the island.

While President de Cespedes was in the interior looking over the damage caused by a hurricane, the soldiers rebelled.

*September 7, 1933*—The question of the day is: Will Uncle Sam be obliged to intervene in Cuba?

The rebels led by swarthy Sergeant Batista are still in control.

*September 13, 1933*—Postmaster General Farley's promise of prohibition repeal by Christmas is beginning to look like a reality. Now that not only Maine but Maryland, Minnesota, and Colorado have turned in their votes for repeal, it needs only seven more.

*September 15, 1933*—Hitler's followers are determined to make Austria a part of Germany. But Chancellor Dollfuss of Austria has made a counterattack. He proposes to steal the Nazis' thunder and make Austria a Fascist state, modeled on Italy.

*September 18, 1933*—By a new edict Jews are forbidden to fish or hunt in Germany.

*September 19, 1933*—In several towns on the border there were riots between the Nazis and the anti-Nazis. The Austrian border police were obliged to fire to break up the mobs in upper Austria, where three of Hitler's Nazis were killed.

*September 22, 1933*—His Royal Highness has got the English Tories worried. The Prince of Wales seems to be becoming radical.

H.R.H. has been touring the country, getting together with what the English like to call the lower classes.

*September 28, 1933*—A great man stepped ashore in New York today off the Italian liner *Conte di Savoia*. The man who—— Well, if it hadn't been for him you wouldn't now be hearing any of these broadcasts. I mean, of course, the father of radio, Senator Guglielmo Marconi. He's to attend the World's Fair at Chicago, where one day next week has been set aside as Marconi Day.

The news from Vienna today indicates that civil war is possible. The Socialist party announces that it will call a general strike throughout the entire country if Chancellor Dollfuss carries out his threat to dissolve the party and proclaim a Fascist constitution.

*September 29, 1933*—It seems too ironic that just as unemployment has been reduced there should be a wholesale walkout on the part of workers. A hundred thousand coal miners are out, and labor troubles are spreading in the automobile industry, in the tool and die plants, in the steel mills.

A high spot was reached today at Leipzig, where five Communists are on trial—charged with having set fire to the German Reichstag. Marinus van der Lubbe, the young Dutch brick mason, expressed himself with scorn and defiance. Today he confessed that it was he who had tried to burn down the Reichstag.

*October 3, 1933*—A young Nazi fanatic tried to kill the Chancellor of Austria, Dr. Engelbert Dollfuss. He had fired two shots and was knocked out with a single punch by Dollfuss's Minister of Commerce. Both bullets hit the fiery little five-foot Chancellor, but neither wound was serious.

Cuba was quiet on the surface today, although the streets of Havana are full of Colonel Batista's soldiers.

*October 5, 1933*—Illinois National Guards are now mobilized at Harrisburg, Illinois.
Fifteen hundred strikers' pickets have been firing into Peabody Mine No. 43, a mine in which a hundred strikebreakers were at work. Several of the strikebreakers were seriously wounded during the night.

*October 9, 1933*—The walkout of steelworkers appears to be at an end.

*October 11, 1933*—There's a wild strike in the California cotton belt.

The trouble between the cotton ranchers and the cotton pickers resulted in bloodshed yesterday and today. Four people were killed and fifteen injured.

*October 13, 1933*—An announcement from Attorney General Cummings that Alcatraz Island in San Francisco Bay is to be turned into an American Devil's Island for incorrigible Federal prisoners.

Admiral Byrd's expedition to the South Pole is on its way. His flagship, the steamer *Jacob Ruppert*, starts tonight on the second leg of her journey to the Antarctic.

*October 16, 1933*—The Germans announce their withdrawal both from the League of Nations and that perennial international comedy known as the Disarmament Conference. The League, for the last year, has been functioning without Japan, and of course also without Russia and the United States. With Germany on the outside also, the poor old League will be more or less of a living corpse.

*October 17, 1933*—The labor troubles in western Pennsylvania seem to be slowly on the mend. Ninety-five hundred workers were on the job today at the seventeen mines of the Pittsburgh Coal Company.

A new transatlantic record for dirigibles has just been hung up. The famous old Graf Zeppelin did the trick. She arrived in Pernambuco, Brazil, a full half day ahead of her schedule!

*October 20, 1933*—Uncle Sam is going to recognize Russia!
The President has invited the Russian Government to send representatives to Washington to discuss problems of common interest to the two countries.

*October 24, 1933*—The gold program announced by President Roosevelt in his radio speech Sunday night, the program for the purchase of newly mined American gold by the government, will start in operation tomorrow.

*October 27, 1933*—The Secretary of the Interior, Mr. Ickes, who is administrator of the Public Works program, announces today a Federal Housing Corporation is going to be established.

Rioting has broken out again in Palestine, rioting between Arabs and Jews. It seems that the Arabs had become incensed because the ascension to power of the Hitler government in Germany has brought a considerable immigration of Jewish people into the Holy Land.

*October 30, 1933*—Late this afternoon the President, General Johnson, captive mine operators, and representatives of the United Mine Workers reached an agreement on the coal strike.

*November 3, 1933*—Mussolini, the black-shirt dictator, plans to put his program for the complete Fascist state in full force by the beginning of the New Year.

The Italians call it the corporative state, the government to consist of representatives of the chief industries of the country, about fifty industries in all, a union of capital and labor.

*November 6, 1933*—Mussolini announces he has taken over Marshal Balbo's portfolio as Minister of Aviation and has made the marshal governor of Libya, the desert colony in North Africa.

Some commentators interpret this as a process of kicking the spectacular Balbo upstairs.

*November 7, 1933*—This is the sixteenth anniversary of the founding of the Soviet Republics in Russia, and this is the first time an official Soviet representative has been formally received in Washington.

Commissar Litvinov arrived in New York this morning on the *Berengaria* and was promptly whisked off to the capital.

*November 8, 1933*—The lid blew off in Cuba again today, and fourteen people are dead, sixty wounded from sniping in the streets of Havana.

So prohibition comes to an end. Curiously enough, it was Utah that administered the deathblow to the Noble Experiment; Utah, the home of the Mormon Church, which forbids the use of alcohol. The sale of liquor will become legal in many parts of the U.S.A. either December 5 or 6. There goes what has been for the last fourteen years one of our principal topics of conversation. What'll we talk about now?

Fiery Fiorello La Guardia was elected mayor of New York by an overwhelming vote.

*November 10, 1933*—One French paper declares that the Reichswehr, Germany's only legitimate military force, has been doubled in strength and that there are now eight hundred thousand men under arms. It states further that the Hitler government is manufacturing artillery night and day and will soon have machinery capable of turning out twenty-five hundred fighting planes a month.

Martial law proclaimed throughout Austria following Nazi disturbances.

*Nobember 13, 1933*—In German elections more than 95 per cent of the voters cast their ballots for Hitler.

*November 14, 1933*—Today Mussolini abolished the Italian parliament. This is part of his program for establishing a corporative state. The Duce says that parliamentary rule is out of date. Henceforth Italy will be governed by a Supreme Council, representing capital and labor, industry and agriculture, commerce and the professions.

*November 17, 1933*—The first American Ambassador to Red Moscow is William C. Bullitt, who has taken a prominent part in the negotiations which brought about this historic event.

*November 30, 1933*—The Bank of France reports a loss of gold during the week amounting to the value of eighteen million English pounds sterling.

*December 5, 1933*—In Scotland, on the banks of Loch Ness, people have been scared by rumors of a monster fish. It is thirty feet long and has two huge humps.

So many people in the Loch Ness region claim to have seen this animal that these reports are not in the same class with the many sea-serpent yarns.

*December 6, 1933*—Tonight the big repeal celebrations will take place all over the country. Hotels and restaurants are stocked up.

*December 22, 1933*—President Roosevelt certainly made a handsome Christmas present to a lot of people who are interested in silver—I mean, of course, that proclamation of last night affirming the program for buying silver.

General Johnson's offices have discovered that the people given jobs by the CWA, the Civil Works Administration, are getting more money than people employed in private industries are receiving under the NRA codes.

*December 28, 1933*—The good ship *Jacob Ruppert* is almost smothered with icebergs amid foaming Antarctic seas. A Mackay radiogram from Admiral Byrd's expedition to the South Pole estimates that they have seen no less than six thousand bergs.

*December 29, 1933*—Premier Duca of Rumania was murdered this afternoon by a young student. The crime took place at a railroad station where the Premier had gone after an interview with the King.

# 1934

Hitler's power grows with giant steps. He has the leaders of the storm troopers executed in a savage purge and causes Chancellor Dollfuss of Austria to be murdered by local Nazis. He signs a ten-year non-aggression pact with Poland. He holds the first of his spectacular meetings with Mussolini. He insists that the Germans believe in themselves as a super-race. The names of his henchmen begin to have a sinister sound—Goering, Goebbels, Himmler. We will hear much more of them as time passes.

In Russia, mass murder follows the assassination of Stalin's lieutenant in Leningrad. In Spain, Red atrocities become common in many places. In France, the Stavisky scandal touches off a heated quarrel that threatens to disrupt the national life.

At home, President Roosevelt presses forward with his schemes for social reform. Drought scourges a wide belt in the Southwest. Bruno Richard Hauptmann is captured and accused of kidnaping the Lindbergh baby. Dillinger is shot down outside a movie house, following one of the biggest man hunts on record.

---

*January 4, 1934*—Uproar in France. A financial uproar. Bank busted. Bank president missing. It's the Municipal Bank of Bayonne, and it blew up to the tune of a quarter of a billion francs. French police have asked Scotland Yard to look for the missing bank president. He is a Russian, Alexander Stavisky.

*January 10, 1934*—Yes, they rang the curtain down today on that Reichstag fire in Berlin. And the last scene was the guillotine. The young Dutch stonemason who was found guilty of starting the Reichstag fire was the victim. Marinus van der Lubbe was executed this morning at Leipzig.

*January 12, 1934*—Not since the days of the affair of Dreyfus has Paris been so indignant as right now—over that bank scandal. Twenty thousand angry Parisians tried to storm the Chamber of Deputies today.

*January 18, 1934*—Dick Byrd is back at his old base once more, the frosty camp he built and named "Little America."

*January 22, 1934*—It turns out that Stavisky, the mysterious Russian head of that French bank who committed suicide, had a police record. An old charge had been pending against Stavisky for years.

*January 23, 1934*—Chancellor Dollfuss protested to the League of Nations and asked for protection against Nazi attacks on Austria. And now a dispatch from Geneva indicates that the League is ready to back up the Austrian Government.

*January 24, 1934*—It looks as if they've put the hooks into the Kingfish! That mayoralty election in New Orleans has gone against him. The first real licking—that is, political licking—that Senator Long has taken in six years.

Three Catholic priests in Bavaria have been sentenced to prison. They are charged with circulating stories of Nazi atrocities.

*January 26, 1934*—A radiogram from Berlin announces the signing of a non-aggression agreement between Germany and Poland. The treaty agreed on between Warsaw and Berlin is for ten years.

The notorious Dillinger gang is now in the city prison out at Tucson, Arizona, after having been tracked all over the continent.

*January 30, 1934*—At four o'clock this afternoon, on his fifty-second birthday, President Roosevelt signed the bill which gives him the immense powers he asked of Congress, power to reduce the gold content of the dollar to sixty cents or even fifty cents.

*January 31, 1934*—By twelve o'clock tonight Samuel Insull must be outside the boundaries of Greece. The Foreign Office at Athens today notified the American Legation that the one-time king of Chicago utilities must be on his way.

*February 5, 1934*—The Austrian Government believes that outside help will be necessary to prevent the absorption of their country by the Hitlerites.

*February 13, 1934*—The little Republic of Austria is now in a state of civil war between government and Socialists.

A bitterly fought battle has been raging in the heart of Vienna. With artillery and machine guns government troops attacked a huge Vienna tenement known as Karl Marx Court. More than four thousand of the disciples of Marx had barricaded themselves inside the building. It was not until shells from Chancellor Dollfuss's artillery had set the building on fire that the defenders evacuated.

France sent a notice to Chancellor Hitler in Berlin today, a note decidedly firm in tone. The gist of it is that France will not stand for the big army of brown-shirt Nazi storm troopers which the German Government now supports. Hitler has several times protested that this is not an army and that his brown shirts are not armed.

*February 14, 1934*—Tonight it looks as though a revolution in Austria is over and Dollfuss, the vest-pocket Chancellor, is still in the saddle.

*February 16, 1934*—Mussolini has sent an unofficial note to London and Paris in which he suggests that Great Britain and France join him in a declaration that the three powers will not tolerate any interference with Austria's domestic affairs. What the big powers fear most at present is a Nazi *Putsch* in Austria.

*February 19, 1934*—Will young Leopold be the wise and effectual King that his father was? That question will be predominant among the glittering dignitaries of all the chancelleries of Europe who will assemble on Thursday for the solemn, stately funeral of Albert, King of the Belgians.

*February 26, 1934*—Tonight McGraw, the little Napoleon, lies dead. And tonight Connie Mack, the long, lanky patriarch of Philadelphia, declares, "John was the greatest of them all."

The passing of John J. McGraw, long-time manager of the New York Giants, definitely marks the end of an era, the era of scrappy, bulldog, bait-the-umpire and hate-your-enemy kind of baseball.

*February 28, 1934*—It's Coronation Day in frosty, wind-blown Manchuria. The former Henry Pu-yi, now the Emperor of the new state of Manchukuo, sits on his modern dragon throne.

*March 5, 1934*—It seems almost unbelievable that Dillinger could have escaped so soon after he was put in prison with all the blaring of publicity that went with it. The fact that he escaped by means of a pistol carved with razor blades out of a piece of wood caps the climax of incredibility.

*March 8, 1934*—In Madison Square Garden last night a trial—civilization against Hitler. Among the prosecutors who thundered against the Nazi dictator were former Governor Al Smith, Mayor La Guardia, and Judge Samuel Seabury. The case in favor of Hitler was presented by nobody.

*March 9, 1934*—Some of the President's critics cry, "Socialism!" To which Postmaster General Farley retorts, "Absurd!" He says, "The New Deal is a new order of *social justice,* if you like, but no socialism."

*March 27, 1934*—The Nazis want to introduce into Christianity the idea of race and racial purity. The Hitlerites are inclined to go back to the old paganism of the primitive Germans, to the great gods Wotan and Thor.

*March 30, 1934*—Hitler told the foreign correspondents in Berlin he wished it were possible for him to meet President Roosevelt and talk things over.

*April 3, 1934*—A severe criticism of Nazi propaganda has been sent forth by Pope Pius. It indicates that the high prelates of the Catholic Church in Germany are in revolt against Nazi ideas.

*April 4, 1934*—The hunt for Dillinger goes on and on—one of the biggest, grimmest man hunts this country ever saw.

A German court says the entire Catholic press in Germany is "a superfluous element."

*April 18, 1934*—General Johnson of the NRA appointed the once fiery and still radical Clarence Darrow chairman of a board to criticize the NRA.

Darrow took the general at his word. He declares that the NRA favors monopoly, that it crushes the small businessman, that it is hard on the underdog in every field of endeavor.

*April 20, 1934*—Though he offers bonuses to other Germans to get married Hitler himself is conspicuously a bachelor. He is a vegetarian, eats sparingly, doesn't drink. Neither does he smoke. His one passion is politics, his only recreation music.

*April 23, 1934*—In Germany ten thousand German Protestants gathered in the old city of Ulm and denounced Hitler's chief bishop. The assembly called upon the Nazi state to keep its hands off the affairs of the Church.

*April 24, 1934*—Dillinger in a battle in the woodlands of Wisconsin. Two more notches on his gun, one of them a Federal agent. The Indiana killer is being hunted by the entire power of the United States.

*May 4, 1934*—The French Minister of War, Marshal Pétain, wants to increase the term of compulsory military service from one year, as it now is, to fifteen months; maybe even two years. This seems to be aimed at Hitler.

*May 7, 1934*—Samuel Insull actually is in our midst again. And Uncle Sam's men certainly took every precaution to insure his staying here until he has answered the charges brought against him.

*May 23, 1934*—It was doom for a desperado who might be called Public Enemy No. 2. A party of officers outshot Clyde Barrow, the notorious Texas rattlesnake and his flaunting girl friend, the cigar-smoking Bonnie Parker.

*May 24, 1934*—Masaryk has just been re-elected President of Czechoslovakia for his third term. Genuine democracies, says Dr. Masaryk, will outride the storm of dictatorships that is sweeping over the world.

*May 30, 1934*—Japan is mourning the death of its great naval hero, Admiral Togo. One of the stateliest funerals ever seen in Japan will be given to the little sea fighter who sank the Russian fleet in the Russo-Japanese War.

*June 8, 1934*—The President's message to Congress presents that long-expected program of social reform. Its great purpose, the President says, is security, security for everybody.

There is unemployment insurance. The President proposes old-age pensions. Then there is a home-improvement program—and land reclamation.

Today the government has classified forty-six counties on its emergency list. That gives us some idea of the colossal scope of the drought in the West.

*June 15, 1934*—Mussolini and Hitler are deep in their discussions of the affairs of Europe. Secrecy surrounds their confabulation.

Over in Europe they call us not Uncle Sam but Uncle Shylock. But I should say that as a debt collector Uncle Shylock is a failure. Of all the millions that were due us today, 477 of them, how much do you suppose we got? One hundred and sixty-six thousand dollars from the little fellow who pays—Finland.

*June 27, 1934*—It is an open secret that Hitler himself would really like his storm troopers shoved into the background for a while. Those brown shirts are responsible for the constant violence, for the virulence of the anti-Semitic movement, and for most of the things that cause criticism of Germany.

*June 28, 1934*—The house of Morgan stands for everything that is conservative. Thomas W. Lamont has gained renown as a Morgan partner. And now his son, young Corliss Lamont, gets himself arrested as a Communist.

*July 2, 1934*—The Nazis struck like rattlesnakes today—struck at the leadership of the storm troopers. Goering presided at the summary executions in Berlin while Hitler did the same in the Nazi plotters' nest at Munich.

Captain Roehm, commander of the storm troopers, like so many of his fellow storm troop leaders, was shot. He was one of Hitler's most intimate friends. They tried to persuade him to kill himself, but he refused and so he was executed.

The situation is enormously confused. But just now Hitler seems to have things in the strangling clutch of an iron hand.

*July 3, 1934*—It would seem that Hitler struck his savage blows at the three chief sources of opposition, sources that we have heard about all along, the Prussian Junker conservatives, the Catholic opposition, and the Bolshevik element among the storm troopers—especially the storm troop rebels.

*July 5, 1934*—Here's another side light on Germany's weekend of terror. They say that many of those lightning-swift executions may be laid to a pale young man who heads the Nazi secret police. His name is Himmler. He is described as Goering's man. He is thirty-three, very blond, aloof, and exceedingly cool. Yes, cool indeed; they say he holds human life cheap.

*July 9, 1934*—The radio address by Rudolf Hess, speaking for Hitler, would seem to mark a turning point of policy—it was so pointedly a gesture of friendship toward France.

*July 12, 1934*—The order has gone out from Berlin that hereafter every program on the air must sign off with the Nazi war cry, "Heil Hitler."

*July 23, 1934*—They say that Dillinger was betrayed by a woman—one of his girl friends who gave the tip that trapped him.

The government agents were waiting, watching, around the movie house. Dillinger came out with the two women. These disappeared as the government men closed in. They got away. It is said that one of the two women raised her hand and fluttered a handkerchief, signaling to the waiting officers.

Then the swift climax and close. Dillinger suddenly saw that he was trapped. He started to run, drawing his automatic. There was a fusillade of shots—and that was the end of the greatest man hunt this country has ever seen.

*July 25, 1934*—I wish I could tell you the meaning of things in Austria right now, the precise state of affairs in Vienna. But I can't. Communications with the troubled city on the Danube are cut off after that wild revolutionary outbreak.

The stately, splendid old city of the Danube was drowsing in the quiet of a summer day. Then suddenly it happened—the revolt, the Nazi *Putsch*. The conspirators struck right in the middle of things, in the very heart of the government. With carefully timed secret moves, and before anyone knew what was happening, they suddenly captured the headquarters of the government. And they seized the heads of the Dollfuss dictatorship, Dollfuss himself, the aged President Miklas, and Vice-Chancellor Emil Fey. Thus with one swift stroke the heads of the anti-Nazi regime were in the hands of their enemies, and along with them the lesser members of their Cabinet.

*July 26, 1934*—Tonight we can get some perspective on the events of yesterday. The Nazi revolt was a murderous, miscalculated affair. The conspirators who seized the heads of the government and sent out a radio broadcast announcing an overturn seemed to have believed that a general Nazi uprising would promptly flare. Nothing of the sort happened. The people were quiet. The forces of the government gathered. So all those Nazi insurrectors could do was to threaten to kill the high officials who were their prisoners.

And they did shoot down Dollfuss, the little man who has long been trying to clamp down an iron hand on the assorted disturbers and terrorists. They shot him down and left him to die slowly, without doctor or priest.

Pope Pius XI denounces the murder of Chancellor Dollfuss as "a damnable and bloody act."

*July 27, 1934*—Hitler's government has been disclaiming all responsibility for the trouble in Vienna.

*August 2, 1934*—Immediately after Von Hindenburg's death this morning Hitler made himself absolute ruler of Germany with the combined title of President-Chancellor.

*August 3, 1934*—Hitler, while taking to himself full presidential powers in Germany, has abolished the name of President. He does this as an act of homage to Von Hindenburg. But the title of President has democratic flavor, characteristic of a republic, which the Hitlerites hate.

Hitler's present title of leader, *der Fuehrer*, smacks of a kind of mystical absolutism.

*August 20, 1934*—Der Fuehrer got a mere 90 per cent majority in the election yesterday. Ninety per cent would seem to be a convincing margin, but then those Fascist totalitarian ballotings have a look of cock-eyed fantasy.

*August 30, 1934*—The new mandate forbids all relations between the Nazis and the Jews. A Nazi is forbidden to be seen in public with a Jew.

Several prominent Jewish families have been made "Aryan" by decree, proclaimed to be of the Aryan race.

*September 11, 1934*—The fire-ruined hulk of the ill-fated *Morro Castle* at Asbury Park is still burning. The strange sight of the great horror-haunted liner stranded on the beach has drawn tens of thousands of sight-seers.

*September 14, 1934*—Juliu Maniu, a dominant figure in Rumanian affairs of state, makes a scathing attack on King Carol's red-haired lady, Madame Lupescu.

"Through her meddling into politics thirteen cabinets have fallen," says he. "She's responsible for all the evil in this country."

*September 18, 1934*—Today the League of Nations at Geneva voted the U.S.S.R. a full-fledged membership.

*September 21, 1934*—Proceedings in a New York court today. The prisoner, Bruno Richard Hauptmann, the central figure in the new break in the Lindbergh case, the man of the Lindbergh ransom money. The only charge on which the New York authorities could hold him was one of extortion. "We want him on a charge of murder." That was the flash from New Jersey. Governor Harry Moore demands him as the kidnaper of the Lindbergh baby.

The case still has two distinct and sharply different angles—the kidnaping and the ransoms. And the dominant question remains: Did the same man do the kidnaping and get the ransom, or was each act done by a different man?

*September 24, 1934*—Hauptmann sticks stubbornly to his story of not guilty. The authorities claim just as stubbornly that, on a basis of handwriting, the ransom notes, and other evidence, they have a convicting case against him.

*October 8, 1934*—Tonight the picture is one of raging battle scattered all over the Iberian Peninsula.

*October 9, 1934*—The procession of automobiles in Marseilles had not progressed far along the broad avenue when two men suddenly leaped through the police line. Pistol in hand, they began firing at the car in which the royal visitor was riding.

King Alexander of Yugoslavia slumped and died. Premier Barthou of France, beside him, was mortally wounded. In the swiftest flash the crime was committed.

The Spanish story tonight is quieting down. The government seems to have a strong grip on the nationwide sweep of revolutionary strikes and insurrection.

*October 10, 1934*—Hauptmann will be tried for murder in New Jersey. This was made certain today when Governor Lehman of New York announced that he would yield to the request of the New Jersey governor and would sign extradition papers.

*October 11, 1934*—Albert Sarraut, French Minister of the Interior, is out. His department is entrusted with the protection of visiting potentates. The failure to protect King Alexander was so startling and calamitous that the Minister of the Interior resigned today.

*October 16, 1934*—The Federal investigation charges neglect of duty by the officer in command of the ill-fated *Morro Castle* and by four of his subordinates.

*October 22, 1934*—They got Pretty Boy Floyd, the last of the Dillinger big shots. In Iowa, Federal agents dropped Pretty Boy with a well-aimed bullet, so that he crept away into a thicket like a wounded animal. Now comes the last word, the wound was mortal. They found him dead.

*November 1, 1934*—Here is an official survey of the havoc caused by the recent Red revolt in the province of Asturias. This is merely one small province, a mining center, but the damage was terrific. The list of people killed runs way up in the thousands. The civil guards of the province were almost wiped out, and even their wives and children killed by the revolutionists. The Reds shot down public officials and especially the local clergy. Throughout the province the insurgents wrecked convents and monasteries.

*November 7, 1934*—Japan, England, and the United States are deadlocked in London, with Japan demanding naval equality, the United States firmly opposing, and England standing in the middle.

*November 16, 1934*—Little Gloria Vanderbilt, the ten-year-old heiress to two million dollars, is ordered by the court to remain in the custody of her aunt, Mrs. Harry Payne Whitney—that is, until the child is fourteen years old. But she will be allowed to make visits to her mother.

In England, Mrs. Alice Hargreaves has died at the age of eighty-two. As a little girl she was the original Alice of *Alice in Wonderland*. Let's believe that today Alice went to Wonderland.

*November 28, 1934*—They got Baby Face Nelson. This most recent Public Enemy No. 1 is dead. His bullet-slashed body was found this afternoon some miles out of Chicago. His pals had tossed the body out of the getaway car.

*December 3, 1934*—The assassination of Kirov, class associate of Stalin, is a pretext for a flare of violent propaganda against the internal enemies of the Soviet.

*December 5, 1934*—The decree was drawn up in the Kremlin on the very evening after Kirov was killed in Leningrad. But it has only now been published.

Hereafter the trials of the enemies of the Soviets shall be conducted "without the participation of either party." There will be no formal prosecution and the accused will not be allowed to present any defense. Execution by shooting will be carried out at once.

*December 12, 1934*—That new plan for saving the country is ready to be placed before the President by its creator, Dr. F. E. Townsend, the California dentist.

They say the Townsend Plan is the most popular utopian formula in the country at the present moment.

When people reach the age of sixty they should be retired, given nothing to do, and two hundred dollars a month to do it on.

*December 25, 1934*—The probabilities are that the biggest Christmas in the world fell to the lot of the Dionne quintuplets. All day presents have been pouring into that little town and are still pouring in for those most famous babies on the globe—also their father, mother, and the kindly physician, Dr. Dafoe.

*December 26, 1934*—The date of the Lindbergh trial is now finally decided. January 2—next Wednesday.

*December 27, 1934*—More than a hundred men and women have been executed as a kind of modern sacrifice to the ghost of the murdered Kirov. It isn't pretended that the holocaust of victims was connected with the assassination. They were merely enemies—class enemies, as the Communists say.

*December 31, 1934*—Gregory Zinoviev and Leon Kamenev, who used to be partners of Lenin, are being sent into exile by Lenin's successor, Stalin, to a frigid island in the frozen Arctic north of Archangel.

# 1935

Mussolini starts the downfall of the League of Nations by invading Ethiopia in spite of its warnings. The world becomes more than ever split between the democracies and the Fascist powers. The Saar votes for union with Germany. Hitler attacks all religious bodies. In Russia, Stalin puts two old Bolsheviks and colleagues of Lenin, Kamenev and Zinoviev, on trial for their lives.

At home, the Supreme Court declares the NRA unconstitutional. Hauptmann is sentenced to die for the Lindbergh kidnaping. Will Rogers and Wiley Post crash to their death in the Arctic waste. Huey Long is assassinated.

*January 1, 1935*—Persia has decreed that its official name hereafter will be Iran.

*January 2, 1935*—We all knew that there'd be something of a carnival spirit here at the Flemington, New Jersey, trial of Bruno Hauptmann. It is a hurly-burly with a touch of grimness.

An interesting feature today was the dramatic proximity of Lindbergh to Hauptmann. Each seemed carefully to avoid glancing in the other's direction.

*January 3, 1935*—When Colonel Lindbergh came to the stand, the prosecutor asked him if he had heard any unusual sound. Lindbergh replied, "Yes," a noise as of something falling outside. The prosecution's theory of the crime is that there was a fall from the ladder and that the child was killed by that fall.

*January 4, 1935*—President Roosevelt summed up his program in one characteristic phrase when he spoke of guaranteeing everyone "the security against the major hazards and vicissitudes of life."

*January 8, 1935*—The highest tribunal of the land declares the NRA oil code to be illegal.

This is the first Supreme Court decision that goes against a major issue of President Roosevelt's New Deal.

*January 9, 1935*—Dr. Condon told his story at length. He was the pedantic schoolteacher all over in his meticulous precision.

He was telling of the mysterious John with whom he made contact, and declared that John was Bruno Richard Hauptmann.

*January 11, 1935*—Albert S. Osborn, one of the foremost graphologists, declared emphatically that it was Hauptmann who had written the ransom notes.

*January 15, 1935*—The people of the Saar Valley have voted for union with Germany. Immediately after the election figures were published, Hitler went on the air and told the people of the Saar that a fifteen-year wrong had been cleared up.

*January 16, 1935*—As the Nazis prepare to take over, refugees are leaving the Saar—Jews, Socialists, anti-Hitlerites in general.

The Zinoviev trial is on.

The opinion in Moscow is that Zinoviev, Kamenev, and their coterie of famous old Communist leaders who are on trial now will not face the firing squad. Not one prominent Bolshevik leader has ever been shot.

*January 18, 1935*—Mrs. Hauptmann is reported to have said that Hauptmann was limping. The prosecution claims he fell off the ladder and was hurt.

*January 23, 1935*—The long-expected Japanese push against China has begun.

*January 24, 1935*—Hauptmann gives you the impression of a hunted creature at bay. He keeps his hands clasped nervously on his knees, loosening them only occasionally to make a gesture.

Hauptmann swore that he was home all evening after supper on the fateful March 1.

*January 25, 1935*—You yourself could come close to writing down Hauptmann's testimony of denial. Take every point of evidence against him and answer it with, "No, I did not. It is not true." That would include everything from the kidnaping itself to the writing of the ransom note, to the meeting with Jafsie.

*January 28, 1935*—Hauptmann as a witness is a man carrying on under the gravest of handicaps. His story that does not sound plausible, his account of how the bundles of bank notes of ransom money were left with him in a shoe box by the dead man, Fisch. Yet he must stick to the tale of many improbabilities if he is to save his life.

*January 29, 1935*—Now what did the cross-examination achieve? The Attorney General did not maneuver Hauptmann into any admission that in itself would mean conviction. But in those many hours of question and answer he undoubtedly built up an impression that Hauptmann was a stubborn, cautious, wary, and defensive witness who was making the best of a story woven full of contradictions and improbabilities.

Today Poland passed legally under the power of a president-dictator. Marshal Pilsudski, of course.

*February 1, 1935*—Today a trickle of water streamed across parched western desert land and one of the greatest of man's labors went into operation. Boulder Dam!

*February 4, 1935*—Today was Colonel Lindbergh's thirty-third birthday—a mere thirty-three years for the Lone Eagle, who has done so much and suffered so much. He sat in court as usual, attending the proceedings that endlessly renewed his melancholy tragedy.

*February 11, 1935*—How important an adventure is Mussolini embarking on? It has been surmised that in one of the clauses of the new agreement France has assured Italy a free hand with respect to African expansion along the Abyssinian line.

*February 13, 1935*—The jury is still out at Flemington—no verdict yet.

*February 14, 1935*—Today the story turns into sheer emotion. That's to be expected after last night's verdict, with the death penalty. Hauptmann's nerve is shaken. He is even weakening, refusing food. But he told the press he was innocent—no confession to make.

*March 1, 1935*—Today's biggest piece of news as sheer panorama and hurrahing is the return of the Saar Valley to Germany.

*March 5, 1935*—I wonder what Mussolini is going to do with those thousands of soldiers in East Africa!

*March 7, 1935*—Today Sir Malcolm Campbell, in that queer-looking contraption of his, more like a mechanical monster than an automobile, blazed along at 276.8 miles an hour.

*March 13, 1935*—The Greek revolution seems to be pretty much at an end—with the flight of the aged former Premier Venizelos.

*March 19, 1935*—There were war planes over Berlin today. That's the way Hitler told the people that Germany had renounced the Versailles Treaty and was rearming, restoring her old militarism.

Less of a spectacle is Hitler's announcement to Germany to fortify the Rhine. That's another thing forbidden by the Versailles Treaty.

Today the Emperor Haile Selassie of Abyssinia again appealed to the League of Nations. He once more calls upon the League to intervene in that dispute along the frontiers of Ethiopia and the Italian African colonies.

*March 27, 1935*—Hitler wants an army, he wants a navy, he wants as strong a force in the air as Britain and France. He wants the Polish Corridor. He wants those portions of Czechoslovakia in which the Germans outnumber the Czechs. And he wants the *Anschluss* customs union with Austria.

Well, it's all over between Japan and the old League of Nations. With bows and banzais the emissaries of His Imperial Majesty, the descendant of the sun, backed politely out of the august body that meets and talks on the beautiful banks of Lake Geneva.

*March 28, 1935*—Captain Anthony Eden, Lord Privy Seal of Great Britain, is conferring with Foreign Commissar Maxim Litvinov of Soviet Russia. Captain Eden, after having taken part in the Berlin palaver, has gone on for some more palavering at Moscow.

*April 1, 1935*—The Supreme Court of the United States has spoken in the Scottsboro case. For the second time that august tribunal has saved Clarence Morris and Haywood Patterson, Negroes charged with raping a white woman, from a death sentence and has ordered a new trial.

*April 4, 1935*—President De Valera has signed a bill declaring that the people of the Irish Free State are no longer British subjects.

*April 10, 1935*—Goering, the Reichsfuehrer's right-hand man, was being married to the beautiful Emmy Sonnemann in one part of Berlin while in another the headsman was swinging his ax. One victim a Jew, the other an Aryan; condemned to death for the murder of the Nazi martyr, Horst Wessel.

*April 12, 1935*—At Stresa, Foreign Minister Laval of France declared today that the three powers represented at the conference had reached an agreement.

Great Britain, France, and Italy have decided to take a common stand toward Germany.

*April 15, 1935*—Today again opaque clouds of murk and dirt hang over the land all the way from Brownsville, Texas, north to Denver, Colorado. There seems to be no end to the dust storms that began last year.

*April 29, 1935*—Hitler's announcement that he is going to build submarines has given Britain a case of Neptunian shivers.

*May 1, 1935*—In Russia, May Day took the form of a huge military demonstration. In Moscow a parade of uniforms and guns from morning till night. With fixed bayonets the helmeted legions of the Soviet marched past the Kremlin while Tovarish Stalin and his staff looked on with grim approval.

A new industry is springing up in the Middle West, the making of dust masks. Thousands of people are ill in the storm area.

*May 10, 1935*—Salutations to the men from the South Pole. There's no need to detail the ceremonies of welcome in Washington for Admiral Byrd and his hardy crew. They're getting all the honors, with a reception by the President, for their Antarctic exploration.

*May 13, 1935*—Marshal Pilsudski, "the Iron Man of Poland," has died.

*May 14, 1935*—A profoundly tragic story has to be told tonight. It's about the serious accident to Lawrence of Arabia that happened late yesterday in England when he crashed his motor bike to avoid hitting a child.

*May 20, 1935*—The Council of the League of Nations has been at it all day trying to find an Italian-Abyssinian solution. The Council received an urgent telegram this afternoon from the Lion of Judah imploring the League to do something, do anything, to avert warfare.

Colonel Lawrence, "Lawrence of Arabia," put in most of the last fifteen years of his life trying to avoid fame. And now England wants to bury him in Westminster Abbey, Britain's hall of fame.

At Cincinnati next Thursday evening, the first baseball game to be played at night under the big arc lamps in the major leagues.

*May 21, 1935*—Der Fuehrer appeared today before the Reichstag and proclaimed that Germany utterly rejects the League of Nations' action in condemning German rearmament.

*May 23, 1935*—Father Coughlin's address in New York last night draws the usual contradictory shouts of yes or no, answering the blistering things the radio priest said, his denunciation of the plutocratic capitalistic system, of the President's veto of the Bonus Bill, and of the newspapers of the land.

*May 27, 1935*—The United States Supreme Court has outlawed the NRA. The august Justices handed down three decisions. Every one of them is a defeat of the gravest kind for the New Deal. The latest from the banks of the Potomac is that the White House was "stunned by the news."

*May 31, 1935*—The most important verdict the Supreme Court of the United States has handed down since that historic Dred Scott decision in the middle of the last century, which did so much to bring the nation to civil war. That's what the President called the Blue Eagle decision. According to the President, the Supreme Court decision puts government regulation of interstate commerce back to the days of the horse and buggy.

*June 3, 1935*—A new queen of the seas, a new Atlantic record! The great *Normandie*, the pride of France's mercantile marine, swept majestically past Ambrose Lightship. She had dashed across from Bishop's Rock on the English coast in ninety-nine hours and five minutes, just a hairline over four days.

Hitler's delegate, Herr Joachim von Ribbentrop, is telling Britain, "You ought to let us have a navy at least 35 per cent as strong as yours." Of course that's dead against the Versailles Treaty, but the Versailles Treaty is now generally recognized as a thoroughly moribund piece of paper.

*June 10, 1935*—Japan has swiftly forced China to withdraw Chinese troops from the great cities of Peking and Tientsin, leaving Japan, tonight, in control of North China.

*June 12, 1935*—The three-year-old squabble over the Gran Chaco is settled. Bolivia and Paraguay are no longer at war.

*June 13, 1935*—There certainly are evidences of nerves in Italy—in the way Rome is clamping down on American journalists. Not only is the New York *Times* banished from the peninsula, but now the Rome correspondent of the Chicago *Tribune* has been expelled.

*June 18, 1935*—The former lord of the Red Army has arrived at Oslo, Norway, and at first nobody recognized him. Trotsky in his day of glory was known for a big mustache. After his exile he added a beard. Now he is smooth-shaven.

*June 25, 1935*—There's definite word from the White House that the President will not ask for any more NRA legislation. The present skeleton Blue Eagle will have to do.

The word from the White House is "Full speed ahead"—full speed for those taxes. Congress is to drive the "tax the wealth" program through during this present session.

The new figures show that the biggest army in the world is Red—Soviet Russia with a million men under arms. Way down the line comes the United States, with a standing army of 140,000 men.

Germany is definitely pledged to England—no ruthless submarine warfare.

*June 26, 1935*—Captain Eden is back in London. The best he could say about his visit to Rome was that his conversation with Mussolini had been "worth while."

*July 3, 1935*—The Abyssinian Government reports violent fighting along the frontiers of Ethiopia and the Italian colony of Eritrea.

*July 8, 1935*—The King of Kings, Haile Selassie, has obviously abandoned all hope of being saved by the diplomats. He is hastily and desperately mobilizing his scanty forces of trained troops and the more numerous wild but poorly armed tribesmen.

*July 12, 1935*—The exodus of Americans from Ethiopia continues. The latest is the departure of eight American Negroes, warned by the American consul that it might be dangerous for them to remain. While in Harlem, Negroes are enlisting to go and fight for Abyssinia.

*July 23, 1935*—A paragraph from Germany—the organization of Catholic War Veterans has been ordered disbanded. And so Goering's threat to put an end to all Catholic societies begins to materialize.

*July 30, 1935*—Berlin sent a formal diplomatic remonstrance to Washington because of the riot aboard the steamship *Bremen* last week when the Nazi swastika was torn down in a riotous demonstration.

*August 1, 1935*—Reports come from Addis Ababa telling of a mass meeting of high chiefs of Ethiopia, the great territorial lords in their lion skins. In full uniform the King of Kings reviewed his chiefs as they marched by at the head of their warriors. And most resplendent of all was Colonel Julian, the Black Eagle of Harlem.

*August 7, 1935*—I'd like to have been on the airplane that took off from Seattle, Washington, at a quarter past one this afternoon. The pilot, Wiley Post; the passenger, good old Will Rogers. One-eyed Wiley and Two-lung Will are bound for Russia. They aren't aiming at any records. They made no rigid plans. Probably their first stop will be Juneau, Alaska. Wiley goes on to Siberia. Will will sojourn in Alaska.

*August 8, 1935*—And now the Nazis are hitting at Freemasons. Hitler's own newspaper proclaims the end of Masonry in Germany. The Masons are accused of conspiring for a world state under Jewish control.

*August 14, 1935*—Hitler's men have turned their attention to the Protestants. No minister who has not been ordained by Hitler's Bishop Mueller will receive a pfennig of salary. Students for the ministry are forbidden to study at any theological schools except those approved by Reich Bishop Mueller.

*August 16, 1935*—The President of the United States expressed what we all feel over the tragic accident. Said Mr. Roosevelt, "I was deeply shocked to hear of the tragedy. Will Rogers and Wiley Post were outstanding Americans who will be greatly missed."

The Eskimo told the story of what happened. A crash on the frozen Arctic tundra. Will Rogers, thrown clear, never knew what hit him. Wiley crushed to death. Fatality hundreds of miles north of the Arctic Circle.

*August 23, 1935*—Mussolini was terse and decisive—epigrammatic. "Italy," he cried, "will pursue her aims, with Geneva, without Geneva, or against Geneva."

*August 26, 1935*—The French War Office has completed more than three hundred new forts. In appearance they are small turrets buried in the earth. The Maginot Line, a wall of steel and concrete between the French and the Germans.

*August 29, 1935*—Once more the fate of the mountains in the royal family of Belgium. Last year it was the mountaineer king—Albert. Killed while climbing a peak. Now Queen Astrid, come to an untimely end while motoring through the mountains, the Alps.

*September 3, 1935*—Sir Malcolm Campbell achieved his life's ambition today. He was out to do three hundred miles an hour in his roaring racer, the Bluebird. And let's say he did it. Although some captious mathematicians may wrinkle their brows and say that 299.874 is not three hundred.

*September 6, 1935*—Last evening we had the Italian delegation to the League walking out on a speech of defense made by the Ethiopian representative. Today we have the official announcement that Mussolini's men will stay out as long as Ethiopia has any part in the deliberations.

*September 9, 1935*—Huey Long has taken a turn for the worse after being gravely wounded. In the Louisiana state capital he was shot by a Dr. Weiss, who fired twice before he was mowed down by bullets from Senator Long's bodyguard.

*September 10, 1935*—President Roosevelt expresses his sorrow over the assassination of Huey Long, who was a formidable political enemy.

*September 18, 1935*—The new Philippine President, Manuel Quezon, will have invaluable help in at least one department. The military defenses of the new Philippine Commonwealth will be organized by no less a martial magnifico than General Douglas MacArthur.

The latest *verboten* in Germany is you mustn't allude to Palestine as the Holy Land.

*September 26, 1935*—The League of Nations today took the strongest action it has ever taken. It said to Mussolini, "Don't you dare go to war, not for three months." The Italians didn't vote. They stayed out of the Assembly room while the fateful ballot was cast against them.

*October 2, 1935*—The Duce announces personally and publicly that he's going ahead with the war in Africa—probably right away. It may be on now.

*October 3, 1935*—Italian planes bombed the spearmen of Ethiopia today. In the forefront of the attacking planes were Mussolini's two sons and his son-in-law, Count Ciano, who commands a squadron which calls itself *The disperati,* meaning the Desperate Squadron.

*October 9, 1935*—Bruno Richard Hauptmann advanced one stage closer to the electric chair today. The judges of the New Jersey Court of Errors and Appeals decided against him.

In the Assembly of the League of Nations the delegates of two countries said, "Count us out in this sanctions-against-Italy business." Those two countries were Austria and Hungary.

*October 14, 1935*—Aksum, the sacred city of the Ethiopians—not much of a city but a great deal of a shrine—is now definitely in Italian hands.

The population of this ancient African holy place consisted principally of priests and monks. They submitted without resistance.

*October 16, 1935*—Secretary of Commerce Roper says the U.S.A. will not join the boycott of Italy.

*October 18, 1935*—The U.S.S.R., Union of Soviet Socialist Republics, has officially notified the League of Nations that it is right on the job with that embargo on Italy. No war munitions, no supplies will be sent to the Duce's country.

*October 24, 1935*—A big battle is reported to be raging in southern Ethiopia.

Dutch Schultz is dying. Two of his henchmen shot with him have died. The other is in a desperate state.

At Newark, New Jersey, the four racketeers were in a room, confabulating about the Schultz interminable income tax trouble with the law, when two gunmen stalked in and blazed away.

*October 28, 1935*—When the late Huey Long was assassinated, we all wondered who would inherit his mantle. Governor Talmadge of Georgia has replaced the Kingfish as the chief baiter of President Roosevelt and his New Deal.

To celebrate the thirteenth anniversary of Fascism, the Duce's men in the north are driving deeper into Ethiopia.

London and Paris are preparing more drastic measures for the boycott of Italy.

*October 30, 1935*—Today's Ethiopian war picture gives us the same scenes of Italian advance with little or no opposition, a few fierce skirmishes, but nothing more.

The League of Nations itself is one of the first sufferers by the sanctions imposed on Italy.

The League has been building itself a new palace. But the beautiful rose marble can be procured only from Italy. It was all cut and ready to be shipped. But since the League passed those sanctions, none of it can be accepted.

*November 5, 1935*—The Japanese militarists in North China issued a warning that if Chinese authorities don't do something about checking the spread of communism the Japanese will.

*November 14, 1935*—Yesterday's anti-British outbreak in Egypt has spread today through towns and villages of the Nile delta. There was fighting from morning till night between government police and the storming members of the Wafd party.

*November 15, 1935*—This was "Sanctions Day," the day on which fifty-one member countries of the League of Nations officially began their historic boycott of Italy—all because of the Duce's invasion of Ethiopia.

*November 20, 1935*—The Social Register has dropped from its august pages the name of the Countess von Haugwitz-Reventlow, former Princess Alexis Mdivani, and before that plain Miss Barbara Hutton. As the consort of the Georgian prince she was to remain in that sacrosanct volume. But her divorce and marriage to the Danish Count have put the five-and-ten heiress beyond the pale of America's nobility.

*December 2, 1935*—The passing of Dr. James H. Breasted deprives the world of the greatest oriental scholar of his day.

*December 5, 1935*—Laval stays in power, meaning he yielded. He gave his promise to take action against the Cross of Fire and the other Fascist groups. So the radical deputies voted to sustain him.

*December 6, 1935*—It was a red-letter day in aviation when the China Clipper took off! And it was again when it completed its transpacific flight by landing at Manila. Today the China Clipper completed the first round trip.

*December 18, 1935*—In Czechoslovakia, Dr. Eduard Beneš has been elected President, to succeed the beloved Masaryk.

*December 23, 1935*—Poor old Blue Eagle. He screamed his last scream on the day the Supreme Court clamped the muzzle on his beak. But a certain part of the organization continued to exist. This afternoon the President signed his name to the final executive order which abolished even the skeleton.

Thus ends a picturesque, sensational, and stormy chapter in the history of American government.

Young Mr. Anthony Eden becomes His Majesty's Secretary of State for Foreign Affairs at the age of thirty-eight. He is the youngest man to be appointed Foreign Secretary since the office was created.

*December 30, 1935*—Was or was not Al Smith invited to the White House, and how many times? Al says not at all.

From the presidential side, the statement that Mr. Smith has a standing invitation to pay a call any time he comes to Washington.

It's a curious petty bit of bickering between the two men whose careers were so singularly tied together and then broken apart.

# 1936

The Spanish Civil War erupts into an inferno of fire and steel, of violent battles, mass murder, and unspeakable atrocities. The rebels under Franco drive steadily forward, wreaking terrible revenge for the bloodstained orgies of the Communist-dominated Loyalists. Russia, too, sees more bloodshed—Stalin executing his opponents, including Kamenev and Zinoviev, after a repulsive mock trial in which the victims confessed everything, groveled, and begged for mercy. Hitler tears up the Versailles Treaty, remilitarizes Germany, and marches into the Rhineland. But he suffers humiliation in the Olympic Games when America wins mainly because of her Negro athletes, led by the great Jesse Owens. Mussolini continues his conquest of Ethiopia.

The news from abroad carries one of the great love stories of all time. Edward VIII abdicates the British throne in order to marry Mrs. Simpson, and the two are known from then on as the Duke and Duchess of Windsor.

At home, President Roosevelt wins an overwhelming victory in his campaign for re-election. Landon carries only Maine and Vermont out of the forty-eight states. Social security begins, but in New Deal circles there is much talk of curbing the Supreme Court because it has balked Roosevelt policies by declaring them unconstitutional. Bruno Richard Hauptmann is executed for the kidnap-death of the Lindbergh baby. Cardinal Pacelli visits the United States.

January 6, 1936—The nine high Justices today declared the Agricultural Adjustment Act unconstitutional in toto, from beginning to end.

January 7, 1936—We hear defiant mutterings in New Deal circles, talk of curbing the power of the Supreme Court, depriving the nine high Justices of their right to knock out congressional laws because they consider them unconstitutional.

*January 16, 1936*—Governor Hoffman of New Jersey today granted a stay of execution, which gives Bruno Richard Hauptmann sixty days more of life. With the chair waiting for him for tomorrow night, the Bronx carpenter is snatched from it.

On the Southern frontier the Italians report a big advance. Rome says that General Graziani's army in the Dolo sector has pushed ahead forty-three miles.

*January 17, 1936*—Tonight Lincoln Ellsworth and his pilot, Captain Hollick-Kenyon, are aboard ship. After being marooned for two months on the Antarctic ice they are once more enjoying civilized comfort.

They were found at Byrd's old camp in Little America.

The two flying explorers made their stupendous sky voyage across the Antarctic Continent with first-rate success—except that they ran out of fuel within twenty miles of their destination. They had to land on the ice and then push their way afoot to Little America, where they found supplies which Byrd had cached for the use of future explorers.

*January 20, 1936*—Hourly bulletins from Sandringham. The King is sinking. Then the solemn bulletin came, "The King's life is drawing to a close."

That melancholy comedian, the League of Nations, faces a titanic question mark. "To oil or not to oil the Duce, that is the question." Shall they slam the big petroleum embargo on Italy?

*January 21, 1936*—Everywhere people are talking about the two Kings of England, the King that was and the King that is, the death of George V and the ascension of Edward VIII.

What kind of King will Edward make?

There's one thing unique about him—he's a bachelor king. Edward has never undertaken the dynastic obligation of marriage and succession.

*January 23, 1936*—In Alabama, the Scottsboro case, the jury found Haywood Patterson guilty of the charge of attacking the two white girls.

He is one of the four defendants. They have all been granted a new trial by the Supreme Court. And now the first of those new trials comes to that same old result.

The jury did not condemn Patterson to the extreme penalty. They recommended a prison term instead, a prison term of seventy-five years.

*January 27, 1936*—The Bonus Bill is law.

If I'm not mistaken, this is the second time since President Roosevelt entered the White House that one of his vetoes has been overridden.

*January 28, 1936*—Remember Leopold and Loeb, the two wealthy, highly educated youths who set out to commit the perfect crime? The kidnap-murder of little Bobby Franks?

There was the flash of a razor today in the Illinois State Prison at Joliet. Richard Loeb, killed by a fellow convict.

The British Empire bowed its head for the funeral of King George. There was the dark pageantry of the funeral cortege in London, the affecting simplicity of the brief Church of England ritual as the monarch was laid to rest.

*January 29, 1936*—General Graziani's vanguard is now only 175 miles south of Addis Ababa.

*February 6, 1936*—At Garmisch-Partenkirchen they staged a Winter Olympic pageant. Hitler was there, presiding.

One highlight was that the American team of winter sportsmen, as they paraded by the Fuehrer, didn't give him the Nazi salute. They executed an eyes-right in salutation.

*February 11, 1936*—The earthly remains of Father Damien are on the way back to his native Belgium, where the order to which he belonged is beginning the procedure to have the martyr to the lepers canonized as a saint—St. Damien of Molokai.

*February 17, 1936*—Adherents of President Roosevelt were rejoicing over the decision of the Supreme Court upholding the constitutionality of the Tennessee Valley Authority.

Riots are raging all over the Iberian Peninsula.

In some respects the election resembles those in many other countries. Every leader says, "We have won." The Rights, the conservatives, claim the victory in the provinces. In Madrid and Barcelona, strongholds of the radicals, the Red flag is flying.

*February 19, 1936*—The first threat to be met by the new Spanish Government of the Left is a military revolt.

Warrants have been issued for the Army's Chief of Staff, General Francisco Franco, and his principal lieutenant, General Manuel Goded. Those military moguls have disappeared and are being sought by the political police.

American aviation is poorer tonight. It has lost a voice that preached flying in season and out. Once it was a voice crying out in the wilderness—back in the days when the flying machine was laughed at.

General Billy Mitchell, prophet of aviation, has flown off on his longest flight—headed west.

*February 21, 1936*—There is a widespread revolutionary movement throughout Spain. Red flags flying in many places. Extreme Socialist leaders are calling for communism, demanding that Premier Azaña's government set up a Union of Iberian Soviets.

*March 9, 1936*—People are asking: Does it mean war—that march of Hitler's into the Rhineland?

France is gloomy tonight because of the mild stand London is taking. The French see that England will not help them oust the Germans from the Rhineland.

*March 10, 1936*—France has declared in favor of peace and demands a solution by peaceful non-military means. France didn't propose an advance of troops into the Rhineland to push out Hitler's soldiers.

*March 11, 1936*—Hitler's answer to the world from the Rhineland is, "Here we are, here we stay."

Hitler is standing pat. The rest of the world running around in circles.

The House of Commons heard King Edward's message. "His Majesty," it read, "desires that the contingency of his marriage should be taken into account." That meant, "Don't be stingy with the allowance, gentlemen, I may have a queen as well as myself to support on the Civil List." The supposition is, of course, that he will follow precedent and select a wife of royal blood.

*March 12, 1936*—Midnight tonight is zero hour for Bruno Richard Hauptmann.

At Trenton, Governor Hoffman gave out the statement, "I have no intention of granting another reprieve."

One faction is asking: Who is King Edward VIII going to marry? The other faction is busy proving that he isn't likely to marry at all.

*March 13, 1936*—Rome is reported today to have told the statesmen in London that Italy will not join in any penalties against Germany—that is, until she herself has been freed from the sanctions.

*March 19, 1936*—The Connecticut River tonight is roaring sixteen and a half feet over the Holyoke Dam. The railroad tracks five feet under water.

Just repeat the same thing over and over, place after place, and you have a picture of New England.

Herr von Ribbentrop stood there, with the Council of the League sitting around a table, and he spoke a reasoned defense of Hitler's action in rearming the Rhine.

The vote was taken. And the Council's decision was unanimous. The League today condemned Germany as a treaty breaker, a violator of Versailles and Locarno.

*March 30, 1936*—The German election has aroused a new case of the jitters. After 99 per cent of the voters have endorsed Hitler's policies, he will be spurred on to fresh aggression.

*April 13, 1936*—Dessye captured. Haile Selassie's northern headquarters taken!

*April 20, 1936*—The Ethiopians are evacuating the capital.

*April 30, 1936*—Haile Selassie declares that Ethiopia will go on fighting to the last man.

*May 4, 1936*—The Italians are annoyed—annoyed because the French gave the King of Kings refuge in Djibouti. The British are doing the same in Palestine. They are receiving the dethroned monarch as Emperor.

In such circumstance the last independent kingdom of Africa comes to an end.

*May 5, 1936*—Even if the Italian occupation of Addis Ababa had been a mere formal procession, the significance of the event would be there—gesture of complete Italian triumph in the face of all the opposition of the League of Nations and the British Empire.

*May 12, 1936*—At Mussolini's order, Baron Aloisi and his Italian delegation have packed up, left Geneva, and gone back to Rome. Tonight the League of Nations is wondering—does that mean Italy is withdrawing from the League?

*May 14, 1936*—Vienna tells us that the policy of the new Schuschnigg dictatorship will be less Fascism and more freedom, and the cultivation of better relations with Nazi Germany.

*May 18, 1936*—The Guffey Act, regulating the coal industry, has been declared unconstitutional.

This makes the ninth defeat which the Roosevelt administration has sustained on the battleground of the Supreme Court.

*May 26, 1936*—Rome is angry about the way London is receiving Haile Selassie.

*May 28, 1936*—Smart London today noticed that the list of King's guests included Mr. and Mrs. Simpson.

She is an American whose charm and beauty have distinguished her in London society. As the Prince of Wales, King Edward was noted for his preference for American girls as dancing partners. Of them all, his favorite dancing partner was Mrs. Simpson. The London papers printed photographs of them together at the seashore on the Riviera, at winter resorts in the Alps, at the fashionable race meets in England. Dancing partner of the Prince of Wales, now dinner guest of the King.

*June 1, 1936*—By a five-to-four decision the Supreme Court put the quietus on the minimum-wage law of New York State.

Thus ends the most momentous session of the Supreme Court in its entire history. Law after law, cardinal points of New Deal philosophy and policy, has it thrown into the wastebasket as contrary to the Constitution of the United States.

*June 4, 1936*—All of France in the throes of a labor revolt.

*June 9, 1936*—The Landonites at the Cleveland convention have been assuring me, and assuring each other, that they have the nomination absolutely in the bag.

*June 12, 1936*—After the nomination of Landon for President it was clear that the delegates were eager to shout, "Vandenberg for Vice-President!" But the Michigan delegation came to bat with a telegram in which the senator once again refused to consider the nomination.

After that the only thing left was to get aboard the second-place band wagon for Colonel Knox.

*June 13, 1936*—In Parliament, Foreign Secretary Eden declared the plain facts that Italy had won swiftly and decisively in Ethiopia, the League of Nations had failed, sanctions had not worked, there was no way to make Mussolini back down, no way to re-establish the independence of Ethiopia.

This week removes from the world of writers and readers two of its best-known figures, for today died Maxim Gorky, while on Monday came the news of the passing of G. K. Chesterton. And so the grim reaper's symbolic scythe has swiftly removed two of the most vividly contrasting figures in the literature of their time—the gloomy Gorky with his drab, somber stories, and the gay, lusty Chesterton with his brilliant paradoxes.

*June 25, 1936*—At the Democratic National Convention, a day of quick action. The delegates elected Senator Joe Robinson of Arkansas permanent chairman, said O.K. to the report of the Credentials Committee, and adjourned.

A two-thousand-word platform to be adopted tonight, all in prelude to the nomination of F.D.R. for a second term.

*July 3, 1936*—The League Assembly has met for the express purpose of calling off sanctions against Mussolini. And not only has the former Conquering Lion of Judah insisted on appearing at the deliberations, like a picturesque reproachful ghost, but on Tuesday he took the rostrum and made his moving and impassioned demand that, instead of calling off the sanctions, the League should keep and increase the penalties, force the Italians to get out of Ethiopia, and restore Haile Selassie to the throne of the Queen of Sheba.

*July 6, 1936*—Good-by to sanctions! The League of Nations today formally ended that sour comedy.

*July 14, 1936*—July 14 in France today, and plenty of trouble! There was a giant military parade of the grim mechanized battalions of France. Hundreds of thousands of Communists giving their salute of upraised fists were held in check along the streets by massed battalions of police.

*July 15, 1936*—By order of Premier Mussolini flags flew and *vivas* resounded today in the public places of sunny Italy. Celebrating the official end of those abortive sanctions imposed by the League of Nations.

*July 17, 1936*—The Townsend Convention is getting tangled up in snarls and complications. The sudden and rather startling get-together of the doctor, Father Coughlin, and the Reverend Gerald L. K. Smith in a third-party drive for candidate Lemke has caused some lively dissension in the Townsend ranks.

A raucous cause for dissension is found in the anger aroused by Father Coughlin's bitter denunciation of President Roosevelt.

*July 20, 1936*—At this moment the fair land of Spain is shut off from the rest of the world like a huge volcano raining with fire and surrounded by a sky-high wall. Not a train, not an automobile, not a horse can pass the land of frontiers. Not a boat can enter its harbors or land a living soul on its wide stretch of coasts. And inside those rigidly closed frontiers, rebellion runs red and fighting is ruthless.

It's an uprising of the Right with a strong Fascist tinge. The condition is nothing more or less than civil war against the leftist government headed by President Manuel Azaña.

As we have heard and read, the head of the revolution is General Francisco Franco. At any rate, he's the actual commander of the rebel troops.

*July 22, 1936*—From one dispatch we learn that the Red flag of communism is flying over the government buildings in Madrid. This indicates that, should the rebellion fail, the popular-front government will be replaced by out-and-out Bolshevik rule.

*July 23, 1936*—There's a reign of terror in beautiful Barcelona; Red mobs looting, burning, and killing. The Communist fury is raging against the churches; ancient, priceless edifices going up in flames.

*July 24, 1936*—Father Coughlin today added a flourish to his apology. In the open letter to President Roosevelt, printed in his magazine, the radio priest said that he was sincerely sorry for what he said about the President—calling him a "liar." He explained that he had spoken the word in the heat of anger, "righteous anger," he qualified.

*July 28, 1936*—The important thing in Spain today was a left-wing government decree ordering all churches and other religious buildings to be confiscated in five days. This would indeed be a heavy blow to the Catholic Church, the archenemy of the Reds and radicals.

*July 31, 1936*—In the shadow of the Château Frontenac, overlooking that superb, incomparable view of the St. Lawrence River, Franklin Delano Roosevelt celebrated the first official visit of an American president to the Dominion of Canada.

*August 4, 1936*—Jesse Owens broke records and won championships today. In preliminary races he crashed the record for the 200-meter sprint. Then in the quarter finals he duplicated that record-breaking performance. Keeping right on with his stride, he went into the broad-jump finals and made a leap of a shade more than 26 feet and 5 inches. That smashed the record by more than a foot and took the championship. All of this follows the performance Owens put on yesterday, when he won the championship for the 100-meter run and tied the record.

All of which makes the brown flash the running sensation of the 1936 Olympics.

*August 5, 1936*—The Executive Council of the A.F. of L. has just pronounced its sentence upon John L. Lewis and his associates; finds Lewis and his Committee for Industrial Organization guilty of insubordination and destructive tactics. And the punishment? Suspension from the American Federation of Labor!

When Jesse broke the tape on the 200-meter dash he won the first Olympic triple crown since 1924. Three championships in one meet. The last man to do it was the Finnish flash, Paavo Nurmi.

*August 10, 1936*—Madrid charges that the rebels today received a second contingent of Italian Caproni planes, twenty-one of them, which were flown from the Caproni factory to rebel headquarters in Spanish Morocco.

*August 13, 1936*—The Fascists exacted a deadly revenge for the execution of those two Fascist generals at Barcelona yesterday. Forty prisoners, officers and men of the government's air force, were led before a firing squad and shot. This we learn direct from the Fascist radio station at Seville.

*August 14, 1936*—Sixteen Bolshevik big shots arrested in Russia, charged with conspiracy, counterrevolutionary activities. But that isn't all of it. Two of the men so accused are Gregory Zinoviev, former chairman of the Executive Council of the Third International, and Leon Kamenev, formerly No. 2 man of the Council of Commissars. The story is that they were acting as agents of the exiled Leon Trotsky.

*August 19, 1936*—If sixteen political leaders in any other country were brought to trial for conspiracy to murder the head of the state, it's a safe bet that they would fight such a charge to the bitter end. But what did those Russians do, the Soviet big shots accused of a plot to murder Stalin? They pleaded guilty, not as men making a reluctant confession, but as martyrs proudly claiming an immortal distinction.

Zinoviev himself while testifying displayed precisely the same attitude. We heard about him last night—his connection with the murder of Stalin's lieutenant, Kirov. Today he made no attempt to deny his guilt. "Yes," he said, "I plotted the death of Kirov." Then asked the prosecutor, "Did you concoct the plan to kill Comrade Stalin?" "I did," replied Zinoviev firmly. "I am guilty of every charge."

*August 20, 1936*—The word comes now that the goal that he and Leon Kamenev and the fourteen other conspirators were aiming at was nothing less than a Fascist Russia.

Trotsky's reply to that is—bosh. All those confessions have been obtained, he says, by the ruthless third-degree methods of the Ogpu, Russia's dreaded secret police. They threaten prisoners with unnamable tortures, then promise them a light sentence if they confess.

*August 24, 1936*—There are reports of increasing insistence that General Francisco Franco's armies are enclosing Madrid from all sides.

*August 25, 1936*—The Soviets are always curt in announcing executions. It was merely stated that the sixteen men convicted of plotting with the exiled Trotsky to kill the Red dictator Stalin have been shot.
Zinoviev and Kamenev. Those two famous veterans of Bolshevism head the list of the confessed plotters just executed.

*August 31, 1936*—The situation in Madrid is so desperate that all the foreign diplomats are leaving the city and taking their staffs with them.

*September 9, 1936*—There was no mistaking the boast in the tones of the German Chancellor as he jubilantly rejoiced over the tearing up of that scrap of paper, the Versailles Treaty.

*September 11, 1936*—Before the delegates of the thirty-two nations the head of the United States Government solemnly pressed a golden key and said, "Boulder Dam, in the name of the people of the United States, to whom you are a symbol for greater things in the future; in the presence of guests from many nations, I call you to life." And the pressure on that golden key did things thousands of miles away in the Far West. It put the greatest power plant in the world into operation.

*September 15, 1936*—There's no dispute about the way Maine voted. The Pine Tree is Republican again.
But is Maine really a barometer? That's what the Democrats are asking today.

*September 21, 1936*—In Toledo the Fascist soldiers are still holding the fort. The destruction of the magnificent old Alcazar did the government militia no good.

*September 22, 1936*—Today Hitler watched a sham-battle attack on Winterburg Mountain. The attacking Red army made a completely mechanized onslaught—war planes collaborating with tanks.
New ways of war are revealed in those military maneuvers.

*September 25, 1936*—General Franco's motorized regiments of Moors and legionnaires are pushing against Toledo tonight—almost within sight of the city.

September 28, 1936—The picturesque and historic side light that stands out from the fall of Toledo is the extraordinary defense of the Alcazar. I can think of nothing like it in modern warfare. Seventeen hundred people holding out three months! Even after their fortress aboveground had been blown up!

September 29, 1936—Reports from Toledo declare that the Reds staged an orgy of killing when the rebel army burst in and relieved the Alcazar. Six hundred priests reported to have been massacred by the enraged anarchists.

September 30, 1936—Not since the year 1801 has the papal Secretary of State ever left Italy, and never has a cardinal holding that office ever visited the United States. So the journey of His Eminence, Cardinal Pacelli, to America becomes extraordinary and astonishing.

October 9, 1936—At a Long Island country home a Roman cardinal has been spending his first couple of days in America, Cardinal Pacelli, papal Secretary of State, a guest of Mrs. Nicholas Brady. His Eminence arrives at an exceedingly interesting moment. It has been widely rumored that Cardinal Pacelli was coming to the United States to look into the political activities of Father Coughlin.

October 15, 1936—British journalism is highly circumspect in dealing with the King. They regard the monarch in his public station as one thing and his private life as another. They don't deal with royalty in the spirit of gossip. That is why today's headline over here is absent over there, the headline—"Mrs. Simpson has sued Mr. Simpson for divorce." And whatever slight mention they do make of this case at law, there is no word of King Edward.

Such is the reserved journalistic slant of the British. Yet in the story of King Edward and Mrs. Simpson, there's one person who seems to laugh at secrecy and concealment, and that is the King himself. He is frank and open in his friendship for the sprightly lady from Baltimore.

October 21, 1936—The reception given to Mussolini's son-in-law in Germany contributes another angle to the tangled European situation. Count Ciano is being greeted as though he were royalty.

October 27, 1936—Deserters from the left-wing ranks tell that there have been thirty thousand executions in Madrid, that great hosts of people of the upper and middle classes have been shot by Red firing squads.

*November 2, 1936*—The giant *Literary Digest* poll includes not only the farms but also the cities. What do we find there? Once more it's Landon. The *Digest* poll tallies pretty closely with the *Farm Journal* straw vote: a Landon victory.

*November 5, 1936*—The Fascist artillery is bombarding the suburbs of the capital of Spain.

Today the rebels announced the fifth column. They have four columns in the field and they have been claiming that in the capital itself their sympathizers have been waiting to rise. These they call the fifth column.

It has been a national phenomenon that President Roosevelt, in all his great triumphs, has never been able to carry his own home county—nor did he do it this year—his neighbors voted against him. Today's tabulation was that he won the nation by nearly ten million, but he lost Dutchess County by 4,407 votes.

*November 6, 1936*—Nationalist troops are now within four miles of the Puerto del Sol. That's the central plaza of Madrid. Four miles would be about the equivalent of eighty American city blocks.

People saw a glimpse of the future today at a press demonstration of R.C.A. experimental television. It was an impressive revelation which left one with the feeling that we are approaching the era of television entertainment. It's not around the corner. It's still somewhere in the future. But it's coming.

*November 10, 1936*—Father Coughlin finds his radio campaign and his Union for Social Justice overwhelmed by the Roosevelt landslide. So he retires to silence and disbands his organization.

Bulletins from Madrid tell us that General Franco's detachments are advancing from one street to another.

*November 11, 1936*—The most furious battle of the entire counter-revolution has been raging all day in the Spanish capital.

*November 12, 1936*—Today Eugene O'Neill, who is the only dramatist who has won the Pulitzer Prize three times, was awarded the Nobel Prize. He is the second American to get it, Sinclair Lewis the first.

With an electric flash across the country President Roosevelt in Washington opened the mighty San Francisco–Oakland bridge.

*November 16, 1936*—At eight o'clock this morning some 250,000 of

Uncle Sam's gray-clad mail carriers started on their rounds to make history. To three million employers they carried the new social security cards.

*November 18, 1936*—Shortly before noon a curt official announcement from Rome startled the world. In terse terms it declared, "The Fascist government has decided to recognize the government of General Francisco Franco in Spain."

Berlin dropped bombshell No. 2 into the international chaos, announcing that Hitler follows suit—recognizes Franco!

The university district in Madrid is described as one large no man's land. Rebels and government soldiers fight from house to house.

*November 24, 1936*—The latest attack by the rebels on Madrid was fought off principally by a regiment of foreign volunteers, Red sympathizers from other countries.

The report from Moscow is that the new Russian Constitution will incorporate many features of the American Bill of Rights, those vital amendments to our Constitution.

*November 25, 1936*—At last we know the details of the much-rumored treaty between Adolf Hitler and the Son of Heaven, His Majesty, Emperor of Japan. Roughly speaking, it is, as Berlin maintains, an agreement aimed at the Comintern, the Third International.

*November 27, 1936*—Today the Madrid government handed in the demand that the League Council be called into immediate session to consider charges against Germany and Italy.

*December 2, 1936*—In England the lid is off the news of the world-famous friendship between His Majesty, King Edward VIII, and the lady from Baltimore. The policy of hush-hush, with which the London government attempted to keep it private, has failed.

Tonight the rumor is current that the King may abdicate. The gossip around Whitehall is that Prime Minister Stanley Baldwin, speaking for a unanimous Cabinet, has advised the King not to think of marrying Mrs. Simpson. If His Majesty insists—and they say he does insist—the Cabinet threatens to resign.

*December 3, 1936*—As predicted, members of Parliament questioned the Prime Minister about the perilous clash between the Cabinet and the Crown in the celebrated case of King Edward VIII and Mrs. Simpson.

Then up spoke the Right Honorable Winston Churchill, former Chancellor of the Exchequer and stormy petrel of British politics. He de-

manded from the Prime Minister an assurance—an assurance that no irrevocable step had been taken. Baldwin gave the assurance—there had
been nothing irrevocable.

That word gave Englishmen the jitters—it could refer only to abdication.

Edward VIII himself is described as unchanging in his determination
to wed Wally of Baltimore.

*December 4, 1936*—Today Prime Minister Stanley Baldwin made
his anxiously awaited declaration in the House of Commons. And he put
his government completely and unchangeably in opposition to the marriage of Edward VIII and Mrs. Simpson.

*December 7, 1936*—"Throughout the last few weeks," said Mrs. Simpson in her statement, "I have invariably wished to avoid any action or
proposal which might hurt or damage His Majesty or the throne." And
she adds, "I am willing to withdraw forthwith from a situation that has
become unhappy and untenable."

So there the matter rests. England, the British Empire, the world now
wait for the King's decision.

*December 10, 1936*—What must be the thoughts of the forty-three-
year-old man who may be most simply named as David Windsor? He was
the world's darling as the glamorous Prince of Wales. He became the most
popular of kings. Now, abdicated.

In a villa on the French Riviera a woman sits and thinks. And what are
her thoughts?

*December 11, 1936*—Less than two hours ago we radio listeners heard
the greatest broadcast of all time. A truly extraordinary thing—in power,
pathos, and simplicity.

The drama of an empire rose to a soaring note of pathos when Edward
embarked upon the theme that has stood first in the eyes of the world.
Remember how he said, "You must believe me when I tell you that I have
found it impossible to carry this heavy burden and responsibility and to
discharge my duties as a king as I would wish to do, without the help and
support of the woman I love."

*December 16, 1936*—The first official act of King George VI was to
make his retired elder brother Duke of Windsor.

*December 24, 1936*—The ex-King celebrated Christmas Eve with a
telephone call to the woman he loves. From the Rothschild castle in
Enzesfeld, Austria, he put in a call to Mrs. Simpson at Cannes, and they
exchanged Christmas greetings.

# 1937

*The Spanish Civil War continues amid scenes of death and destruction. War in China flares up again. Japan seizes Shanghai and deliberately bombs the American gunboat Panay. Japan, Germany, and Italy sign the anti-Comintern Pact aimed at Russia. Meanwhile Stalin's fury is turned against his internal enemies—a holocaust of executions, including the leader of the Red Army, Marshal Tukhachevsky. A terrorist vendetta between Jews and Arabs breaks out in Palestine.*

*At home, controversy over the possible packing of the Supreme Court goes on. However, President Roosevelt raises a storm when he appoints Justice Black in the normal way, for the new Justice is criticized as a former member of the Ku Klux Klan. The greatest disaster on the American scene is the burning of the German dirigible Hindenburg at Lakehurst, New Jersey. The death of John D. Rockefeller removes one of the powerful labor barons of a previous era, the wizard who founded Standard Oil and made a legendary fortune out of it.*

*January 4, 1937*—Nineteen thirty-seven opens with on every side either a strike or a menace of a strike.

*January 7, 1937*—There was a battle in the Flint plant of Chevrolet —two thousand strike-sympathizing workers fought with others who stick with the company.

*January 8, 1937*—Today a telltale command was given. The left-wing government of Spain ordered the entire civilian population of Madrid to leave the city.

*January 12, 1937*—The auto strike takes on a more serious aspect, with the mobilization of National Guardsmen in Michigan. Governor

Frank Murphy announced the calling out of the state soldiers to stand guard in the strike-beleaguered town of Flint.

There's savage word of more Red massacres in Spain, the merciless killing of hostages by the anarchists of Bilbao.

*January 18, 1937*—That truce in the automobile strike is definitely all off. And now the situation is, if anything, worse.

*January 21, 1937*—The principal task of the Secretary of Labor is to remedy the sit-down strike situation. That's the biggest stumbling block in negotiations for labor peace in the auto world. General Motors refuses to go into a peace parley until the strikers have ceased their sit-down occupation of factories, while the workers insist on remaining seated.

*January 22, 1937*—Labor leader John L. Lewis had issued a demand that President Roosevelt intervene in the auto strike in favor of the union. Today President Roosevelt's reply was given—and it's a rebuff for Lewis.

*January 27, 1937*—On the strike front today ten General Motors plants, Chevrolet factories in Michigan and Indiana, reopened with forty thousand men going back to work. It was accomplished without disorder, though large numbers of union pickets surrounded the plants.

*January 28, 1937*—The flood of the Ohio is now surging into the Mississippi.
The fight against the river right now is represented by fifty thousand men, flood fighters. For a stretch of a thousand miles they are strengthening the levees, patrolling the dikes.

While the situation is in suspense on the Mississippi River, they are reckoning the damage in the Ohio Valley.

*January 29, 1937*—The levee system along the Mississippi is holding up as the flood moves southward—although there are indications of danger at various places.

*February 2, 1937*—Today, Circuit Court Judge Gadola granted the injunction requested by General Motors. He agreed with the company's contention that sitters-down were illegally occupying company property. So the court decreed, "Move out, leave the premises."

*February 5, 1937*—The most sensational of the half dozen proposals that emanate from the White House is the one about the Supreme Court. This would give the President the power to appoint a new member to the Court for every Justice who is over seventy and who shows no signs of retiring. Such appointments not to increase the number of the Court to more than fifteen.

The addition of six New Deal members would radically change the complexion of the Court with reference to liberalism and conservatism, pro-New Deal and anti-New Deal. The phrase inevitably suggests itself—packing the Court.

*February 8,* 1937—In Flint, the center of the sit-down strike, the tension is more acute than ever. The city is on tenterhooks, expecting martial law to be declared at any moment.

*February 11,* 1937—The sit-down strikers have just moved out of the factories in Flint.

The strike was settled last night, when the union and the company agreed on terms.

*February 18,* 1937—A climactic battle of thunder and death is on to cut the eastern communications of Madrid and surround the city. This must mean that Franco's mechanized legions have advanced so far and into such strategic territory that the only thing for the Socialists to do is to force them back—or else.

*February 23,* 1937—There's nothing definite about the number of Ethiopians who have been executed in Addis Ababa. Mussolini ordered drastic measures in reprisal for the tossing of a hand grenade at Viceroy General Graziani, who was injured by the explosion.

*February 24,* 1937—Sit-down strikes are spreading like an epidemic. From coast to coast there is a series of them. Judging from the reports that pile up, they involve everybody, including the butcher, the baker, and the candlestick maker. Shoemakers in New Hampshire, pressmen in Ohio, watchmakers in Illinois, boat builders in Connecticut, munitions makers in California.

*March 2,* 1937—Word today indicates that Germany is building fighting aircraft faster than had been expected. Germany now has at least two thousand up-to-the-minute warplanes of a most modern sort, and by next year Hitler may have as many as five thousand.

*March 4,* 1937—The German Ambassador in Washington put in a formal complaint today—protesting to the State Department against things said by Mayor La Guardia of New York. But the State Department has no command over declarations made by the mayor of any city.

La Guardia took a savage public fling at Hitler. In a luncheon speech he said that at the coming World's Fair they should have a chamber of horrors, and in that chamber of horrors they should put an effigy of Reichsfuehrer Hitler, brown shirt and all.

President Green of the American Federation of Labor today gave a command to expel all unions affiliated with John L. Lewis's C.I.O.

*March 5, 1937*—"Will Franklin Delano Roosevelt seek a third term?" Today inferences were being drawn from what the President said last evening. And surprisingly one of these inferences is, yes, he may. He may seek a third term.

The President says his ambition is to turn over the country in good shape to his successor. But suppose he thinks the country is not in good shape—then he may not turn it over to any successor. He might decide that he needs a third term to put the nation into proper condition to turn over to a successor afterward.

*March 9, 1937*—Sit-down strikes have closed all of the Chrysler plants in Detroit—nine of them.

*March 16, 1937*—Bitter fighting continues to the northeast of Madrid, with the left-wingers continuing to assert that they're battling against Italian divisions.

*March 18, 1937*—Amelia Earhart began her equatorial flight around the world in high style—setting something of a speed record from the Pacific coast to Honolulu.

*March 22, 1937*—A new note in the Supreme Court controversy. The Court itself has spoken—and through the mouth of none other than the Chief Justice, Charles Evans Hughes. And the declaration is, "No." If you increase the number of Justices in the country's highest tribunal you will not make it more efficient.

*March 23, 1937*—A hundred thousand strikers are staging their protest in Detroit against any eviction of the sit-downers there.

*March 25, 1937*—The truce signed last night was followed by quick action today. The sit-downers in the plants promptly ratified the agreement the union leaders had made, ratified and obeyed, vacated.

*March 26, 1937*—Today Colonel Isham is back in New York with a whole new heap of Boswell and Johnson papers—the matchless prize among which is an original diary kept by Dr. Johnson, a manuscript in the handwriting of the great lexicographer.

*April 1, 1937*—Nikolai Bukharin will soon go to trial before the tribunal of Red justice in Moscow. He's a famous old Bolshevik, a companion of Lenin, one of the topmost leaders of the Red revolution.

*April 5, 1937*—Nobody knows how many men and women were lined up in front of a firing squad for treason by Yagoda, former head of the Ogpu, the Russian secret police. Only last January we learned of the treason trial in which Yagoda sent thirteen former Bolshevik big shots to their death. And now he's in prison himself.

*April 27, 1937*—Squadrons of rebel bombers have destroyed the old town of Guernica. It's important as a matter of strategy, and it was once the capital of the Basques—a city of sacred and historic memories to those hardy mountaineers of northern Spain. Eight hundred people are said to have been killed in Guernica today, the town shattered by the bombs.

*April 30, 1937*—France and Britain are also going to investigate the charges that Guernica, the historic city of the Basques, was deliberately and ruthlessly destroyed by the "black birds," as the people of Bilbao call the German bombing planes. Meanwhile Nazi Germany, hotly denies the accusation.

*May 3, 1937*—In that cut-and-dried ceremony, which took a bare twenty-five seconds, Mrs. Wallis Warfield Simpson became a free woman after waiting in virtual exile for six months. She's free now to become H.R.H., the Duchess of Windsor.

*May 7, 1937*—Tonight I'm in Rome, and once more I can say that the most important item of news here is the same as everywhere. But this time it's tragic. The Zeppelin disaster. That calamitous event at Lakehurst, New Jersey. The horrifying inferno that destroyed the Hindenburg.

*May 10, 1937*—She was at a height of about two hundred feet. Suddenly a detonation at the stern of the ship. It was very loud. In a few seconds immense flames were enveloping the entire ship, and she sank very rapidly to the ground. The ground crew were madly running for safety, the first members of the crew and passengers frantically crawling from the burning wreckage.

*May 12, 1937*—The King and Queen are moving up the aisle of Westminster Abbey. The Queen is in the lead, with six lovely peeresses carrying her train. Then the King, with nine peers and pages carrying his still longer train. The King and Queen kneel and pray alone before the great golden altar.

Then followed the hour-long ritual of which you have heard and read so much: the coronation oath, the anointing, and the crowning of both the King and Queen.

May 20, 1937—The German Embassy has protested to the State Department over Cardinal Mundelein's criticisms of Hitler.

May 26, 1937—Today they solemnized a funeral which seems like the inevitable long delayed. John D. Rockefeller passes into the grave.

His stupendous philanthropies earned him the esteem of the nation and the world until, at the end, he was like a national monument lingering from times gone by—John D.

May 28, 1937—Stanley Baldwin retired as Prime Minister of Great Britain.

Edward abdicated, and Baldwin resigns.

Baldwin advised His Majesty to summon Sir Neville Chamberlain to be the next Prime Minister.

June 1, 1937—Amelia Earhart landed this afternoon at San Juan, Puerto Rico, and started refueling for continuation of her flight around the world.

June 3, 1937—The great salon in the Château de Cande was aglow with flowers. No wedding ceremony has ever been more beautifully arranged. Everything was flowers, the blooms and blossoms of Touraine.

There was the Yorkshire clergyman, the Vicar of Darlington, the poor man's parson, who was defying his church and ecclesiastical superiors by giving religious marriage to the exiled English King and the twice-divorced American woman.

June 11, 1937—A court trial of magnitude and terror without precedent began in Soviet Russia today.

Today facing a court of dread are eight of the foremost Soviet generals. Heading the lugubrious list is Marshal Tukhachevsky, who was Assistant Commissar of War, Russia's youngest marshal, a soldier of international reputation.

It is officially announced in Moscow that they have confessed—confessed to the charges against them, espionage, plotting to get the Red Army beaten in war, Trotskyism, and the scheme to restore capitalism.

June 18, 1937—News continues to stream out day by day of the terror raging in Red Russia. More and more arrests on charges of sabotage, wrecking, conspiracy, Trotskyism. One Communist newspaper prints a list of denunciations—seventeen hundred persons accused. And today we hear of mass arrests of Soviet railway officials. Stalin at death grips with his enemies; death is right—much of it.

*June 21, 1937*—Those three Soviet aviators flew from Moscow to Vancouver Field, near Portland, Oregon—flew it via the North Pole.

*June 29, 1937*—Amelia Earhart in dark New Guinea tonight! Amelia now faces the most perilous part of her trip—across the vast Pacific.

*July 5, 1937*—Somewhere in the middle of the boundless Pacific Ocean are two people, the best known of them a woman—out there to-night floating helplessly upon the waves, indefinite miles away from res-cue. For hours the radio signals from Amelia Earhart and Fred Noonan grew fainter and fainter, less and less intelligible—up to several hours ago. And for those several hours—no signal.

*July 7, 1937*—The gist of the Royal Commission's report has been an open secret for some time. The new British plan is an old, old Roman plan—Roman, Assyrian, Babylonian, and Greek, for that matter. Partition is the word; split Palestine up into three districts, a Jewish state, an Arab state, and a third which would be a territory ruled by Britain under a mandate from the League of Nations. That mandate territory would cover the holy places of Jerusalem and Bethlehem.

*July 8, 1937*—Today the world-wide Jewish reaction to the British Palestine Plan announced yesterday is one of opposition verging from mild complaint to bitter refusal.

*July 12, 1937*—George Gershwin, the boy who grew up on the side-walks of New York and became one of the world's most accomplished musicians—one foot in Tin Pan Alley, the other in Carnegie Hall—now gone from the scene. He died at the height of his fame.

*July 13, 1937*—The fighting in China continued bitterly all day. Ad-vancing Japanese troops fought their way to the ancient walls of Peiping.

*July 19, 1937*—A dispatch from Shanghai declares that the Chinese Government has definitely refused Japan's ultimatum to withdraw China's forces from northern China.

*July 20, 1937*—The man has died without whom there would be no broadcasting. Guglielmo Marconi, inventor of radio.

*July 21, 1937*—Both Mussolini and Hitler absolutely decline even to discuss withdrawing their so-called volunteers from Spain.

*July 23, 1937*—President Roosevelt is described as taking a mild attitude toward yesterday's final defeat of his plan to enlarge the Supreme Court. His stand today is represented to be that it was his duty to tell Congress what he thought ought to be done, and it was up to Congress to do as it thought best.

That's somewhat in contrast to the famous White House letter to Senator Barkley—that Dear Alben epistle, in which the idea seemed to be that the President should tell Congress what to do and then Congress should go ahead and do it.

*July 26, 1937*—The Japanese are in Peiping.

*July 27, 1937*—War has not been declared between Japan and China, but that means nothing because war is raging right now.

*July 29, 1937*—Another king was crowned today. The enthronement today of King Farouk as the sovereign of Egypt—as the twentieth-century Pharaoh.

*August 9, 1937*—The extraordinary demonstrations in favor of Pastor Martin Niemoeller were followed by a queer announcement. The prosecution of the Reverend Niemoeller is to be postponed, indefinitely postponed. Nor is he the first clergyman to defy Hitler's iron-fisted government and get away with it. This postponement follows swiftly upon the acquittal of another pastor, Dr. Dibelius.

*August 12, 1937*—President Roosevelt today did the thing about which there has been so much controversy. He names a Supreme Court member to succeed ex-Justice Van Devanter, and his nominee is Senator Black of Alabama.

The Japanese today disembarked some thousands of fighting men at Shanghai.

*August 13, 1937*—The battle of Shanghai is raging.

*August 16, 1937*—The leader of the objectors to President Roosevelt's new Supreme Court appointment was Senator Burke of Nebraska. He insisted that his colleague, Senator Black, be summoned before the committee to answer questions, to tell whether it was true that he used to be a member of the Ku Klux Klan.

*August 20, 1937*—Shanghai is burning as desperate battle rages through the streets.

*August 25, 1937*—In Spain, Santander has fallen. The last important government stronghold on the Bay of Biscay.

*August 27, 1937*—Today London insisted on "full satisfaction" for the shooting of the British Ambassador to China by a Japanese aviator.

*August 30, 1937*—The Mikado's high command has launched a fresh and tremendous drive, an invasion of the province of Shantung, one of the richest in all China.

*August 31, 1937*—Will Franklin D. Roosevelt run for a third term? Today the President's mother repeated what she had to say yesterday about the possibility of a third term. In Paris, Mrs. Sara Delano Roosevelt said once again, "My son does not want to run for a third term."

*September 6, 1937*—Today 70,000 of Japan's crack troops were hurled in a hammerhead blow against an army of 150,000 Chinese near Shanghai. Meanwhile the Mikado's airplanes darkened the skies, raining bombs of destruction on the secondary China line, one hundred miles long and to the west of Shanghai.

*September 13, 1937*—The Chinese high command describes its evacuation of the Shanghai area as a strategic move.

*September 14, 1937*—Political opinion continues to seethe today over Supreme Court Justice Black and the Ku Klux Klan. The general tone of the comment is severe—holding that a member of the hooded order is unfit for the Supreme Court.

*September 15, 1937*—The Chinese feel that the worst blow they have received yet was administered not by the Japanese attacks but by President Roosevelt's order forbidding the shipment of arms to the Far East in vessels owned by the United States.

*September 17, 1937*—London and Paris announce that the neutrality ship patrol is off—discontinued. The maritime cordon to keep war supplies from the Spanish belligerents never did amount to much, was more or less of a farce.

*September 22, 1937*—The destruction of Nanking is on! A hundred of the Mikado's war pilots rained bombs upon the Chinese capital this morning.

*September 24, 1937*—Shanghai, Nanking, Canton, and now Hankow.

The air fleets of Japan are striking far and wide over China while the outside world looks on with horror.

*September 27, 1937*—Many foreign potentates have paid state visits to Berlin, but none of them ever got such a tumultuous reception as did Benito Mussolini, Premier of Italy and head of the Italian Fascisti.

*October 1, 1937*—Mr. Justice Black is going to tell us tonight, "Yes, I was once a member of the Ku Klux Klan." Mr. Black will tell us over that nationwide hookup that he joined the Klan while his political career was still young, joined it just as most people join a lodge. He resigned more than ten years ago, when he discovered the real nature of the Klan and its activities.

*October 12, 1937*—Word just in—Nanking bombed again.

*October 15, 1937*—The latest right off the wire is: "Martial law in the Holy Land."

*October 18, 1937*—To end terrorism in the Holy Land the British authorities are burning the homes of the Arab terrorists. Today the Arabs answer by bombing the orthodox Jewish quarter of Jerusalem.

*October 19, 1937*—Hitler formally asserts that Germany will support the Germans living in Czechoslovakia.

*October 21, 1937*—Election news from Soviet Russia, where the Red regime is busy preparing for the coming of democracy with voting, candidates, ballot boxes, and all that! Today's announcement of executions—fifty-five!

*October 27, 1937*—The fall of Shanghai! The Chinese resistance around Shanghai was finally broken today.

Emperor Hirohito has just issued word to the world that Japan will continue the war in China until victory is achieved.

*November 1, 1937*—Rome announces today that the rumored anti-Communist pact with Germany and Japan is a fact.

*November 3, 1937*—Thomas E. Dewey, a new figure on the political horizon. Running for district attorney in New York County, he actually ran up a bigger majority than La Guardia himself.

*November 11, 1937*—Today an official spokesman of the Chinese

Army admitted that all resistance to Japan at Shanghai was at an end.

*November 18, 1937*—The exodus from Nanking continued today. Most of the Americans have gone.

*November 30, 1937*—The Japanese seized an American vessel, tore down the American flag, and tossed it into the Whangpoo River.

*December 1, 1937*—The Irish Free State is no more. That doesn't mean another revolution has taken place or that Eamon De Valera has decided to give his country back to King George. No, the Emerald Isle just changes its name. In future it's to be known as Eire, and that's Irish for Ireland.

*December 7, 1937*—The Japanese are surrounding Nanking tonight.

*December 10, 1937*—Right now Nanking seems as good as captured.

*December 13, 1937*—The President received a visit from Secretary Hull, who brought with him official reports of the sinking of the *Panay*, the killing of one member of her crew, and the wounding of two officers.

Apologies have already been forthcoming. The doors of our State Department had hardly opened today when Japanese Ambassador Saito arrived. He brought expressions of his government's regrets.

The Japanese insist that their plane mistook the American gunboat for a Chinese craft.

*December 17, 1937*—The full story of the *Panay* was finally available today. Official reports were filed by survivors in Shanghai. Three points are to be noted:

First, it is completely confirmed that the attack was deliberate, and no accident. The Japanese planes bombed from high altitude and from low altitude. Also, there was machine-gunning from the Japanese planes and Japanese ships. The American flag was plainly visible, flying all the time.

*December 23, 1937*—The Japanese have done the expected thing at Nanking—they've set up a government there under their own domination.

# 1938

*This is a year of colossal diplomatic victories for Hitler. He seizes Austria, demands the Czech Sudetenland, gives all of Europe a bad case of war jitters, and compels Chamberlain and Daladier to come to Munich and bow to his demands. Chamberlain returns to London, where, in one of the most ironic speeches in the history of European international relations, he declares that Britain and Germany will never go to war with one another again. But Winston Churchill criticizes the Munich agreement as a fearful defeat. Meanwhile, Anthony Eden has resigned from the Chamberlain Cabinet, claiming that the Prime Minister is endangering the democracies with his appeasement of Hitler and Mussolini.*

*In Russia, Stalin continues to claw to death the remnants of opposition to his monstrous tyranny. In Siberia his generals defeat the Japanese in undeclared warfare along the border of Manchuria. There is more fighting in China, more terrorism in Palestine.*

*At home, there is resentment among the oil companies whose holdings in Mexico have been seized by the Mexican Government. Richard Whitney, five times president of the New York Stock Exchange, goes to jail for misusing securities in his care.*

---

*January 12, 1938*—John Bull is building himself an air fleet of ten thousand fighting planes.

*January 14, 1938*—This was another big conference day at the White House. Distinguished representatives of industry came to discuss the state of American business. But before the conference gathered, President Roosevelt gave business something to think about.

Abolish all holding companies was his demand. Put an end to those corporations whose purpose it is to hold stock in other corporations and thereby maintain control of them.

*January 27, 1938*—The Niagara bridge collapsed this afternoon, the span so sentimentally favored by honeymooners. The ice jam finally won the battle. Tonight the bridge lies in the water below the Falls, a tangled mass of wreckage.

*February 4, 1938*—Von Blomberg, decidedly a Hitler general, lost favor with the upper hierarchy of the German Army because of his marriage—he married a girl secretary, a carpenter's daughter. German Army tradition is that an officer must marry a woman of rank and fortune. So Hitler's man, Von Blomberg, was forced out. And now Hitler himself takes the post of Chief of National Defense, immediate and supreme master of the German Army.

*February 7, 1938*—The die was definitely cast today by the Executive Council of the American Federation of Labor. All hopes of peace in the union world are at an end. The Council today formally and officially expelled three unions connected with the C.I.O. First and most important, the United Mine Workers of America, the one of which John L. Lewis is chief, expelled.

*February 8, 1938*—The trial of Pastor Niemoeller in Germany took a dramatic turn today. That leader in the Lutheran Church abruptly dismissed his own lawyers, refused to be represented by them any longer. He is being tried secretly for being a leader among the Lutheran clergy in opposition to the Nazi regime.

*February 15, 1938*—All day long there have been sensational rumors of German troops concentrating to the north of Austria.

These military aspects are a spectacular background for the fact that right now the government of Austria must cast the die—must decide what to do about the demands Hitler made to Chancellor Schuschnigg: that Austrian Nazis be given key positions in the Vienna Cabinet.

*February 16, 1938*—Late this afternoon came a fresh bulletin reporting a still more formidable rumor: Hitler not yet satisfied! Austrian Chancellor Schuschnigg has not gone far enough to please him in forming that Cabinet with Nazis in the key positions.

*February 18, 1938*—The latest from Vienna is an official declaration by the Austrian Government which states that Germany agrees to forgo any interference by the Nazi party in the internal affairs of Austria.

*February 21, 1938*—The most important part of Anthony Eden's farewell today was contained in the words, "Propaganda against this country by the Italian Government is rife throughout the world." And he added, "I myself pledged this House not to open conversations with Italy

until hostile propaganda ceased. This propaganda has not ceased." Then
he added that neither Italy nor Germany has shown any respect for international obligations.

The British Prime Minister's reply to his former Foreign Minister is
being described tonight as an emotional piece of political strategy. For
he told the Commons that Mussolini has agreed to negotiate with Britain
on terms almost identical with those that Eden has demanded.

From Vienna comes a tale of ominous doings. The beginning of the
demonstrations against the Jews that everybody had expected. Among the
Jews in Vienna there is a state of panic.

*February 22, 1938*—The House of Commons supports Prime Minister
Chamberlain in the Cabinet crisis over the resignation of Anthony Eden
and the peace talks with Fascist Italy.

It is announced by Barcelona that Franco has captured Teruel.

*February 23, 1938*—Fear in Czechoslovakia. More reports from
Prague. This time a quotation from the chief of the Czechoslovakian
general staff. Said he, "This country must be prepared for a brutal, quick
attack by motorized forces, assisted by an air force, without any warning."

*February 24, 1938*—Nazi Germany will not interfere with the internal affairs of Austria. Schuschnigg specifically stated before the Austrian parliament that Hitler will not play a policy of making Austria Nazi.

Czechoslovakia declares its determination to resist any German aggression.

*February 28, 1938*—Ominous news again from Austria. In the city
of Graz, in the province of Styria, the Nazis continue to defy the government, wearing their uniforms and swastika emblems.

*March 2, 1938*—Stark melodrama right from the beginning of that
trial of the twenty-one former Bolshevik leaders. Tragic irony was present
in the mere personalities of those prisoners who are believed to be
doomed. There among the accused was Henry Yagoda. As head of the
Ogpu, the Russian secret police, in his time he sent thousands to premature graves.

Then there is Dr. Levin, the famous Russian physician, superintendent
of the Kremlin hospital. He's the one accused of having murdered the
writer, Maxim Gorky, at the instigation of Trotsky. He has confessed it,
told in detail how he did it.

*March 3, 1938*—Eyes at the trial are on Bukharin, the famous old Bolshevik chief, who one time was regarded as Lenin's heir.

Alexei Rykov, who was a member of the first Cabinet of the U.S.S.R., told of a plot to seize the Kremlin itself, storm into that sanctuary of Bolshevism, and there arrest Stalin.

*March 8, 1938*—The former Ogpu chief admitted virtually everything. Said he was guilty in the liquidation of his superior, Menzhinsky. Specifically he also confessed that he ordered the medical murder of Maxim Gorky.

*March 10, 1938*—Here's a late flash—civil war threatening tonight in Austria.

*March 11, 1938*—I am in Washington tonight. And my first direct news of the seizure of Austria by Germany came from Secretary of State Hull, whom I was with at the time.

German troops have reached Vienna. A motorized Nazi unit dashed all the way to the Austrian capital today, came rolling into the city, and its commander is Goering, Hitler's right-hand man.

Schuschnigg has resigned.

*March 14, 1938*—Adolf Hitler, to the cheers and screams of thousands, today entered in triumph the ancient capital of the Hapsburgs. The last conqueror to ride triumphantly into Vienna was the Emperor Napoleon.

And so Austria becomes part of the German Empire.

Among the Jews—hysteria, panic. Many of them trying to flee across the frontier today were arrested.

*March 15, 1938*—Brief word from the land of the Soviets. The eighteen men convicted in the latest mass trial have been shot. This was announced by the Stalin government today. Eighteen doomed! Eighteen executed!

The central European spotlight focuses more and more on Czechoslovakia. Today the French Ambassador to London made a demand on the British Government—or rather renewed a demand: that London make an outright declaration of British support for France in guaranteeing Czechoslovakia against any German attack.

Stalin's government repeats that it will back France in defending Czechoslovakia.

*March 17, 1938*—Tonight the great and historic city of Barcelona lies in a stupor, a paralysis of fear, an exhaustion from sheer horror and panic. Everywhere are scenes of frightful devastation: ruins, blasted streets and boulevards, scattered bodies, the wounded moaning for help.

The reason of war for the air bombing is simple to see—the Franco forces determined to put the finishing touch of demoralization upon the capital of left-wing Spain.

*March 21, 1938*—The seizure by Mexico's President Cardenas of all foreign oil properties, principally American, precipitated a crisis, a money crisis. There were long lines in front of the Bank of Mexico today asking for hard money instead of the paper peso.

*March 23, 1938*—The horror over the bombings in Spain has shocked the Vatican. Pope Pius has instructed his diplomatic envoy at Salamanca to make a new and urgent protest to Generalissimo Franco.

*March 24, 1938*—Great Britain will not guarantee Czechoslovakia against Hitler! That was point No. 1 in the Chamberlain pronouncement.

*March 30, 1938*—General Franco's drive is getting farther and farther into Catalonia, closer and closer to Barcelona. This morning the rebel armies captured Alcatraz, eight miles from Lérida. Not the "Rock," the island prison in California. But the original Alcatraz.

*April 4, 1938*—Franco's men are hammering at the gates of Barcelona.

*April 5, 1938*—Cardinal Innitzer of Vienna advised Austrian Catholics to vote Nazi in the forthcoming plebiscite. And that was the cause of something of a stir in Rome, with the statement that the pro-Nazi action of the Austrian bishops was taken without consultation with the Vatican.

The German bishops, headed by Cardinal Faulhaber of Munich, decided not to issue a pastoral letter, as the Austrian bishops did. They'll not advise German Catholics to vote Nazi in the election. Their policy is silence.

*April 7, 1938*—Refugees crossing the French border today report that the policy of wholesale executions has been revived in Barcelona. The left-wing Tribunal of Espionage and High Treason is at its grim work again.

*April 11, 1938*—A stalwart, handsome, well-groomed man, once a leader in the highest financial and social circles, stood at the bar of justice today, Richard Whitney, five times president of the New York Stock Exchange. There to be sentenced for theft of securities whose value ran up into large figures.

*April 14, 1938*—The predominant story of the day is the presidential message to Congress proposing four and a half billion dollars of spending and lending, forty-five hundred million for priming the pump.

*April 15, 1938*—The Spanish rebels have reached the sea. Franco's battalions have at last cut left-wing Spain in two.

*April 21, 1938*—One of the cardinal points of the London-Rome reconciliation is the recognition of Mussolini's conquest of Ethiopia.

*April 25, 1938*—There was a demonstration today outside No. 10 Downing Street. A large crowd was shouting, "Hurrah for Dev; well done, Dev!" meaning Eamon De Valera, Prime Minister of Ireland. The occasion was the formal signing of that treaty between John Bull and what Bernard Shaw called his "other island."

The tariff war is at an end; Ireland now has the rich markets of England and Scotland for her dairy and livestock.

The momentous topic in European foreign offices today was the new Czech crisis. New and more drastic demands for autonomy by the Sudeten Germans.

*April 27, 1938*—The Nazi government issued a new edict today, a regulation for Jews that bids fair to crush them. Hermann Goering, as economic dictator, issued a decree empowering Hermann Goering, as administrator of the Four-Year-Plan, to use all assets owned by Jewish people. Thereupon he issued another decree ordering Jews in Germany to register and list everything they own.

*April 29, 1938*—There were frightful events at the great Chinese city of Hankow today, air battle and air bombing. Battle in the blue, and hideous devastation on the ground.

*May 3, 1938*—Adolf Hitler arrived in Rome by train at 8:30 P.M.—Roman time—midafternoon here.

The Hitler special train, after a triumphant journey through Italy, arrived at Rome, where the Fuehrer was greeted by King Victor Emmanuel and Duce Mussolini.

*May 4, 1938*—There was one significant fact that struck all foreign observers. The cheering demonstration for the Nazi chief was polite, not tumultuous. The applause that greeted the cars of the dictators had a distinctly formal sound to it.

*May 10, 1938*—Hitler's triumphal return to Berlin is accompanied by remarks concerning the one discordant element in his triumphal visit to Rome. That discordant element was the attitude of the Vatican, such as the Pope's expression of displeasure because of the swastikas displayed in the Eternal City. In Nazi quarters it is being said that the Vatican attitude was outrageous and that the Hitler government may retaliate by denouncing the concordat between the Nazi Reich and the Catholic Church.

*May 19, 1938*—Tonight the great Chinese city of Soochow is in flames—and in the hands of the Japanese.

*May 25, 1938*—Today there was a funeral of those two Sudeten Germans killed last week by Czech police. As might have been expected, it was turned into a monster demonstration for Hitler and for a Sudeten *Anschluss* with the Nazi Reich.

*May 27, 1938*—Czechoslovakia will not withdraw those mobilizations of troops from the German frontier, German protests notwithstanding. This was announced tonight in Prague.

The Czechs seem to be bucked up by assurances of support they are getting from Paris and London.

*June 6, 1938*—Japan, under her new Army Cabinet, answered the protests of England, France, and America by bombing populous Canton for the eighth day in succession this afternoon. The carnage and destruction were perhaps the worst ever yet suffered by a city under air bombardment.

*June 7, 1938*—The Japanese have answered the world-wide protest against the bombing of Chinese cities. Today they answered it in words—announced that the bombing is to be intensified.

*June 8, 1938*—From Vatican City we learn that Pope Pius has registered a formal protest with Franco against the bombardment of civilian populations.

*June 15, 1938*—The word from Berlin is that a new anti-Jewish drive is imminent. Leaders of the Nazi party admitted it. The intention is to Aryanize all stores and establishments owned by Jews throughout the Reich.

*July 7, 1938*—Two British cruisers ordered to Haifa in the Holy Land.

And that's an indication of the gravity of the present trouble, the fighting between Arabs and Jews.

*July 12, 1938*—A typical American country jury had its say today. Said it about six American Nazis.

Today the verdict of that Riverhead, Long Island, jury was—guilty.

Fuehrer Fritz Kuhn promptly announced that the verdict would be appealed.

*July 18, 1938*—A solo flight from New York to Dublin under the most incredible circumstances, made by a young man named Corrigan! Said he, "Me break a regulation? Why, I was heading for Los Angeles."

*July 21, 1938*—Paraguay and Bolivia signed a treaty today calling off the Gran Chaco dispute.

*July 22, 1938*—Moscow refuses the Tokyo demand to get the Red Army troops off that disputed hill on the border of Manchukuo and Siberia.

*July 26, 1938*—The Japanese report there has been fighting in the disputed area along the frontier of Japanese-controlled Manchukuo and Russian Siberia.

*August 2, 1938*—Today battle was raging in that strategic area which joins the borders of Siberia, Manchukuo, and Korea. Infantry charges, dashes by tanks, artillery fire, and air raids by Soviet planes into Japanese-controlled territory.

*August 8, 1938*—Diplomatic observers still claim that this fierce fighting between Japanese and Russians at Changkufeng is merely an incident and that it won't result in any large-scale war.

*August 11, 1938*—Japan and Soviet Russia have concluded an armistice and are trying to settle the boundary question that had their armies fighting.

*August 12, 1938*—Today that question again—how much did Jimmy Roosevelt make out of his insurance business? In *Collier's* the President's son answers by printing his income tax figures from 1933 to 1937. He doesn't deny that being a President's son helped him to write insurance. He says frankly, "I got into places I never could have if I wasn't the son of the President."

*August 18, 1938*—Tonight world-wide attention is focused on a speech

President Roosevelt made in Canada today. "The United States," said he, "will not stand idly by if domination of Canadian soil is threatened by any other empire."

President Roosevelt seems to expand the Monroe Doctrine to include everything from the Canadian Arctic Ocean to the tip of Cape Horn.

*August 22, 1938*—It looks today as though the Czechoslovak republic, erected at Versailles largely through the pressure of President Wilson, is in for great changes.

*August 25, 1938*—It's only natural that there should be quite a row about the congressional committee investigating un-American activities. There is a chorus of protests from the advanced liberal thinkers who frown on Red-baiting as a bad thing but don't mind baiting the Nazis.

*August 26, 1938*—The British announce they have things under control in the ancient city of Jaffa in the Holy Land. All day they struggled against the Arab violence which flared after a frightful bomb explosion in the market place at Jaffa. The infernal machine blew up with horrible effect—sixteen Arabs killed, thirty wounded. That caused the Arabs to run wild with savage attacks upon the Jews.

*August 30, 1938*—The Sudeten Germans have decided to turn down the compromise proposal the government of Prague has offered them. The Czech offer is a cantonal plan, something along the lines of the Swiss cantons. Each minority in the country to have large right of local rule such as the Swiss enjoy.

At last reports Lord Runciman, the British mediator, was trying to get Konrad Henlein, the Sudeten Hitler, to take back the turndown and negotiate on the Swiss basis.

All accounts represent England and France as in unison, mutually determined to stop a Hitler march into Bohemia.

*September 1, 1938*—Cárdenas says that Mexico will pay the American companies no indemnity for the oil.

The new Nazi regime in Austria orders the abandonment of all religious schools. That, of course, includes Jewish schools, but more than any other it suppresses Catholic parochial schools, so prominent and influential in Austria.

*September 5, 1938*—Pope Pius, at his summer home at Castel Gandolfo, celebrated Mass today, a Requiem Mass for Patrick Cardinal

Hayes, Archbishop of New York, who died yesterday—foremost Catholic prelate in the United States.

*September 6, 1938*—There's a massing of troops on the German border—at the renowned Maginot Line, the ring of steel. This is the French answer to the massing of the great German military power just beyond the border.

And Great Britain, too, has mustered the armed force of the Empire, defense on the alert, as if waiting for quick action.

All this as Czechoslovakia prepares to hand its final compromise offer to the Sudeten Germans, which means to Hitler.

*September 7, 1938*—The Czechoslovaks are furious over an editorial in the London *Times*. The Thunderer, as it used to be known in newspaper circles, calmly suggests that the Czechoslovak territory inhabited by Sudeten Germans be ceded to Hitler.

*September 9, 1938*—Today the London newspapers carried big scare-heads about the possibility of war. In New York the stock market broke because of the fear that war was near.

*September 12, 1938*—This was a day the world anxiously awaited. The day of Hitler's final speech to the Nazi Congress at Nuremberg.

Downing Street looks upon Hitler's declaration as nothing short of an ultimatum to President Beneš of Czechoslovakia.

In Czechoslovakia itself the tension has been tightened to the point of terror.

The French Cabinet has vested Premier Daladier with extraordinary powers. He is authorized to take all necessary measures to help Czechoslovakia.

*September 13, 1938*—Hitler's Nuremberg oration yesterday was immediately followed by disturbance among the Sudetens, a series of incidents that increased in violence all day today.

To this uprising the Czechoslovak Government answered with drastic swiftness—proclaiming martial law in the key Sudeten sections. All public meetings and parades forbidden, and any act of rioting punishable by death. Drumhead court-martial, four judges, all death sentences to be executed within two hours.

The latest figures available at this moment show that, with nearly all of the election returns in, Senator Tydings of Maryland has beaten his opponent.

Once more the New Deal purge has failed.

*September 14, 1938*—Chamberlain proclaimed an epoch-making decision before the Commons. He told how he sent a personal message to Hitler. A message in which he used these unprecedented words: "In view of the increasingly critical situation I propose to come over at once to see you, with a view to trying to find a peaceful solution."

A brief reply from the Nazi Fuehrer stated that he would be ready to meet His Majesty's Prime Minister tomorrow.

*September 15, 1938*—Neville Chamberlain this morning flew from London to Munich. The aged Prime Minister had never flown before, never been up in a plane.

From Munich, Chamberlain took a special train to Berchtesgaden, a little town high in the Bavarian Alps.

Within an hour of his arrival Chamberlain was taken by car from the hotel to Hitler's hermit retreat high on the mountain. Hitler served tea to his English guest, and the conference began.

The Prime Minister himself spoke to the newspaper correspondents as follows: "I had a very friendly talk with Herr Hitler. I am returning to London and will meet Herr Hitler again sometime later."

*September 16, 1938*—Prime Minister Chamberlain returned home by plane today from his visit to Hitler.

A decree was issued in Prague today outlawing the Sudeten German party, ordering the abolition of the Nazi organization in Czechoslovakia, their storm troops to be disbanded, their property to be seized.

*September 19, 1938*—The official announcement of surrender to Hitler was made from London today.

For days it has been a foregone conclusion that the British Cabinet would fall in line with Prime Minister Chamberlain. And now it's also official that Premier Daladier and his colleagues have climbed on the band wagon.

*September 21, 1938*—A tragic message came from Prague. It was an official announcement at the end of a long and painful session of the Czechoslovak Cabinet, and its words were: "Under irresistible pressure, from both the British and French governments, the Czech Government has been forced to accept with pain the proposals elaborated in London."

In short, surrender; complete, humiliating, abject! Surrender, but at least peace. From London we then learned Prime Minister Neville

Chamberlain has ordered an airplane to take him to the Rhineland, where he'll meet Chancellor Hitler.

*September 22, 1938*—Over the River Rhine came a spare, aged Englishman, Neville Chamberlain, Prime Minister of Great Britain. Having flown from London, and having put up at a hotel on the other side of the stream, he took a boat across to meet Hitler.

Meanwhile in Prague angry crowds were marching through the streets, menacing crowds shouting against the partition of Czechoslovakia, wrathful crowds cheering the Army and demanding weapons, enraged crowds calling for war.

*September 23, 1938*—Here's a dispatch from Vienna. A report that there are extraordinary movements of troops toward the frontier of Czechoslovakia and what used to be Austria. In other words, Hitler is preparing to attack Czechoslovakia on two sides.

Here's a late flash—the President of Czechoslovakia has ordered the Czech Army to mobilize. Two million men are at this moment getting ready, jumping into their uniforms.

*September 26, 1938*—For the second time in two weeks the world listened while that master of excited declamation made history.

Hitler shouted, "Now I notify President Beneš that German patience is at an end. We're going to have that Sudeten territory and we're going to have it now."

The Czechs are continuing their preparations for war.

France also is openly making preparations for war.

In London the Air Ministry called up all members of the defense units of the auxiliary air force. And gas masks are being distributed throughout London.

Americans are being urged to leave Europe and come home as soon as possible.

*September 27, 1938*—Prime Minister Chamberlain's address today to the British Empire and the world was as important in tone as it was in substance.

He said in outright fashion that however much Britain might sympathize with little Czechoslovakia, threatened by big Germany, that alone would not persuade his government to plunge the world into war.

The Czechs have turned down completely the Hitler ultimatum demanding Sudeten possession by October 1.

*September 28, 1938*—Neville Chamberlain today, in a voice that trembled with the emotion it couldn't conceal, uttered these words in the Commons: "I have now been informed by Chancellor Hitler that he invites me to Munich tomorrow morning and that he has also invited Premier Mussolini and Premier Daladier." Then he continued: "Signor Mussolini has accepted. There is no doubt but that Monsieur Daladier also accepts. I need not say what my answer will be."

Pandemonium broke loose as the aged Prime Minister of Britain sank back, tears streaming down his wrinkled cheeks. The whole House had jumped to its feet, cheering.

*September 29, 1938*—Germany, England, France, Italy cheering with unrestrained joy because the word tonight is peace. As all the world knows, the Munich conference of four met for the third time today—Hitler, Chamberlain, Daladier, and Mussolini—merely to arrange minor details and sign the agreement.

Hitler is to have his march into Czechoslovakia on Saturday, as he has demanded so stubbornly even at the peril of war.

*September 30, 1938*—After the Big Four signed their agreement yesterday—and signed away Czechoslovakia while doing it—Prime Minister Chamberlain and Fuehrer Hitler had another meeting today. And they issued a statement that Great Britain and Germany would never go to war.

The latest news tells us about German soldiers trooping jubilantly across the Czechoslovak border and taking possession of the fringes of territory assigned for the first day's occupation.

There is plenty of bitter feeling in Prague, the bitterness of enforced surrender. Czech crowds staged demonstrations today in anger and protest. And the Soviets are not wiring felicitations or sending flowers. They're calling the peace pact a sellout. But the rest of the world seems to be happy about it all.

When the Prime Minister himself returned to England, an immense crowd received him with roaring cheers.

In Paris today one of the great French newspapers started a subscription to buy a house in France for Prime Minister Chamberlain.

When French Premier Daladier returned to his office in Paris he found it simply crammed with flowers, his desk heaped with telegrams and cables of congratulations.

Naturally the Italian Fascists are acclaiming the decisive part Mussolini played in his last-minute intervention with Hitler. They say the Duce did the trick.

One interesting angle is the part President Roosevelt played. It develops now that, in addition to his message to Mussolini asking him to appeal to Hitler, the President sent a whole string of similar messages to various nations.

It appears that, while the President's message was being sent to Rome, Mussolini was already making his fateful telephone call to Hitler and the four-power peace conference was already agreed upon.

*October 3, 1938*—The English today were recovering from their transports of last week's jubilation. Said Clement Attlee, the Labor leader, "There's no doubt it was a tremendous victory for Hitler. And," he added, "one of the greatest diplomatic defeats this country and France ever sustained."

At Eger, the town which has become the capital of Sudetenland, there was wild rejoicing today. Fuehrer Hitler made his triumphal entry and formally accepted possession of his new domain from the hands of Konrad Henlein, the Sudeten leader.

*October 5, 1938*—Today Dr. Eduard Beneš resigned as President of Czechoslovakia!

The consequences of the British and French surrender at Munich are becoming manifest with great speed.

The sacrifices that Chamberlain made for peace have already virtually produced a Germany that dominates Europe from the North Sea to the Black Sea, from the Baltic to the Aegean.

In the British House of Commons today there was another attack on Prime Minister Chamberlain. The most biting, the most formidable yet. The man who delivered it, that fighter of fighters, the Right Honorable Winston Churchill. He described the Munich Agreement as "a defeat without war."

*October 11, 1938*—Days of Nazi rioting against the Catholic Church in Vienna, with the swastika crowd storming the archiepiscopal palace and Nazi crowds howling against Cardinal Innitzer.

*October 19, 1938*—German honors for Colonel Charles A. Lindbergh. The Hitler government today conferred a decoration upon our flying colonel. The Distinguished Service Cross with the Star and the Order of the German Eagle.

*October 21, 1938*—The Japanese captured the metropolis of South China, marched in, and tonight have Canton in their possession.

*October 25, 1938*—Hankow falls, as Canton fell, without resistance.

*October 26, 1938*—Here is a late dispatch which tells of the decision the British Government has just made with reference to Jewish immigration in Palestine. It's from Jerusalem. It concerns the number of Jewish immigrants who will be admitted in the next six months. The number—forty-eight hundred; that many Jewish homeseekers may go to Palestine between now and the thirty-first of March.

*October 27, 1938*—Today Premier Daladier banished the Communists from the French parliamentary majority—the Popular Front.

*November 1, 1938*—In troubled Palestine the Arab general strike goes on, tying up industry and activities that depend upon Arab labor.

*November 2, 1938*—The House of Commons today gave Chamberlain an overwhelming vote of confidence.

*November 9, 1938*—That wounded German diplomat in Paris is dead. In spite of three blood transfusions the bullets of the seventeen-year-old Jewish assassin finally proved fatal today.

The assassination of Vom Rath has aroused a fresh fury in Germany against the Jews.

*November 14, 1938*—The Nazi treatment of the Jews has aroused such a storm of public disgust in England that the Cabinet doesn't dare even talk of negotiations with the Fuehrer at the present time.

*November 15, 1938*—Tonight the attitude of the American Government is exceedingly clear—outright indignation toward Nazi Germany for the persecution of Jews.

*November 24, 1938*—Once more the British Government declares that the answer to the refugee problem is not Palestine.

France and Britain agree to keep on building their armament so as to match the military strength of the Rome-Berlin Axis.

*December 1, 1938*—The government of Rumania today continued its drastic measures to suppress the Iron Guard. Jewish communities were guarded against attacks by anti-Semitic fanatics.

*December 2, 1938*—In the Italian Chamber of Deputies, in the presence of the French Ambassador, Fascist deputies staged a demonstration with shouts of "Tunisia! Savoy! Nice! Corsica!" Demands that these French possessions be handed over to Italy.

*December 6, 1938*—Today a stately scene was staged in Paris as France and Germany signed their agreement not to go to war.

*December 12, 1938*—The victory of the Nazis in the Memel election evidently has the statesmen of the world worried.

In Memel itself and throughout Lithuania, of course, there's extreme tension.

*December 22, 1938*—An agreement at Lima! The delegates of the twenty-one Pan-American nations have finally okayed a declaration of Western Hemisphere solidarity.

At the State Department called Dr. Hans Thomsen, the German chargé d'affaires. Dr. Thomsen told Acting Secretary Sumner Welles that the German Government expected the United States Government to make an expression of regret because of the anti-Nazi speech made by Secretary of the Interior Ickes. To this our Acting Secretary replied, "No, emphatically no!" He said the German protest was in singularly ill grace.

*December 28, 1938*—In Catalonia the rebel armies of General Franco continue to hammer their way ahead. They're converging in two lines like huge military pincers, crushing the government forces between them.

# 1939

*This is the year of war. Hitler's continuing aggressions leave Britain and France no alternative. He seizes all of Czechoslovakia. He demands the Polish Corridor and forces the Allies to guarantee the integrity of Poland. He signs an agreement with Stalin, crushes Poland in a lightning campaign featuring a co-ordination of tanks and planes that foreshadows gigantic battles to come, and divides the spoils with his partner in crime from Moscow. Britain and France declare war, but after the German conquest of Poland hostilities subside into the lull of the "phony war." Hitler opens his peace offensive. His opponents fail in their attempt to assassinate him at the Munich beer hall where the Nazi movement began.*

*Stalin attacks Finland, and the world is startled by the Finns' heroic defense of their soil. In Siberia, the Manchurian border fighting goes on. Violence in Palestine increases after the publication of the British White Paper, which satisfies neither Jews nor Arabs. In Spain, the Civil War finally ends, but its toll will shortly become pale in the shadow of World War II. In Rome, Cardinal Pacelli becomes Pope under the title of Pius XII.*

*At home, President Roosevelt signs the Neutrality Act but warns that we cannot remain indifferent to what is happening abroad.*

*January 4, 1939*—There was a conspicuous difference between President Roosevelt's message today and those that went before. Hitherto his emphasis was always on the American scene. So it struck sharply upon the ears of listeners that his opening sentence today read, "As this Seventy-sixth Congress opens, there is need for further warning for putting our house in order in the face of storm signals from across the seas."

*January 6, 1939*—Germany, says Lindbergh, has by all odds the greatest military air fleet in the world.

*January 11, 1939*—The Senate Commerce Committee had Secretary Harry Hopkins on the grill, dragging in that famous quotation attributed to Hopkins: "We will spend and spend, tax and tax, elect and elect." Hopkins again denied vehemently that he had ever said anything of the sort.

*January 13, 1939*—Hungary today officially swung into the orbit of the Rome-Berlin Axis. The Budapest government formally joined the German-Italian-Japanese alliance against communism.

*January 16, 1939*—A battle of huge proportions is now raging around Barcelona.

*January 19, 1939*—The issue in question is the fortification of Guam. Japan objects. One Tokyo spokesman declared that if we created a mighty naval base at Guam it would be like pointing a pistol at Japan.

*January 26, 1939*—The taking of Barcelona today was drama that turned into sheer spectacle. Not a shot was fired, not a sign of resistance! Instead houses everywhere hung out bed sheets for white flags, and many displayed the Franco colors, the traditional red and gold of old Spain.

*February 1, 1939*—A debate which started quietly in the Senate today developed into an angry and momentous fight. The issue was peace. The opposition presently came out with a flat charge that the President was preparing to shove us into another European war.

*February 2, 1939*—Secretary Ickes declares there is no danger of Uncle Sam's being involved in any war under the present administration.

*February 3, 1939*—President Roosevelt certainly was emphatic today in denying the story about the American frontier being in France. He declared he never said any such thing.

*February 6, 1939*—Premier Negrin of republican Spain crossed the French frontier this morning, and President Azana fled across yesterday.

*February 10, 1939*—Today passed away Pope Pius XI, the two hundred and sixty-first pontiff of the Roman Catholic Church, with the one last word on his faltering lips—peace!
    The Pope dies, a Pope is elected amid wonder and suspense. Who will be chosen?

*February 15, 1939*—The British Government has just decided unanimously to accord recognition to Franco as the de facto government in Spain.

*February 23, 1939*—The House of Representatives chucked out the Guam item today. No authorization for the fortification of that distant island in the Pacific.

*March 2, 1939*—Eugenio Pacelli is a Roman, a native of the Eternal City—and tonight crowds along the Tiber are cheering the Roman Pope.

The new pontiff is indeed well known here in the United States, having visited in this country extensively in 1936.

*March 6, 1939*—There is not a single Communist in this new Madrid junta. The latest is that the junta is arresting Communists.

*March 7, 1939*—There has been bitter fighting in Madrid all day between the Communists and the forces of the defense junta.

*March 10, 1939*—The Communist revolt in left-wing Spain was at its greatest fury today.

*March 15, 1939*—Today Adolf Hitler rode triumphantly into Prague. A dramatic symbol of his complete control of the ancient countries of Bohemia and Moravia.

Heinrich Himmler, the dread chief of the Gestapo, sent eight hundred Nazi secret police into Prague. The Nazi press in Bohemia and Rumania have already opened an anti-Jewish campaign, so there's little doubt of what will happen.

Viscount Halifax, His Majesty's Foreign Secretary, made an announcement in the House of Lords. He said that Hitler had sent his troops beyond the frontiers laid down at Munich and had done so without consulting any of the other four powers who signed the Munich Agreement.

*March 16, 1939*—Prague is fairly normal tonight, with German troops on guard—the Czech people sullenly angry, but they can't do a thing about it.

Today in Prague, Nazi storm troopers at the Czechoslovak bank loaded eighteen truckloads of gold.

*March 21, 1939*—The United States formally refuses to recognize the German seizure of Czechoslovakia.

*March 23, 1939*—Rumania signed on the dotted line—Rumania now inside of the German orbit. King Carol's regime okayed a buying and selling agreement that makes it economically a vassal of Germany.

*March 28, 1939*—There was no formal surrender of Madrid. The defense junta fled. Whereupon the Franco sympathizers swarmed into the open, took possession of the city—seizing the radio station at once and putting on their own jubilant broadcast.

It was a drama of the fifth column, that famous fifth column so often mentioned in the Spanish Civil War.

*March 29, 1939*—The Republic of Spain is dead. Its obituary was announced today in a broadcast from Burgos, which announced that the almost-three-year-long war has ended.

*April 3, 1939*—There was a growing chorus of voices in Europe today. It was chanting, "Stop Hitler!"

*April 7, 1939*—Today's miniature war in Albania must have been little more than skirmishing. King Zog's entire Army numbers only about twelve thousand men, with a dozen pieces of artillery.

The main focus of resistance was at Durazzo, Albania's No. 1 seaport. Durazzo has been captured by the Italians.

Spain today formally lined up with Germany, Italy, and Japan in the anti-Communist alliance.

*April 11, 1939*—The Italian occupation of Albania goes on.

*April 13, 1939*—A joint declaration made by Great Britain and France guaranteeing the integrity of Greece and Rumania. This momentous declaration was made by Prime Minister Chamberlain in an address to the House of Commons and by Premier Daladier of France in an official statement issued at Paris. Having already guaranteed Poland, they now give similar assurance to Greece and Rumania.

*April 14, 1939*—What the President had to say today in his Pan-American address has set off verbal high jinks in the national capital.

Said he, we have a right to oppose totalitarianism as a doctrine and a practice in Europe.

The controversy boils down to this: one side saying, "He's keeping us out of war," the other side retorting, "He's getting us into war."

*April 21, 1939*—The Soviets are proposing immediate conferences of the Army staffs of the three powers—British and French generals to get together with the Red Army high command to discuss plans of battle for war with Hitler's Germany—if and when.

*April 24, 1939*—A Massachusetts prelate, the Most Reverend Francis J. Spellman, Auxiliary Bishop of Boston, now becomes Archbishop of New York.

*April 27, 1939*—The House of Commons has just passed the bill for compulsory military service in peacetime.

*April 28, 1939*—Hitler won't go to a world conference such as President Roosevelt suggested. The brown-shirt dictator made that emphatic with bitter words.

The other nation that comes to the forefront tonight is Poland—with Hitler denouncing the Polish-German non-aggression treaty and voicing a direct demand for Danzig and for a strategic highway across the Polish Corridor.

*May 4, 1939*—The downfall of Litvinov in Russia has stirred up all sorts of speculation. The obvious surmise is that the Foreign Commissar, so prominent for many years, was chucked out of office because Stalin has turned against the Litvinov policies of lining up with the Western democracies. Some think they even may presage a turning of Soviet policy toward Germany.

*May 5, 1939*—Poland refuses to let Hitler take Danzig—but Poland leaves a way open for future negotiation.

*May 9, 1939*—The Nazi press is talking about a possible agreement with Moscow.

*May 12, 1939*—The Polish Government today turned down the Soviet proposal for a four-power military alliance.

*May 17, 1939*—Today the British Government in London made public that long-expected White Paper. The British propose to establish an independent state in Palestine, which will be united by treaty with Great Britain for ten years.

As soon as the White Paper was published, the Jewish Agency issued a statement denouncing it.

In Quebec there was an imposing military and naval display to welcome the King and Queen.

*May 18, 1939*—Today in the troubled land of Palestine there were mingled solemnity and violence—solemn protest and violent protest. All because of yesterday's British White Paper, London's decree that the Holy Land shall be an independent nation with a two-to-one majority of Arabs, the Jews in a permanent minority.

*May 22, 1939*—When Boss Pendergast of Kansas City was indicted, it was a stunning surprise to the Democratic party in Missouri. Everybody in the Middle West thought the old kingmaker of Kansas City was immune, impregnable. Well—today's surprise was even more. It was like a thunderbolt. Tom Pendergast pleading guilty of income tax evasion. Yes, the man who had made governors and held United States senators in the palm of his hand admitted that he had defrauded the United States to the tune of $429,000.

*May 23, 1939*—Two hundred and forty feet below the surface of the sea lies the United States submarine *Squalus*, which sank today—sixty-one men aboard.

In Canada the royal visit continued on its triumphant way today, with King George and Queen Elizabeth speeding out into the spacious lands of the Canadian midwest—where Indians gazed with astonished eyes at the ceremonies for the sovereigns of empire.

*May 24, 1939*—Today, on the first trip from the *Squalus*, 240 feet below the surface, the diving bell brought up seven men. Three hours later eight were hauled to the surface, making a total of fifteen. Thirty-three in all were saved. Twenty-six lost.

*May 26, 1939*—A report comes from Berlin that the German Government has ordered the Nazi press to drop its attacks on Russia.

*May 31, 1939*—Uncle Sam's Navy has been scouring the Pacific for that gay adventurer, Richard Halliburton. He sailed from Hong Kong on March 4, San Francisco-bound, on a Chinese junk called the *Sea Dragon*, with a crew of thirteen—some of them Americans, some Chinese. Halliburton, from the bridge of his romantic *Sea Dragon*, reported the position of his junk on March 24, and then apparently the vast Pacific swallowed the *Sea Dragon*.

*June 2, 1939*—The latest news is the worst of news, about the British submarine tragedy.

The tide was rushing in fast, and water was pushing strongly against the submarine standing on its head. It pushed the *Thetis* right over, and the stern disappeared in a swirl of water.

The air running short inside! No more signals! Silence!

*June 8, 1939*—The weather was warm, and so was the welcome. President Roosevelt began it when he greeted the King-Emperor with friendly informality.

There was an incessant pandemonium of cheers as the royal and presidential procession in sleek automobiles rolled slowly along Pennsylvania Avenue, the Avenue of the Presidents.

*June 9, 1939*—King George and Queen Elizabeth made a visit to the Capitol under the great dome, where they met members of the Congress of the United States.

*June 15, 1939*—King George VI and Queen Elizabeth left American shores amid cheers. They arrived amid cheers, and loud acclaim is what they received all the way across Canada and here in the United States.

*June 20, 1939*—The Mikado's men have turned on the electricity at Tientsin. Yesterday they put a fence of high-tension wires around the concession, and today they turned on the current, making it death to touch the wires. They're enforcing the blockade with the ever present threat of electrocution.

*June 22, 1939*—The reports from Tientsin seem more and more provocative. The Japanese, at the concession barriers, are still doing their utmost to humiliate British subjects. The British consul told the newspapermen that again a man had been stripped naked. Another was forced to undress down to his shorts, with a crowd of Chinese staring at him.

*June 26, 1939*—As for Tientsin, the argument is still a deadlock, and Prime Minister Chamberlain continues to talk peaceably about it.

*June 27, 1939*—There's an uneasy impression in the world that, in spite of the lull in the European crisis right now, things are stirring dangerously under the surface and there may soon be another flare-up worse than ever.

Today the Japanese commander at Tientsin gave the order—no more of the strip act which so humiliated and embarrassed the British.

*June 28, 1939*—This afternoon aviation history was made when a great clipper plane took off from the sea base at Port Washington, Long Island. The Dixie Clipper, making the first flight on the regular passenger schedule of the Pan American transatlantic service.

*June 29, 1939*—The controversy is focused more sharply than ever on Danzig, which adjoins the Polish Corridor.

*June 30, 1939*—The Poles are saying tonight that any coup in Danzig, whether it comes from inside the city or from without, will be regarded by the Polish Government as a cause for war.

*July 4, 1939*—A new Nazi outrage against Cardinal Innitzer is reported today, another Nazi attack upon His Eminence of Vienna. He was showered with insults and bombarded with a barrage of missiles—eggs and potatoes.

President Roosevelt today took a fling at the arms embargo, which the House of Representatives put back into the Neutrality Bill. The President said that this act was an encouragement to Nazi Germany and Fascist Italy.

*July 6, 1939*—The Chamberlain government has at last stated its position definitely about Danzig and Poland. Great Britain will fight with Poland if there is any one-sided change in the status of Danzig.

*July 13, 1939*—Moscow reports that Russian and Mongolian detachments have driven Japanese and Manchukuan invaders beyond the borders of Soviet Mongolia.

*July 27, 1939*—John L. Lewis charges Mr. Garner with being responsible for attacks on labor during this session of Congress. He wound up by describing the Vice-President as "a labor-baiting, poker-playing, whiskey-drinking, evil old man."

*August 2, 1939*—The state of California won a naval victory today. It was a victory over the gambling fleet which has been holding forth on the high seas of the Pacific twelve miles offshore, near Los Angeles.

The California attorney general's men boarded the ships, arrested the skippers, confiscated the strongboxes which held thousands of dollars, and, adding insult to injury, threw overboard into the deep blue Pacific all their expensive gambling paraphernalia.

*August 3, 1939*—One of the most interesting military questions of the day concerns the actual strength of the mighty fortifications that line the frontier of Germany and France—the Maginot Line on one side, the Siegfried Line on the other.

Japan is at last joining the Nazi-Fascist Axis in a formal military way.

*August 4, 1939*—The Chinese national capital of Chungking was savagely bombed today.

*August 9, 1939*—In Berlin the campaign in the Nazi newspapers against Poland continues with increased vehemence.

*August 18, 1939*—In Germany high Nazi officials are quoted as saying today that Hitler will have a quick solution of the Danzig issue even if it leads to war. And not only Danzig—the Polish Corridor also.

*August 21, 1939*—Another of the prime sources of anxiety in Europe today was the news of a trade agreement between Stalin and Hitler, Soviet Russia and Nazi Germany.

Here's a late and most important-sounding bulletin: Foreign Minister von Ribbentrop will leave on Wednesday, for Moscow to conclude negotiations for a German-Soviet non-aggression pact.

*August 22, 1939*—Just think of today's painful plight of the high-ranking top-lofty members of the Franco-British missions. They are still in Moscow; something like magnificent bigwigs with the rug suddenly pulled out from under them—just sitting on the floor with blank expressions.

Just as the Nazis' diplomatic drive for Danzig in the Polish Corridor was coming to the verge of war, Hitler explodes the bombshell that there will be no Soviet Russia, no Red Army on the side of the democracies if war should come.

Warsaw is talking defiance, saying that the German-Russian treaty doesn't mean so much, won't make any great difference. Poland never did expect any important help from the Soviets, had always rejected the idea of the Red Army entering Poland as a defender.

*August 23, 1939*—The word from London is that the British are prepared for the worst.

In the British Isles every place where raiding airplane bombers might strike is prepared for a black-out.

*August 24, 1939*—France is virtually mobilized.

One graphic scene was witnessed today in Berlin. A crowd of German Nazis, dozens of them, went to the Soviet Embassy and rang the doorbell. They were admitted and walked in solemnly. In the antechamber they shouted all together, "Heil Moscow."

President Roosevelt sent a personal message to King Victor Emmanuel in behalf of the maintenance of peace, asking the Italian monarch to use his good offices to avert war.

A call for peace was addressed to the whole world from the Vatican.

*August 25, 1939*—A treaty, a British-Polish treaty of mutual assistance, Britain guaranteeing to fight if Poland should be attacked. Today's diplomatic document made it formal, official, and permanent.

*August 28, 1939*—The Duke of Alba has given assurance to both Great Britain and France that no Spanish naval bases and no airdromes will be used by any belligerent.

*August 29, 1939*—The Pope is taking air-raid precautions to safeguard St. Peter's and the Vatican.

*August 30, 1939*—An official order of mobilization was proclaimed today in Poland.

King Victor Emmanuel of Italy replied to the appeal for peace sent to him by President Roosevelt. The Italian King thanked the President for his efforts and added the information that the Italian Government is doing everything possible to bring about peace with justice.

*August 31, 1939*—Britain mobilized today. They are beginning the evacuation of children from London.

Hitler requires that Poland hand Danzig over to Germany at once, the bottleneck of the Polish Corridor to be placed under the administration of an international commission, governed by an international group, delegates of Great Britain, France, Italy, and Russia. The Polish port of Gdynia to be retained by Poland. The international supervision to continue for not more than a year, by which time a plebiscite would be held.

The Supreme Soviet took a vote on the Nazi-Communist treaty—and ratified it unanimously, okayed it without argument.

*September 1, 1939*—War it is, with Germany and Poland fighting a major campaign tonight—and Great Britain and France about to plunge in.

It's a heavyhearted thing tonight to begin the reciting of war bulletins. Today the German command announced an advance all along the line, drives into Poland on three sides, pushing on everywhere—"lightning advances," Berlin calls it.

Warsaw was bombed several times today.

London and Paris took simultaneous action. Each instructed its Ambassador in Berlin to present Hitler with an ultimatum. If Nazi Germany doesn't draw back at this last moment and recall its armies from Poland, Great Britain and France will intervene in the struggle.

Chamberlain declared that Great Britain and Poland were still ready to negotiate when Hitler struck this morning.

With war breaking out, Premier Molotov today addressed the Supreme Soviet, the Communist parliament, and played up that suddenly discovered comradeship between Stalin and Hitler. He was just as emphatic about it as the Nazi Fuehrer had been earlier in the day.

Every American is thinking—what about ourselves? Will we be drawn in? That question was answered today by President Roosevelt. I think the President was echoing the vast majority of Americans—let's do all we can to keep out of it!

*September 4, 1939*—The Jews in Palestine will fight for the British if necessary. This was announced in London today by the Jewish Agency. They still object to the British White Paper of last May. Nevertheless, they will help Britain in the war.

German forces by land, by sea, and by air are smashing ahead on every front against the Poles.

*September 5, 1939*—At thirty-six and a half minutes past one today, Eastern standard time, the United States became neutral. That is, officially. At precisely that second the great seal of the Department of State was affixed to President Roosevelt's Neutrality Proclamation.

What about the western front? There seems to be no real fighting there.

The Germans claim to be driving deep into Poland, the Corridor isolated, Hitler's southern army smashing its way toward the great industrial city of Krakow.

German dispatches reported that Hitler's troops, striking from the north, had driven to within fifty miles of Warsaw.

*September 6, 1939*—Tonight the German armies are closing in on Warsaw from four directions. The defenders of the unhappy country are feverishly digging in along the line of the Bug River not more than ten miles from Warsaw.

*September 7, 1939*—It may well be that today's declaration by Prime Minister Chamberlain is of decisive importance. He gave Poland the most solemn assurance that Great Britain will not make peace on the basis of a defeated Poland.

The Polish war continues apace. Military experts are surprised at the swiftness of the German drives that are plunging deep into Poland.

Today was the seventh day of battle, and in seven days the Germans claim to have occupied one third of Poland, and that one third the industrial area so vital to national resistance. Today the principal battle was waged to the north and west of Warsaw.

A gigantic artillery duel is going on between the Maginot Line and the Siegfried Line.

The Germans announced that Westerplatte has surrendered—that little place which has been to Poland what the Alcazar was to the nationalists in the Spanish Civil War. Or you might call it—the Polish Alamo.

*September 8, 1939*—The German high command this afternoon announced the capture of Warsaw.

The President proclaims a state of limited national emergency.

*September 11, 1939*—Mobilization of Soviet Russian troops on the

Polish frontier. The troops are being concentrated in western Russia to disarm and intern the Polish soldiers who cross the border fleeing from Hitler's armies.

Today's reports from Poland present a continuation of the perhaps decisive battle that was raging yesterday.

*September 15, 1939*—Today swift-striking columns of Hitler's mechanized Army struck all the way to Brest-Litovsk.

*September 18, 1939*—According to the latest dispatch from Berlin, the advance guard of the mechanized German Army met the forerunners of Stalin's Russians at Brest-Litovsk.

A semi-official statement is made in Berlin that Hitler and Stalin have drawn up an agreement covering six points for the partition of Poland.

What will England do? Fight Russia? No word!

*September 21, 1939*—President Roosevelt's peace pledges, as spoken today, are decidedly worth repeating. "This government," he told Congress, "must lose no time or effort to keep the nation from being drawn into the war. Our acts," he emphasized, "must be guided by one single hardheaded thought—keeping America out of this war."

*September 22, 1939*—The high commands of the German and Soviet Russian armies announce the division of the conquered country between them. The surprise is how much of Poland Soviet Russia gets. Half of the ill-fated nation.

Warsaw has still not surrendered—is still making a magnificent, desperate, hopeless defense.

The Rumanian Government is taking ferocious vengeance for the Iron Guard assassination of Premier Calinescu. Reports from Bucharest today tell of hundreds and hundreds of executions in reprisal.

*September 26, 1939*—Chamberlain indicated that, so far as the Allies were concerned, the war was more economic than military. No tremendous charge by the British and French armies against the Siegfried Line, but slow economic strangulation—that's the idea.

*September 27, 1939*—Tonight we have one bit of war news that is not contradicted, the long-expected surrender of Warsaw.

*October 3, 1939*—The British Prime Minister indicated in strong terms that the Nazi peace offensive would be rejected, but he also said that Hitler's peace proposal would get at least formal consideration.

*October 5, 1939*—Latvia, as everybody anticipated, is now branded with the Bolshevik "B." She signed a treaty tonight which makes Latvia a vassal of the Soviet.

*October 6, 1939*—London characterizes the Nazi Fuehrer's proposals as vague and obscure—and they certainly seem none too clear and precise.

Hitler was somewhat clearer when he started threatening. He said if the Allies refused to make peace it would be a fight to the finish, and that would be "a triumph of destruction."

*October 12, 1939*—Today marks the close of one phase of the present war—the peace offensive. The British reply to Hitler was stronger than the French reply. Prime Minister Chamberlain's rejection was more positively spoken than that given by Premier Daladier on Tuesday.

*October 13, 1939*—A conference of the northern powers was called today. King Gustav of Sweden invited the kings of Denmark and Norway and the President of Finland to gather at Stockholm on October 18. The main purpose will be a demonstration of Scandinavian solidarity. And this, of course, has reference to the peril of Finland.

*October 16, 1939*—An attack by a squadron of a dozen Nazi bombers on the Scottish coast.

*October 17, 1939*—Today the Germans struck at Scapa Flow from the sky.

A sensation harked back to last week, the torpedoing of the great battleship, the *Royal Oak*. It was announced in the British Parliament that the *Royal Oak* had been torpedoed at Scapa Flow while lying at anchor within the naval stronghold. Somehow a German U-boat managed to sneak through the defenses guarding the channels, through mines and nets.

*October 19, 1939*—Why has not Great Britain done something about the Soviet invasion of Poland? The Allies guaranteed Poland against aggression and declared war on Hitler when Hitler invaded.

Today in the House of Commons the British Government gave the explanation. Great Britain did not guarantee Poland against aggression by Soviet Russia, against aggression by anybody except Nazi Germany.

*October 26, 1939*—Prime Minister Chamberlain made it official today that the German pocket battleship *Deutschland* is on the loose. It turns out now that it was the *Deutschland* which captured the *City of Flint* and sent that American ship to Murmansk. Right now the pocket battleship is somewhere in the North Atlantic seeking new victims.

Moscow refuses to recognize the British blockade of Germany.

*October 31, 1939*—Molotov denounces Great Britain and France for fighting Germany. He termed it "senseless" and "criminal." He called Great Britain the "aggressor."

*November 2, 1939*—Italy today came to terms with Greece—on a non-aggression pact.

*November 3, 1939*—Tonight President Roosevelt has on his desk a bill for his signature. And there's no need to ask whether he'll sign it. It's the Neutrality Bill, cutting out the arms embargo.

It certainly was rather astonishing for Moscow to accuse little Finland of wanting to go to war with giant Soviet Russia.

*November 6, 1939*—The French Government is going to go the limit to wipe out the Communist party from the French Republic.

*November 8, 1939*—Hitler had hardly finished delivering his fiery speech at Munich today when a terrific explosion crashed out in the cellar of the beer hall where he had been speaking. The Fuehrer himself escaped. But several of his followers were killed instantaneously.

The same beer hall where the famous and futile Nazi *Putsch* was born sixteen years ago.

*November 22, 1939*—Today in Great Britain first official mention was made of a thing that has been rumored but hardly believed, a new weapon of war—the magnetic mine—reported as responsible for the recent terror of sinkings on the sea.

In the fantastic story of the beer-cellar bomb plot to kill Hitler the Nazis today continued to blast against Otto Strasser. They are hammering away at the charge that the conspiracy originated with him, the one-time ace-high Nazi and colleague of Hitler.

*November 27, 1939*—It was Hitler's pocket battleship, the *Deutschland*, which sank a British cruiser off the coast of Iceland last week.

*November 28, 1939*—The Soviets have just denounced their non-aggression pact with the little northern republic, Finland.

*November 29, 1939*—The Soviet Premier told the world that Russia could no longer stand the unbearable situation which the hostility of the Finns has forced upon the poor Soviets.

After that Molotov ordered the armed forces of the Soviets to be ready for an emergency.

*November 30, 1939*—The Soviet invasion struck frightfully through the sky, a swift bombing raid against the Finnish capital—Helsingfors, as it was called in the older Swedish fashion—Helsinki, as the Finns call it.

The Red Army is reported to be invading all along the extended border from above the Arctic Circle to the Gulf of Finland.

Late reports tell that the Finnish Army is resisting bravely, with heavy artillery fire.

Yesterday, at the last minute, Washington sent to both governments an offer to mediate. The Bolsheviks rejected American mediation coldly.

*December 1, 1939*—American indignation over the ruthless assault on Finland continued to seethe today. President Roosevelt expressed it in one of the most strongly worded denunciations he has ever made.

*December 4, 1939*—The Russo-Finnish War continues to be one of the surprises of this year's history. Even the official newspapers of the Soviets publish a partial admission that the Red armies are encountering serious difficulties.

*December 5, 1939*—The latest bulletin from Helsinki tells of heavy fighting all day in the Karelia sector, the part of the Finnish border nearest the great city of Leningrad.

Fritz Kuhn was sentenced today and gets two and a half to five years in prison.

*December 12, 1939*—Soviet Russia has just turned down the League of Nations' demand that the Red Army stop its invasion of Finland.

*December 14, 1939*—Tonight, outside of the harbor of Montevideo, warships are steaming back and forth. Their searchlights are sweeping the dark waters with a flash of brilliant beams. The death watch, they are calling it—British warcraft ready for the kill if the German pocket battleship *Graf Spee* should try to get out into the Atlantic. The *Graf Spee*, damaged, ripped by shells, after yesterday's sea fight.

The League of Nations acted promptly today in expelling Soviet Russia. In other affairs the League was known to procrastinate and drag things out—but not now in the case of the invasion of Finland.

*December 15, 1939*—This afternoon the official announcement came through that the government of Uruguay gives the German pocket battle-ship seventy-two hours to leave—three days.

Finland today appealed to Soviet Russia to resume negotiations.

*December 18, 1939*—The Argentine authorities are interning the crew of the scuttled *Graf Spee*.

Reports that the Finns have won a crushing victory on the Karelian Isthmus.

*December 19, 1939*—The Finnish Government will soon get a ship-ment of forty-four American fighting planes.

*December 20, 1939*—The suicide of the captain of the *Graf Spee* caps the climax of that astounding drama of the sea.

The Russian Reds have been launching the most ferocious attack of the whole Finnish campaign.

*December 22, 1939*—Today French Premier Daladier told his Cham-ber of Deputies that France is sending what he described in so many words as "real military aid" to Finland.

*December 25, 1939*—In the Far North the Finns are chasing the Red battalions up toward the Arctic Ocean. There seems to be a Red Army disaster amid frightful Arctic cold.

The most important story in many a day was President Roosevelt's ap-pointment of an American emissary to the Vatican to work for peace in collaboration with Pope Pius XII. It was followed in the papers this morn-ing by the response of the Roman pontiff—his warm welcome of the Presi-dent's action and his suggestion of a five-point program for moral peace.

*December 26, 1939*—In the center of the eastern front the Finns are on Russian soil in places.

*December 28, 1939*—Today's reports from the Russian side indicate that Red dictator Stalin is rushing huge new masses of troops to the battle line.

# 1940

The year's news is headed by the list of Hitler's victims—Denmark,
Norway, Holland, Belgium, France—all knocked over like ninepins
as the Nazi tyrant turns the "phony war" into total war. He occupies
a ring of territory facing Britain along a tremendous arc from the
Norwegian Arctic to the Pyrenees. But Britain, now led by Winston
Churchill, fights back against the blitz from the sky and all-out submarine warfare. Most of the British Army on the continent is saved
at Dunkirk, and Churchill pledges a fight to the end, whipping up the
spirits of his countrymen with the most stirring eloquence of the war.

Meanwhile Mussolini joins Hitler and attacks Greece, only to be
defeated. The Finnish war ends with the imposition of harsh Soviet
terms. In Mexico, Stalin's old antagonist, Trotsky, is assassinated, apparently at the Red tyrant's orders.

At home, President Roosevelt smashes the old precedent by winning
a third term over Wendell Willkie. He repeats that our troops will not
go to war. But he puts an embargo on scrap iron for Japan and leases
British bases. The first American boys are drafted for service in the
armed forces. John L. Lewis resigns as head of the C.I.O. and is
succeeded by Philip Murray.

---

*January 4, 1940*—Dispatches from Helsinki today continue to tell of
the victories the Finns have been winning. The latest accounts describe
what are mostly follow-up operations, chasing defeated Red Army units in
the Arctic North.

The news of trouble in Ireland tells of many arrests, the De Valera
government rounding up members of the outlawed Irish Republican
Army.

*January 12, 1940*—Here is a familiar headline—Little America. The
two Byrd ships had a rough time breaking through the heavy drift ice
they encountered. It seems to be unusually icy down there on the south

polar continent this year. But they reached their goal and have now begun to work for further exploration on the southern continent, claiming great areas for the United States, frozen areas said to be rich in mineral wealth.

*January 15, 1940*—The latest is that the fear of any German invasion of the Low Countries is even less today than it was in the middle of November, when the last scare was raised and came to nothing.

*January 22, 1940*—Naturally there is much debate over that speech by Winston Churchill, First Lord of the British Admiralty, the speech in which he invited all small neutral countries to get in the war, on the Allied side, of course.

*January 23, 1940*—The Finns charge that Soviet planes today attacked parties of civilian refugees. Wanton killing.

*January 25, 1940*—Today in Washington three thousand checks were mailed, and this began the payment of old-age benefits for social security.

*January 29, 1940*—More rumblings from the unfortunate country that used to be Czechoslovakia. A dispatch from Prague reports that the Nazi police are arresting more people in the protectorate, trying to stamp out an agitation against the Hitler regime.

*January 31, 1940*—The British Government is to take over the entire shipbuilding industry of Great Britain. The announcement was made to the House of Commons by Chamberlain today.

*February 7, 1940*—We learn that the Russians have been again using a stunt they practiced in peacetime with benefit of much publicity, dropping soldiers in parachutes. The Finnish Government today issued instructions to the population on how to deal with parachutists.

*February 12, 1940*—There was jubilation in Berlin today over the new trade treaty between the Nazis and the Bolsheviks.

*February 15, 1940*—The Finns today report that the Mannerheim Line is holding fast against continued Soviet attacks.

*February 16, 1940*—Congress today voted against the proposal to fortify the island of Guam.

*February 21, 1940*—For the first time this nightly Sunoco program of ours is being televised as well as broadcast. In fact, Major Lohr, head of

NBC, who is here with me on this historic occasion, has just remarked that this is the first sponsored program ever to go out by television.

*February 27, 1940*—Today's declaration by Winston Churchill to the House of Commons is striking chiefly because of things he admitted. The First Lord of the Admiralty told the members of Parliament that Britain has abandoned its former great naval base at historic Scapa Flow. The British fleet has deserted its naval stronghold at Scapa Flow because of the torpedoing of the great battleship *Royal Oak* in the harbor by a German submarine. Also, Scapa Flow was razed at times by Nazi bombers.

*February 28, 1940*—Finland will get her loan from the United States, any sum up to twenty million. But she mustn't use it to buy the things she needs most—weapons, ammunition, planes, cannon. The bill to that effect was passed by the House, passed to the accompaniment of raucous jeers.

*March 1, 1940*—The war in Finland still shows the Red Army battering at the gates of Viipuri. The Mannerheim Line is being broken.

*March 4, 1940*—The Finns are still hanging onto Viipuri.

*March 7, 1940*—Britain's 28,500,000-dollar, 85,000-ton liner, the *Queen Elizabeth*, docked at New York this afternoon.
Tonight the biggest ship in the world is in her berth alongside those other oceanic queens, the British *Queen Mary* and the French *Normandie*. Like them, she is here for the duration of the war, safe from the perils of the war zone.

*March 11, 1940*—Practically the entire civilized world was waiting today for news from one special quarter. What's happening in Moscow? How are the Finns getting on in their peace parley with Stalin?
That seems to be the only actual fact that we have tonight. The Russians and the Finns are still dickering.

*March 12, 1940*—Here's a dispatch just handed me. It is officially announced that Finland and Russia have concluded their peace negotiations, and the war is at an end.

*March 13, 1940*—The whole world tonight realizes that the terms of the Russo-Finnish treaty are even worse than we thought they might be. The cost of peace to the Finns is heavy and bitter.

*March 15, 1940*—The world has been asking the ominous question: When will the war really blaze forth with murderous violence? Word comes increasingly that the people of Great Britain and France are becoming impatient with the stalemate state of affairs, the siege tactics, the half a war. "Do something," is being demanded more and more, demanded in London and Paris. "Do something"—the cry was raised in the British House of Commons today.

The end of the war was made official in Finland today. The Finnish parliament voted to ratify the harsh treaty with Soviet Russia.

*March 18, 1940*—For a few hours today the most important place in the world was the Brenner Pass. If the walls of those mountains between Italy and Austria had ears, they could tell a tale that all of us would give a good deal to hear: what passed between Mussolini and Hitler; what was decided by the Duce and the Fuehrer in that historic mountain pass?

*March 20, 1940*—Startling news with our breakfast coffee this morning: France at the present moment is without a government, that is to say, without a cabinet. But more spectacular still is the fact that the probable new Premier, Paul Reynaud, will push the war against Hitler with an iron hand.

*March 28, 1940*—The Supreme War Council of the Allies met today in London, with Prime Minister Chamberlain and Premier Reynaud leading the proceedings. In this conference Great Britain and France affirmed their decision to stand together.

*March 29, 1940*—Today the German soldiers raised huge banners inscribed with the biblical injunction, "Love thy neighbor." And at the same time loud-speakers blared out slogans of peace. All this for the benefit of the French troops, who could see the signs and were deafened by the roaring slogans. They replied with artillery and machine-gun fire, which we are told vanquished the loud-speakers and the painted signs.

Molotov warned London and Paris against the idea that they could hit at the Soviets as a way of hurting Nazi Germany. The Foreign Commissar indicated, however, that Stalin was not playing Hitler's game, not playing anybody's game but his own.

*April 4, 1940*—Prime Minister Chamberlain today spoke in a tone of large optimism. He said that he was ten times as sure that the Allies would win the war as he was when the conflict began.

*April 9, 1940*—At about midnight our time, 5 A.M. over there, the break of day, the armed forces of Nazi Germany launched their attack.

They did it with amazing swiftness. They invaded Denmark by land and from the sea.

The government of Denmark submitted under protest. It couldn't do anything else.

Simultaneously the Germans were invading Norway.

It's a topsy-turvy war. Today Hitler, with one blow, sweeps the war northward through Scandinavia to the Arctic coast.

*April 10, 1940*—Reports were current all day that the Norwegians were about to surrender.

The little Norwegian Army continues to put up a fight.

Today Denmark is apparently quiet, the occupation complete.

*April 11, 1940*—Churchill said, "The naval battle is still proceeding." And he indicated that the battle was all over the place, not concentrated particularly in the Skagerrak.

He related that last night sixty German warplanes struck at Scapa Flow.

The Germans, on their part, deny that there was any battle in the Skagerrak.

*April 15, 1940*—Tonight we have a new light upon the Nazi invasion of Norway. It can be summed up in one short sentence. The amazing swiftness and success of the operation were achieved by treachery. Pro-Nazi Norwegian commanders in several key positions handed those positions over to the invaders.

*April 16, 1940*—Today brings still another Swedish report of one more big naval engagement in the Skagerrak. One gets the impression that some of these Swedish battle stories are on the order of the great Scandinavian fabulist, Hans Christian Andersen.

*April 17, 1940*—The Germans announce that they now have tanks and armored cars in Norway.

*April 18, 1940*—Today a series of air raids which London claims did heavy destruction to Nazi flying equipment. Berlin admits the attack and once more places emphasis on British bombs blasting a city of Norwegian civilians. One might suspect that the Nazis were laying the ground for an air attack on some British city.

Britain rejects the independence demand made by Gandhi and the All-India Congress.

*April 24, 1940*—Chancellor Hitler of Germany today appointed one of his gauleiters as commissioner of Norwegian occupied territory. The man appointed to Norway is named Terboven, who was gauleiter at Essen, the German Pittsburgh.

British bombers attacked German air bases in Denmark and Norway.

In Paris today the conviction was even stronger that the Nazis are about to walk in on Sweden.

A new treaty between Nazi Germany and Rumania! This is described as another link in the protective chain that Hitler has been forging for himself in the countries that encircle Germany.

*April 25, 1940*—President Roosevelt today issued a proclamation that a state of war exists between Norway and Germany.

The presidential proclamation now gives Norway the status of a belligerent, subject to the cash-and-carry provision of the American Neutrality Law.

*May 3, 1940*—London tonight officially confirms what was insistently reported all day—the Allied evacuation of the port of Namsos, which completes the British and French withdrawal from central Norway.

The President stated that the Washington government is working actively to keep the European war from spreading to Italy and the Mediterranean. The No. 1 center of uncertainty continues to be Italy.

*May 6, 1940*—Pope Pius has received a report from the Cardinal Primate of Poland, a report on the treatment of the Polish Catholic clergy by the Nazis. It is a harrowing document.

Pulitzer prizes: the thousand-dollar prize for the best novel goes to John Steinbeck—yes, you guessed it, *Grapes of Wrath*; a thousand dollars to Carl Sandburg for his life of Abraham Lincoln; a thousand dollars to Ray Stannard Baker for the seventh and eighth volumes of the *Life and Letters of Woodrow Wilson*; a thousand dollars to William Saroyan for his play *The Time of Your Life*.

*May 7, 1940*—Churchill, one of the vividest personalities on earth, was today placed virtually in complete command of the British war effort.

*May 9, 1940*—The big question in London is: Will or will not the Prime Minister resign?

The shake-up in the Red Army is more than a mere change of com-

manders—Timoshenko succeeding Voroshilov. The political commissar is
out, that type of army official peculiar to communism.

*May 10, 1940*—The most startling thing in the startling war picture
tonight is the surprise tactics of the air employed in the newest German
blitzkrieg.

Surprise air tactics of that sort occurred in a score of places in Holland,
in Belgium. In many places German troops are operating behind the lines
of Dutch and Belgian defense. Something new in warfare.

Meanwhile aid is rushing swiftly. The British Expeditionary Force,
stationed for so long in northern France, hurled its mechanized units into
Belgium today.

This evening the Cabinet of Great Britain met at No. 10 Downing
Street, the storied home of British prime ministers. Facing his colleagues,
Prime Minister Chamberlain announced his resignation.

Today the newest stroke of Nazi terror unleashed, the latest blitzkrieg
hurled with lightning violence at the Low Countries and menacing Britain itself. In such tragic circumstance did Neville Chamberlain announce
his resignation.

And so he resigned, making way for Winston Churchill, the new Prime
Minister of Great Britain—the man of whom it had so often been said
that he would never be Prime Minister.

It was announced today that military guards have been stationed at all
vulnerable points in the British Isles.

*May 13, 1940*—Even when we discount many claims of the Nazis, it
does look as though Hitler's machine were driving relentlessly on.

From what the German high command says, it becomes evident that
their tactics in the Low Countries are much the same as they were in
Poland. First a ferocious bombardment from the air, then a heavily armed
and extremely rapid motor column tearing ahead, speeding round all
strongly fortified places and leaving them to be reduced later at leisure
by the main body of the Army.

One undeniable and significant fact is that Queen Wilhelmina fled to
England late today.

The Germans are attacking everywhere along the Maginot Line.

All in all, it is quite obviously, as Winston Churchill puts it, the fiercest
battle in history.

In the eastern and southern parts of Belgium the highways are now
jammed with pathetic streams of refugees.

The seat of the government of the Netherlands has been transferred to London.

*May 14, 1940*—The Netherlands gave up the fight today.

In London, Queen Wilhelmina of Holland formally established a refugee government today.

Great Britain is rushing its new type of defense force—sharpshooters to guard against parachute troops.

*May 15, 1940*—All through the day the German high command has been crowing in notes of triumph: "We have broken the Maginot Line! We have destroyed the legend that it is impregnable!" And indeed it was admitted that they had advanced ten miles west of the River Meuse.

Here's a bulletin just in. The German advance guard is now reported to be only eighteen miles east of Brussels.

*May 16, 1940*—Paris tonight is jittery with wild rumors—panicky reports that the Germans have broken through.

Premier Reynaud officially stated that the government is, using his words, "in Paris and will remain in Paris."

Premier Reynaud revealed that the German assaults have created what he called "big pockets." These big pockets threatening the Allies from the rear. But, he added, the French high command has reported to him that they have the situation "under control."

Correspondents with the British tell us that the fighting in Belgium is not at all like the trench battles of the World War. Now there are no permanent fortified lines. It's movements on wheels, sudden changes of position, the Germans using little heavy artillery, depending upon the swift strokes of air bombing instead. The whole battle a confused changing maze of thrust and counterthrust.

There's one rather ghostly bit of news in the Swiss situation. Today the League of Nations got ready to move from Geneva.

*May 17, 1940*—The unbelievable thing has happened. The motorized cohorts of the Nazis have swept into France.

The deadly peril to France is reflected in the order of the day, issued by General Gamelin. "Every French unit which is unable to advance," he commands, "must accept death rather than abandon that part of the national territory entrusted to it."

The French say that the lightning-swift German stroke through the Maginot Line and into France caught the Allied command at least partly off its guard. Huge British and French forces had been thrown northward into Belgium to keep the Germans from making a sweep down through

Belgium as the Kaiser's Army did in 1914. So much was sent north into Belgium that the extension of the Maginot Line to the south was left comparatively weak—and the Germans broke through.

There's a report in Rome that Mussolini is only waiting to see whether or not Hitler wins a full-sized victory.

*May 20, 1940*—Tonight the Nazi striking force is turned like a spearhead toward the Channel ports. Their spearhead of course is aimed straight at the heart of Britain.

The Allies are attacking. That's the big word from all Allied fronts tonight: attack, attack, always attack! It is characteristic of the new generalissimo of the Allied forces, Maxime Weygand. He's a true disciple of old Marshal Foch, the modern master of the attack school.

The night scene over France and Belgium tonight is pictured for us as one huge inferno.

*May 21, 1940*—Tonight the battle scene in France is a picture of indescribable terror. Paris reports that the Nazi fleet of the air has unleashed its complete fury, a sky drive of staggering intensity. The German Air Force has gone wild, raging along what Paris calls the red zone. That red zone of flame and havoc extends across the northern angle of France, where the German mechanized cohorts have driven to the English Channel.

Today came an official explanation, the stark truth. Making a statement to the French Senate, Premier Reynaud used these words: "The nation is in danger."

A pitiful state of affairs in France was told briefly but vividly today in a cable from the American Red Cross abroad. A desperate food shortage because of the hosts of refugees, Belgian and French, from the battle area. Five million refugees is the report.

*May 22, 1940*—Who is the real commander-in-chief on the German side? Who gives the orders? The commander of the Sixth Nazi Army says he makes all his reports to Adolf Hitler personally and takes his orders only from Hitler.

There's one word that appears in almost every dispatch from the front. The word "chaos." No town in northern France knows when a deadly motor caravan may sweep through the streets. Armored Nazi divisions pop up almost at any time, any place.

Just about the wildest and most incredible of all the incredible stories coming from France is the story of the way the Nazis captured Abbeville. Apparently the French have no home guards for such places. The consequence was that a small lightning detachment of German motorcyclists swept into town under cover of darkness, promptly scattered to all the key points in Abbeville and seized them.

On a London newspaper tonight was a huge banner proclaiming, "Government Control of Everybody and Everything."

The United States Senate in record time has passed the Army Supply Bill appropriating $1,823,000,000.

*May 23, 1940*—A Berlin spokesman described Hitler's war plan under four headings: First, the capture or annihilation of the Allied armies encircled in Flanders. Second, the possible capitulation of France. Third, a whirlwind attack on Great Britain by air and sea. The fourth, peace, concluded on Hitler's own terms.

Another prominent Englishman was arrested—though that's not so much of a surprise. Sir Oswald Mosley, the British Fascist leader.

*May 24, 1940*—The battle of Flanders continues as the greatest military engagement of history, threatening the English with worse disaster than an army has ever known, or perhaps the Allies may stage the greatest escape in the history of war.

*May 27, 1940*—The Germans declare that Calais is now in their hands and that therefore they'll have only a short time to wait before starting on the venture that has long been their dream—the dream of strafing England.

German spokesmen report that the British are fighting a desperate rearguard action, evacuating the beleaguered Allied troops from Dunkirk and Ostend and Zeebrugge. All three of those ports are being fiercely bombed from the air.

The British Ambassador in Rome has advised all British nationals to get out and go home.

*May 28, 1940*—Tonight the British Minister of Information, Alfred Duff Cooper, made a radio broadcast to the British people and said, "It will be necessary to do our utmost to withdraw our armies from the position they now occupy." By what Channel ports can the B.E.F. go? Apparently only one harbor is free of Nazi control tonight. Paris reports that the Germans have not captured Dunkirk. But that is a small and insufficient port, which, moreover, at this moment is in flames from Nazi air bombardment.

Today the Prime Minister, before the House of Commons, spoke of the

Belgian surrender in these terms. "I have no intention to suggest to the House," said Churchill, "that we should attempt at this moment to pass judgment on the action of the King of the Belgians in his capacity as commander-in-chief of the Belgian Army."

*May 29, 1940*—In Flanders tonight the Allied Army is outnumbered, hemmed in, jammed into two pockets; completely cut off.

Paris admits the position is critical.

The most discussed man in the world today is the latest monarch without a throne, Leopold, King of the Belgians. The French tonight have just one word to describe his order to surrender his Army. Treachery!

They claim for one thing that he did not ask for help until the Germans were already well over the border, when it was already too late. And they say he thus drew the French into a trap when they came to his aid. They repeat that there was no military reason for the Belgian surrender and that, counting on Belgian support, they had determined to keep their strong force in Flanders based on six Channel ports.

*May 30, 1940*—Let's take a look at some of the heresies that caused the downfall of Billy Mitchell. He wrote these words: "Neither armies nor navies can exist unless the air is controlled over them." To that aphorism he added this: "No missile-throwing weapons can actually stop an air attack. The only defenses against aircraft," he added, "are other aircraft."

Those are the military heresies which Billy Mitchell loudly proclaimed in season and out. Today they seem truisms too obvious even to mention —today when President Roosevelt has called for an American air force of fifty thousand planes, and when sky power is predominant on the battlefield in Europe.

Berlin reports the British Expeditionary Force is pinned in a narrow strip against the coast, with no chance for escape—units demoralized under terrific attack, the B.E.F. disintegrating as it vainly tries to evacuate by ship.

The question tonight is: How many men are the Allies succeeding in getting out at Dunkirk? How many are being evacuated, and how many will remain to be taken prisoners?

*May 31, 1940*—The Chief Executive of the United States, in addressing the Congress, referred to the possibility of this country getting into the war.

Tonight the British have every reason in the world to bless the London fog—at least the part of it that extends across the English Channel. This is based on word from the Nazi German side. Today the official German

News Agency announced thick fog, dense mist covering the Channel shore, a blinding blanket over Dunkirk, where the Allies are laboring at the desperate task of getting their trapped armies out of northern France. The German report declares that today the heavy fog greatly impeded the operations of the Hitler air force striking at Dunkirk. The white mist protected the evacuating Allied troops from air bombs. This Nazi statement would indicate that tens of thousands of British lives have been and are being saved—by the fog, the old pea-souper which is such a nuisance in London.

They are being moved out by every sort of craft that the seagoing land of Great Britain can muster. A London dispatch speaks of a rescue armada of hundreds of ships that today sailed in and out of Dunkirk Harbor—barges, tugs, and even ancient stern-wheel steamers. Some of the almost innumerable craft are making as many as four trips across the Channel in twenty-four hours, a ferry service.

*June 3, 1940*—Reconnaissance planes come back from flights over the German lines with warnings of fearful import. Hitler has got a terrific concentration of armies massed north of the Somme—armies, tanks, bombers, all his panoply of war—ready for a do-or-die attempt to smash through General Weygand's lines.

Some 222 British naval vessels and more than 665 other British ships and boats were used in the evacuation of the British and French soldiers from the Dunkirk area.

*June 4, 1940*—Prime Minister Winston Churchill today gave the British House of Commons an account of the battle of Flanders and he did not gloss over the Allied defeat with any cheery optimism. The charge of complacency can no longer be brought against the London government. Churchill described the battle in these words: "A colossal military disaster."

Britain and France will fight on. The Prime Minister made that pledge. He put it in these vivid phrases: "We shall fight in France, on oceans, on landing grounds, in fields, and in the streets. We shall never surrender."

*June 5, 1940*—It looks now as though the fighting in Flanders was a mere prologue to the gigantic battle that rages tonight. On a front 110 miles long, an army of 700,000 soldiers, 2,500 tanks, 1,000 dive-bombing planes, and 15,000 other motorized vehicles hurled themselves in a Nazi frenzy upon the defenders.

*June 6, 1940*—Britain's R.A.F. is hitting from across the Channel, blasting vital areas behind the German line, to break the attack.

Premier Reynaud, in telling of the violent magnitude of the German offensive, made this comment: "I am very satisfied with the French answer." He said there was what he called "reason for hope."

The question of American armament for the Allies is a headline tonight—with the revelation that our ambassadors to London and Paris have been putting in urgent appeals to Washington.

*June 7, 1940*—The giant clash of arms was christened with a new name today. The Allied Supreme Commander, General Weygand, called it the "Battle of France." That indicates the supreme importance of the cataclysmic struggle which now has completed its third day of overwhelming violence.

*June 10, 1940*—Benito Mussolini, in his characteristic dramatic way, told his people that the hour had come. It was time for Italy to strike at the back of France—France reeling from the onslaught of Teutonic fury.

Elsewhere, too, this was a black day for the Allies. First of all, the humiliation of the surrender of Norway. Then the British Admiralty had to admit a serious naval loss. Two of Hitler's pocket battleships sank the big British aircraft carrier *Glorious*, a 22,000-ton ship, off the coast of Norway.
King Haakon, by the way, with his family and staff, arrived safely in London today.

Paris admits that the situation is serious but insists that it isn't desperate. But the Germans declare that the fate of France is sealed, that they are flanking General Weygand's armies at the edge of the Maginot Line.

*June 11, 1940*—All day long there was an exodus from the capital of France, tens of thousands of refugees streaming to the south. And everywhere there were preparations for defense—barricades across streets, barbed wire, guns. The Army command in control of the city, and the word was that Paris will resist to the last stone of the last building!

Rome reports fighting in East Africa, with the Italians from Ethiopia invading British and French Somaliland.

After the President's speech of last night—the President's "stab in the back" speech—in Italy, the reaction to the indignant rebuke was rather reserved. The newspapers didn't mention it, but in government circles they said, as the United Press dispatch phrases it, "the gravest criticism of

Italy ever received from the head of a state which was not at war with
Italy."

*June 12, 1940*—Tonight the Nazis are hammering at the gates of
Paris.

A bulletin from Tours reports that the Supreme Council of the Allies
met somewhere in France. Premier Reynaud, Prime Minister Winston
Churchill, General Weygand, Marshal Pétain, British War Minister
Anthony Eden, and General Sir John Dill, Chief of the British Imperial
General Staff. It was the first meeting of the Council since the French
Government left Paris. What happened at the meeting nobody knows but
those who took part.

*June 13, 1940*—The French have officially declared Paris an open
city.

The Council of Ministers of the French Government met at Tours today and decided to continue the battle.

Today in Paris it was revealed that Premier Reynaud sent an appeal for
help to President Roosevelt last Monday.

*June 14, 1940*—This day an historic event occurred. For the fourth
time in history German troops marched into Paris.

The Germans are advancing at such a rate that the French Government
has left Tours, about a hundred and fifty miles south of Paris, and gone
to Bordeaux, which is on the extreme southwestern coast of France.

The German Army is far down behind the Maginot Line, ready to attack it in the rear.

Here's an extremely significant dispatch from London. I'll read it
verbatim, as the United Press gives it: "Great Britain, it was understood
today, has agreed to accept whatever future political and military decisions France is forced to make—carrying on the war alone against Germany
if the French should be compelled to give up."

*June 17, 1940*—In the history of radio there never was such a
poignant moment as that which occurred early this morning. First we
heard a voice shaking with suppressed emotion as it delivered in French
the last word in tragedy for the gallant people of France. It was eighty-
four-year-old Marshal Pétain, famous the world over as the hero of
Verdun, now the head of France's new government. It took him barely
five minutes to convey his message of catastrophe, surrender, complete
capitulation.

Tonight we know that the gallant old marshal—the hero of Verdun—
could have done nothing but what he did.

Meanwhile, though Pétain gave the order to cease firing, they are still fighting in France. Hitler's hordes continue their sweep toward the Pyrenees.

In our own national capital, the reactions to the French surrender were quick and spectacular. President Roosevelt issued an order freezing all French credits, one billion dollars' worth.

Here's the big surprise of the day. A radio message from Britain to France has just been intercepted. It conveyed a new offer for a complete union between the two countries. The citizens of one country to become citizens of the other. A new nation or commonwealth to consist of Britain and her vast empire and France and her great empire.

*June 18, 1940*—Prime Minister Churchill, in the House of Commons today, spoke these measured words: "France's government," said he, "will be throwing away great opportunities, and casting away their future, if they do not continue the war in accordance with their obligations—from which we have not felt able to release them."

Churchill sounded this warning. "The Battle of France is over," said he, "and the Battle of Britain is about to begin."

*June 20, 1940*—Somewhere in France today the plenipotentiaries of France met high German officers and were given the Hitler terms for an armistice.

*June 21, 1940*—This afternoon, at a quarter past three, Hitler, the Nazi dictator, stepped into a railway dining car near the French town of Compiègne. It was an old dining car which for years had been kept bright and trim—as a shrine of French victory. Today Hitler stalked in and sat down in the very chair which Marshal Foch occupied twenty-two years ago when he dictated to defeated Germany the terms of utter defeat and surrender.

The armistice ceremony of 1918 was fairly closely reproduced, except that it was the other way around—Germany dictating conditions to France, with Hitler playing the leading role.

Colonel General Keitel read a preamble that began with a lot of Nazi rhetoric. It contained the familiar contention that the German Army was really not defeated in 1918 but that the war was lost by weakness and treachery at home.

When Colonel General Keitel finished reading it, he handed to the French emissaries the real terms—a document of precise detailed conditions. That ended the ceremony. It lasted hardly more than ten minutes. Then both parties left the historic dining car. Hitler strutted off amid a blare of military bands. The three French generals retired to a tent provided for them nearby.

The latest from the armistice front—Hitler has ordered the historic dining car to be taken to Germany and set up in Berlin as a trophy of victory.

*June 24, 1940*—Military experts over here are claiming that the Nazi and Fascist terms imposed on France are moderate from a military standpoint. From the standpoint of the rest of us, they are pitiful, crushing, devastating. For the time being, France's entire seaboard on the English Channel, on the Atlantic coast, and along the Mediterranean will be in the hands of foreign soldiers.

London declares unequivocally that the terms accepted by the Pétain government make France a virtual ally of Hitler and Mussolini.

Incidentally, General de Gaulle has been officially rebuked, reduced in rank to a colonel, and will be court-martialed in his absence for his failure to obey orders and come home.

On the Italian front, the Fascists also announce that they have penetrated the French line. In some places they were attacking the French from the rear while the Nazis were crushing them from the front.

*June 25, 1940*—The Japanese battle fleet on its way to the coast of Indochina—that rich French possession in southern Asia. And Tokyo declares that hereafter it will consult the native authorities in Indochina, and not the government of France, on questions concerning that part of the world.

*June 26, 1940*—Both Fuehrer and Duce exude loud confidence that it won't take them long to knock out the United Kingdom.

*June 27, 1940*—Tonight, sometime, the Republican presidential candidate will be chosen.

*June 28, 1940*—So it's Willkie and McNary.

Stalin, the Red dictator, accomplished his latest grab today. Red Army troops marched into the Rumanian province of Bessarabia and the northern part of Bukovina.

London has decreed a defense area along the entire east coast of England—from London to Scotland. A strip twenty-five miles deep is now devoted entirely to defense measures, armed guard against possible German landings along the coast.

Today the British Government took another step toward breaking relations with the government of France—the regime headed by Marshal Pétain. London recognizes the French National Committee set up in London by General de Gaulle, the committee which refuses to recognize the armistice made by the Ministry in France.

*July 1, 1940*—Uncle Sam is going ahead on his new two-ocean navy.

*July 3, 1940*—Today the squadrons of German bombers swept over southern England in waves—raid after raid.

*July 4, 1940*—At Oran, in North Africa, French Morocco, were three French battleships and a number of cruisers and destroyers. A British squadron, consisting of three battleships, an airplane carrier, and other craft, steamed into port and presented an ultimatum.

Berlin reports, quoting French sources, that the warships of France were not ready, did not have steam up—and they were in harbor and could not maneuver. Yet they returned the British fire and fought it out as well as they could.

Some of the French fighting ships managed to break through the British line of attack and get away.

The British have promised not to bomb the Vatican.

*July 5, 1940*—France today broke off diplomatic relations with Great Britain.

*July 9, 1940*—And the British have struck again at the French fleet—and in the most formidable way. With air bombs and water bombs they attacked and disabled the great French battleship *Richelieu*, which we now learn was lying in the West African harbor of Dakar.

The British report heavy destruction wrought by the R.A.F. bombs blasting ports from which the Nazis are preparing their invasion of England. And London states that the German air raids against England today were heavier than ever, working up to what the British believe to be "the blitzkrieg tempo," presaging the attempt to invade Britain.

*July 11, 1940*—Today Great Britain was bombed from dawn until far into the night.

*July 12, 1940*—Once again today waves of Nazi bombers swept over England, blasting far and wide.

*July 16, 1940*—Today the United States spoke in opposition to the reported agreement between Great Britain and Japan. Secretary of State Hull declared himself against the arrangement about which we heard last night. The British closing the Burma Road—that Burma Road which is a main source of war supplies for the Chinese Nationalist regime.

*July 18, 1940*—On the subject of the vice-presidency, the Great White Father has spoken. And his running mate is to be the Secretary of Agriculture, Henry A. Wallace.

*July 19, 1940*—Today's Hitler suggestion for peace was included in a long harangue by the Nazi Fuehrer. The prominent points are two. No. 1—peace. No. 2—or else!

*July 22, 1940*—Last week Hitler said to the British, "Submit or be destroyed." Tonight we have Britain's reply. Here it is! "Thanks, we'll do neither."

The Nazis today were making a target of President Roosevelt. It was a newspaper attack in the controlled German press. They accused the President of being to a great extent responsible for the war and for what they called "the irrational attitude of England toward the present situation in Europe." In other words, they blame Mr. Roosevelt because the British won't yield to Hitler's threats.

*July 26, 1940*—Japan is reported to be taking a grave view of yesterday's action by the United States Government in the matter of oil and scrap iron. These materials are greatly needed by Japan, and now they are placed under the system of licenses—which looks like a move toward an embargo.

*July 29, 1940*—The word from France today is that the Pétain government is going to bring to trial three ex-premiers, at least two other Cabinet ministers, and the ex-commander-in-chief of the Army.

The Premiers are Eduard Daladier, Paul Reynaud, and Leon Blum. Among the other ex-Cabinet ministers to be tried are Georges Mandel, former Minister of the Interior; Pierre Koh, former Air Minister. The ex-commander-in-chief, Generalissimo Maurice Gustave Gamelin—the man who, when the war broke out, was hailed by all Frenchmen as the soldier who would save France.

*July 30, 1940*—Al Smith today came out for Willkie. Al bitterly denounced the third-term nomination and declared it sounded "the death knell of the Democratic party."

*July 31, 1940*—President Roosevelt took another dramatic step toward national defense today. He put an embargo on the exporting of aviation gasoline from this country.

*August 1, 1940*—There was an official declaration of policy in Soviet Russia today. Foreign Commissar Molotov made a series of statements to the gathering of the Supreme Soviet. They can simply be described in these terms: favorable to the totalitarian powers, Nazi Germany, Fascist Italy, and Japan. Hostile to Great Britain, and—for that matter—to the United States.

*August 7, 1940*—Italian victories in Africa! The British admit that the Italians are on Egyptian territory.

*August 9, 1940*—President Roosevelt today announced some betting odds—100 to 1. That's a long shot—and what does it apply to? It's 100 to 1 that the National Guard and the Regular Army will never be sent for service outside of the United States or its possessions. So said the President. Meaning no new A.E.F.

*August 12, 1940*—All day today Nazi bombers in mass formation roared over England and, for the first time, as far as the north of Ireland.

*August 15, 1940*—Churchill told the House of Commons today that the country should beware—Britain still in imminent danger of an intensive invasion from the Nazis.

*August 16, 1940*—In Washington, President Roosevelt went to the length of permitting a direct quotation of these words: "The United States Government is holding conversations with the Government of the British Empire with regard to acquisition of naval and air bases for the defense of the Western Hemisphere and especially the Panama Canal."

*August 20, 1940*—The British Prime Minister stated that Great Britain is ready to let the United States establish naval bases in British-American possessions—such as Newfoundland and the West Indies. This would involve no transfer of British sovereignty, but is offered on a lease basis. Churchill specified leases of ninety-nine years.

The British-American arrangement opened wide horizons in the Winston Churchill address. He said, "Undoubtedly this process means that these two great organizations of English-speaking democracies, the British Empire and the United States, will have to be somewhat mixed up together."

The British Empire and the United States—somewhat mixed up together; does this suggest some kind of British-American union? Well, Churchill said it was inevitable. "I could not stop it if I wished," said he. "No one can stop it. Like the Mississippi, it just keeps rolling along. Let it roll!" he exclaimed, and he added this bit of Churchillian eloquence: "Let it roll on full flood, inexorable, irresistible, roll on to broader lands and better days."

*August 21, 1940*—Tonight the whole world is conjecturing what lies back of the murderous attack in Mexico on Leon Trotsky, the onetime war lord of the Red Armies of Russia. His last conscious words were, I quote: "I will not survive this attack. Stalin has finally accomplished the task he attempted unsuccessfully before."

*August 26, 1940*—Today Goering's airmen dropped bombs on County Wexford in Eire.

The De Valera government promptly registered a protest with Berlin—also a claim for damages.

*August 27, 1940*—Today the British were remarking on the sheer discomfort of London's nightly experience—millions of people kept in air-raid shelters hour upon hour, spending almost the whole night there.

*August 28, 1940*—The latest grapevine is that Hitler doesn't want to start anything on a big scale against Britain until he gets the Balkan mess cleared up.

*August 29, 1940*—Three French colonies now have decided to cast their lot with Great Britain instead of Marshal Pétain's Government of France. They are the Lake Chad area, the Cameroons, and New Caledonia.

*September 3, 1940*—Great Britain and Germany observed the first anniversary of the war with the usual day of air battles.

London reports that still another French colony has broken with the government of Marshal Pétain. This time it's Tahiti, that haunt of Polynesian romance.

*September 4, 1940*—The Fuehrer spoke to his faithful at Berlin today, shouted in characteristic phrases. The British, he said, have been crying that Hitler does not come. So the Fuehrer screamed to his people, "My answer is, keep your shirts on, he is coming."

*September 5, 1940*—Stirring days in the Balkans, alarming days; first of all, one prophecy comes true. Rumania comes definitely within the orbit of the Rome-Berlin axis. King Carol, for the time being at least, is nothing more than a figurehead. General Antonescu, the new Premier, is virtually the dictator.

*September 6, 1940*—Somewhere along the valley of the Danube a special train is rolling under heavy guard toward Switzerland. That train carries the living embodiment of one of the great romances in history. Ex-

King Carol of Rumania rides into exile with the great love of his life, Magda Lupescu.

Wendell Willkie today gave his opinion regarding this trade of fifty destroyers for air and naval bases. The G.O.P. candidate declared that putting over this negotiation without the consent of Congress was the most dictatorial and arbitrary action of any president in the history of the United States.

*September 9, 1940*—For the third successive day Goering's bombers dropped a shattering air attack on London.

*September 10, 1940*—Today witnessed a wholesale exodus from London—women and children going, such children as are left. A flight of women. If the air raids go on, the bombed city on the Thames will be a metropolis merely of men.

Today's German communiqué describes "the first cross-channel artillery duel."

*September 11, 1940*—It became known today that a bomb had fallen even on Buckingham Palace.

The main purpose of Prime Minister Churchill's broadcast today was to give his people a rough idea of what they must expect. Most important of all was the warning that Britons must be ready for a gigantic attempt to invade the British Isles, maybe next week.

*September 12, 1940*—Tonight, once again, London is the scene of air battle.

British retaliation goes on! An eye for an eye. Berlin was bombed again.

*September 13, 1940*—King George and Queen Elizabeth were in the palace when it was hit—but they were uninjured.

The House of Lords was hit, one wing of the stately Parliament building. And fire bombs were flung into Downing Street, near famous No. 10 —the home of the Prime Minister.

*September 16, 1940*—Conscription became the law of the land shortly after three o'clock this afternoon, when President Roosevelt signed the bill.

It was made public today that Goering had taken part personally in one of yesterday's raids over Britain.

*September 17, 1940*—Bombs fell again on some of the most famous places in the British capital—Piccadilly, Berkeley Square, Mayfair, Oxford Street, and Bond Street.

What about that invasion? Churchill warned it was likely to come.

Cairo today announced the Fascist capture of Sidi Barrani, the oasis where the motor road to Alexandria begins.

*September 26, 1940*—President Roosevelt's embargo of scrap iron is certainly no surprise. Everybody understands that the embargo is directed against Japan.

*October 4, 1940*—The Hitler-Mussolini conference is not at all illuminated by the official communiqué issued as the two dictators parted company. It's the usual meaningless nothing—merely stating that the heads of the two nations discussed all problems in a spirit of complete cordiality.

*October 8, 1940*—In the House of Commons today Prime Minister Churchill made an announcement—and this is the main thing behind the crisis in the Far East. Great Britain is going to reopen the Burma Road as a route for war supplies to Nationalist China in its fight against Japan.

*October 10, 1940*—Marshal Pétain of France today gave clear expression of his opinion that Nazi Germany will win the war.

Wendell Willkie today was flaming his way through New England, blazing with attacks against a third term.

*October 15, 1940*—In the Balkans there are continuing reports of Soviet mobilization on the Rumanian frontier—facing the Germans.

*October 17, 1940*—In India civil disobedience began today. Mahatma Gandhi's new campaign of non-violence against British rule.

The Moscow newspaper *Red Star* stated flatly that the German air offensive against Great Britain has failed.

*October 18, 1940*—Out in Asia that Burma Road is being bombed. The Japanese are carrying out the threat they made that they would blast the winding tortuous highway when it was opened by the British.

*October 22, 1940*—Today Hitler had a meeting with Laval, Vice-Premier of France. The Berlin announcement states that the conference occurred somewhere in France—Hitler going to the conquered country.

*October 23, 1940*–It is now known that Hitler and Mussolini have not only Italian but German planes, tanks, and men concentrated for an advance upon Egypt.

Willkie's progress throughout the country continues to be stormy. Not only were eggs thrown at him in Chicago, but he was loudly and deliberately booed at Indiana Harbor while talking to a crowd of some ten thousand steel workers.

*October 24, 1940*–London is saying that Hitler's meetings with Franco and Pétain are simple evidence that the Nazi warfare against Great Britain has failed and Hitler needs allies. This evokes an angry denial in Nazi Germany.

Last night the President gave a pledge against war more strongly and specifically than ever before.

*October 28, 1940*–War in Greece following the Italian invasion. It seems definite that the Greeks are not giving in to Mussolini and are fighting back for all they are worth; also that the British are helping them.

*October 29, 1940*–The scene, a stately hall in one of the great government buildings in Washington. The place crowded. On the stage were the instruments for the drawing–and here we find a note of dramatic reminiscence. A huge goldfish bowl full of capsules, and each capsule with a number. It was the same goldfish bowl that was used for draft lottery drawing in the World War, the draft that sent millions of young Americans to fight in France.

Secretary Stimson was blindfolded with the historic strip of cloth left over from World War days. He reached into the goldfish bowl and picked out a capsule. The names of the first American boys to be drafted this time.

Athens has not been bombed, although Italian planes did blast the harbor of Piraeus. The hope on both sides is that neither Athens nor Rome will be bombed–those two cities of such great fame in the ancient times of our civilization.

*October 30, 1940*–Marshal Pétain today gave the French people an inkling of what he had discussed last week with Adolf Hitler. He had agreed, said the aged marshal, to work in collaboration with the Nazis.

*November 1, 1940*–The latest straw vote returns add New York, Connecticut, and Missouri to the Willkie column.

Little is clear about the Italian invasion of Greece. The Greeks claim successes, and the Italians are bringing up heavy forces for their drive.

*November 5, 1940*—Early election figures indicate that Willkie is running far more strongly than the Republican ticket did four years ago. Of course, he was expected to do that. And the question is, can he do enough better to overcome the terrific Democratic majorities of 1936? For the most part, the scattered returns are what they usually are at this hour on presidential Election Day—a tantalizing puzzle.

*November 6, 1940*—President Roosevelt's lead over Wendell Willkie grows larger every hour. F.D.R. has about three and a half million more than Willkie. The latest figures show the President with 54.2 per cent of the vote, Willkie with 45.8 per cent. The Democrats have carried Congress.

*November 11, 1940*—General de Gaulle and his Free Frenchmen at last have a foothold on French soil. It is official tonight that Libreville capitulated. The capital of Gabon in French Equatorial Africa gives the leader of the Free Frenchmen an entering wedge into the French colonies.

*November 12, 1940*—Molotov conferred with Hitler for two and a half hours—and heaven knows what decisions were arrived at.

An epitaph of Neville Chamberlain, who has died, was spoken today with solemn formality. Spoken in the House of Commons, where Neville Chamberlain played his historic part as Prime Minister. Spoken by his successor, Winston Churchill. "He was," proclaimed Churchill, "deceived and cheated by a wicked man."

*November 13, 1940*—Before that raid at Taranto, the Italian fleet was superior to the British naval forces in the Mediterranean. It was with bombing planes taking off from an airplane carrier that the British swooped down on the heavily guarded Italian fleet hiding there in what they once regarded as an ideal refuge. And here's the score reported by the British Admiralty: One 35,000-ton battleship with her forecastle under water, listing heavily to starboard; one 35,000-ton battleship beached with her stern under water, listing heavily to starboard; another battleship of the same class damaged, but details withheld pending further investigation; two cruisers listing to starboard, surrounded by fuel oil; two auxiliaries with their sterns under water.

*November 15, 1940*—In Berlin the statement was made that the raid on Coventry was in revenge for the British bombing attack on Munich a few days ago, when Hitler and the Nazis were having an anniversary celebration in the Nazi beer-cellar shrine.

Today Coventry was a scene of such devastation that the descriptions appear fantastic.

President Roosevelt today proclaimed American neutrality in the Italian-Greek conflict—extending the provisions of the United States Neutrality Law to cover it.

*November 18, 1940*—Mussolini took his oratorical full-dress regalia out of mothballs today and gave the Fascist citizens a treat, an old-time bit of Mussolini spellbinding. The Duce's devoted subjects waited in vain for him to say anything about those army foot races in Greece, not a word about the crack Italian division smashed by the poorly equipped Hellene Army.

It still appears beyond doubt that the Greeks have accomplished one of the dramatic and exciting upsets of the war. They have kicked the invader out and they command the mountain passes into Albania.

Uncle Sam and Britain have agreed on sites to be leased in Bermuda, the Bahamas, Jamaica, Antigua, St. Lucia, and British Guiana.

*November 19, 1940*—The government of Eire will positively not give Britain any bases on any Irish coast. That news comes from the fountainhead, President De Valera himself.

*November 20, 1940*—Hungary formally signed up in what the Nazi-Fascist people are calling the "New Order in Europe."

*November 22, 1940*—The C.I.O. did the expected today. The delegates at Atlantic City elected Philip Murray president of the Congress of Industrial Organizations. The nomination was made by John L. Lewis—keeping his promise to resign as head of the C.I.O. if President Roosevelt were re-elected.

*November 27, 1940*—Mussolini's mouthpiece, Virginio Gayda, announces that a big Italian offensive is about to begin—against Greece.

Today's blood purge in Rumania bids fair to become one of the most ferocious of all.

The political prisoners who were shot today were of course anti-Nazi.

*November 28, 1940*—The frightful terror in Rumania continues—

Iron Guardists killing prominent political opponents in savage vengeance. Here's later word: German troops being hurried to Bucharest.

*December 2, 1940*—Tonight Southampton was one of the most spectacular scenes of devastation in all Britain.

News from Rumania tells today of a triumphal march of German troops through the streets of Bucharest: in honor of King Michael and the dictator, Premier Antonescu.

*December 3, 1940*—The Nazi statement is that Germany has at least a hundred U-boats now prowling the Atlantic in groups.

The adventure into which Mussolini entered so lightly, as it seemed— has turned into the bitterest kind of war—with the Italians still trying to stem the onset of the surprising Greeks.

*December 5, 1940*—Bulletins from Rome indicate that the Italians are strictly on the defensive.

*December 6, 1940*—Two things happened in dramatic juxtaposition today. The Greeks captured the Italian base at Porto Edda and Marshal Badoglio resigned as Chief of Staff of the Italian Army.

*December 9, 1940*—Cairo announces that advance British forces in the western desert had made contact with Italian troops over a broad front.

*December 10, 1940*—What Hitler had to say today expanded the Nazi notion of the war as a revolution. With many words and much excited rhetoric he told the huge assemblage of workers in Berlin that it was a struggle between the have-nots and the haves, between Nazi theories about the workers on one hand and British capitalism and gold on the other.

*December 11, 1940*—There is a British victory to report tonight— a British desert blitzkrieg. They took Sidi Barrani, an advance post far out on the western edge of the Egyptian desert.

*December 12, 1940*—In Italy things are restive.
Is the Fascist regime about to collapse? Is Italy about to be knocked out of the war? Or will defeat mean that Nazi Germany will take control in Italy?

*December 13, 1940*—The Italian Army in Egypt is facing still more desperate disaster.
There are reports that the Fascists may ask for an armistice in Greece.

*December 16, 1940*—The British have captured what was the last Italian stronghold on Egyptian soil.

*December 17, 1940*—In the North African war, the British are still attacking—pushing on past the border of the Italian province of Libya.

*December 18, 1940*—Today the R.A.F. is hammering away at all ports from which Hitler could attempt to cross the Channel.

Laval today made his position clear quite candidly to Ralph Heinzen of the United Press. He believes in a new order in Europe. He's anti-British. He believes France must reach friendly understandings with Germany, Italy, and Spain. That's the only way she can become an important member of the new Europe.

All talk in Washington today centered around that sensational proposal made public by President Roosevelt yesterday, the proposal to lend or lease war material to the British.

*December 23, 1940*—That was indeed an extraordinary speech broadcast today to the Italian people by Prime Minister Churchill. "One man against the crown and the royal family of Italy, against the Pope and all the authority of the Vatican and of the Roman Catholic Church, against the wishes of the Italian people who had no lust for this war, has arrayed the trustees and inheritors of ancient Rome on the side of ferocious pagan barbarians." So spoke Winston Churchill.

*December 30, 1940*—Early today Prime Minister Winston Churchill walked down one street and up another, climbing over smoldering wreckage and wading through puddles of water. As the Prime Minister passed down the street, a woman called out to him, "What about peace, Mr. Churchill?" In characteristic fashion he turned, walked straight up to the woman, looked at her a moment, then said: "Peace? When we've beaten them."

*December 31, 1940*—One of the Fascist papers declares that the United States must now be considered the enemy of Germany and Italy.

# 1941

*Pearl Harbor. For Americans this is the event of the year—the Japanese striking savagely at our naval base in Hawaii even as their emissaries are talking peace in Washington. The troops of the Mikado hit strategic points throughout the western Pacific area. Wake, Guam, and Hong Kong quickly fall. Battles rage in the Philippines and in Malaya, where Singapore is the prize. General MacArthur commands our defense, but it is evident that he is pitifully undermanned.*

*The second greatest event of the year is the German-Russian war— Hitler turning ferociously on his partner, sending his armies hurtling into the Soviet Union. He wins titanic victories in the South and sweeps into the Ukraine. But the Russians fight back fiercely, scorch their earth, and hold both Moscow and Leningrad. The British help the Russians by pounding Hitler's Reich from the air. Resistance in the occupied territories grows, so does the execution of hostages. But the Germans have a strong foothold in the Mediterranean since their conquest of Greece and Crete while bailing Mussolini out. And their panzer divisions are already operating against the British in North Africa.*

*The strangest story of the year concerns Rudolf Hess, a prisoner of the British after hopefully flying to Scotland with a proposal for a common front against Russia.*

*At home, President Roosevelt signs the Lend-Lease Bill and the repeal of the Neutrality Act. In a dramatic meeting at sea he confers with Winston Churchill. All of this becomes of secondary importance when the bombs begin to fall on Pearl Harbor.*

*January 3, 1941*—Ireland today sent a stiff protest to Nazi Germany— because of the bombs that have fallen on Irish soil.

*January 6, 1941*—In his historic speech today the President asked for greatly increased appropriations to meet new needs for our own safety. "I also ask this Congress for authority and for funds enough to manufacture additional munitions and war supplies of many kinds, to be turned over to those nations which are now in actual war with aggressor nations."

*January 7, 1941*—In North Africa the British are near the No. 1 Italian base at Tobruk. That is sixty miles east of Bardia, which the British captured over the weekend.

*January 10, 1941*—R.A.F. war planes today bombed the Germans in the area of Calais. The significance lies in the word *today*, as meaning daytime. Hitherto the R.A.F. bombings have been at night, under cover of darkness.

*January 14, 1941*—President Roosevelt today used strong language— "rotten and dastardly." He was provoked by the statement from Senator Wheeler of Montana, condemning the President's bill for "All Out Aid" to Britain: "A New Deal A.A.A. program—plowing under every fourth American boy."

*January 20, 1941*—Somewhere in Europe two men met secretly, the two arch dictators, Hitler and Mussolini. Over here the United States was inaugurating a president, a president whose hope it is to upset the plans of the dictators.

Athens reports that Piraeus, the classic seaport of the old city, has just been attacked by Italian bombers.

*January 21, 1941*—Great Britain today took one of the most drastic steps possible in a democratic nation—the drafting of labor. Every person of working age is to be registered.

Britain today struck its first blow against the British Communist party, suppressing two Red publications, one—the London *Daily Worker*.

*January 22, 1941*—The capture of Tobruk is official. With the Australians in the lead, Sir Archibald Wavell's forces crashed through the last lines of a fierce resistance by the Italians.

*January 23, 1941*—Before the Foreign Relations Committee of the House of Representatives, Colonel Lindbergh announced himself against the Lend-Lease Bill. "I am opposed for two reasons: First, it's one more step away from democracy; second, it's one step closer to war—and I don't know how many more steps we can take and still be short of war."

The capture of Tobruk brings the number of prisoners the British have taken in the North African campaign up to more than a hundred thousand—including sixteen generals.

Today Admiral Kichisaburo Nomura sailed from Japan to take his post as the new Japanese Ambassador to Washington.

*January 29, 1941*—General Sir Archibald Wavell's Army of the Nile is forging ahead towards the Italian stronghold of Benghazi.

Government bonds for everybody, that's the latest plan of the Treasury. Everybody who has money, everybody who has a job, to buy bonds, just as in the last war.

*February 4, 1941*—The Foreign Relations Committee of the Senate heard some more testimony today concerning the Lend-Lease Bill.
Dr. Charles A. Beard is one of the leading historians of the nation. He says that the measure would involve us in the war. "It is," he added, "a bill for waging an undeclared war."

*February 5, 1941*—In France the duel seems to be on between old Marshal Pétain and Pierre Laval, Hitler's friend.

*February 7, 1941*—The British capture of Benghazi climaxes a campaign distinguished for dash and brilliance. The Italians abandoned the chief city in the eastern part of Libya without a fight.

*February 10, 1941*—In France it becomes more and more clear that the principal power is devolving upon Admiral Darlan, Minister of the Navy and commander-in-chief of the fleet. Tonight Marshal Pétain, the chief of state, named Darlan to succeed him in the event of his death or inability to function as chief of state.

*February 11, 1941*—The Free French forces have made another dashing advance through the desert—striking at Libya from the south, capturing Italian outposts in the Sahara.

*February 13, 1941*—United States consular officials have advised Americans to leave Japan and Japanese-occupied territories.

*February 24, 1941*—Hitler announced that, beginning April, the long expected all-out attack on Britain will take the form of a colossal, deadly U-boat campaign.

Japan's Foreign Minister, Matsuoka, today told his parliament that all of Oceania ought to belong to Japan, and the white races must get out.

*February 26, 1941*—German troops in Libya! Hitler's motorized units came to grips with an outpost of the British Army near a place called Agedabia, about a hundred miles southwest of Benghazi.

*March 3, 1941*—Bulgaria is now a part of the Nazi system, virtually a part of Hitler's Reich; also, Nazi troops are at the borders of Greece.

*March 5, 1941*—The people of Sofia today had their first taste of what it means to become subjects of Hitler. They had to stand by while Nazi motorized military equipment rumbled through the streets of the capital.

The war lords of the Rising Sun executed a quick surprise move and landed a large expeditionary force within a few miles of the borders of French Indochina.

*March 11, 1941*—At ten minutes of four this afternoon, President Roosevelt signed the Lend-Lease Bill; thus making H.R. 1776 the law of the land.

*March 12, 1941*—A British expeditionary force has landed at Athens and also at Salonika.

Here's today's comment from Berlin on the Lend-Lease Act.
Nazi spokesman repeated over and over again the threat by Hitler that none of our materials will reach the British anyway, because Nazi U-boats and bombers will take care of that, sink any ships carrying war materials to Britain.

*March 14, 1941*—The British call it the Battle of the Full Moon. And it's raining bombs again tonight. The third night in succession.

*March 18, 1941*—London tonight repeats that Great Britain has warned Italy that, if Athens is bombed, the Royal Air Force will bomb Rome.

*March 19, 1941*—Hitler tonight has Yugoslavia on the Nazi side.
The Yugoslav Government agrees to suppress all influence opposed to the Axis powers throughout the country.

*March 24, 1941*—The people of Berlin last night had a taste of what Londoners have been going through. The Royal Air Force made the most vigorous attack yet upon Hitler's capital.

*March 26, 1941*—More rioting in the streets of Belgrade and other cities of Yugoslavia. The subjects of Prince Paul, the Regent, are seething with helpless fury at the signing of that pact with the Nazis.

The Mikado's Foreign Minister arrived with great pomp and ceremony at Berlin today.
Matsuoka said: "Our place is at the side of Germany."

*March 27, 1941*—A dispatch from Belgrade states: "A spontaneous people's uprising against recent events swept boy king Peter II to the Yugoslav throne in the dark hours before dawn today. Tonight," the dispatch continues, "people crowded the streets of Belgrade shouting, 'Down with the pact! Down with the Germans! Down with Hitler.'"
Belgrade broke into a pageant of British and American flags. Tens of thousands hurrahed the names of Churchill and Roosevelt.

*March 28, 1941*—Germany has just delivered a warning to Yugoslavia.

*April 2, 1941*—Throughout Germany the newspapers teem with screaming headlines, abuse of the Serbs, accusations against the Yugoslav Government.

*April 3, 1941*—Late today a dispatch flashed from British headquarters at Cairo saying that Benghazi has been abandoned because of a sweeping attack by a German armored column.

*April 4, 1941*—President Roosevelt has ordered the construction of 212 merchant vessels for Britain—and for the other democracies.
He revealed that $500,000,000 of war material has been released to the democracies, Great Britain and Greece.

*April 7, 1941*—The official Nazi news agency claims that Hitler's Army has advanced some twenty-five miles down the Struma Valley; that panzer divisions have smashed through stubborn resistance and passed by forty-five places—driving a spearhead into both Greece and Yugoslavia.
The German radio announces today that Nazi and Italian troops have now advanced as far as Tokra, a point on the Libyan coast forty miles east of Benghazi. Another column has reached a place called Seledin, forty-five miles southeast of Benghazi, in the interior.

*April 9, 1941*—Hitler's motorized hordes broke the line in the Balkans, the strong Metaxas line, in three days.
The swastika is now on the shores of the Aegean. Salonika gave up without a blow.
The sending of that British expeditionary force to Greece weakened the Army of the Nile. The German high command announces that Hitler's

General Rommel has taken Derna, where they say they captured two thousand troops, including six British generals and a huge amount of booty.

*April 10, 1941*—Nazi German troops today marched into Zagreb, the second largest city of Yugoslavia.

The British in North Africa have lost three of their top-ranking generals, captured in battle with the Germans and Italians.

An agreement with the government of Denmark was signed yesterday.

The United States undertakes to guarantee the status of Greenland as a Danish colony.

The United States acquires the right to establish bases in Greenland.

*April 11, 1941*—German tank units, having cut across southern Serbia, turned fast and went south.

They clashed with the British—the first fighting between the Empire forces and the panzer units in the Balkan struggle.

*April 14, 1941*—Somewhere in Greece, the British and the Greeks are fighting along a new line of defense.

The Nazi high command declares that the Yugoslav forces have been smashed.

British spokesmen in London make no attempt to conceal the gravity of that ferocious drive of the panzer divisions toward the Suez Canal.

There is fierce fighting at Tobruk, which the German advance guard left in the rear.

*April 15, 1941*—Berlin today told of a thrust of sixty miles into Greece. Athens and London report that their forces retreated forty or fifty miles.

President Roosevelt today named a chief director of the Lend-Lease program—Harry Hopkins.

*April 16, 1941*—Around classic Mt. Olympus, which the British are holding, the Nazi attack is two-headed. The Germans make the boast that they have broken through around that fabled mountain and have trapped a large British force.

*April 17, 1941*—Here's the latest: a Greek dispatch announcing that the Germans are near Larissa—well to the south of Mt. Olympus—in the plains of Thessaly.

*April 18, 1941*—The fate of Yugoslavia was formally confirmed by London today. The armies of the Balkan kingdom have surrendered.

*April 21, 1941*—In London it is virtually acknowledged that the evacuation of Sir Archibald Wavell's army will be only a matter of time— that, in short, the game is up in Greece.

*April 23, 1941*—The English and the Anzacs are still fighting—on Greek soil. They're battling on to the bitter end almost at the gates of Athens, even though the Greek armies of Epirus and Macedonia made their unconditional surrender, leaving the British in a sorry position.

*April 24, 1941*—London says the British are still holding Thermopylae.
Here's the latest—the first admission from the Allied side that the British are evacuating Greece.

*April 28, 1941*—In Greece, the Nazi armies are engaged principally in mopping up. There still remains a handful of British troops fighting in the Peloponnesus. But that again is only a delaying action to complete the evacuation.

The Nazis announce that two of their swift motorized columns have invaded Egypt from Libya.

The resignation of Colonel Lindbergh from the Army Reserve.
The specific words from the President that provoked Lindbergh's resignation were Mr. Roosevelt's remarks last Friday, comparing Lindbergh and other isolationists to the Copperheads of the Civil War.

*April 29, 1941*—Neutrality patrols of the United States Navy are operating as far as two thousand miles out in the Atlantic, a part of the plan to maintain a safe channel for shipments of war supplies to Britain.

The War Department today accepted Lindbergh's resignation as colonel.

*May 6, 1941*—Molotov steps out as Premier, but he remains as head of Soviet Foreign Affairs.
Who succeeds Molotov as Soviet Premier? The answer is striking. Stalin. For the first time the Red dictator has taken an official post in the Soviet Government. Hitherto, his formal status has been that of a functionary of the Communist party—which, of course, is all-powerful. Now Stalin becomes Premier.

*May 9, 1941*—At Tobruk the Axis forces are making their most violent assault—masses of tanks forcing their way into one section of the defenses.

Moscow has dismissed the diplomatic representatives of Belgium, Norway, and Yugoslavia. The Soviet reason is given in these words—"loss of sovereignty." Because Belgium, Norway, and Yugoslavia have been conquered by the Nazis, their governments are not considered as having any official standing.

*May 12, 1941*—The No. 3 Nazi Rudolf Hess landed on Scottish soil Saturday night with a broken ankle—landed by parachute.

Hess now, we hear, is in a hospital in Glasgow.

Why did the No. 3 Nazi flee? All the world wonders.

The British Houses of Parliament tonight are not merely damaged. They're a shambles.

The havoc was done by seven high explosive bombs and a shower of incendiaries.

*May 13, 1941*—Berlin intimated increasingly that Hess went on a peace mission—all on his own.

London states that Rudolf Hess is in a hospital bed—recovering from those injuries incurred in his parachute jump, a broken ankle principally. But he is not insane!

*May 20, 1941*—In the black of night on the island of Crete, men are dropping out of the sky—floating down. Nazi parachute troops are landing. Likewise, huge transport planes are coming to earth—disgorging swarms of blitzkrieg soldiers. And, strangest of all—gliders. Wings without motors, swooping down silently out of the sky. Huge gliders towed by warplanes, until they're near enough to coast in.

London tells us that the Nazi air invaders are holding onto ground they seized.

The air invasion of the island of Crete is perhaps the most startling and theatrical stunt of the present war.

*May 21, 1941*—The story of Crete tonight sounds more and more like something invented by Jules Verne or H. G. Wells.

Tonight in Berlin military spokesmen were telling how wave upon wave of German soldiers have been dropping from parachutes and landing by air transport. Berlin claims they have been rapidly seizing key positions on Crete.

However, said Churchill, the situation is well in hand.

*May 22, 1941*—Prime Minister Churchill today reported to the House of Commons on the battle of Crete. "It's a most strange and grim battle that is being fought. Our side has no air support, and the other side has little or no artillery or tanks. Neither side," he added, "has any means of retreat."

All R.A.F. fighter squadrons are being withdrawn from Crete. The rugged and mountainous island is poorly supplied with flying fields.

The battle of Crete is now turning into a full-dress conflict of German air power and British sea power. It's a major test, which will decide whether air control can prevail over sea control in the conquest of an island—conquest across some seventy miles of water.

Unique in military history!

*May 23, 1941*—Darlan declared that the Vichy government will not turn over the French fleet to Nazi Germany. Nor would Marshal Pétain yield the French colonies to the Nazis.

*May 26, 1941*—The British may already have their revenge for the loss of the great battle cruiser *Hood*. The Admiralty announces that the German battleship *Bismarck*, which sank the *Hood* with an unlucky shot in the magazine, was herself hit today.

*May 27, 1941*—The naval and air battle off Crete is still continuing.

*May 28, 1941*—The United States has had an opportunity to reflect upon the momentous utterance made by its President.

Renewed promise that the United States will support Great Britain! That the principle of freedom of the seas will be supported. And instantly comes the question—does it mean war?

In the battle of Crete, Berlin announces today that the resistance of the defenders has been broken.

Berlin today states that the entire crew of the *Bismarck* went down with the ship, including Admiral Luetjens—Germany's No. 1 sea fighter. The number aboard the pride of the Nazi Navy? About fourteen hundred.

London has already stated that there were few survivors of the fifteen hundred aboard the *Hood* when the great ship exploded. Which would bring the combined British and German losses to twenty-nine hundred. That much destruction of human life in the startling epic of the ocean that began with the clash off Greenland.

*May 29, 1941*—Berlin claims the capture of Candia, the largest city of Crete.

London calls the situation in Crete desperate.

*June 2, 1941*—Another conference in the Brenner Pass; Hitler and Benito cooking up fresh war plans.

*June 3, 1941*—From Rome we have an indication that the meeting between Hitler and Mussolini was largely concerned with the possibility of American intervention in the war.

Moscow today withdrew its diplomatic recognition of the kingdom of Greece. Greece conquered by the blitzkrieg machine, Stalin's Foreign Office says, "We recognize you no longer."

Lou Gehrig was buried today. The great first baseman, the Iron Horse, colleague of Babe Ruth on the New York Yankees. Stricken at the height of his prowess, victim of a rare and incurable malady. At his funeral, a distinguished list of pallbearers, headed by Mayor La Guardia of New York.

*June 4, 1941*—Early this morning in that castle at Doorn, the ex-Kaiser died—almost a forgotten man.

*June 11, 1941*—Tonight we have the President's first report to Congress under the Lend-Lease Law. We have already transferred war materials worth seventy-five million dollars, actual shipments to Britain, also to China. But principally Britain.

*June 13, 1941*—We have a statement from the Soviets denying that Nazi troop movements are aimed at Russia. Yet the official Soviet news agency declares that heavy forces of German troops have been withdrawn from the Balkans and are moving to eastern Germany, the Soviet frontier.

There are still no bombing attacks against Britain—although the moonlight nights are ideal for air raids.

Britain strikes from the air at Germany, but Germany does not reply. London wonders—what does it mean?

*June 16, 1941*—President Roosevelt certainly produced a sensation by ordering all German consulates closed.

A fierce battle in North Africa. Sir Archibald Wavell's desert fighters have pushed their lines to within forty miles of Tobruk, where the Australians are still withstanding a desperate siege.

*June 17, 1941*—The Soviet mystery is still mysterious. There's no further enlightenment anent the rumors of a break between Stalin and Hitler.

The suspicion increases that the German command is massing its forces —for something.

*June 19, 1941*—There appears to be a giant duel behind the scenes— something like a monster struggle in the dark. Hitler making drastic demands on Stalin—that's the supposition. Nothing is really known about the state of affairs between Nazi Germany and Soviet Russia; but everything points to some sort of hidden tug of war—diplomatic war as yet.

*June 20, 1941*—There is still no clarification about the state of affairs between Nazi Germany and Soviet Russia.

Soviet scientists have opened the tomb of Tamerlane in Samarkand. They uncovered a marble slab weighing three and a half tons, and under this giant slab a sarcophagus of marble. In this kingly coffin, a skeleton. One leg is shorter than the other—Timur the Lame.

*June 23, 1941*—Hitler on the march again—this time into Russia.

The official Berlin news agency says the Nazi legions have smashed the Soviet defenses in many places along that seventeen-hundred-mile battle line.

Moscow, however, insists that the attacking Germans have been hurled back with heavy losses, and that the Red line has only been dented in a couple of places.

Tomorrow is June 24, and on June 24, 1812, an army of six hundred thousand crossed the river Niemen, invading Russia. Thus beginning that historic and disastrous invasion by Napoleon.

There's no guarantee that Russia will also be the end of Hitler. Russia today may be a pushover.

The principal question among military observers right now is how long can they hold out? The German high command estimates one month.

Winston Churchill said over the air yesterday that all forms of dictatorship are hateful to us but that the immediate issue is to stop Hitlerism.

Will the Lend-Lease Act now be applied to help Communist Soviet Russia?

Senator Harry Truman of Missouri said we ought to help whichever side seems to be losing and let them kill each other off—as many as possible.

*June 24, 1941*—Peace—between the exiled government of Poland and the Stalin regime in Moscow!

Great Britain is sending a military mission to Russia, high officers to collaborate with the Red Army chiefs in the fight against the Nazis.

In the Commons, Foreign Secretary Anthony Eden announced a virtual British-Soviet alliance—mutual aid.

The President pledges all possible aid to Soviet Russia—material aid.

*June 26, 1941*—The principal blitzkrieg advance would seem to be in the North, from Central Poland and the Baltic states. Hitler's mechanized legions are thrusting a wedge possibly in the direction of the important city of Minsk.

Finland is definitely in the war tonight—on the side of Germany.

*June 27, 1941*—Moscow today tells of a Red Army withdrawal from areas of Poland and Lithuania—nearly all of Lithuania. So the Germans have driven to the former Soviet border—Russia proper.

Tonight the Red Army is defending itself against what threatens to be a catastrophe.

*June 30, 1941*—Marshal Pétain has handed the Soviet Russian Ambassador his passports.

The Free French proclaim their sympathy and solidarity with the Soviets.

*July 1, 1941*—Tonight the Nazi blitzkrieg is claimed to have reached the Berezina River—on an eighty-five-mile front.

Will the blitzkrieg lines hold until encircled Red Army segments are forced to surrender or be annihilated?

Britain's Royal Air Force continues to take full advantage of the absence of the bulk of the Nazi air force now so busy in Russia.

A dispatch reads as follows: "The greatest force of R.A.F. bombers I've ever seen in daylight since the war's beginning roared across Dover Straits this evening."

President Roosevelt stated today that he still hopes the United States can stay out of the war, but he refrained from predicting that we would.

*July 2, 1941*—On the extreme northern front, the Germans have beaten back the Red armies that were defending the Dvina River, have crossed it, and are pushing through Estonia toward Leningrad.

*July 3, 1941*—Stalin's radio speech today clearly indicated the possibility of much greater Red Army withdrawals—almost unlimited retreat.

He proclaimed the policy of what the Chinese call "the scorched earth."

A German dispatch tells that blitzkrieg forces are pushing across vast areas of utterly devastated land—every village burned, everything destroyed as far as possible.

Moscow is being fortified, streets barricaded, preparations for a house-to-house defense.

*July 4, 1941*—Berlin states that twenty thousand Red Army troops in a body have deserted to the Germans, after killing their political commissars.

Neutral observers in Britain are of the opinion that the blitzkrieg is running behind schedule—is not up to the time table which the German high command had set.

*July 7, 1941*—Tonight the Stars and Stripes float at Reykjavik, the capital of Iceland. Armed forces of Uncle Sam's Navy are occupying that island up north in the middle of the Atlantic.

The President said that the conditions laid down by the Icelandic Government were perfectly acceptable to the government of the United States and would be observed.

*July 9, 1941*—The Italians admit that it can't be denied the Russians are fighting with unexpected spirit and tenacity.

*July 14, 1941*—Here's the comment of the newspaper owned by the family of Mussolini's son-in-law, Foreign Minister Count Ciano.

"The resistance of the Russians gives life to insidious doubts and uncertainties." A remarkable admission to be made in a paper owned by the son-in-law of Hitler's ally, Mussolini.

*July 15, 1941*—The focus of war news tonight is on the city of Kiev—capital of the Ukraine. Berlin tells of a terrific battle raging around that most important place.

It's official now—Great Britain and Soviet Russia are allies, full-fledged allies.

*July 16, 1941*—Today's important war news tells us more about a Russian counterattack. Even the Nazi high command admits it, acknowledges for the first time that the Reds are striking back, taking the initiative.

*July 17, 1941*—The greatest of all battles is being fought along the entire front of eighteen hundred miles. Nine million men locked in a struggle of mad violence—nine million men and an incalculable weight of machines.

The Nazis admit that the Red forces are counterattacking fiercely.

The re-establishment of political commissars in the Red Army may be highly significant.

As representatives of the Communist party, they are to share authority with the officers commanding the troops in battle.

In Berlin a propaganda representative today admitted that the marking of "V" was on the increase in the conquered countries. He said it was an expression of peoples' hope for a German victory over Communist Russia. That sounds like a tall one—the Nazis trying to take over the British "V" campaign for themselves.

*July 18, 1941*—Nazi armored forces have driven on past Smolensk, and have broken through the Stalin line along a front of a hundred and eighty miles.

*July 23, 1941*—The Nazis admit that terrific battles around Smolensk and to the southwest of Novgorod have put the brakes on the progress of their panzer attacks.

The second phase of the blitzkrieg on Russia is not going so well.

*July 24, 1941*—The armed forces of Japan are landing at strategic naval bases in French Indochina.

A London political spokesman declared today that the Japanese move into Indochina did not constitute a military threat to Britain's great base at Singapore.

*July 28, 1941*—President Roosevelt today sent to the Senate his nomination of Douglas MacArthur, formerly Chief of Staff of our Army, as lieutenant general in command of our forces of the Far East. General MacArthur's headquarters will be in the Philippines, where he is now in the capacity of field marshal of the Philippine Army.

Tonight a prominent Nazi military expert warned the German people that they must not expect any quick results from the drive into Russia.

*July 30, 1941*—Japanese Prime Minister Konoye has prepared four decrees, mobilizing Japan for total war.

*July 31, 1941*—The fiercest flare of war is in the Leningrad area. Berlin claims that Leningrad will soon be captured.

*August 4, 1941*—The Mikado's government has stopped the sailing of all Japanese ships to the United States.

*August 5, 1941*—The Presidential yacht *Potomac* is somewhere out on the Atlantic, and Winston Churchill may be aboard. Indications from London today were insistent—that the Prime Minister of Great Britain may have flown by plane to confer at sea with the President of the United States.

*August 7, 1941*—Rabindranath Tagore died today at the age of eighty. Philosopher, mystic, poet, winner of the Nobel prize—and sage of India.

*August 11, 1941*—This morning the Russians admitted that the Nazi invaders had gained large territory in their drives on both Leningrad and Odessa.

*August 12, 1941*—German offensive number three was in full blast today. This is stated in a Moscow dispatch, which describes the present flare of battle as the third full-force blitzkrieg attack.
Berlin pictures the battle in the Ukraine as an overwhelming military triumph.

*August 13, 1941*—Tonight there seems no doubt the Hitler steam roller is rolling over the Ukraine.
Here's a British estimate of the Russian situation. Losses on both sides prodigious.

In London an official statement describes Admiral Darlan as a dictator, placed in the strongest possible position for forcing on the French people measures of further surrender and collaboration with the Axis.

There's another flare-up of guessing about a meeting between President Roosevelt and Prime Minister Churchill.

*August 14, 1941*—How many attended the meeting? Roosevelt and Churchill—we know.
On what vessel did they foregather? We don't know, but probably a warship and not the presidential yacht, *Potomac*.
The eight-point program pledges the governments of the United States and Great Britain to effect a peace settlement that will eliminate Nazi tyranny—destroy it.

The Nazis say they regard the oceanic confabulation as "unimportant."

*August 15, 1941*—The army of Marshal Budenny is conducting an orderly retreat, a strategic withdrawal—say the Soviets. They admit that the blitzkrieg forces have advanced more than sixty miles in the Ukraine.

*August 18, 1941*—Odessa is encircled, with the Russians trying to escape by the thousands.

*August 22, 1941*—In occupied France, the German military authorities announce that the death penalty will be inflicted on anybody caught working for the De Gaulle cause. And this also applies to anybody shielding British aviators shot down in France.

*August 27, 1941*—At Versailles, the shooting of Pierre Laval, thrice premier of France and pro-Nazi.
Laval telephoned his wife that the bullets have been extracted and he will recover.

One entire Red Russian army wiped out! This happened, say the Nazis, between Smolensk and Lake Ilmen, 265 miles west of Moscow.

*August 28, 1941*—Red Army engineers have smashed the Dnieper Dam with high explosives, shattering that vast barrier and opening a deluge of water down the river.
The Stalin policy of scorched earth has come to a spectacular climax.

*August 29, 1941*—The Hitler-Mussolini get-together, as announced today, might well be called "the world's best-kept secret."
They've been touring the Russian war front since Monday, and not a rumor has come drifting.

Averell Harriman, son of the great railroad magnate of the past generation, will head the American Military Mission to Soviet Russia.

*September 1, 1941*—The radio address by President Roosevelt began as though we were actually at war. He said: "The task of defeating Hitler may be long and arduous."
After that he went on: "We shall do everything in our power to crush Hitler and his Nazi forces."

Today's news is that the Red armies are counterattacking vehemently. That isn't merely a claim from Moscow; the Nazis themselves admit it.
The Nazis talk about the tremendous number of tanks that the Reds are throwing into the fight. Some time ago Hitler announced that most of the Russian mechanized equipment had been destroyed.

*September 2, 1941*—There are continuing reports that Finland is in a mood to make peace—the Finns quite satisfied with getting back the territory the Red Army took from them winter before last.

London gives us a report that the first American warplanes have arrived in Soviet Russia.

*September 3, 1941*—The Royal Air Force has finally been able to give Berlin the works. Flight after flight of heavy bombers roared over the great capital on the Spree and treated Berliners to a night-long bombardment from aloft.

*September 4, 1941*—The first tanker of American aviation gasoline has reached Soviet Russia.

*September 8, 1941*—The German-Finnish ring has been closed around Leningrad, and the city is now cut off from all communication by land.

In France subterranean terrorism is said to be growing against Vichy and against the Nazis.

*September 11, 1941*—It seems to be clear that the blitzkrieg forces have been driven back in places, though Berlin insists that the Germans still hold firmly such key points as Smolensk and Gomel.

*September 12, 1941*—What will Hitler do about President Roosevelt's order to the Navy—to clear German submarine and surface raiders out of a large area of the North Atlantic?

In Britain the Roosevelt declaration is received with unmitigated rejoicing.

*September 16, 1941*—One of the world's rulers fell from power today —the Shah of Persia, Riza Shah Pahlevi. He leaves his throne as the British and Soviet forces draw near the city that was his capital. The occupation of Teheran by Empire forces and units of the Red Army may be expected at any time.

Today in Paris notices were posted announcing the execution of ten Frenchmen, hostages. The Nazis describe them as Communists. They were shot in accordance with German threats to take reprisals for attacks on Nazi soldiers in the occupied area.

*September 17, 1941*—The latest from Berlin is that the armies of the south are crashing into the Crimea and have isolated the great Russian naval base at Sevastopol.

*September 19, 1941*—Berlin announces the capture of Kiev.

More executions were announced in Paris today. The victims of Nazi firing squads are described as Communists, charged with terrorism and anti-German "manifestations."

*September 22, 1941*—Tonight's war story—from Berlin. Staggering if true—almost half a million men, four armies, cut to pieces! And it is ominous that Moscow has nothing to say about all this—in the Ukraine.

In Berlin it was announced that in one month 295 people have been executed in the countries occupied by the Nazis.

*September 23, 1941*—Tonight, to the east of Kiev, a great part of Marshal Budenny's southern Soviet army lies encircled.

*September 29, 1941*—Britain's bombers descended upon Italy with an all-out raid that gave Mussolini's country its first real taste of air war. The heaviest bombers of the Royal Air Force were sent against Genoa, Turin, Spezia, and Milan.

In Russia, Moscow was reporting with considerable exultation that winter is acomin' in. Snow around the Kremlin itself, while in the extreme northwest the invading Nazi troops are snowbound.

*October 1, 1941*—The tri-power conference for aid to Russia ended today. The United States and Britain agreed to grant the Russians "practically every requirement which Soviet military and civil authorities desire."

*October 2, 1941*—We have a formal White House declaration expressing the President's belief that the Communist regime in Moscow may grant liberty of conscience to the Russian people.

There is said to be an absolute reign of terror in Bohemia and Moravia, those provinces now in a state of semi-insurrection, with the Nazis applying ferocious repression.

*October 3, 1941*—The Hitler speech today was notable because the Nazi dictator gave his version of the reasons for the war against the Soviets —that sudden end of the Hitler-Stalin friendship. Hitler today stated that the Soviets had made a series of demands on Nazi Germany, presented by Stalin's Foreign Minister Molotov on a visit to Berlin. Germany to allow the Red Army to take as much of Finland as it liked, similar demands concerning Rumania, the right to send Red Army troops into Bulgaria, and Soviet control of the Dardanelles.

Hitler said that his generals had informed him that they could not guarantee a successful invasion of Britain as long as the Red Army stood at their backs, as the entire Nazi air force would have to be used against Britain.

Averell Harriman, President Roosevelt's emissary to Moscow, has urged Stalin to grant liberty of conscience in the Soviet Union. This was stated by Mr. Roosevelt today.

*October 6, 1941*—Hitler, throwing all his power—every tank, every plane, every armored division, against the Red Army of Marshal Timoshenko around Smolensk.

Military soothsayers are shaking their heads over the Nazi strategy. Even with all the millions of soldiers in the German armies, Hitler's front is too long.

*October 7, 1941*—Moscow describes the offensive on the central front as an all-out Hitler attempt to take the Soviet capital before winter sets in—those famous snows of Russia.

Finland today told Great Britain that the Finns will not step out of the war.

*October 8, 1941*—The Nazi panzer divisions, with the full weight of three million soldiers and virtually the entire German air force, have crashed through the pick of Stalin's Army. They have advanced seventy miles and have captured Orel, an important town and a key place on the main railroad line leading from Kharkov to Moscow.

One effect of Hitler's latest drive is to arouse impatience in Russia because the British are doing nothing to relieve the pressure on the Red armies.

The appeal from Russia for action in the West caused grave anxiety in Britain. The British are sympathetic and say, "Maybe we should, but how?"

*October 9, 1941*—President Roosevelt asked Congress today to repeal the section of the Neutrality Law that forbids the arming of American merchant vessels—he wants that done immediately.

*October 10, 1941*—The British word is that Hitler has hurled four million men into the battle. The purpose is no less than to surround Moscow and the whole central Soviet army in one stupendous encirclement.

The British people meanwhile are demanding action to save the Red Army situation. Threats that Churchill will be held responsible in Parliament if the Red Army should fall.

Averell Harriman, chief of the American Mission to the Kremlin, stated he was convinced that the Soviet Army would fight to the last—the Soviets realizing that they have the United States and Great Britain behind them.

*October 14, 1941*—In the London House of Commons, Prime Minister Churchill was queried today about the possibilities of a British invasion to help the Red Army. He was pressed for an answer but refused to give one.

*October 15, 1941*—There was a report in London today that a patriot Serbian army numbering no fewer than a hundred thousand is in the field, in what used to be Yugoslavia.

*October 17, 1941*—The new Japanese Premier is General Tojo. A general heading the Mikado's government sounds ominous. Konoye was too moderate for the war lords.

*October 20, 1941*—Hitler's advance guard is now within forty miles of the Kremlin, though the Russians put the distance at sixty miles. The Reds are counterattacking desperately along a front of three hundred and fifty miles.

Immediately after the Nazis in France had executed their eightieth French hostage, another German officer was killed.

*October 21, 1941*—The German drive against Moscow has slowed down almost to the tempo of siege operations. The besiegers are before Moscow in a semicircle that threatens to close around the city, but no rapid progress of the closing movement is reported.

*October 22, 1941*—The Nazis executed fifty French hostages in reprisal for the assassination of Lieutenant Colonel Holtz at Nantes. But before the firing squads had done their work another German officer, a major, was murdered at Bordeaux.

*October 23, 1941*—Stalin is said to be in direct command—in spite of his appointment of a general to succeed Marshal General Timoshenko. The ousting of Timoshenko constitutes a headline, the first removal of a high Soviet commander.

*October 24, 1941*—The battle of Moscow is in a condition of stalemate. Berlin says it's because of the weather—heavy and continuous rain—which has turned the Moscow area into a morass. The Germans paint a picture of mechanized equipment bogged in the mud.

*October 27, 1941*—On the banks of the Don, the armies of Hitler are at the gates of Rostov, and pointing for those rich oil fields of the Caucasus.

*October 31, 1941*—An article by Joseph E. Davies in *American Magazine* gives us a new interpretation of the Stalin blood purge, those garish Moscow trials and the orgy of executions.

The former Ambassador to Moscow says he now realizes that it was a case of Stalin eliminating the fifth column in Soviet Russia, blotting out pro-Nazi elements. Speaking of the Moscow trials, Davies goes on: "It appears that they indicated the amazing foresightedness of Stalin and his close associates."

*November 5, 1941*—Saburo Kurusu, a high ranking envoy of the Mikado's government, is on his way to the United States. The way his mission is being described in Tokyo, it's an eleventh hour effort to preserve the peace between Japan and the United States.

Wendell Willkie is making ready with a hot retort to the Republicans in Congress who want to read him out of the G.O.P. His reply will be that the party should purge itself of isolationists and become a party of aggression against Hitler.

*November 7, 1941*—London tonight gives us an official version of one of the dramatic episodes early in the war—the death of Balbo, No. 2 man to Mussolini. Royal Air Force headquarters in the Middle East explains that there was a surprise British air raid. Fascist anti-aircraft guns went into action, and Fascist airplanes took off to fight. Balbo was in one of these, and his plane was hit by one of his own anti-aircraft shells and crashed in flames.

*November 11, 1941*—The war in Russia is pretty much at a standstill. The Moscow front is a morass of snow and mud, and only local operations appear to be possible.

*November 13, 1941*—No doubt you have all heard the news about the administration victory, the outcome of the Neutrality battle in the House. The Senate passed it; and now the Lower House has done likewise.

Soon our ships will be free to visit any port in the world. No more neutrality restrictions.

The American neutrality news was received in London with cheers.

*November 14, 1941*—President Roosevelt today ordered the withdrawal of the Marines from China—the treaty cities, Peiping, Tientsin, and Shanghai. This coincides with the arrival of the special Japanese emissary in this country, Saburo Kurusu.

*November 17, 1941*—Hitler's armed forces tonight are nearer the Caucasus.

The capture of Kerch, the Russian fortress at the east end of the Crimea, gives Hitler complete control of the Sea of Azov.

*November 18, 1941*—General Tojo, Premier of Japan, appeared before his parliament today and declared that the armed forces of the Mikado are fully prepared to meet any eventualities.

Meanwhile, Ambassador Admiral Nomura and Special Envoy Kurusu were closeted for two hours and three quarters with Secretary Hull.

*November 19, 1941*—The British today began their offensive in North Africa. They launched a powerful drive against the Italians and Germans, and scored a fifty-mile advance.

The special emissary from Tokyo and the Japanese Ambassador to Washington are waiting for fresh instructions from their government after their conferences with President Roosevelt and Secretary of State Cordell Hull.

*November 20, 1941*—The British are within ten miles of Tobruk.

Emissary Kurusu and the Tokyo Ambassador have received the instructions for which they had been waiting. So the diplomatic parleys were renewed at once.

*November 21, 1941*—The British report a big tank battle on the desert—in front of Tobruk.

Late news from the Moscow front. The blitzkrieg has broken through to the north of the city.

Violent fighting is going on, and the Soviet forces are gradually withdrawing—under terrific pressure.

The battle of Moscow seems to be approaching its climax.

*November 24, 1941*—The British spokesman at Cairo talks about a gigantic nonstop tank dogfight, the outcome of which may decide who shall control Libya. Both sides admit the fight is raging with extreme fury.

Moscow is in extreme peril.
However, there's a heavy snow falling, which may save the Soviet capital. Radio Moscow broadcasts that the weather is getting colder and colder, with many German soldiers dying from exposure.

*November 25, 1941*—Cairo tells us that the huge maelstrom of tanks south of Tobruk is slowing down—because of great losses on both sides.

On the Moscow front the defense is still holding.

*November 26, 1941*—On the Libyan desert tonight, the British are going all out for a quick victory. The Anzac defenders of Tobruk broke through the Axis lines to take part in the main engagement.

Late this evening Secretary Hull received Ambassador Nomura and Special Envoy Kurusu. Whereupon the Secretary formally handed the Japanese a definite plan for settling Far Eastern affairs. The plan is not made public.

*November 27, 1941*—Today in Washington, Special Japanese Envoy Kurusu and Tokyo Ambassador Nomura had a forty-five minute conference with President Roosevelt at the White House.

Today's headline from the battle of the desert told how troops of the main British drive have at last joined forces with the defenders of Tobruk.

In Russia the battle for Moscow goes on as before—with the Nazi forces progressing slowly in their attempt to encircle the city.

*November 28, 1941*—It's up to Tokyo now—that's the word from Washington. The fate of the Japanese-American negotiations for a settlement in the Pacific depends entirely upon the response that the Mikado's government makes to the terms that the United States has laid down.
From official sources in the capital we learn that Uncle Sam demands that Japan must consent to get out of China and Indochina and renounce all policies of aggression. The belief is that Tokyo can hardly accept these conditions. So the Japanese-American negotiations would seem to be at the point of collapse.

The conflict south of Tobruk continues with mechanized violence, with the Axis panzers fighting strongly.

Moscow is now half surrounded, with the Germans pushing on.

*December 1, 1941*—Negotiations with the Japanese envoys are still going on, in spite of those defiant words from Japanese Premier General Tojo at Tokyo. Special Envoy Kurusu said his chief, the Premier, had been misquoted.

At Singapore a state of emergency was proclaimed for the entire Straits Settlements, including the great naval base.

From Manila comes a report that a fleet of Japanese warships, sixteen heavy cruisers, and several aircraft carriers, is concentrated around the southern Caroline Islands.

*December 2, 1941*—A British fleet steamed into Singapore today, including a brand-new thirty-five-thousand-ton man-of-war, H.M.S. *Prince of Wales*, flying the flag of Admiral Sir Tom Phillips.

*December 4, 1941*—Tomorrow morning at eleven o'clock the Japanese reply to the United States will be presented. Ambassador Nomura and Special Envoy Kurusu will transmit the message from Tokyo—replying to President Roosevelt.

*December 5, 1941*—The White House has just released the contents of the Japanese message.

Tokyo flatly denies that the recent landing of troops in Indochina has any aggressive significance.

It is evident that the Japanese want to keep on talking. And this may be the old dodge of sparring for time—stalling.

From Russia the news is: bitter fighting and bitter cold.

*December 8, 1941*—This may have been the most momentous weekend in the history of our country. Reports are pouring in from the Pacific.

The Navy still gives out no information about what happened at Pearl Harbor. But the White House admitted that fifteen hundred were killed in Hawaii, fifteen hundred wounded, and an old battleship, presumably the *Oklahoma*, capsized.

At twelve thirty-five the President addressed the joint session. He gave a picture of what happened. He called it "a day that will live in infamy." He did not tell us the full extent of the damage the Japanese raid inflicted at Pearl Harbor. He didn't tell us whether the Japanese told the truth when they claimed to have destroyed two battleships, damaged four heavy cruisers, and sunk an aircraft carrier.

A few minutes after four, he signed the resolution declaring that the government and the people of the United States were at war with the

Japanese Empire—the war which was already more than twenty-four hours old.

In the Pacific struggle Thailand invaded—the Japs besieging Hong Kong, bombing Singapore, landing troops on the Malay Peninsula.

Britain's formal declaration against Japan came several hours before our own. A British Cabinet doesn't have to ask permission of its Parliament.

Here's news which on an ordinary day would have taken up half my time on the air—Hitler has given up hopes of taking Moscow this winter. The Nazi spokesman said it was the Russian winter that had licked them.

*December 9, 1941*—The scope of the Japanese campaign became clearer today. It extends over immense spaces of that greatest of oceans—the Pacific.

Berlin today quotes a Japanese military spokesman as declaring over the radio that the Japanese have landed in the Philippines.

Tokyo claims that the Japanese have taken possession of both Guam and Wake Island.

The Japanese assault against British Hong Kong is by both land and air.

The Japanese tell of taking Thailand without a hitch. Yesterday their regiments entered Bangkok, the Siamese capital. There is severe fighting in nearby Malaya, where Nipponese troops have made landings.

*December 10, 1941*—Tonight from the War Department we have War Communiqué No. 1. It reads: "Information received last night from the Commander General, Far Eastern Command [that means Mac-Arthur] reveals the defeat of a hostile attack against the west coast of Luzon."

Here's War Communiqué No. 2. It admits the landings of enemy forces on the northern coast of Luzon.

Prime Minister Churchill told the London House of Commons today that the thirty-five-thousand-ton *Prince of Wales*, the pride of His Majesty's Navy, and the thirty-two-thousand-ton battle cruiser *Repulse*, had been sent to the bottom. He gave no details. He said he didn't have any.

*December 11, 1941*—The Italian and German declarations of war were so little a surprise that the State Department in Washington hardly bothered to receive them.

*December 12, 1941*—By now everybody knows about our first hero in the war of the Pacific. All day long, newspaper stories and radio broadcasts have been hailing the name of Colin Kelly, who sank the Japanese battleship *Haruna*.

He plunged almost into the mouths of the blazing Japanese guns, it seemed, before he released his stick of bombs. Then Colin Kelly, plane and all, vanished in the tremendous explosion that made an end to the Japanese battleship.

*December 15, 1941*—It turns out that our Pearl Harbor loss in battle-ships is less than two. Though both the *Oklahoma* and the *Arizona* lie at the bottom of Pearl Harbor, the *Oklahoma*, which capsized, can be easily and readily salvaged. We also lost three destroyers and a mine layer.

General MacArthur's armies have cooped up the Japanese invaders of Luzon into three small areas.

In Malaya, the British are having a tough time, but they are holding their own. The Japanese have started a determined blitz down the penin-sula.

*December 16, 1941*—Tonight the danger point in the war appears to be Malaya. British reports tell of powerful Japanese drives southward through the jungle country.

The goal of the Japanese is Singapore.

The situation at Hong Kong is serious for the isolated British defenders. The Japanese, having taken the mainland section of the Crown colony, are concentrating on the narrow strip of water across which lies the island.

In Libya the Axis reverses continue. The British, driving on in the desert, report that they've isolated the German tank forces west of Tobruk.

The Red Army announces new progress, today reoccupying the city of Kalinin, north of Moscow.

*December 17, 1941*—Admiral Kimmel at Pearl Harbor has been re-lieved of his command.

*December 18, 1941*—General MacArthur reports that his forces there have inflicted a defeat upon Japanese patrols and motorized troops. The first official account of offensive action by the Americans in the Philip-pines.

For the third time today the Japanese demanded the surrender of Hong Kong—and for the third time this was rejected.

In Libya the British report that their main forces have now driven as far as two hundred miles. The Axis in retreat, trying to avoid encirclement.

In Russia the Red Army continues driving on, recapturing one place after another—the Nazis drawing back all along the line.

*December 19, 1941*—The British evacuated Penang. This means that the Japanese have advanced about a hundred miles and are now about three hundred and twenty miles from the Singapore naval base, their supreme objective.

Today President Roosevelt made Lieutenant General Douglas MacArthur a full general.

News from Wake Island, and it's the same, heroically the same. The tiny garrison of marines has sustained two more air attacks by the besieging Japanese. But they're still fighting back.

*December 22, 1941*—The battle of Lingayen Gulf is now raging a hundred and fifty miles north of Manila. This is the first great land battle in our war with Japan.

Adolf Hitler has fired his professional commander-in-chief and taken over the leadership of the Army himself.

The dismissal of Von Brauchitsch may be interpreted as blaming the field marshal because the campaign in Russia fell short of Hitler's promise —Christmas in Moscow.

A few minutes ago the wires from Washington brought us the news that British Prime Minister Winston Churchill is in this country, conferring with President Roosevelt.

*December 23, 1941*—The Japanese have landed on Wake Island.

*December 24, 1941*—The Japs bombed Manila violently today, and they were air raiding indiscriminately far and wide.

The Japanese have finally taken Wake Island—have overcome the forces of the United States Marines after more than two weeks of constant attack.

The number of Americans at Wake was only four hundred.

They fought off fourteen Japanese attacks and sank four enemy warships.

There were disturbances in Berlin last night when a hospital train arrived. Throngs of people broke through the police lines and were horrified when they saw the condition of the wounded coming in from the Russian winter war front.

*December 25, 1941*—In the surrender of Hong Kong the British garrison had to yield largely because of lack of water.

Water mains and connections were destroyed by sky bombardment.

In North Africa the British have captured Benghazi.

*December 26, 1941*—The Prime Minister of Great Britain addressed the Congress of the United States today.

"I avow my hope and faith," proclaimed Churchill, "that in the days to come the British and American peoples will, for their own safety and for the good of all, walk together in majesty, in justice, and in peace."

Manila is an open town tonight. The Philippine Government has moved to some other place—just where it is not disclosed.

From the battlefronts around the city we hear of the heaviest kind of fighting.

On the eastern side of Malaya the enemy has penetrated to within 225 miles of Singapore.

In the battle of the North African desert, the British Imperials announce that they are driving broken forces of the Axis into a sector ninety miles beyond Benghazi.

*December 30, 1941*—General MacArthur described the bombardment of Manila after its defense against air raids had been removed. The enemy, he said, mercilessly bombed civil installations, churches, the cathedral, hospitals, convents, private dwellings.

*December 31, 1941*—In the Crimea the Red forces captured the important town of Kerch and are trying to drive across the peninsula to relieve the siege of the great naval base of Sevastopol.

# 1942

---

*This year is a complicated one, with a tangle of military events all around the world. The Japanese continue their rapid drive in the Pacific all the way from Burma to New Guinea. For the British, the saddest moment is the fall of Singapore; for Americans, the fall of the Philippines, after the heroic defense of Bataan and Corregidor, and the Bataan death march.*

*But our counteroffensive gets under way too. General Doolittle leads his planes in a bombing attack on Tokyo. Our Navy wins the battles of the Coral Sea and Midway Island. And our Marines begin the long road back when they land on Guadalcanal, where a hideous battle in the jungle quickly develops.*

*In Russia the Germans push their invasion onward into the death-trap of Stalingrad. In North Africa, Marshal Rommel becomes famous as the Desert Fox—until he is caught between the British under General Bernard Montgomery and the American landings under General Dwight D. Eisenhower. Most of North Africa is quickly seized, with Rommel pushed back into Tunisia.*

*Hitler retaliates by occupying all of France, but he loses the French fleet when it is deliberately scuttled by the crews. He faces more unrest among the captive peoples, especially in Yugoslavia, where General Mikhailovitch and his Chetniks are now waging a real war. All the while the British are smashing the Nazi homeland from the air. They are cheered by the arrival of the first American soldiers.*

---

*January 1, 1942*—Today's bulletin from General MacArthur indicates a unified battle front around Manila.

*January 2, 1942*—This afternoon an agreement was announced pledging the Allied countries to a fight to the finish. No separate peace.

Tonight General MacArthur's forces appear to hold defense lines across the country just north of the Bataan area.

*January 6, 1942*—In his war message to Congress, President Roosevelt gave us a grim picture of the task ahead. "We have already tasted defeat," said he. "We may suffer further setbacks." And he added, "We must face the fact of a hard war, a long war, a bloody war, a costly war."

*January 7, 1942*—An intense battle on again in the Philippines. The Japanese are pushing a savage mass attack to drive General MacArthur and his small army into the sea.

The news from Singapore? Not so good. The Japanese have advanced 420 miles in twenty-eight days, and military experts in London consider that phenomenal, considering the nature of the ground over which they had to fight in Malaya.

*January 8, 1942*—Tonight's navy bulletin includes a citation by President Roosevelt honoring all the Wake Island marines under the command of Major Devereux.

Alarming news from Singapore. British officials are talking of moving their Malayan headquarters to the Netherlands East Indies.

There are widespread reports of bitter dissension between the German Army command and the Nazi politicians, army opposition to Hitler policies.

*January 9, 1942*—Radio Saigon today quotes an official Tokyo newspaper as announcing that Japan is ready to invade North America.

*January 12, 1942*—The forces of the Netherlands were standing off a succession of hard attacks from the Japanese all day. They were fighting stubbornly on the large island of Celebes, with American and Australian planes sharing in the air attack on Japanese vessels.

*January 13, 1942*—The Dutch military authorities now admit the fall of Tarakan, the rich oil island off the coast of North Borneo.

*January 14, 1942*—Secretary of the Navy Knox said he doesn't believe that there has been any German rout in Russia. He thinks it's just a withdrawal.
Prime Minister Winston Churchill two weeks ago stated definitely that the Nazi withdrawal on the eastern front was a retreat in good order.

President Roosevelt surprised the country last night when all of a sudden he announced the appointment of Donald Nelson to be the chief for all war production—one-man control.

*January 15, 1942*—General MacArthur's forces were attacked heavily today in their defense lines across the Bataan Peninsula. But they're holding their positions with "courage and determination."

*January 16, 1942*—The wildest violence of war is blasting at the defense lines held by General MacArthur's Americans and Filipinos across the head of the Bataan Peninsula. The Jap attack is largely one of infiltration, trying to get through in small parties, detachments of jungle and mountain fighters seeking to slip by the strong points and penetrate to the rear.

A dispatch from Rangoon states that British-Burmese troops are in contact with the enemy. In other words, that a battle of Burma has begun.

The Jap invasions of Borneo, Celebes, and other islands of the Dutch East Indies are continuing.

*January 20, 1942*—After a twenty-four-hour period of relative quiet the Japs are again assailing the American-Philippine defense line across the Bataan Peninsula.

The Soviets report a striking success—one of the most signal victories that they have scored in their huge counteroffensive. The town of Mozhaisk has been recaptured, and Moscow describes it as one of the key points of the Nazi winter defense line.

*January 22, 1942*—New Britain is the first Australian possession to be invaded by the Japanese.

Devastation reigns on the east coast of Borneo. The Dutch have applied the scorched-earth policy to their biggest Borneo oil port.

General MacArthur reports that the Japanese have landed another entirely new army.

It is commanded by General Homma, described as an able strategist.

The Nazis are striking back in Libya. British headquarters at Cairo reports that General Rommel's panzer forces today made a reconnaissance in force—an advance of about ten miles.

*January 23, 1942*—MacArthur reports that the Japs are trying to wear down the Americans and Filipinos by assaults on a twenty-four-hour-a-day schedule, and never mind the casualties.

At Britain's Far Eastern naval base tonight they are saying: "The battle of Singapore."

The war today stretched out to its widest extension thus far when Japanese troops landed in the Solomon Islands, four thousand miles east and south of Singapore, which is at the other end of Japan's far-flung battle line.

The Japs today invaded New Guinea, and that's the island nearest to Australia.

The sudden Axis drive in Libya is spectacular.

General Rommel has driven ninety miles eastward from El Agheila. Cairo today doesn't know whether this is merely a reconnaissance in force or a regular offensive.

Congress today voted $12,500,000,000 to provide the Army with 33,000 planes.

*January 26, 1942*—Once more we have an A.E.F. in Europe—or perhaps we should call it the vanguard of an A.E.F. Yes, the Yanks are over there, over in Northern Ireland.

*January 27, 1942*—In the Australian Parliament today the demand was made for the recall of all Australian Air Force units and air equipment from Europe and from Africa.

The arrival of American soldiers in Northern Ireland was protested today by Irish Prime Minister De Valera.

*January 28, 1942*—The Japanese are advancing on five fronts, a battle line without parallel in the military history of the world, stretching from Burma to Polynesia. To visualize it you may imagine a war front that reaches from the Rio Grande to the North Pole.

The British command has ordered the evacuation of the northern coast of Singapore Island itself.

The defenders of Singapore must now make a last stand.

*January 29, 1942*—The Australians are still complaining about the British attitude toward the battle of the Pacific. Today War Minister Forde took issue with something Prime Minister Churchill said the other day—the Churchill statement that a Japanese invasion of Australia was most unlikely. "We cling to our own view of the danger," says the Australian Minister of War, and says that an invasion is a logical possibility.

The latest report from Libya places the German panzer divisions sixteen miles southeast of Benghazi. General Rommel made a lightning shift of his attack, swung to the north, and struck at the Benghazi area.

In Russia the Red Army has launched a big offensive on the southern front—the Ukraine. They are striking in the neighborhood of Kharkov.

Brazil's break with the Axis leaves only two Latin-American republics still maintaining normal diplomatic contacts with our war enemies; these are Argentina and Chile.

*January 30, 1942*—The Japanese dropped leaflets, and in one the Japanese commander addressed our General MacArthur in these words: "Sir. You are well aware that you are doomed. The end is near. You have already cut rations by half. I appreciate the fighting spirit of yourself and your troops. Your prestige and honor have been upheld." The enemy commander goes on to request that General MacArthur surrender. Needless to say, the request has not been fulfilled.

*February 2, 1942*—In the Philippines, MacArthur's men have just been through the most savage battle yet.

Tonight the enemy faces the Empire defenders across the Strait of Johore, where there is a shattered and broken causeway. Such is the terrain for the siege of Singapore.

In the Indies the Dutch are putting up a desperate fight against the Japanese invaders in West Borneo.

The Japs are driving with redoubled ferocity toward the rich islands of Sumatra and Java.

In the Libyan desert the spearheads of General Rommel's panzer divisions have swept ahead still farther toward the Egyptian frontier. Already they are a hundred miles beyond Benghazi.

*February 3, 1942*—It is apparent now that the American and Filipino forces hold a front about halfway down the Bataan Peninsula.

*February 4, 1942*—General Rommel's drive has advanced 324 miles in an amazingly short time. The British have had to retire fifty miles in two days.

*February 5, 1942*—The Red Army reports that it has broken through on the Smolensk front—and that's about the most important sector on the long winter battle line.

*February 6, 1942*—In Libya the Nazi panzers are within fifty miles of Tobruk.

*February 9, 1942*—By seizing the island of Pulau Ubin, the Japanese misled the British defense into expecting an attack in force on the northeastern part of Singapore Island. A devastating artillery bombardment from the west prepared the way for the crossing of Johore Strait.

Tonight a queen of the Atlantic lies in ruins. At a Hudson River dock workmen had been transforming the luxurious French liner *Normandie* into the U.S. transport *Lafayette*. The naval authorities this evening explain that the blaze was touched off by an acetylene torch, which was being used by one of the workmen. The great liner was swept by fire at its dock.

*February 10, 1942*—The fall of Singapore is only a matter of hours.

Another Japanese move, the ultimate goal of which is Java, is an advance down the east coast of Borneo. In short, everything points to the conclusion that the forces of Nippon are girding themselves for a final all-out attack on Java, the heart of the Netherlands East Indies empire.

Australia today went on an absolute war basis.

*February 11, 1942*—The Japanese have just demanded the unconditional surrender of Singapore. The demand was refused.

*February 12, 1942*—A dark veil of doubt and uncertainty shrouds great and famous Singapore tonight.

*February 13, 1942*—The Singapore story tonight can best be summarized in the words of the enemy! "The British are determined to die in order to live up to the ideals of British prestige."

Those two Nazi battleships, the *Scharnhorst* and *Gneisenau*, were bombed in the harbor at Brest. They were supposed to have been battered and battered—time and again. But today they started their run through the Channel at the fastest kind of clip.

The Germans used weather and visibility to good advantage, concealing their dash in the dimness of fog and rain, also smoke screens which they laid. They got through to Germany.

Our naval attack on the Gilbert and Marshall Islands arouses the first loud victory cheer that we've had in this war. Heavy damage. Sixteen enemy ships destroyed, five being warships.

*February 16, 1942*—On top of the fall of Singapore comes the Japanese occupation of Palembang in Sumatra, one of the greatest oil fields in the world.

Sixty thousand of the British imperial forces have capitulated at Singapore.

*February 17, 1942*—In Russia the Soviets report that they have taken the key city of Novgorod on the northern front between Moscow and Leningrad.

*February 18, 1942*—The news of the Japanese advance in Burma is distressingly similar to the story of Singapore and the Malay Peninsula.

*February 19, 1942*—Port Darwin in North Australia bombed today. It was the first enemy assault against the mainland of the continent of Australia.

*February 20, 1942*—The Japs have invaded Bali. Bitter fighting has been raging on that bit of earthly paradise, and the latest would seem to indicate that the Japs have captured Bali.

The Japs have invaded Portuguese Timor, just across Timor Sea from the strategic Australian port of Darwin.

*February 24, 1942*—In Burma, Rangoon is ready to stand siege.

A Japanese submarine shelled the California coast last night. The Japs fired twenty-five shots at an oil refinery at Elwood, California, near Santa Barbara. There was only slight damage. The shells were from 5-inch guns. This indicates that the Japs were using one of their huge submarines.

*February 25, 1942*—Rangoon an inferno of flames tonight!
The British themselves, we are told, set fire to the city to make sure that the Japanese will find nothing but a heap of smoldering ashes.

With the occupation of both Bali and Timor, the Japanese have severed communications between Java and Australia.

*February 27, 1942*—Over in France the war-guilt trials are being held. Former Premier Daladier stated that France had 3,600 tanks and armored cars while the German blitzkrieg was launched with two thousand. The French Army was superior in the number of its tanks. But the Nazis massed their tanks to strike a heavy blow while the French high command dispersed its own armored equipment into small groups. Daladier stated that De Gaulle, the youngest French general, had repeatedly urged his superiors to revise their tank tactics.

*March 2, 1942*—In Java the Japanese troops are pushing on and on—toward Batavia, the capital; and toward Soerabaja, the great naval base, the last important Allied naval base in that part of the world.

Here's another echo of the clamor for the appointment of General MacArthur as commander-in-chief of the Pacific. It comes from Australia. An influential newspaper in Sydney declares: "MacArthur has all the qualities needed to make a man acceptable to the Australians."

*March 4, 1942*—The air support of the United Nations in Java apparently has collapsed.

*March 9, 1942*—The amazing resistance of General MacArthur and his men has brought about a shake-up in the Japanese high command. Lieutenant General Yamashita, the Jap who took Singapore, is now the Mikado's No. 1 man in the Philippines.

The Japanese tonight have Rangoon and south Burma. With Rangoon definitely in enemy hands, the threat to India becomes more sinister every day.

The Reds are preparing most systematically for the expected Nazi drive in the spring. They have removed numerous factories from the country near the fighting front—taken them all the way to Tashkent, in the depths of Central Asia.

*March 10, 1942*—From all parts occupied by Japanese troops there have come stories of atrocities unequaled since the hordes of Genghis Khan overran the world.

*March 11, 1942*—It is hardly news that British Sir Stafford Cripps is going to India. Churchill told the House that Cripps was going to offer dominion status if all the factions of Hindustan make peace and settle their squabbles.

*March 12, 1942*—From Corregidor, that tiny fortress of the United States which guards the entrance to Manila Bay, a report that at least fifteen hundred Japanese bombs have fallen on Corregidor.

*March 13, 1942*—The Japs are now thrusting down through the Solomon Islands.

*March 17, 1942*—General Douglas MacArthur tonight is in Australia, taking charge of the defense of that continent.

The President ordered MacArthur to Australia last month. Even so, the general sought and gained a delay so that he could complete his arrangements for the continuing defense of Bataan. Then finally he obeyed the order, arriving in Australia today.

The Bataan commander on the scene is General Wainwright, who has been MacArthur's right-hand man.

*March 18, 1942*—In Burma the long-expected battle for Mandalay has begun.

*March 19, 1942*—A report from Switzerland states that all the big-time German generals have returned to the eastern front, which carries implications of that Hitler spring offensive.

*March 20, 1942*—Prime Minister Curtin of Australia revealed today that the naming of the American general as supreme commander was actually proposed by Australia, and he added that President Roosevelt agreed.

*March 23, 1942*—The Russians appear to be considerably pepped up by the arrival of Airacobra fighter planes from the United States in considerable numbers.

*March 24, 1942*—The Japs today struck heavily at Port Moresby, key point on the southern coast of New Guinea.

Sir Stafford Cripps has begun his conferences with Indian leaders.

The German command has thrown into the fighting along the Russian front more than thirty-eight divisions—about a half million men.

*March 27, 1942*—Today in India, Sir Stafford Cripps and Mahatma Gandhi held what may have been a fateful conference.

The Japs are smashing at Corregidor with torrents of high explosives.

London admits the Japanese Navy controls the Bay of Bengal.

In London, King Peter of Yugoslavia called upon his people to rally to the leadership of General Mikhailovitch, the commander who is leading an unrelenting guerrilla campaign against the Nazis.

*March 30, 1942*—The Australians and Americans have control of the air over the northern approaches to Australia.

No more electrical gadgets! That's the latest order of the War Production Board. Factories turning out electrical appliances will be converted to munitions work.

*March 31, 1942*—The battle in the Philippines has turned into a day-and-night bombardment—by Japanese artillery as well as enemy bombing planes.

We hear of heavy Nazi air raids against the Soviet port of Murmansk—trying to destroy supplies already landed there, and trying also to put the harbor out of commission.

*April 2, 1942*—The Royal Air Force struck again today at Nazi-controlled France. This time they smashed at ports along the Channel.

*April 3, 1942*—Cripps today was informed that the Nationalist party of India will not accept the offer of dominion status after the war. They demand full freedom right away.

*April 6, 1942*—There is not too much optimism in Washington tonight. The resistance on Bataan has been extraordinary and heroic. But it can hardly go on forever against such odds.

While the statesmen were talking at New Delhi, a Japanese fleet was attacking the eastern coast of Hindustan.
It came at a dramatic and ironic time.

*April 7, 1942*—The Indian Nationalist Council declares full national resistance to Japanese invasion whether India comes to an agreement with the British Government or not.

*April 8, 1942*—General Wainwright and his tiny army in the Philippines are being pounded more and more fiercely. The Jap commander, General Yamashita, has thrown more and more fresh troops into the drive.

*April 9, 1942*—This, tonight, is a nation saddened but proud. The tragedy of Bataan had to happen, as we all knew. Perhaps most of us last night did not expect the dark news today, the end so sudden and complete.
When General Wainwright yesterday reported the desperate situation caused by the Japanese break-through, President Roosevelt instructed him to use his own judgment about what action to take. The general asked the Japanese for an armistice, which means surrender.

The epic of Bataan has ended, but that of Corregidor remains. General Wainwright has transferred his command to the fortress.

In Australia, General MacArthur vows his determination to lead storming forces back to Bataan.

*April 10, 1942*—On the island fortress of Corregidor there are tonight 3,500 United States marines and sailors of the fleet who eluded the enemy thrust that broke through the lines of the worn-out defenders of Bataan.

As for the remainder of the heroes of Bataan, it would appear that they are prisoners.

*April 13, 1942*—Japanese General Yamashita is using everything he has to break down Corregidor, our last bastion in the Philippines. The island has endured twenty-two bombing raids in the last forty-eight hours.

Today the British War Council announced that the chief command over all the Commandos has been given to Captain Lord Louis Mountbatten, cousin of King George VI and son of Prince Louis of Battenberg, who was First Sea Lord of the British Admiralty in 1914. The family changed the name of Battenberg to Mountbatten during the last war.

*April 17, 1942*—The recall of American Ambassador Admiral Leahy from Vichy, France, is officially described as for the purpose of consultation. Yet it is quite clear that the return of our Ambassador is a definite expression of American hostility toward Laval.

Today in London an island was decorated. Malta—which has endured more than two thousand air raids. King George awarded to the people of that fortress the George Cross, a civilian decoration granted for supreme courage under fire.

*April 20, 1942*—Tonight we are still getting all our information from the enemy about that air raid on Tokyo.

Several reports, but no two of them are the same.

It seems that the damage was considerable, and that the consternation on the part of the Japanese was even more.

One paragraph in the conflicting reports from Tokyo indicates that some of the bombs dropped not far from the imperial palace. Whether Tokyo was bombed by American planes we won't know until our high command deems it militarily wise to publish the whole truth.

Laval's broadcast to the French people was a typical Nazi performance. The gist of it was that France must go Nazi if it wishes to escape Bolshevism.

*April 21, 1942*—The President himself revealed today the base from which the American bombers flew when they blasted Japan last weekend. Their air base was Shangri-La. The President indicates that there's a secret American landing field in that beautiful utopia in a mythical Tibet, the paradise inhabited by monks who are forever young, as described by James Hilton in his novel, *Lost Horizon*.

*April 23, 1942*—An American bomber landed in the Far Eastern territory of Soviet Russia. It happened last Saturday, and that was the day Japan was bombed. This immediately raised the surmise that the American plane took part in the air attack on Tokyo. And the American pilot says he did.

With a disabled American bomber landing in eastern Siberia, where did the Tokyo bombers take off, and where did the others go?

Tonight's dispatch, via London, states that the Russians are interning the crew of the bomber, because Soviet Russia is neutral in the war with Japan.

Soviet Russia states that Nazi Germany has concentrated nine tenths of all available German troops on the Russian front—preparing for the much expected offensive.

*April 27, 1942*—Mikhailovitch and his Chetniks, as the guerrilla bands are called, have been giving the Nazis more trouble than the people of any other occupied country.

*April 28, 1942*—The news from Burma would indicate that the entire eastern sector of the Chinese-British defense has collapsed.

*April 30, 1942*—This was the eighth day of the all-out R.A.F. air assaults, in which four thousand British planes have taken part. In the eight-day period the R.A.F. has lost one hundred planes—a low cost, says London.

The Nazis strike back in what are called Baedeker raids, referring to that famous Baedeker guide to historic places in Europe. The Nazi air corps is hitting at old and venerated cities in England as a sort of spite revenge.

*May 1, 1942*—The latest Hitler-Mussolini meeting was held in the deepest of secrecy at Salzburg, in Austria.

*May 4, 1942*—The Dutch radio today announced that the Nazi authorities had shot seventy-two Netherlanders, and seven others have been sentenced to life imprisonment.

*May 5, 1942*—At this moment the Japs are storming Corregidor with that culminating type of assault—landing. Swarming across in boats under a violent fire of shells and bombs.

*May 6, 1942*—Corregidor has fallen. Lieutenant General Wainwright's last communiqué told how the island bastion's 12-inch naval guns kept firing at the enemy to the end.

That end had been in sight ever since the message that Yamashita's storm troops had made a landing on Corregidor.

Moscow continues to tell of attacks by the Red Army all along that 1,800-mile Russian front. The Soviet Government reports that it is being admirably helped by an ever increasing flow of materials from the United States and Great Britain.

*May 7, 1942*—The War Department today announced the total of soldiers, sailors, marines, and civilians who must have been captured at Corregidor, minus the casualties during the past few days. The figure is 11,574 Americans and Filipinos.

*May 8, 1942*—The battle of the Coral Sea is still being fought—so far as we know. Warships of the United Nations have struck swift and telling blows against the Japs, with a smashing of enemy naval forces and the sinking of ships.

The battle of the Coral Sea occurs in fabulous waters, bounded by Australia and the Great Barrier Reef on the west, and by strings of islands and archipelagoes on the north and east. The Japs were pushing an invasion fleet to seize more strategic islands, and were intercepted by American and British naval forces.

*May 11, 1942*—Twenty-one enemy ships destroyed or damaged in the battle of the Coral Sea. Such is the report from General MacArthur's headquarters in Australia.

*May 12, 1942*—The horror of Nazi executions in Holland is accompanied by indications of widespread organization by the patriotic Dutch.

And in France the horror of the killing of hostages continues.

*May 13, 1942*—It looks as though the expected Nazi drive against Russia were really under way. The Germans claim a spectacular victory in the Crimea, taking some forty thousand prisoners.

The main British army is still fighting its way out of Burma into India under the most difficult conditions.

General Joe Stilwell personally has accomplished incredible feats of physical endurance. Commanding Chinese units, he risked his life repeatedly during the desperate days in the dusty valley below Mandalay.

*May 15, 1942*—President Roosevelt today signed the congressional bill for the Women's Army Auxiliary Corps, and promptly directed Secretary of War Stimson to mobilize 25,000 women.

The commander of the petticoat army has been named—Mrs. Oveta Culp Hobby, an executive vice-president of the Houston *Post* and wife of the publisher of that paper.

*May 19, 1942*—Today the secret was disclosed. The American bombing raid that hit Tokyo was led by Brigadier General James H. Doolittle, better known to fame as the irrepressible daredevil Jimmy Doolittle of a thousand hair-raising exploits in the sky.

There is one thing that Jimmy Doolittle does not tell—the bases from which the American bombers operated. That secret, which has puzzled the Jap enemy so much, is still concealed.

*May 20, 1942*—The Russians say that the battle before Kharkov has resolved itself into such a tangle of tanks and men that the planes on either side have been unable to intervene because the fighters are so mixed up and also because of the clouds of smoke.

The German city of Mannheim is largely in flames and ruins tonight. From an R.A.F. raid.

*May 22, 1942*—While we are all singing the praises of Brigadier General Jimmy Doolittle, let's blow the trumpets for another flying general—Claire Chennault, of the Flying Tigers.

In the ninety days following December 21, the Tigers destroyed 457 Japanese planes. And Chennault's lads have never had more than forty-four pursuit ships in their outfit.

*May 25, 1942*—The Chinese and British in Burma took an unmitigated beating, said General Stilwell today.

*May 26, 1942*—Moscow reports indicate clearly that the Red Army is on the defensive. Marshal Timoshenko's drive, which smashed forward day after day, has now stopped.

*May 27, 1942*—The long-expected Axis attack in Libya has begun. Nazi commander-in-chief Rommel sent his tank spearhead seventy miles across the desert, led by strong squadrons of dive bombers. Battle is now raging in the area known as Bir Hacheim.

*May 29, 1942*—Ferocious Nazi penalties are to be inflicted on masses of people in Czechoslovakia unless there is an arrest of the men who shot Heydrich, the No. 2 leader of the Gestapo—Heydrich, called the "Hangman."

Two hundred prominent Czechs, including several government officials, are being held as hostages—to be executed if the hunted men are not apprehended.

Should the Hangman die, the Czechs will face a still more brutal ordeal.

*June 1, 1942*—The Nazi plan of retaliation for British raids is quite clear. Every time an important industrial center of Germany is bombed, the Germans pick some quiet, ancient, and particularly beauitful English town and do all they can to devastate that. This time it was Canterbury, with its 770-year-old cathedral. Historic buildings wrecked by bombs and gutted by fire.

The British who bombed Cologne, by the way, report that they did not hit the splendid cathedral there.

*June 3, 1942*—Japan strikes at the back door of the continent of North America. They bombed Dutch Harbor on the island of Unalaska, our main base in the Aleutian Islands.

The second phase of the battle of the Libyan desert has begun. Rommel has found a gap in the line of British mine fields. Through this he is bringing up a flock of armored reserves for a new direct attack on Tobruk.

*June 4, 1942*—The death of Heydrich the Hangman brings a new wave of Nazi terror upon unhappy Czechoslovakia. The Nazi killers are avenging their big Gestapo man. More than two hundred Czechs have already been shot, and it is believed that a host of other victims will perish in reprisal for the mortal attack on Heydrich the Hangman.

*June 5, 1942*—Today's word from our naval command in Hawaii related that a mighty sea and air battle was developing—this as a sequel to yesterday's Japanese thrust against Midway Island.

*June 8, 1942*—The sea and air engagement at Midway was a brilliant victory for American ships and planes. The main battle fleet of the Mikado is in full retreat, presumably toward its bases in Micronesia.

*June 10, 1942*—In the battle of Sevastopol the Nazis are nearly in possession of that great Crimean fortress.

The battle has reached the hand-to-hand stage, and the Soviet defenders are putting up a last-ditch resistance.

*June 12, 1942*—Nazi Germany officially states that the big Hitler offensive in Russia is about to begin. The present fighting is described as a prelude to the expected all-out attempt.

*June 15, 1942*—In the Libyan campaign the battle is raging some fifteen miles from Tobruk.

*June 16, 1942*—We have little news from the Aleutians—that area is shrouded by storm and fog. But it is assumed that a big naval and air battle is still going on, the third to be fought in the Pacific. The Coral Sea, Midway Island, and the Aleutians.

Tobruk is now under siege again.

*June 19, 1942*—Today President Roosevelt and British Prime Minister Winston Churchill again sat in conference. The exact place is being kept a secret. We are merely told "somewhere in the United States."

*June 22, 1942*—Here is the latest from Tobruk—its loss is a disastrous blow.
Rommel is not sitting on his laurels but is preparing to sweep on as fast as he can toward the Nile.

An amazing thing was heard in France today—the chief of state imploring his countrymen to go to work for the Germans. Pierre Laval used these words: "Workers of France, go to Germany and work for your conquerors or else they will not release any of the 1,250,000 French prisoners they hold."

*June 24, 1942*—Cairo dispatches tell of a great dust cloud rising from the Libyan desert—meaning that Nazi Field Marshal Rommel's columns, after several fights with British tank units near the Mediterranean, are swinging southeast to the Egyptian border.

*June 25, 1942*—The Nazi panzers are now from sixty-five to seventy miles inside Egypt—and it certainly looks like a dash aimed at the Suez Canal. The issue of Egypt is in a supreme crisis tonight.

The European theater of operations has a commander—designated today—Major General Dwight D. Eisenhower, who hitherto has been on the War Department General Staff. General Eisenhower is a Texan, as are quite a few of our high-ranking officers. He is a West Pointer, fifty-two years old. He arrived in London today, after having conferred with President Roosevelt and Prime Minister Winston Churchill on Monday.

*June 26, 1942*—President Roosevelt and Prime Minister Churchill have been talking things over with Soviet Ambassador Maxim Litvinov. The question of a second front is brought into still greater prominence.

*June 29, 1942*—Mersa Matruh is gone. The Nazis hold the railroad, Britain's Eighth Army is in retreat, and Rommel is but eighty miles from the gates of Alexandria.

The speed of Rommel's hammerhead blows has been utterly bewildering.

Hitler is making good his threat of an all-out effort to get the Caucasian oil fields before winter comes. The Nazis are pressing on the entire 1,800-mile Russian line.

*June 30, 1942*—Rommel is now beyond the Qattara Depression and has an open road ahead—only eighty miles to Alexandria.

*July 1, 1942*—The British are making ready to blow up the Suez Canal—if necessary.

Sevastopol has fallen after twenty-five days of one of the fiercest sieges in history.

*July 2, 1942*—The thunder of cannon can now be heard in Alexandria.
Yesterday a desperate daylong battle, the British fighting with savage determination—and holding their own.

Today in London, Prime Minister Churchill stated that the British on the desert have been reinforced and that the battle of Egypt has by no means been decided. He said the British were ready to begin an offensive against the German panzers, and were confident. But Rommel struck first. "On June 13," related Churchill, "we had about three hundred tanks in action. By nightfall not more than seventy remained."
That apparently was the blow that decided the battle in Libya—the British in one day losing 230 tanks while Rommel lost only a few.

*July 3, 1942*—There is still no decision in the battle of Egypt, which was in its third day today. But it is clear that the British have checked Rommel.

Berlin states that Hitler's war machine is smashing forward along a front of 180 miles in southern Russia.

*July 6, 1942*—Both Berlin and Rome admitted that the British have been growing stronger and stronger in the desert battle.

From the moment Auchinleck took command of the Eighth Army, the seemingly unstoppable Rommel was first slowed, then stopped, then pushed back.

*July 7, 1942*—Soviet Russia concedes that the military situation of the Red Army is gravely endangered. It looks as if the old swift blitzkrieg might be rolling again.

The new commander of the American air forces in Europe is a veteran pilot. Major General Carl Andrew Spaatz made his mark as a flying man in the previous world war.

*July 8, 1942*—In Egypt, Rommel is reported to be digging in—going on the defensive—sixty-five miles from Alexandria.

*July 13, 1942*—Soviet Marshal Timoshenko and his armies are fighting still another round of the fiercest battle so far. Hitler's generals have thrown hundreds of new tanks into the fight for Voronezh. They are within 190 miles of Stalingrad.

*July 14, 1942*—In Russia a great crisis of the war continues to build up in the south—along the river Don. The huge German offensive is making progress everywhere.

*July 17, 1942*—Moscow states that today the Germans continued their advance to the big bend of the Don.

*July 22, 1942*—In Egypt the British have captured a ridge at the northern end of the line held by the Germans, west of El Alamein.

*July 23, 1942*—Soviet forces are systematically retiring to the line of the Don—the big bend of that river.

Heavy fighting is going on all along the forty miles from the Mediterranean coast to the Qattara Depression. The British have scored advances.

*July 27, 1942*—The British Government is trying to squelch the clamor for an immediate second front in Europe.

*July 28, 1942*—The Nazi war machine now occupies the entire area within the large deep loop formed by the river Don. To the east lies all-important Stalingrad and the river Volga.

*July 29, 1942*—German panzers are being thrown forward in a supreme attempt to slice off the Caucasus, cut off most of the Soviet oil, capture Stalingrad, and gain control of the entire lower Volga region all the way to the Caspian Sea.

It is not surprising that Moscow is pressing fresh appeals for a second front in Western Europe.

*July 30, 1942*—Soviet Russia today rang with calls and exhortations to stop the retreat.

*July 31, 1942*—Berlin states that its war machine has driven 112 miles south of the Don—that deep into the Caucasus.

About the situation in the Aleutians: How many Japs are in the islands that they have seized? Not more than ten thousand. So said a navy spokesman late this afternoon.

*August 4, 1942*—The Red Army retreat continues. The Germans are nearing the Caucasus.

*August 6, 1942*—Queen Wilhelmina of the Netherlands addressed a joint session of Congress in Washington. She said her kingdom's aims are to recover its lost territories and to join in post-war plans to prevent future wars.

*August 7, 1942*—Tonight's Berlin bulletin states: "German troops are engaged in a struggle with newly arrived enemy forces."

It speaks of "masses of infantry and tanks." Russian reinforcements—reserves.

*August 10, 1942*—The battle of the Solomon Islands.

Our forces have landed in the Tulagi area, the wild islands north of New Guinea.

The Government of India today outlawed the India Congress party.

More than two hundred leaders of the Congress party are under arrest, including Gandhi.

*August 11, 1942*—The battle of the Solomon Islands is accompanied by thundering repercussions. Americans are striking at the Japs far and wide to aid the marines on the beaches of Tulagi.

The Japs are bringing to bear everything they can to beat off this first United Nations offensive.

Gandhi's campaign of non-violence grew more violent today than ever. Twenty-eight people have been killed in the Bombay area alone.

Moscow gives out bad news about Stalingrad. There the Nazis are attacking at two critical points, north and south, threatening to close a pincer around the city.

*August 12, 1942*—The Red armies are holding firm opposite Stalingrad, and the Germans have not made any positive impression during the last day or two.

*August 13, 1942*—The German population is becoming increasingly affected by what they call "bomb-shelter nerves."

The great battle of the Solomon Islands is still going on.
Stories from Australia put a focus of attention on the name Guadalcanal.

In the Caucasus the panzer forces are pushing on toward the Caspian Sea.
Moscow tells of little change in the front near Stalingrad.

*August 17, 1942*—An official navy communiqué states that the shore positions that were seized by our marines in the Solomons have been consolidated and are now firmly established.
The Navy adds further that several landings have been made on islands in the Guadalcanal-Tulagi area.

The official announcement that Prime Minister Winston Churchill has just returned from a conference with Stalin sets the whole world guessing. Washington and Moscow as well as London are agog with speculations about the opening of a second front.

In Europe our air fleets are now working with the British Royal Air Force.

*August 18, 1942*—There is a change in command for the British in Egypt. Auchinleck is replaced. General Sir Harold Alexander has been named to succeed him.

The southern claw of the German pincer movement aimed at Stalingrad seems to have been smashed up badly.

*August 19, 1942*—Commandos landed at Dieppe, on the coast of Britanny, landed with not only men and guns, but with tanks. With the British were not only Canadian Commando troops, but a force of American "rangers."
They destroyed a huge Nazi battery of 6-inch coast-defense guns, a

radio station, an anti-aircraft battery, and a vast munitions dump. They were speedily attacked by the Germans, who announced that they had inflicted several hundred casualties on the Allies.

The Nazis are making their final drive for Stalingrad.

*August 20, 1942*—Today's news elaborates the mighty commando raid in Dieppe with a wealth of vivid descriptions.

Premature discovery made by the Nazi E-boats was the reason why the commandos were beaten back at a place called Berneval.

The Commandos scored their swiftest victory at Varengville. There, with only a slight loss to themselves, they captured a No. 1 objective, a battery of 6-inch naval guns.

And so it went until at the appointed moment, according to schedule, the radio flashed the word "Evacuate."

In Washington, Wendell Willkie, after a conference with President Roosevelt, announces that he is going on a mission to Soviet Russia.

*August 21, 1942*—A fearful four-day struggle continues to storm at the gates of Stalingrad, with the Nazis hammering violently—yet without making much progress apparently.

*August 24, 1942*—The reports from Russia are so grave tonight that it seems as though only a miracle can save Stalingrad.

Moscow admits that the Nazi hordes are now pouring across the Don, only forty miles west of Stalingrad.

The Russian officers are saying to their men: "Hold on at all cost. There is no room for any further retreat."

*August 25, 1942*—Moscow reports that the Nazi war machine is plunging ahead both north and south—trying to close the two pincer claws around Stalingrad.

*August 26, 1942*—The Russians are now digging in for the siege of Stalingrad.

*August 28, 1942*—The battle of the Solomon Islands was renewed with greater fury than ever today.

*August 31, 1942*—The Nazi Government has warned correspondents not to prophesy that Stalingrad may fall at any moment.

*September 4, 1942*—The state of affairs at Stalingrad is illustrated by a Soviet slogan sounded today—make Stalingrad a Red Verdun.

*September 7, 1942*—In the air over Western Europe the British, Canadians, and Americans are carrying on what is described as a non-stop aerial offensive.

*September 8, 1942*—Churchill again pledged a second front, and referred to the recent great Commando raid on Dieppe as a prelude.

*September 15, 1942*—Berlin admits that the Soviet forces still control most of Stalingrad and are resisting street by street, house by house.

*September 16, 1942*—Every house in Stalingrad is now a barricaded pocket of resistance.

*September 17, 1942*—Although the Germans are now in Stalingrad, are within the city limits, they still face a terrible battle.

*September 22, 1942*—The surprising word from Stalingrad is that the Nazis have been driven back at points.

*September 23, 1942*—The battle of Stalingrad tonight is on its thirtieth day. With the city a shambles, a scene of carnage.
The tide of battle continues to flow in the littered ruins of what once boasted of being a model city.

The Jap high command has been able to reinforce its troops on Guadalcanal.

*September 24, 1942*—Moscow reports that Soviet troops, striking in a powerful counteroffensive northwest of Stalingrad, have broken through the first German defense line.

Moscow newspapers today had most of their front pages covered with a huge photograph of Willkie and Stalin, standing together and smiling.

*September 25, 1942*—Over in Russia, Wendell Willkie visited the Moscow battle front of the Red Army today.

*September 29, 1942*—In London today Prime Minister Churchill certainly did try to put his foot down on the second-front controversy. In his most measured tones he urged people to stop demanding an immediate invasion of Nazi-controlled Europe.

The battle for Stalingrad was in two phases today—the Nazis driving deeper into the ruined city and, the Red Army smashing forward in a flanking counterattack.

The Soviet counterattack is to the north of Stalingrad, where the Red Army drive is grinding away—with the intention of cutting in behind the Nazis in the city.

*October 1, 1942*—Moscow reveals today that the defense of Stalingrad was organized by the man after whom the city was named—Stalin.

He grimly decreed the elimination of what Moscow calls "panicmongers and cowards." Before the defense of Stalingrad began, the frightened and halfhearted were what they call "eliminated."

*October 2, 1942*—Willkie is getting a great reception at Chungking, capital of Nationalist China, as President Roosevelt's envoy.

*October 5, 1942*—The Germans have launched a new and ferocious drive on Stalingrad.

*October 6, 1942*—In London, Prime Minister Churchill today refused to discuss the Stalin demand for a second front.

The last time Wendell Willkie had a headline thing to say was in Moscow, where he trumpeted the Soviet demand for a second front. At Chungking today he stated that after the war all Asiatic nations must be completely independent.

*October 7, 1942*—The fate of Stalingrad still hangs in the balance.

*October 8, 1942*—The apparent miracle seems to have happened at Stalingrad—the Nazi war machine has definitely failed in its battle for the city.

The Berlin radio puts it in these words: "It is no longer necessary that the rest of the city be captured."

*October 12, 1942*—Soviet Marshal Timoshenko's counteroffensive is roaring forward above Stalingrad.

*October 13, 1942*—In the Caucasus the Nazi war machine seems to be stalled in its drive against the oil-well area. Meanwhile it is growing cold at the battle fronts—the approach of the Russian winter.

*October 15, 1942*—A critical battle is raging on Guadalcanal.

Acting Secretary of State Sumner Welles expressed American gratification that Soviet Russia agrees that Axis war criminals should be punished.

Today Axis planes again raided Malta—as they have been doing constantly since October 10.

*October 16, 1942*—The Nazis are making a climactic attempt to storm Stalingrad.

*October 19, 1942*—The latest Nazi assault on Stalingrad has been going on for six days now.

*October 21, 1942*—In Stalingrad the Germans are making a desperate effort to take the city before winter begins in earnest.

A great battle is going on in the Balkans between German, Croatian, and Bulgarian troops and the Chetniks under General Mikhailovitch.

President Roosevelt today signed the biggest tax bill in the history of the United States. It will make every American who is earning more than $624 a year pay an income tax.

*October 22, 1942*—It was revealed today that a few airmen of General Doolittle's bombing of Japan are missing. This follows Japanese claims of holding some of the Doolittle air raiders as prisoners.

*October 23, 1942*—There is alarming word about Captain Eddie Rickenbacker, American ace of the air in the last war and prominent figure in this one. A late army bulletin just in announces that Eddie Rickenbacker is overdue on a flight out over the Pacific.

*October 26, 1942*—Admiral Darlan uttered a warning in Morocco that in case of any attack on her African colonies Vichy France will not fail to use every defense available.

*October 27, 1942*—The battle of the desert continued today—with the British Eighth Army smashing more deeply into the Nazi defense position. It is now under the command of General Bernard Montgomery.

*October 28, 1942*—A giant naval and air battle is raging in the Solomons.

General MacArthur's forces are pounding away at the Japanese in New Guinea.

Soviet Marshal Timoshenko's relief army is fighting its way to the rescue of the defenders of Stalingrad, and is advancing along a broad front.

*October 29, 1942*—It was announced today that just about the greatest road-building project in history has been completed—the Alcan Highway. "Al" for Alaska, and "can" for Canada. Traffic is already moving along the 1,600-mile thoroughfare that provides direct communication between Alaska and the United States.

*October 30, 1942*—The Nazis today pushed forward for another gain at Stalingrad.

This news is balanced by the Russian drive into the Nazi line south of Stalingrad.

*November 2, 1942*—We now have control of the waters around the Solomons, the Japs having withdrawn their huge fleet, a considerable part of which was badly crippled.

*November 4, 1942*—In the battle of El Alamein, British General Montgomery's Eighth Imperial Army is pushing Rommel's Afrika Korps back in earnest. The Nazis and Italians are retreating along the coastal roads.

*November 5, 1942*—The victory of El Alamein grows in dimensions by the hour. Rommel's Afrika Korps is now on the run, with Montgomery in hot pursuit.

*November 9, 1942*—The United States invasion of North Africa so far is a complete success. General Eisenhower's advance guard is rolling toward Tunis at breakneck speed. A constant stream of American reinforcements is being landed at Algiers and other points in the teeth of desperate attacks from Nazi dive bombers.

The capture of Algiers, practically without bloodshed, has put the American Army in a commanding position.

One of the questions unanswered is the whereabouts of Admiral Darlan, commander-in-chief of all the armed forces of Vichy France. He was in North Africa.

One guess is that General Eisenhower invited Admiral Darlan to get on the band wagon and throw in his lot with the Allies.

Darlan has been violently anti-British.

General Henri Giraud, who escaped from a Nazi prison last spring, is taking over command of all Free French forces in Africa.

American planes under the command of General Jimmy Doolittle are already operating from French airports in North Africa.

*November 10, 1942*—Tonight the American flag is flying at the great French naval base of Oran.

The advance forces of the great offensive are now driving eastward toward Tunis.

Today American General Eisenhower announced that General Giraud is in Algeria to organize the French forces that will battle side by side with the Americans.

Switzerland reports that the Nazi Fuehrer and the Fascist Duce are together right now, trying to figure out what to do. Mussolini is said to be greatly alarmed by the possibility of an American-British attack on the Italian peninsula.

*November 11, 1942*—All of Morocco and all of Algeria are now in American hands. Our armies under General Eisenhower have won control after a campaign of seventy-six hours, a lightning drive that exceeded all hopes.

Nazi and Italian troops are streaming into previously unoccupied France.

Although Marshal Pétain did make a formal protest against the entry of German troops and declared that it had violated the armistice, the Germans are moving on Marseilles, also Toulon, the great naval base, home of the French fleet.

The order to French troops in Algeria and Morocco to cease firing was issued by Admiral Darlan. He said he spoke with the authority of Marshal Pétain.

*November 12, 1942*—American troops pushing eastward through Algeria are making fast headway toward Tunis.

Today the story was told how in the days preceding the invasion a group of patriotic Frenchmen from North Africa got in touch with American representatives and suggested that an American general be sent secretly to meet them at Algiers—an undercover mission.

The War Department selected Major General Mark W. Clark—forty-six years old, slim and sharp-eyed, an able soldier and an astute diplomat. He arranged a trip that would make the thrills of a mystery novel seem pale. Much of the story of how they went is a military secret. In North Africa today General Clark said: "I used planes, trains, ships, submarines, canoes, automobiles—and everything but mules."

French officers agreed to collaborate with the forthcoming American offensive. They gave to the Americans complete plans of all French military installations in North Africa, the disposition of troops, the type of equipment and garrisons, and data on what French leaders could be counted on as friendly. They even made an arrangement to have the airfields outside Algiers delivered over to General Jimmy Doolittle's air force.

The secret mission headed by General Clark laid the important groundwork for the invasion of French North Africa.

*November 13, 1942*—The British Eighth Army has occupied Tobruk, and is now chasing Rommel across Libya.

Admiral Jean François Darlan has gone over to the Allies, lock, stock, and barrel.

Eddie Rickenbacker may be alive. Today the War Department announced the rescue of Captain William T. Cherry, who was the pilot of the Rickenbacker plane when it vanished in the Pacific three weeks ago. He was discovered on a life raft, after drifting on the ocean ever since October 21. So may it not be possible that Rickenbacker, too, may be alive and adrift?

The President has just signed the bill to lower the draft age to eighteen.

*November 16, 1942*—The British and Americans rolled over the border into Tunisia today. They encountered a whole division of ten thousand Axis troops. These launched a counterattack somewhere near Bizerte, and the fight is on.

Hitler has elected to stand in Tunis as long as he can.

A complicated political situation has developed in North Africa. Admiral Darlan is now head man of the French in North Africa, with the consent of our own high command.

In London, General Charles de Gaulle of the French National Committee does not agree. A statement was issued, saying: "General de Gaulle and the French National Committee announce that they are taking no part whatsoever nor assuming any responsibility for negotiations in North Africa with representatives from Vichy."

*November 17, 1942*—Here is a statement made by President Roosevelt late this afternoon: "I have accepted General Eisenhower's political arrangements made for the time being in northern and western Africa."

Eddie Rickenbacker has been picked up in the Pacific. He was on a life raft with Colonel Hans Adamson and Private John Bartek.

*November 18, 1942*—Marshal Pétain has made British-hating, Hitler-loving Pierre Laval the virtual head of the French state.

The statement issued by President Roosevelt describing the acceptance of Admiral Darlan as a temporary expedient has not satisfied the British. They and many Frenchmen believe Darlan to be a traitor and a quisling.

*November 19, 1942*—In North Africa the trap is closing rapidly around the old desert rat, Field Marshal Rommel. The British chasing him from the east, Americans and British pushing through Tunisia against him from the west, and the desert column of Free French and Americans thrusting up at Rommel from the south—Lake Chad, across the Sahara. Rommel is a resourceful commander, but to escape the triple threat he'll have to be a miracle man.

*November 24, 1942*—The Germans at Stalingrad are in serious trouble. Already they are almost cut off from the main Nazi forces.

In Dorchester, Massachusetts, the management of a grocery store has posted a sign which reads:
"Please be kind to our employees. They are harder to get than customers."

*November 27, 1942*—Tonight the great French naval base of Toulon is a shambles, its harbor in ruins, and the ships that once were the pride of the French Navy are on the bottom of Toulon Harbor, either scuttled or blown up.
Officers and sailors of the French Navy did it to keep the fleet from falling into Nazi hands.

Hitler has definitively canceled the armistice. All of France is now under German martial law.

*December 1, 1942*—Hitler's forces are defending the area of the city of Tunis and the naval base of Bizerte.

Great Britain today was presented with a sweeping plan for post-war economic reform. It proposes a sort of social security program reaching from the cradle to the grave of every Britisher—a kind of insurance to cover the economic contingencies of life for everybody.

*December 4, 1942*—General MacArthur now has his headquarters on the island of New Guinea. For the first time since the desperate days of Bataan he is leading an army in person.

*December 7, 1942*—In Tunisia the Americans and British are now on the defensive. The Germans are counterattacking.

*December 9, 1942*—The news from Africa is a shade more encouraging today. The Nazis were forced back.

*December 10, 1942*—Hitler has fired the Chief of Staff of the German Army and appointed another. Chief of Staff General Halder was at odds with Hitler's war policy. He disagreed with the Nazi Fuehrer over the strategy in Russia.

General Zeitzler is the new Chief of the General Staff.

Australians and Americans have captured that key Jap strong point, Gona, in New Guinea.

*December 11, 1942*—The battle in Tunisia is still impeded by rain and mud, slowed down to a halt at most places today.

*December 14, 1942*—In Libya the British today were chasing Rommel again. The Nazi Afrika Korps abandoned its fortified positions at El Agheila without a fight.

*December 16, 1942*—The British are chasing Rommel as fast as they can, in the hope of catching him before he is able to get his battered army into Tunisia.

*December 21, 1942*—The extent of the sweeping Soviet advance in southern Russia is indicated by the fact that the Red Army is threatening the city of Millerovo. This place is two hundred miles southwest of Stalingrad, far in the rear of the Nazi forces, between the Volga and the Don. The Russian rush, you might call it, has encircled twenty-two German divisions in the area before Stalingrad.

Rommel's North Afrika Korps is averaging fifteen miles a day, which is rapid retreating.

In Burma, British General Wavell continues his advance into that Japanese-occupied country, the British pushing down along the Bay of Bengal.

*December 23, 1942*—The Red Army today is back in the Ukraine, that rich province which first tempted Hitler to his Russian adventure.

*December 25, 1942*—All day long a heavy censorship was clamped down on French North Africa, and consequently no new illumination was shed on the assassination of Admiral Darlan. General Giraud, the commander of the French African army, has been given the task of maintaining order.

*December 28, 1942*—The Red Army has twenty-two Nazi divisions in a trap between the Volga and the Don. The word from Moscow is that the Soviets have a double ring around those twenty-two divisions.

The fighting there is in deep snow and with the thermometer below zero.

*December 31, 1942*—Hitler today addressed a New Year proclamation to the German Army, and this pronunciamento by Der Fuehrer featured the words, "It will be a difficult one but certainly no more difficult than the past one."

# 1943

*The tide has turned irrevocably against the Rome-Berlin Axis. The Germans lose their Sixth Army at Stalingrad and begin a big-scale retreat in Russia. They are swept out of North Africa, Sicily is taken from them, the battle of Italy begins—and their Fascist partner collapses. Mussolini falls, and Italy surrenders.*

*The big political development of the year is the Teheran Conference—the first meeting of Roosevelt, Churchill, and Stalin. The second front in Europe is decided on; command of it goes to General Eisenhower.*

*But there are sinister signs of Soviet hostility. Moscow claims that the part of Poland occupied by the Russians in 1939 belongs to Russia. Stalin indicates that he intends to have a Communist Poland after the war.*

*In the Pacific there are more American victories—Bougainville, Tarawa, the Bismarck Sea, and others. The rollback of the Japanese line across the Pacific is gathering momentum.*

---

*January 7, 1943*—Today the Germans for the first time admitted that they were on the retreat in southern Russia—the Caucasus.

*January 8, 1943*—The situation of the German army in the Caucasus is desperate, the trap closing on them.

*January 11, 1943*—Secretary Ickes made it known today that he had received instructions from President Roosevelt to give the Russians preference on whatever they want, and whatever we can supply, in munitions of war.

Colonel Andrew Summers Rowan has died in a San Francisco hospital at the age of eighty-five, the man whom President McKinley picked to carry the message to Garcia.

*January 12, 1943*—The Russians are sweeping on into the Caucasus, with the Cossacks leading the charge.

*January 15, 1943*—The Communists have the best underground organization in France, and have provided the fighting French with valuable information.

The Red Army is on the offensive—in the Leningrad area, in the V sector west of Moscow, before Stalingrad, in the big bend of the Don, and in the Caucasus.

*January 19, 1943*—Red Army forces have driven to within eighty miles of Kharkov.

The British Eighth Army drove today to within less than fifty miles of Tripoli.

*January 21, 1943*—The United States forces on Guadalcanal have a new commander—Major General Alexander M. Patch of the Army. He succeeds Major General Alexander A. Vandegrift of the Marines.

The marines who fought so long and bravely have been taken out to enjoy a well-earned rest.

*January 22, 1943*—Tripoli has fallen to the British.

The German high command announces bluntly that its army before Stalingrad is surrounded and that Red Army forces have broken through its defenses.

*January 25, 1943*—A division of Fighting French troops under General Jacques LeClerc has fought its way north 1,200 miles from French Equatorial Africa.

The Nazi Propaganda Ministry is getting the German people ready for the announcement that the Sixth Army at Stalingrad has been wiped out.

*January 26, 1943*—Moscow announces tonight that the liquidation of the huge German army in front of Stalingrad is virtually complete.

Prime Minister Winston Churchill has conferred with President Roosevelt at Casablanca, in Morocco.

*January 27, 1943*—Elmer Davis, Director of the Office of War Information, had this to say about the Casablanca Conference: "It has opened the way for a global offensive against the Axis in all parts of the world."

The French leaders, Giraud and De Gaulle, did not get together on political issues. With all the cheering over the Casablanca Conference, that fact could not be concealed.

The guns of the Red Army continue to blow to smithereens what is left of the German army at Stalingrad.

Flying Fortresses made their first raid over Hitler's Reich. In broad daylight they heavily bombed Wilhelmshaven, one of the biggest naval bases.

*February 1, 1943*—The Nazi high command acknowledges the German disaster at Stalingrad.

The vanguard of General Montgomery's British Eighth Army crossed the border from Tripolitania in two places.

*February 2, 1943*—Today the President's office was jammed for the White House news conference.

The unconditional surrender declaration at Casablanca? The President expanded that by saying there will be no negotiated armistice, as there was at the end of the last war.

He spoke optimistically of the meeting that he and the Prime Minister arranged between Giraud and De Gaulle—the French leaders who have been in disagreement. His tone indicated that he expected the French North African administration and the Free French to collaborate.

F.D.R. said he left Churchill at Marrakech. Churchill was sketching then—he's something of an artist. He was making drawings of the distant white summits.

Moscow announces that all the Germans in Stalingrad have finally been wiped out.

*February 3, 1943*—The naval and air engagement in the Solomons is continuing.

Today the German high command announced officially what Moscow stated yesterday—that the Nazi forces at Stalingrad have been wiped out. The bad news was broadcast by the Berlin radio and followed by music, the funeral march from the opera, *Götterdämmerung*.

Of late the Nazis have been hammering the Germans with a rhetoric of defeat—with the Stalingrad fanfare as a climax today. Are they trying to frighten the Germans with a new fighting desperation by enlarging upon the threat of Soviet invasion?

*February 4, 1943*—The Japanese are making a desperate attempt to land reinforcements and supplies on Guadalcanal—the Isle of Death.

*February 8, 1943*—The Berlin high command continues to try to give the impression that the Russians are advancing because the Germans are executing a strategic withdrawal according to plan.

*February 11, 1943*—Prime Minister Winston Churchill, in the London House of Commons, stated that one of the Casablanca decisions was: unified command in North Africa. All the Allied forces in North Africa are to be commanded by our own American General Eisenhower.

The battle for Guadalcanal ended officially yesterday. Actually, we knew it was all over last Tuesday, but the Navy reckoned that the fighting was not formally over until one last Jap force in the north of the island had been eliminated.

*February 15, 1943*—The Royal Air Force last night dealt a couple more terrific blows at the Axis. One, another raid on Cologne, with those massive blockbuster bombs.

Meanwhile another R.A.F. formation was in southern Europe smashing at the great city of Milan and the foremost Italian naval base at Spezia.

In Africa our troops have taken the brunt of a hard attack by one of Marshal Rommel's panzer divisions in the area west of Faïd Pass. United States forces were pushed back eighteen miles.

*February 16, 1943*—The Soviets announce the greatest victory of the present Red Army offensive in southern Russia—the capture of Kharkov.

New demands are being made for the release of Gandhi, the latest being urged in the Indian parliament. One British leader characterized the Mahatma's hunger strike in these words: "A pistol again is held at our forehead."

*February 17, 1943*—Rommel's North Afrika Korps, pushing through Faïd Pass, has driven forward for thirty-five miles.

President Roosevelt and the First Lady waited to greet a guest arriving by train. Madame Chiang Kai-shek, wife of the Generalissimo. They took her to the White House, where she will stay during her visit to Washington.

*February 18, 1943*—A broadcast by Nazi Propaganda Minister Goebbels threw out suggestions aimed at driving a rift between Soviet Russia, Britain, and the United States. He asked: "What would England and the United States do if the worst happened and the European continent fell into the hands of the Bolsheviks?"

The senators and representatives listened to a slender, elegant lady from China. Madame Chiang Kai-shek, arguing that in the Japanese we have an even more formidable enemy than in the Germans.

*February 22, 1943*—The swift tank columns of Marshal Rommel have advanced sixteen miles farther in their blitzkrieg through the American lines.

*February 23, 1943*—In Britain a powerful demand for a second front follows the Red Army Day statement by Stalin—that Russia is bearing the whole burden of the war against Hitler.

The Afrika Korps is driving through a mountain gateway called Kasserine Pass.

*February 24, 1943*—Prime Minister Winston Churchill today refused to liberate Mahatma Gandhi.

*February 25, 1943*—General Eisenhower witnessed the final stage of the battle when the Germans were thrown back at Kasserine Pass.

*February 26, 1943*—The Germans, after having abandoned Kasserine Pass yesterday, are still in retreat.

Moscow reports that German resistance has stiffened all along the southern Russian front.

George Bernard Shaw came out with a blast against the imprisonment of Gandhi: "The King should release Gandhi unconditionally and apologize to him for the mental defectiveness of his Cabinet."

*March 2, 1943*—In Tunisia the battle on the American front is receding to where it started.

The official Russian news agency declared that the part of Poland Russia seized is really Russian in character and belongs to the Soviets.

For days a big Jap convoy has been reported moving toward New Guinea. Today the news is: the giant convoy has been beaten up and scattered by our planes.

*March 4, 1943*—From the coast of New Britain to the coast of New Guinea the waters are strewn with the wreckage of Japanese ships and airplanes. The battle of the Bismarck Sea was a spectacular victory.

*March 8, 1943*—General Montgomery and the British Eighth Army have given Nazi Marshal Rommel and his Afrika Korps such a going over that the Germans have taken to the hills back of the Mareth line.

*March 9, 1943*—Admiral Standley declared in Moscow that Stalin is deliberately keeping the Russian people ignorant of the war help that the United States is extending to the Red Army—the Russians not being told about Lend-Lease.

*March 11, 1943*—The Soviet high command admits the battle on the Kharkov and Donets River front is critical.

*March 12, 1943*—Soviet forces have lost the city of Kharkov.

*March 15, 1943*—Our airmen have been bombing the Japs in the Aleutians again.

The Russians in the south tonight are being hammered on a front 120 miles long.

Farther north they are driving ever closer to the big goal, Smolensk.

*March 17, 1943*—In London today Prime Minister Winston Churchill declared once again that the British Empire, with its vast colonial possessions, is to be maintained.

*March 18, 1943*—Hard-boiled Lieutenant General Patton, at the head of his tanks, rolled into Gafsa, near the Tunisian coast, and took it away from Rommel.

The Russians and Germans along the Donets River are in their greatest test of strength since Stalingrad.

*March 22, 1943*—General Montgomery's British Eighth Army now has a wedge inside the Nazi-held Mareth line.

Hitler announced yesterday that the eastern front has been stabilized.

*March 23, 1943*—It really looks tonight as if Rommel were in a desperate trap, with fatal coils closing around the old Fox of the Desert.

The Americans are hitting the Germans from the west, while the British are smashing from the east.

*March 29, 1943*—Montgomery and his British Eighth Army have burst into the Mareth line on a twenty-five-mile front. The Desert Fox has escaped, for the time being, into the Gabès bottleneck.

*March 30, 1943*—The Afrika Korps is in retreat northward.

Last night's Royal Air Force raid on Berlin was one of the most devastating of the war.

President Roosevelt stated this afternoon that negotiations between the United States and Soviet Russia are going to be held in the near future—talks concerning world arrangements after the war. The President added that he was still hopeful of meeting Stalin—and of talking over post-war planning with him.

*April 2, 1943*—The Nazi Afrika Korps is retreating north to join with Von Arnim's Germans in the Bizerte area.

*April 7, 1943*—The latest from North Africa is an official bulletin that the British Eighth Army has linked up with the Americans.

*April 8, 1943*—The Northwest African Strategic Air Force, under the command of Major General James H. Doolittle, in the past week has bombed sixty-two Axis ships. Nine sunk, others were left in flames or sinking.

One suprising fact on that long Russian front is the tenacity with which the Germans are holding out at Kuban in the Caucasus. For a while after the Russians had cleared them out of the oil fields and driven them to the coast, it looked as though they would push the Nazis right into the Black Sea. But that was months ago, and today the Germans are holding out as doggedly as ever at Kuban.

*April 9, 1943*—The North Afrika Korps is now cornered with other German troops in the Tunis-Bizerte pocket at the tip of Tunisia.

*April 12, 1943*—Rommel has been able to take the cream of his troops into the protection of a bristling loop of defenses.

*April 14, 1943*—General Eisenhower was asked about Rommel, his antagonist. Is Rommel a great strategist, as the Germans claim he is? General Eisenhower responded in the affirmative. "Rommel," said he, "certainly is a great general. He is not a superman. But, commanded by him, the German army in Tunisia is a force which must not be under-estimated."

*April 16, 1943*—In London today the exiled Polish Government announced that it was asking the Red Cross to investigate statements that the Russians killed ten thousand Polish officer prisoners. The statements to that effect are being made by Nazi propaganda.

*April 19, 1943*—In the North Pacific more raids on the Japs at Attu and Kiska, where the Nipponese are working persistently on new airdromes.

*April 20, 1943*—Soviet Russia is reacting bitterly to the demand by the exiled Polish Government for a Red Cross investigation of Nazi charges that the Russians massacred ten thousand Polish officers near Smolensk. The Moscow retort is that the killings were done by the Nazis and blamed on the Soviets, and that now the Polish Government in London is collaborating with the Hitler trick.

*April 21, 1943*—The Far Eastern murder gang has executed some of the captured American fliers who raided Tokyo. This was announced today by President Roosevelt.

The War Department gives us the pledge this afternoon that the Doolittle raid will be repeated with bombings ten times as great, a hundred times—the Japs to be bombed time and again, without end, until they are blasted to utter defeat.

*April 23, 1943*—In North Africa the assault upon the Nazi stronghold is in full blast. Today both British armies drove forward in a thundering advance.

*April 26, 1943*—Soviet Russia broke off relations with Poland in the question of the mass murder of Polish officers.

The Moscow note says that the exiled government of Poland has put itself in a position hostile to the Soviet Union.

*April 28, 1943*—The word today that the Americans have captured three hills in Tunisia keeps emphasis on the character of the fighting over there, desperate foot-by-foot battling in rugged, mountainous country that has been heavily fortified by the enemy.

*April 29, 1943*—The Russian battle front has come to life again. The Soviet generals have begun a long-expected drive to clear the last remaining Germans out of the Caucasus.

*May 3, 1943*—The Americans have taken Mateur, one of our chief objectives in Tunisia. The key to the whole system of Nazi fortifications defending the Bizerte naval base and Tunis.

*May 6, 1943*—In Tunisia the British First Army pushed ahead ten miles today.

The Red Army has broken through on the Kuban front in the Caucasus. So says Moscow.

*May 7, 1943*—Tunis has fallen, and Bizerte has fallen.
It's all over for the Nazis now in North Africa.
The British at Tunis have reached the sea, and this cuts the Axis armies in two—the southern group now separated from the northern.

*May 11, 1943*—On the Cape Bon Peninsula the Germans were expected to produce another Bataan, but they are yielding in such fashion that the Cape Bon fighting may be regarded as at an end.
A note about Rommel. He has been out of North Africa ever since March 11, two months ago. He commanded the retreat all the way from Egypt to Tunisia and then left North Africa.

Prime Minister Churchill has arrived in Washington for another conference with President Roosevelt.

*May 12, 1943*—The battle of Tunisia has ended.
The final chapter was written today with the surrender of the Nazi commander-in-chief, General von Arnim.

*May 13, 1943*—In North Africa the Axis prisoners are said to total around a hundred and seventy-five thousand.
President Roosevelt and Prime Minister Churchill were closeted with their advisers at the White House.

*May 14, 1943*—Tonight our soldiers are fighting in a nightmare of a place. Like the other islands of the long Aleutian chain, Attu is the top of a lofty mountain that rises from the floor of the deep sea. It rises steeply to snow-clad mountains, with beaches at the base of the peaks.
Attu is one of the rainiest places on earth. There may be 250 rainy days a year, and an almost perpetual fog envelops the island.

From London comes grim and evil word about anti-Semitic atrocities in Warsaw. The entire ghetto at Warsaw has now been wiped out, a section that contained forty thousand Jewish people.
The ghetto in Warsaw resisted the Nazi killers, the forty thousand Jews fighting with what few weapons they could procure. It was a ten-day battle, with Nazi tanks rumbling through streets, their guns blazing. They overpowered the feeble weapons of the defenders—until the last flicker of resistance was suppressed.

*May 17, 1943*—The Attu operation is proceeding.

*May 18, 1943*—Last night the bombers of the R.A.F. raided far and wide into Germany again. But the news today concentrates on the catastrophic event of the night before—the smashing of the great dams in the Ruhr Valley. Word from within Germany indicates that the floods from the broken dams have been the greatest disaster inside Naziland since the war began.

*May 19, 1943*—Our soldiers on Attu are in a continuous line across the neck of land that connects the main part of the island with the smaller section extending east. And that cuts the Jap forces in two.

The address that Prime Minister Winston Churchill made to Congress today was designed to meet a good deal of congressional criticism.

Churchill said the theory of licking Hitler first was agreed upon by himself and President Roosevelt when they conferred in Washington during the month after Pearl Harbor. "It was evident," said he, "that, while the defeat of Japan would not mean the defeat of Germany, the defeat of Germany would mean infallibly the ruin of Japan."

As for an invasion of Europe, that will come "in due course," said Winston Churchill today.

*May 20, 1943*—Tokyo says tonight that more than two thirds of the Japs on Attu Island have been wiped out.

*May 21, 1943*—The Japanese naval and air commander, Admiral Yamamoto, who once boasted that he would write the terms of the peace in the White House, was killed in action, says Tokyo. He was flying in air battle on what Tokyo calls "a foremost front." That might mean anywhere in the Pacific where the Japs are facing the Americans.

The battle of Attu is about over.

*May 24, 1943*—In the Mediterranean it became clear today that the Allied air command is aiming to knock out that strongly fortified Italian island of Pantelleria, midway between Sicily and Tunisia.

Secretary of State Hull today welcomed the disappearance of the Communist International, which has been abolished by Moscow. Stalin takes this action to bring about a better understanding with his allies. The end of the Comintern, the Secretary said, will contribute to the co-operation necessary not only for winning the war, but for agreement after the war.

*May 25, 1943*—On Attu the remaining Japanese have been pressed back more tightly into the narrow peninsula where they are fighting with their backs against the sea.

The island is living up to the meteorological infamy of the Aleutians. American soldiers are driving through sleet, snow, and rain.

The latest in the Allied air war against Fascist Italy was a huge and devastating affair, with great formations of bombers striking at military centers in Sardinia.

*May 26, 1943*—Just a year ago today the Soviets and Great Britain signed their mutual-aid treaty. Today Moscow newspapers repeated the pledge that neither Great Britain nor Stalin's Russia has any intention of interfering with the domestic affairs of other countries. This is pointed up by the recent abolition of the Comintern.

*May 28, 1943*—The Red Army is smashing against what is called the Kuban bridgehead, the Black Sea peninsula which is all the Germans have left of their one-time large conquests in the Caucasus.

*May 31, 1943*—The first news that the battle of Attu had ended came via Tokyo. The official bulletin said the Attu garrison was believed to have perished in a final assault on American positions.

*June 2, 1943*—Warships are joining the warplanes in battering the island of Pantelleria—the rock fortress that commands the strait between Sicily and North Africa.

*June 8, 1943*—Fighting broke out again today in Los Angeles, the battle of the zoot suit—the conflict between soldiers and sailors and the ferocious jitterbugs. The latest news tells that one sailor was stabbed and three others were badly beaten.

It seems like fantastic nonsense when we hear how gangs of jitterbug youths are attacking uniformed fighting men of the nation.

*June 9, 1943*—The surrender of Pantelleria was demanded yesterday, but refused.

The argument for surrender was enforced by the most violent naval bombardment that Pantelleria has endured. The volcanic island looked like an erupting volcano.

*June 10, 1943*—Pantelleria has surrendered. Once called the "Italian Gibraltar."

Moscow today celebrated the first anniversary of Lend-Lease to Soviet

Russia. The Moscow newspapers gave full and glowing accounts, telling of American aid, with expressions of gratitude and cordiality.

*June 14, 1943*—Allied air power is being concentrated on Sicily.

*June 16, 1943*—Charlie Chaplin got married today. He is white-haired, fifty-four, and has been wedded three times previously. His bride is eighteen—Oona O'Neill, daughter of the playwright, Eugene O'Neill.

*June 17, 1943*—Several French Catholic archbishops have signed a joint pastoral letter protesting against the conscription of French workers for compulsory labor in Germany.

*June 18, 1943*—The British Government has named a new viceroy of India, Field Marshal Sir Archibald Wavell, who until now has been British commander-in-chief in India, and who earlier in the war scored dazzling victories in North Africa.

Still another bombing of Sicily, that steppingstone island which more and more looks like the next target for invasion.

*June 21, 1943*—Race riots in Detroit. Tonight, eleven dead. Thirty-five hundred police are on special duty. The State Director of Civilian Defense has mobilized one thousand machine gun home guards and a thousand auxiliary police. At State Police headquarters five hundred troopers are standing by.

Governor Kelly has declared martial law in three counties.

General Eisenhower has received a communication from people on the captured island of Pantelleria. Sixty-seven inhabitants signed it, and the gist of it was to thank Eisenhower for saving them from Mussolini and Hitler.

*June 22, 1943*—In North Africa today the feuding French factions came to an agreement on one important subject. Who is to control the French armed forces fighting the Nazis?

The committee today named General Giraud as the commander-in-chief of the French forces in North and West Africa, and named De Gaulle as commander-in-chief in the other territories of the French empire.

Detroit was quiet today on the riot front. The aftermath is a slump in production at Detroit's many armament factories because of the absence of Negro workers. Deterred by the orgy of violence, thousands failed to show up at their jobs today.

*June 28, 1943*—The French radio, controlled by the Nazis, announces that ninety-six divisions of German troops have been sent to positions where they are ready for an attack. Forty divisions are in France, Belgium, and Holland; sixteen divisions on the French Mediterranean coast; fifteen in the Balkans; and fifteen in Italy.

*June 30, 1943*—Winston Churchill made another of his great speeches today. He predicted large-scale action in the Mediterranean by the end of summer and reiterated the slogan "Unconditional surrender."

*July 1, 1943*—The American invasion of Rendova in the New Georgia group of islands is proceeding according to plan.

*July 2, 1943*—The occupation of Rendova Island has been completed by regular army troops, all resistance crushed.

On New Georgia Island the Marines advanced all day toward Munda.

*July 5, 1943*—The war in Russia has come to life again. The Germans began their long-expected offensive. They attacked on a front of 160 miles between Orel and Belgorod.

*July 7, 1943*—Tonight's German communiqué makes the first enemy claim of any real success in the current offensive, and states that the main Russian front facing Kursk has been broken.

*July 9, 1943*—Soviet Russia admitted today that the situation at Belgorod is serious, as the Nazi drive continues to smash forward and make progress.

The latest from New Georgia Island relates that the United States Marines are now only three miles from the Japanese air base at Munda.

*July 12, 1943*—The invasion of Sicily is on. The British, Canadians, and Americans are forging ahead so quickly in Sicily that the news can hardly keep up with their advance. The towns captured stretch all the way from historic Syracuse, one third of the way up the east coast, to Licata, on the southern coast. That gives the Allies a triangle of 147 square miles.

Some stories of the invasion forces tell us that most of the Sicilian prisoners have surrendered with smiles, not to say enthusiasm.

The general commanding the American forces in Sicily is none other than Lieutenant General George S. Patton, Jr.

*July 13, 1943*—The general picture in Sicily is one of continuing progress—satisfactory and according to plan.

The German and Italian radios seem to be writing off the loss in Sicily as a foregone conclusion.

*July 14, 1943*—The German offensive in Russia seems to be turning into a Russian offensive. The Russians are attacking, and soon may have a full-fledged counteroffensive under way.

In Sicily tonight the Allies hold more than a hundred and seventy-five miles of coast line.

*July 15, 1943*—The British, Canadians, and Americans are proceeding right through Sicily.

*July 19, 1943*—Timoshenko smashed into the German lines at Orel today for a distance of six and a quarter miles.

The bombing of Rome. A great force of R.A.F. and U.S. bombers dropped explosives and incendiary bombs on the huge railroad yards on three sides of Rome. Also on the many airfields just beyond the Seven Hills.

No bombs whatsoever were dropped on any of the classic architecture with which Rome abounds. Both pilots and bombardiers were instructed to be particularly careful to avoid any damage to religious and cultural monuments.

The Americans are well on the way to cutting off the entire western part of Sicily.

The Italian forces are cracking up, surrendering by units.

The most desperate fighting is now going on around Catania, where most of the Nazi force is concentrated.

*July 20, 1943*—In Sicily, Italians are surrendering in defiance of their own military command.

But, at the eastern tip of Sicily, the Germans are putting up a terrific battle in front of Catania.

*July 21, 1943*—Soviet Russia announces a move that may be of considerable importance in the politics of war and post-war. In Moscow an "Anti-Nazi German National Committee" has been formed. Its members are Germans opposed to Hitler. Its purpose, as described, is to overthrow the Nazis and establish a democratic regime in Germany.

*July 22, 1943*—The Germans at Catania are still giving Montgomery's Eighth Army a stiff fight. But from the rest of Sicily we hear of nothing but progress.

*July 23, 1943*—Tonight the battle of Sicily has definitely reached its final phase.

*July 26, 1943*—Well, the inevitable happened, as you know. Italian fascism crashed in ruins—with the fall of Mussolini.

At the end of one day of the Marshal Badoglio regime rigid controls are on.

Censorship is stricter than ever. We have no information as to the whereabouts of Mussolini and the Fascist leaders.

In Sicily the Canadian Army has carved its way twelve miles nearer to Catania. The Germans have been able to reinforce the Hermann Goering division which is responsible for the desperate defense of Catania.

*July 27, 1943*—Tonight the peninsula shaped like a boot remains an enigma—shrouded by censorship, enveloped in silence.

As for our policy toward the new regime in Rome, the President re-affirmed that our demand is still one of unconditional surrender.

In the war of the air based on Britain, the name in the news once more is Hamburg. That great German seaport has been smashed five times in sixty hours. In one raid alone 2,300 tons of bombs were dropped on Hamburg.

*July 28, 1943*—Tonight Rome comes out officially for peace. A Rome radio broadcast states that the purpose of the government that overthrew Mussolini is to get Italy out of the war. The new Victor Emmanuel-Badoglio regime declares that its intention is to yield to the Allies.

*July 29, 1943*—"Stop helping Germany and the Allies will bring you peace!" The message was sent by General Dwight Eisenhower, the Allied commander-in-chief in the Mediterranean.

It was addressed to the Italian people, and to the house of Savoy. This means that the Allies are prepared to dicker with King Victor Emmanuel as the legitimate head of the Italian nation.

Hitler's troops have been moving in large numbers through the Brenner Pass. These are said to have occupied all the big Italian bases at the head of the Adriatic Sea.

*July 30, 1943*—There is still silence from Italy. The belief is that the Badoglio government is conducting surrender negotiations with General Eisenhower.

In Sicily the Allied forces are pressing on against the stubbornly de-fending Germans at the eastern tip of the island.

*August 2, 1943*—The blockbusters that fell on Naples notified Badoglio and the Italian people that the Allies are tired of waiting for the surrender of Italy.

In Sicily the armies of the Allies forged ahead today on a front sixty miles long.

*August 3, 1943*—In Sicily, British-American and Canadian troops have smashed a breach in the Mount Etna lines.

*August 4, 1943*—In Russia the Germans are evacuating the Orel salient.

*August 6, 1943*—Tonight the Soviet armies are driving against Kharkov.

*August 9, 1943*—The German defense in Sicily is collapsing. The Nazis have already begun escaping by small boats and barges across the narrow Strait of Messina to the mainland of Italy.

*August 10, 1943*—Churchill's arrival today was preceded by the wildest kinds of rumors—even that Mussolini was being brought over to stand trial.

*August 11, 1943*—President Roosevelt will meet Prime Minister Winston Churchill in Quebec.

The Red Army trap is closing swiftly. Nazi troops and war materials are pouring out of Kharkov in a desperate attempt to escape.

*August 12, 1943*—The evacuation of German and Italian troops from Sicily is now in full swing.

*August 13, 1943*—Rome bombed again, Berlin hit, heavy raids launched against the two great industrial cities of northern Italy—Turin and Milan.

*August 17, 1943*—The final act of the Sicilian campaign was performed by the Americans. This morning U.S. armored units pushed into Messina.

A superoffensive. Berlin uses that term in describing a Russian assault launched southeast of Kharkov.

*August 18, 1943*—The Germans apparently are abandoning southern

Italy. They are evacuating the tip of the peninsula just opposite the tip of Sicily, and are pulling northward.

*August 19, 1943*—The Allied high command has completed a master plan for a United Nations march to Berlin. At Quebec, President Roosevelt and Prime Minister Churchill have approved it! That's the unofficial news from the historic old heights of Abraham tonight.

The plan includes a definite choice of a spot on the coast of Europe for a beachhead.

American warships have been shelling the mainland of Italy—for the first time in all history.

German divisions have been roaring down the Brenner Pass. There are already six or more Nazi divisions on the peninsula.

*August 23, 1943*—Kharkov fell yesterday.

Getting at Japan was uppermost at Quebec today. All we learn is that the attack on Japan will be launched at the same time as the coming knockout blow against the Germans!

*August 24, 1943*—Himmler becomes Minister of the Interior—Himmler, the ruthless head of the dreaded Gestapo. This means that virtually all Germany now goes under the direct rule of the Hitler secret police. Himmler, Hitler—two evil birds of a feather, or at least of similar names.

*August 26, 1943*—From India comes the first reaction to the appointment of Lord Louis Mountbatten as Allied commander in Southeast Asia. The Americans in New Delhi greeted the news with cheers. They take it as a guarantee that the time is at hand for the big push against the Japanese.

During one of the recent Allied raids on Milan bombs fell on the Convent of Santa Maria delle Grazie. When they cleared the debris away, they found Leonardo da Vinci's painting of The Last Supper miraculously intact!

*September 1, 1943*—Harry Hopkins—who lives at the White House—predicts that both Germany and Japan will be defeated by 1945.

*September 3, 1943*—At dawn today boats put out from the Sicilian shore—myriads of Allied landing boats—dashing across the strait to the mainland of Italy. The weather was perfect, and the sea was calm. In a brief time they were across, and now it was a scene of landing boats running aground on the beach, with soldiers leaping out and tanks and armored cars rolling off. A bridgehead was promptly established—the Italian peninsula invaded with little resistance.

*September 6, 1943*—In New Guinea, Australian and American troops are pushing swiftly inland from the beachheads they seized in their surprise attack over the weekend.

*September 7, 1943*—The capture of the toe of the boot is complete. British Eighth Army forces have made their way across the Aspromonte Mountains and have come down on the other side—to the other coast.

*September 8, 1943*—President Roosevelt and Prime Minister Churchill heard the word of the Italian surrender this morning and were not surprised. They knew about it all the time.

Today, following General Eisenhower's announcement of the capitulation, Badoglio broadcast his own statement on the Rome radio.

General Eisenhower suggests that the Italians might help to drive the Germans out of Italy.

And so Italy has surrendered—the first of three major Axis countries to be knocked out of the war.

The official Nazi news agency comes out tonight with raging fury, calling the Italian surrender open treason.

*September 9, 1943*—Early this morning the greatest sea-borne invasion in history landed on the Italian coast. The goal—Naples, the great Italian harbor.

The landings were far greater than those that hit Sicily—the biggest ever. They were supported by a tremendous naval and air bombardment.

The invasion force is the American Fifth Army, under the command of General Clark—the officer who made the adventurous trip to North Africa in negotiating for the surrender of the French colonies there.

*September 10, 1943*—American and British troops under General Clark have crushed five powerful German counterattacks. The Nazis are fighting stubbornly. We are informed today that the landings, previously described as being generally in the vicinity of Naples, were actually made in the Gulf of Salerno, which is to the south of Naples. Nazi troops have seized Rome.

The Berlin radio repeats that a phony government of resurrected fascism is to be headed by Mussolini. He'll be made the Duce again—by German armed force.

*September 13, 1943*—The British Eighth Army, on the toe of the Italian boot, was having a fairly easy time today and advancing rapidly.

But at Salerno the soldiers of the American Fifth Army were having the toughest fight of their lives. The Nazis kept their strongest shock troops and their heaviest tank divisions to throw in against General Clark's men.

*September 14, 1943*—We needn't pay too much attention to the Nazi boasts about a defeat of the Allied forces at Salerno.

However, from our own side we do know that the situation at Salerno is serious. American and British troops have been driven back by ferocious Nazi counterattacks.

*September 15, 1943*—The state of affairs in the battle of Salerno is clearer tonight. We have a fairly precise picture of the American Fifth Army holding firm on the beaches against one German assault after another, an interminable series of panzer drives launched from the advantage of higher ground.

Today the bedeviled Italian people heard something with a familiar sound—a proclamation by Mussolini.

Today's pronunciamento asserts the re-establishment of the Fascist state —though with a difference. This time it's called a Fascist republic. Meaning the end of the monarchy, no more king—by implication, the king is dethroned.

*September 17, 1943*—Today occurred one of those junctions of forces that are so dramatic in war—when armies are battling toward each other and then make contact. This happened in the fight at Salerno, when patrols of the hard-pressed Fifth Army joined forces with advance units of the British advancing from the south.

The Yugoslav partisans are said to be consolidating their hold on sixty miles of Yugoslav coast—and that's just across the Adriatic from the Italian coast, which is being occupied increasingly by British forces.

*September 20, 1943*—The Allied armies in Italy have now thrown their siege lines around Naples.

Long convoys of German trucks are hurrying north tonight, through the mountain passes, in swift retreat from the Salerno front.

*September 22, 1943*—At Naples the picture is grim and ugly. Naples looks like a smoking volcano—as seen from distant viewpoints held by the Allies. The Germans are carrying out extensive demolitions, destroying things with explosions and fire.

*September 24, 1943*—The Russians have now swept to the river Dnieper. And Smolensk is being encircled by Russian troops.

Word from Switzerland is that the phony Fascist government of the puppet Mussolini has been set up in the city of Bologna.

*September 29, 1943*—The Allied Fifth Army under General Mark Clark has broken through the enemy mountain line defending Naples and has thrust down onto the level Neapolitan plain. This means that they are advancing across flat land on both sides of Mount Vesuvius.

*September 30, 1943*—There has been a conference between Marshal Badoglio and General Eisenhower. Its purpose was to consider means of making the Italian military effort against the Germans more effective.

*October 1, 1943*—The capture of Naples was made certain when the Allied forces broke through the mountain barrier ringing Naples on the south. That is, when they smashed the Nazi defenses and advanced on both sides of Vesuvius.

The Germans did a thorough job of demolition in the harbor, blowing up buildings and docks and ships, doing everything they could to make the great port of no use to the Allies.

*October 4, 1943*—General Mark Clark's Fifth Army is pushing the Germans in the direction of Rome, and Corsica is now almost entirely in Allied hands.

*October 5, 1943*—All along the hundred-mile front across the Italian peninsula heavy fighting is on.

*October 7, 1943*—The Red Army has again forced its way across the Dnieper, which Hitler said last week was to be held at all costs.

*October 8, 1943*—Tonight in Italy, General Clark's Fifth Army is along the entire length of the river Volturno, from the ancient city of Capua to the sea.

The exiled Yugoslav Government is under attack as not really representing the Yugoslav people. This ties in with the feud between the Chetniks of General Mikhailovitch and the Communist partisans in Yugoslavia.

From the three bridgeheads established on the German-held side of the Dnieper, the Russians are advancing steadily.

*October 11, 1943*—In ten days the British and Americans have dropped something like twenty thousand tons of bombs on Hitler's Reich. And in the last three days they bagged three hundred German planes.

*October 12, 1943*—Suppositions that the Nazis might take Pope Pius XII away as a prisoner are strengthened by a story today which states that the Hitler people have made the Pope "an offer." They have advised him to leave Rome, and have offered him a place of refuge.

Today's Italian declaration of war against Nazi Germany produces one of the most curious twists in the history of war and statecraft. The Allies grant to Italy the status of a co-belligerent in the war. At the same time the armistice with Italy remains in force, without any change—that armistice of unconditional surrender. And this leaves Italy still in the position of a surrendered enemy. Allies remain technically at war with their new ally.

Badoglio, in his declaration, uses savage language in describing what he calls "German arrogance and ferocity."

*October 14, 1943*—The Allied armies in Italy have broken through the first line of Nazi defenses before Rome. The Fifth Army is pouring across the Volturno.

In Yugoslavia the two separate armies of patriots fighting the Nazis may join the forces under General Mikhailovitch, who was War Minister of Yugoslavia, and another army fighting under the command of General Tito Brozovich.

*October 20, 1943*—Red Army forces are a third of the way across the big bend of the Dnieper. Large Nazi forces are imperiled.

*October 21, 1943*—The Yugoslav guerrillas now dominate the entire east coast of Croatia and Dalmatia.

*October 25, 1943*—It looks like a race to decide whether the Germans can pull their troops out of the Crimea before Stalin's hordes sweep down to the Black Sea.

*October 27, 1943*—Virtual civil war is raging among the Yugoslavs.

*November 1, 1943*—The U. S. Army and Navy today began an amphibious operation on the west coast of Bougainville Island in the northern Solomons.

It is a daring stroke which bypassed enemy bases to the south of Bougainville. The Japs have a force of thirty thousand men on that large island.

MacArthur repeated his complaint about not having enough to fight with. If he had his way he would hit the Japs at two, three, or four points all at once, but he has not the necessary men and equipment.

*November 2, 1943*—Today American marines were swarming over mountains on Bougainville, after their surprise landing at Empress Augusta Bay.

*November 5, 1943*—Powerful Japanese naval reinforcements are moving toward the focus of battle in the area north of the Solomons.

*November 8, 1943*—Soviet Russia will pay us back for all the help we have sent through Lend-Lease—will pay in full. So says Stalin.

*November 9, 1943*—In Algiers, General Giraud has resigned from the French Committee of National Liberation—resigned as co-president with General de Gaulle, meaning that De Gaulle now is in full control. Leaders of the anti-Nazi underground in France gave their support to De Gaulle.

*November 10, 1943*—The Japs are making desperate attempts to hold that island of Bougainville, where the Marines are smashing at them with everything the Marines have got.

Tonight we have an explanation concerning Soviet Russia and Lend-Lease. The elucidation given by War Production Chief Donald Nelson tells us that Stalin's promise of repayment does not apply to Lend-Lease—but only to such goods as the Soviets receive from the United States after the war.

*November 11, 1943*—The Russian spearhead west of Kiev is spreading out like a huge mushroom. The news is that they are hurling Hitler's columns back to what used to be the Polish border.

*November 16, 1943*—A MacArthur spokesman today stated: "The Southwest Pacific has something less than five per cent of American military resources." Of all the equipment of war that this country has piled up, less than one twentieth has been sent to fight the Japs.

*November 22, 1943*—The Gilbert Islands in mid-Pacific have been invaded. Marines and U.S. infantry have established beachheads on the Makin and Tarawa atolls, although they ran into desperate resistance from the Japanese garrisons.

*November 23, 1943*—Two islands that we have invaded in the Gilbert group are now "securely in our hands." Makin and Abemama. But there is bitter fighting on Tarawa. The Marines are having a desperate battle.

*November 24, 1943*—The battle of the Gilbert Islands is virtually finished after the savage fight for Tarawa.

More than a thousand fires are reported to be raging in the capital of
Hitler's Reich. That nightmare metropolis is today the most heavily
bombed of all German cities.

*November 29, 1943*—Tonight we are informed from foreign sources
that President Roosevelt and Prime Minister Churchill have been in Cairo
for several days. Travelers from the Middle East report that Premier Stalin
is at Teheran, the capital of Persia.

It may be assumed that a Roosevelt-Churchill-Stalin conference will take
place in Teheran.

*November 30, 1943*—The secret is out—how Churchill, Roosevelt,
and Chiang Kai-shek had a long series of conferences in Egypt, and how
Churchill and Roosevelt thereupon left the land of the Nile, going to meet
Stalin, presumably in the land of Medes and Persians.

*December 1, 1943*—Messrs. Chiang Kai-shek, Roosevelt, and Churchill, in the Cairo Declaration, present definite terms of peace to be imposed
on Japan.

The Chinese are to get Formosa back and everything else they have
lost to Japan. Korea is to be set free. And the Japs will be deprived of the
islands they have gained as a result of World War I, those immensely
strategic isles that stretch out into the Pacific.

Today in Washington the casualty figures for the conquest of the Gil-
berts were announced.

On Tarawa atoll alone, in a mere seventy-six hours of fighting, our
losses were almost as high as they were on Guadalcanal during the weeks
of savage struggle there.

*December 2, 1943*—No official news tonight from the conference of
the Big Three. There still is considerable difference of opinion about the
location of the conference. Most of the European radios insist Roosevelt,
Churchill, and Stalin are in session at Teheran.

*December 3, 1943*—At last it is official. President Roosevelt, Prime
Minister Churchill, and Premier Marshal Stalin did meet at Teheran.

*December 6, 1943*—The joint declaration, signed by Messrs. Roosevelt, Churchill, and Stalin, states:

First, as to the war: there will be a triple front against Hitler. The
Western Allies will open another front, presumably in France.

Second, as to the peace: they are sure that their concord will make it
good and lasting.

The declaration winds up with a highly idealistic statement of confidence that the day is coming when all the peoples of the world may live free lives, untouched by tyranny.

*December 6, 1943*—The United States Fifth Army is rolling. They have captured three more heights of Mount Maggiore. The battle is increasing in fury every hour.

*December 8, 1943*—In Yugoslavia the British Government is now giving most of its support to Tito and his partisan army of guerrillas. Civil war is raging between General Mikhailovitch and his Chetniks on one hand and Tito's partisans on the other. Britain now swinging to the Soviet-supported partisans. "For the simple reason," stated the parliamentary Under Secretary today, "that the resistance of the partisan forces to the Germans is very much greater."

*December 9, 1943*—Bewilderment and despair in Bulgaria. In the Bulgarian parliament deputies, regardless of their Nazi overlords, complained openly against the use of Bulgaria as a military base by the Germans, saying it will inevitably result in Bulgaria's becoming a battlefield.

*December 10, 1943*—It was disclosed tonight that President Roosevelt has made a tour of the battlefields of North Africa, an aerial tour—by plane. The President was on his way, homeward bound.

*December 13, 1943*—We now have a definite idea of one angle of Premier Stalin's foreign policy in Europe after the war. He has already laid the foundations for a three-power alliance in Eastern Europe—the Soviet Union, Czechoslovakia, and Poland. There is a definite provision that Russia and Czechoslovakia will not meddle in each other's internal affairs.

*December 15, 1943*—A Senate subcommittee on military affairs refused to okay the promotion of Lieutenant General Patton. Secretary of War Stimson admitted that General Patton had actually slapped two soldiers and verbally abused a third.

*December 16, 1943*—President Roosevelt today is back, safe and sound, somewhere in the United States.

*December 17, 1943*—President Roosevelt today held the first White House press conference since his return from the Big Three conference.
He stated his belief that the Teheran Conference will prevent another war in this generation.

On the island of New Britain the Americans are mopping up.

*December 20, 1943*—In Italy two columns of American troops are driving on the town of Cassino, that historic site of the first Benedictine monastery and an important highway junction on the road to Rome.

Marshal Tito, head of the partisan guerrillas, today announced the formation of a Yugoslav National Committee of Liberation. Tito's forces claim to be the legitimate government of Yugoslavia. Today Marshal Tito demanded that the Allies stop supporting the royal government in exile, together with its Minister of War, General Mikhailovitch, and his Chetniks.

*December 21, 1943*—On the river Dnieper front, the battle line in the great bend, the Nazis are in retreat, retirement, flight.

*December 23, 1943*—Today we find that stretch of shore near Calais given another name—the "Rocket Coast." It all goes back to the much talked of secret weapon of the Nazis, which concealed menace is being more and more defined as a giant rocket projectile with which the Nazis intend to bomb Britain from the shore of France.
The British response is to bomb the "Rocket Coast."

*December 24, 1943*—The President made known the name of the general officer appointed to be commander-in-chief of the second front in Europe. The commander selected at Teheran to lead the combined attack of the Allies on the fortress Europe is General Dwight Eisenhower.

*December 28, 1943*—The second front will be launched in northwestern Europe. So say the Chiefs of Staff in Washington. Northwestern Europe could mean anything from the northern tip of Norway to the western tip of northern France.

The Eighth American Air Force, operating out of Britain, gets a new commander, and he is Major General James H. Doolittle.

The first official proposal has been made for the trial of Hitler and other Nazi war criminals. Formal demand has been submitted to the United Nations by the exiled government of Czechoslovakia.

*December 29, 1943*—Today the German war commentator, Captain Ludwig Sertorius, declared: "Invasion is relatively near."

Washington today was busy interpreting President Roosevelt's formal abandonment of the term "New Deal," which now goes out the window. One assumption is that it's a move in the direction of a fourth-term campaign, a maneuver to pacify conservative Democrats in preparation for the Democratic Convention.

*December 30, 1943*—The Marines, after five days of fighting at the tip of New Britain Island, have seized their major goals—the two landing strips built by the Japs.

Stalin, in a special announcement, revealed that the Red Army has scored a giant break-through in the northwestern Ukraine. The German front has collapsed, and the Red Army tonight is rolling at a swift rate toward the pre-war border of Poland.

*December 31, 1943*—Hitler today issued a proclamation and reviewed the old year. And it's hard to find fault with what he said: "The year of 1943 brought us the heaviest setbacks."

As for the new year, all he could see ahead was a second-front invasion. He tried to reassure the German people by telling them how strongly the invasion coasts were fortified.

Today's news from Russia continues yesterday's tidings of overwhelming Soviet advance and corresponding German retreat—the Nazi front in the Ukraine apparently in a state of disorganized collapse.

# 1944

*Hitler's power begins to crumble, and there is a second unsuccessful attempt to assassinate him. General Eisenhower hurls his men into France, where they advance at breakneck speed—suffering only one real defeat, the Battle of the Bulge. Otherwise, it is a race to get to Germany first. General de Gaulle assumes political power in France.*

*At the same time the Russians are driving forward at the other end. Marshal Zhukov commands the center and batters his way into East Prussia as other Soviet armies begin to swamp the nations of Eastern Europe. In Italy the slow, dogged advance under General Clark continues.*

*In Greece the British return only to find a Communist rising on their hands. In Yugoslavia there is civil war between Mikhailovitch's Chetniks and Tito's Red partisans. Communist conspiracy begins to look uglier in the liberated nations.*

*In the Pacific it is a year of great and costly American victories— Eniwetok, Saipan, Guam. MacArthur keeps his promise and returns to the Philippines.*

*At home President Roosevelt wins a fourth term. Senator Harry Truman of Missouri is the new Vice-President. Former Vice-President Henry Wallace begins to demand a more pro-Soviet foreign policy.*

---

*January 3, 1944*—President Roosevelt has given to the government his home at Hyde Park, New York.

This is in line with the President's promise of a library at Hyde Park and a repository for official papers of his presidency.

*January 4, 1944*—A late dispatch from Allied headquarters tells of the first big Japanese counterattack in the Cape Gloucester area of New Britain. The Japs made a large-scale attempt to dislodge the American Marines, but were beaten back by the leathernecks.

*January 5, 1944*—The slow advance in Italy continues, with the Fifth Army pushing on through deep snowdrifts.

The Polish *Daily News*, which is published in Chicago, today prints an editorial headed: "Russia, Friend or Foe?" The Polish editorial asks: "Is Russia entering Poland as an ally or as an invader?"

*January 6, 1944*—Moscow tells of a Polish group formed in the Soviet capital, a group calling itself the "Union of Polish Patriots."

The new Polish outfit, sponsored by the Soviets, comes forward today with a bitter blast against the exiled Polish Government stationed in London, calling it "reactionary."

A new fighter plane, tested in the U.S. and Britain, has no propellers. It is sent through the air by a system of jets—and that sounds remotely like the principle of rocket blasts.

*January 10, 1944*—A Moscow announcement: "The territories of the western Ukraine have become a part of Soviet Russia, and the territories of western White Russia have become a part of Soviet White Russia." The point of it all is, of course, that what the Soviets call the "western Ukraine" and "western White Russia" are precisely the areas that the Soviets took from Poland under the terms of the Hitler-Stalin pact.

*January 11, 1944*—The story was ended today for Count Ciano, former Foreign Minister of Fascist Italy and son-in-law of Mussolini. He was executed by a firing squad this morning.

When the Fascist Grand Council voted to overthrow Mussolini, Ciano was one of the majority that turned against his father-in-law. It was for this act that he has now been condemned and executed by the puppet Fascist regime.

*January 13, 1944*—In Poland one Soviet thrust advanced today to a point forty-eight miles beyond the old Polish border.

*January 14, 1944*—The gateway to the corridor through the Pripet Marshes is now in the hands of the Russians, and disorganized and fleeing Nazis are being driven into the wilderness of the swamps.

Eleven hundred war planes flew against the French invasion coast by daylight today.

Senator Bridges of New Hampshire today declared: "Americans want to know how Poland, which was the only full ally that England and France had at the beginning of the war and which has been so horribly ravaged, is to be rewarded for its loyalty and supreme sacrifices."

He stated this in a call upon President Roosevelt to tell, in the senator's words, "what really happened at Teheran."

*January 18, 1944*—President Roosevelt declared that he is as much mystified as anybody else by that Russian charge of British negotiations with Hitler's Foreign Minister, Ribbentrop.

The Russian communiqué declares that the whole series of Soviet offensives from Leningrad to the Black Sea is now linked up into what Moscow calls "one vast battlefield."

*January 20, 1944*—The siege of Leningrad is now lifted completely, just twenty-nine months from the day that it began, August 21, 1941.

*January 21, 1944*—Moscow disavows that *Pravda* story. The Deputy Foreign Commissar of the Soviet Government informed the British Embassy at Moscow that no official of the Russian Government was responsible for the publication of that report about Britain's wanting a separate peace.

*January 24, 1944*—Pope Pius XII will stay in Vatican City, come what may.

*January 26, 1944*—Seven more attacks against the Marshall Islands. The Japs in that archipelago are taking an incessant beating from the air.

Today Soviet Moscow charged Nazi Germany with that monstrous crime of which the Germans accused the Russians. That is—the murder of eleven thousand Polish officer prisoners in the Katyn forest, near Smolensk.

Secretary of State Cordell Hull announced today that Soviet Russia has rejected the offer of the United States to mediate the Soviet-Polish dispute.

*January 27, 1944*—A report has been released tonight almost too shocking and horrible for comment. More than fifty-two hundred Americans captured in the Philippines have died from starvation, thirst, torture, and wanton murder in two Japanese prison camps. The number of Filipino soldiers treated in like fashion is even larger.

The beachhead at Anzio now reaches to within twenty miles of the Eternal City.

The Germans are rushing other troops to that beachhead front, by plane and by glider, as fast as they can.

The headquarters of Marshal Tito Brozovich, leader of the Serb partisans, announces that Tito's armies have cleared the Nazis out of 70 per cent of central Bosnia.

*January 31, 1944*—On the beachhead below Rome a battle has been going on for forty-eight hours and growing more intense with every hour.

Here's the picture in Berlin: Every railroad station crowded with would-be refugees trying to get away from the German capital after the third raid by the Royal Air Force in four nights. In those three nights the R.A.F. dropped more than fifty-six hundred tons of bombs.

*February 1, 1944*—The American landings, officially reported by Admiral Nimitz today, are on both Kwajalein Island and Roi Island.

Today Foreign Commissar Molotov entered a proposal to permit each one of the sixteen Soviet republics to form its own relations with foreign powers.

From Washington we have instant comment that the whole thing would increase the Soviet voting power in any future international body—sixteen states of the U.S.S.R. voting independently instead of one Russian government.

*February 2, 1944*—The Red Army has swept across the border of Estonia.

*February 3, 1944*—Infantry reinforcements and mechanized equipment have been landed on Kwajalein. There the Japs are still fighting desperately with the 7th Infantry.

Admiral Nimitz has issued his first proclamation as military governor of Kwajalein. He proclaims the abolition of the Mikado's powers.

*February 4, 1944*—In the Southwest Pacific a striking Allied success was scored on Bougainville when our ground troops drove clear across the island.

The battle for Rome has developed into the bitterest conflict of the whole Italian war.

*February 7, 1944*—It is evident tonight that the Nazis are determined to throw the Fifth Army back into the Tyrrhenian Sea.

*February 8, 1944*—From the sector of Cassino we have a new and striking expression—the Battle of the Monastery—which applies, of course, to the ancient Benedictine Monastery of Monte Cassino. A late dispatch tonight tells how American and German troops fought today with machine guns, rifles, and grenades in the shadow of the towering battlements of the first monastic buildings of the Western world.

*February 9, 1944*—In the Cassino area Fifth Army troops are driving in a culminating effort to capture that much blasted place.

At Seattle tonight Vice-President Wallace denounced what he called the "American Fascists of Wall Street." He said they have the wrong kind of economics, while, on the other hand, it is different in Soviet Russia. "Nearly everyone in Russia," said the Vice-President, "feels that he is working for the welfare of the whole nation. He has no fear whatever of being exploited for the sole profit of the management or stockholders."

*February 10, 1944*—The Fifth Army units made up of British and Americans battling on the Anzio beachhead below Rome are in real danger, and it would be a great mistake to minimize it.

*February 14, 1944*—On the northern Russian front three Red columns are driving from different directions toward Pskov, the gateway to Latvia and Estonia.

*February 15, 1944*—An end came today to one of the most historic structures on this earth—the ancient Benedictine Monastery of Monte Cassino.

Yesterday leaflets were dropped on the monastery, bidding the monks to take shelter from the bombardment that was coming. And today squadrons of planes bombed the Monastery of Monte Cassino. With the explosion of one bomb, the gleaming blue dome fell to pieces and others tumbled its walls. After the air bombing Allied guns poured shells into what remained of the first monastery of Western Europe—which tonight lies in ruins.

Today Mussolini disclosed that it was his own decision that sent Count Ciano, his son-in-law, before the firing squad.

American forces have completed the conquest of the Solomon Islands.

*February 16, 1944*—The capital of Finland was bombed tonight, Helsinki enduring a rain of Soviet high explosives.

*February 17, 1944*—The latest news from Anzio, a strong German armed force has just begun the second big offensive there.

*February 18, 1944*—The amphibious operation against Eniwetok is a good deal on the order of the Kwajalein affair, only more so. That is, this newest atoll assault was prepared by an even more stupendous bombardment, with warships and planes hurling an even greater weight of high explosives. The landings were made skillfully and efficiently.

South of Rome, all around the perimeter of that Anzio beachhead, the Germans were attacking today, and were beaten off time and again with heavy losses.

*February 21, 1944*—The war news is good tonight from all over the globe, even from the Anzio beachhead. General Mark Clark's forces just below Rome are on the offensive again.

So anxious is Hitler to drive the Fifth Army into the Tyrrhenian Sea that he detached nine crack divisions from the army of General von Mackensen, in Russia.

The latest on our great naval victory at Truk is that the Japanese admit it. Radio Tokyo announced today that His Imperial Majesty's navy had lost two cruisers, three destroyers, thirteen transports, and 120 planes at Truk.

The latest bulletin from Admiral Nimitz tells of the capture of the island of Eniwetok.

*February 22, 1944*—Stalin repeated the contention that there was only one real front—the battle line in Russia. No second front.

*February 25, 1944*—In his recent statement to the House of Commons, Churchill reiterated the Allied intention of dealing with King Victor Emmanuel and Marshal Badoglio. And this was assailed today by the aged Count Sforza, leader of the Italian political elements hostile to the King. He repeated the demand—"King Victor Emmanuel must go."

The Nazi loss of great strongholds in Russia is getting to be monotonous. And today we have another—Vitebsk.

*February 28, 1944*—Adolf Hitler has given out one of his characteristic orders to his troops on the northern front: that his army must hold Pskov at all costs; fight to the last man.

*March 1, 1944*—The German secret weapon is a tank without a crew, a small, low-slung tank guided by wireless. It carries a 1,000-pound explosive charge, which is detonated by remote control. And so, in effect, the tank without a crew amounts to a rumbling land torpedo. The Russians saw that same contraption in action—the "beetle," they called it. And today a whole swarm of beetles scurried across the plain at the Anzio beachhead, heading for the British and American lines—the German idea being to touch them off when they arrived at a strong point.

Allied artillery opened upon the crawling beetles, and promptly knocked fourteen of them out—while others failed to keep going—apparently because of some mechanical failure. So the beetles were a washout.

*March 2, 1944*—General Mark Clark's Fifth Army has successfully withstood the shock of Field Marshal Kesselring's third attempt to throw the Allies back into the sea.

*March 3, 1944*—The fate of the surrendered Italian fleet was revealed by President Roosevelt today. It is to be divided between the United States, Great Britain, and Soviet Russia. The Soviets will receive about a third of the Italian warships, said the President—either that or the equivalent.

*March 8, 1944*—Rear Admiral Land, Administrator of War Shipping and Chairman of the Maritime Commission, said that American shipments to Russia at the end of last year were 33 per cent above schedule, and added that this was one reason why the Soviets were able to seize the offensive and hold it month after month.

There is heavy fighting on the Willaumez Peninsula of New Britain, on which the Marines landed Monday.

*March 10, 1944*—Washington has asked Dublin to break relations with enemy Germany and Japan, and kick out the diplomatic representatives of the Axis powers. But the De Valera government of Eire has refused, and insists on maintaining its neutrality.

Yesterday, in the London House of Commons, Prime Minister Winston Churchill stated: No, there was no intention of giving the Soviets one third of the Italian warships.

So what did President Roosevelt have to say today? He indicated that he was fully in accord with the Churchill statement, explaining that his own declaration of some days ago had been misinterpreted.

*March 13, 1944*—The Red armies are advancing all along a front of five hundred miles, all the way from Poland to the Black Sea. Marshal

Zhukov is now only about a hundred miles away from the old Czech border, and only fifty-two miles away from Rumania.

*March 14, 1944*—Gayda was killed in the bombing today. Virginio Gayda, the Italian journalist who for years was in the limelight as the No. 1 Fascist newspaperman and Mussolini's spokesman.

*March 16, 1944*—General MacArthur's men are tackling another island in the Admiralty group. The island is called Manus. And it's the largest of them all.

Another air raid on Truk.

*March 17, 1944*—Tonight the Nazis are still holding on to a corner of the shattered town of Cassino.

The surprise of the whole thing is that the Germans should hold any part of Cassino at all after the cataclysmic bombardment of the day before yesterday, which churned the town into a chaos of tumbled masonry.

*March 20, 1944*—The Nazis have taken over full control of Hungary. Admiral Horthy and the Hungarian generals are Hitler's prisoners.

*March 21, 1944*—The news from Burma is not good, with word today that the Japs now are within fifteen miles of the border of India.

Tonight Soviet troops have driven nineteen miles into the Rumanian province of Bessarabia.

Finland has rejected the terms of peace advanced by the Soviets.

*March 22, 1944*—Tonight in the city of Naples people are gazing at a spectacle of wonder and fear—a great tip of fire that flows blood red in the sky. It is the crater of Vesuvius, which has undergone a strange and ominous transformation. The top of the mountain has become incandescent, the volcanic summit red-hot, and it glows in the night like a giant ruby with a blood-red glare.

Tojo is becoming gloomier and gloomier—with good reason. The news today quotes him as giving warning to the Tokyo parliament that the Japanese military situation has become increasingly serious during the past six weeks.

Bombs on Rabaul, bombs on Wewak, bombs on New Guinea!

The Japs are across the Indian border at several points, and are trying to push their way to a place called Imphal.

*March 24, 1944*—The eruption of Vesuvius has subsided.

*March 27, 1944*—The Japanese invasion of India appears to be gaining headway.

*March 28, 1944*—The first great battle of the Japanese invasion of India is raging today on the edge of the plain of Manipur.

*March 29, 1944*—The attempt to take Cassino has been a failure, and the war is stalemated there.

The Dies committee today denounced the Political Action Committee of the C.I.O. as being Communist-controlled.

*March 30, 1944*—The four Japanese columns driving into the state of Manipur have been checked by British planes and heavy artillery.

*March 31, 1944*—A blow to the Allied cause was announced today—the death of General Wingate, leader of Wingate's Raiders. He was killed in Burma in an airplane crash—the Allies losing one of the fabulous personalities of this war.

*April 3, 1944*—The Red Army is driving across Rumania on a broad front.

In Washington, Secretary Hull is enthusiastic about that announcement from Moscow that the Soviet Union does not want any territory in Rumania.

Nazi newspapers from now on are forbidden to publish maps, that is, maps which show readers how the eastern front has changed.

*April 4, 1944*—There is ominous friction between the Polish underground and the invading Soviet armies.

*April 5, 1944*—This afternoon Wendell Willkie called together the newsmen who had been accompanying him on his campaign trips in Wisconsin and Nebraska. He told them he was withdrawing from the contest for the Republican nomination. This following the Nebraska primary—which he lost to Dewey.

*April 10, 1944*—The Red Army's entry into Odessa is the culmination of a drive that has covered more than nine hundred miles.

*April 13, 1944*—General MacArthur has proclaimed that young Dick Bong of Poplar, Wisconsin, Captain Richard Ira Bong to give him his title, is the ace of aces in the war against Japan, having just bagged his twenty-sixth and twenty-seventh Jap planes.

The Japs have begun a final all-out attempt to capture Imphal.

*April 14, 1944*—Tonight in North Africa, General Giraud was put on what is called the "reserve command list," meaning retirement. This ends the long competition between De Gaulle and Giraud, with De Gaulle finally winning out so completely that Giraud gives up the command of the French forces fighting the Nazis.

*April 17, 1944*—Sevastopol is in flames tonight while three Russian armies are fighting their way into that once great fortress.

A story from London tonight seems to indicate that the invasion hour draws near. The British Government has put an embargo on code telegrams by the diplomats of neutral nations.

British imperial troops have counterattacked the Japs besieging Imphal and are clearing the road to Kohima.

*April 18, 1944*—The British Government has suspended all travel between Britain and Cork, in southern Ireland—another precaution for the invasion.

In Russia, the Crimea, the Soviets have captured Balaklava—made famous by Tennyson's *Charge of the Light Brigade*.

*April 19, 1944*—In India the British have broken the siege of Kohima.

*April 20, 1944*—The Japanese invasion of Manipur has been definitely stopped.

One rather astonishing event in Russia today was a half page in a Moscow newspaper praising the United States. It was the Soviet Army paper, *Red Star*, which said: "The war production of the American people will play a great role in the final rout of Hitlerite Germany."

*April 21, 1944*—General Patton is in the British capital! Patton in London means that Patton will play a part in the invasion.

London announces the greatest air assault thus far, with the pre-invasion sky offensive coming to an all-time peak.

At Imphal the imperial forces drove forward today in fierce attacks.

*April 24, 1944*—MacArthur's swoop down upon the Japs in northern New Guinea seems to grow in importance by the hour. The general himself is on the spot.

Nobody may leave Britain except on business of urgent national importance which cannot be postponed.

The American air fleets that attacked Europe today are described as numbering upward of three thousand.

*April 25, 1944*—We hear of various trophies taken by American soldiers from dead Japs, and tonight's news tells of one of the most curious —a baseball bat autographed by Paul Waner of the Brooklyn Dodgers.

It is believed to have been signed by Paul Waner at the time when big-league players made a tour of Japan in 1931. Paul Waner was then at the height of his career as one of the greatest hitters in baseball.

*April 26, 1944*—In Chicago tonight soldiers of the United States Army took over one of the greatest mail order houses of the nation— Montgomery Ward & Company.

The whole thing began with a labor dispute in which Montgomery Ward refused to sign a contract with the union on the grounds that it had not been shown that the union represented employees of the company.

Over in England there is a man who hears the roar of bombers overhead, and it has driven him nearly mad. He is Rudolf Hess, that strange prisoner of war in Britain—the former No. 2 Nazi who flew to Scotland on a fantastic mission of peace. At his place of detention somewhere in England, Hess can hear the fleets of bombers overhead day and night as they fly to bomb Germany. He is a flier himself, and knows what it means— the doom of Naziland.

A new protest against the Allied bombings of Nazi cities was made public in London today—the Bishop of Birmingham joining other Anglican churchmen who denounce the obliteration air assaults designed to wipe out Nazi cities.

*April 27, 1944*—Sewell Avery, president of Montgomery Ward & Company, is sixty-nine years old but he's rugged—and it took two soldiers to throw him out of his own office today. Each of the two soldiers grabbed one arm and one leg of the sixty-nine-year-old business executive, carried him downstairs and through the store, and then threw him on the sidewalk. This was done by the order of Attorney General Biddle himself, who explained that Avery had refused to turn over the books of Montgomery Ward to government officers, refused to call a meeting of the staff, refused to co-operate in any fashion.

Perhaps the most important story of the day is the news of the recent meeting between General MacArthur and Admiral Nimitz. They have co-ordinated their plans so that in future operations they can throw the full weight of the forces under their command against the Japanese in concerted operations.

At midnight last night the population of the British Isles, some fifty million people, became completely isolated from the outside world. By government order, all travel abroad ceased, even for diplomats—except the envoys of the United States, Russia, and the British dominions.

*April 28, 1944*—Late news from Denmark tells us that Nazi troops are concentrating on the peninsula of Jutland and Danish civilians are being evacuated.

*May 1, 1944*—In Burma, American tanks are now in action with General Stilwell's army. The first time American tanks have been used on the continent of Asia.

*May 2, 1944*—The War Department reveals that Lend-Lease planes are being flown to Soviet Russia by Red Army pilots, by what is called "the northern air route." Meaning, presumably, via Alaska. They have been doing it for two years. But it is disclosed only now.

*May 3, 1944*—In Congress today there were scathing denunciations of Soviet Russia because of Stalin's attitude toward Poland. A series of lawmakers called on the United States to take a stand to defend Poland against the Soviet demands.

*May 4, 1944*—The German Army has declared an entire province of Holland a prohibited zone, the province of Zeeland.

German generals are making tours of inspection among the garrisons of the Atlantic coast, giving the soldiers pep talks.

*May 5, 1944*—On the ground at New Guinea the news continues—

Japs are surrendering. They are not so determined to die for their Mikado any more.

Mahatma Gandhi to be released. The Mahatma will emerge from his place of imprisonment tomorrow.

All along, the British Indian government refused to release him unless he gave a formal pledge that he would do nothing to impede the war effort. This Gandhi consistently refused to do. And now he's been released unconditionally, without any promise, because of his illness. It's apparent that the British do not want him to die on their hands and become a martyr.

*May 8, 1944*—The Japanese were attacked again on a big scale in the Manipur hills in eastern India.

*May 9, 1944*—The Montgomery Ward employee election turns out to be a victory for the union.

So what do we have tonight as a result of all the noise and excitement? Montgomery Ward is back in the hands of its owners, who will negotiate with the union.

Headline from Russia—Sevastopol captured. This completes the Russian reconquest of the Crimea.

*May 10, 1944*—While the Japs continue to lose out in their invasion of India, our own forces are scoring new successes in northern Burma. That is, forces of American-trained Chinese under the command of Lieutenant General Stilwell.

The new Secretary of the Navy was named today, previous reports turning out to be true. The President has chosen Acting Secretary James V. Forrestal to succeed Frank Knox.

*May 16, 1944*—In Italy the fury of battle is raging near that much embattled place, Cassino.

In Burma, General Stilwell's Chinese troops are continuing their push down the valley of the Mogaung River.

*May 18, 1944*—A Chinese-American army has advanced fifty miles up the Mogaung Valley in Burma and has captured the main airfield at Myitkyina.

After all these months Cassino is finally in the hands of the Allies.

*May 22, 1944*—The weather has improved in Europe, and consequently the air war is again on an around-the-clock schedule: on a bigger scale than ever.

*May 23, 1944*—A new republic is due to appear on the roster of the nations of the earth—Iceland. Today the people of that island up toward the Arctic Circle completed a referendum in which they definitely decided to sever their bonds with the King of Denmark and become entirely independent.

*May 25, 1944*—We have been waiting for months for this news from Italy: the main body of the Fifth Army has joined up with the forces at the Anzio beachhead.

At his news conference today the President was asked about his hospital checkup and the fourth term, but he parried all questions with gay quips and laughter.

*May 29, 1944*—Around the Imphal plain, in India, the British and the Japs are fighting more desperately than ever.

*May 30, 1944*—At Buffalo a Congress of Polish Americans demands what it calls "Atlantic Charter treatment for post-war Poland." In other words, Polish Americans ask that the country of their ancestors be given the good treatment provided for in the Atlantic Charter.

*June 1, 1944*—American soldiers today had their first view of the Eternal City.

*June 2, 1944*—Heavy American bombers flew from bases in the west, hit the Nazis, and kept going straight to the land of the Soviets. And so today began shuttle bombing—with Soviet bases as one terminus.

Today Pope Pius XII spoke for moderation in the war, moderation in victory. He expressed the fear that the policy of total victory and unconditional surrender would only cause the Germans to fight to the final gasp of desperation.

*June 5, 1944*—Rome has been captured. Columns of American tanks, armored cars, and infantry moved down the broad Via dell' Impero, which seven years ago Benito Mussolini pointed out to me, as we stood on the balcony of the Palazzo di Venezia, as one of his proudest achievements.

President Roosevelt commented on the fall of the first of the three great capitals of the Axis powers, and said, "One up and two to go."

*June 6, 1944*—Tonight's communiqué just in from D-day invasion headquarters summarizes the news. "Allied forces," it says, "have succeeded in their initial landings in France; and fighting continues."

The vaunted Atlantic wall was not so formidable as had been anticipated.

Allied troops are battling in the streets of the Norman city of Caen. That place is nine and a half miles inland.

The events of today were studded with records. The greatest fleet of ships ever to set sail—four thousand ships and thousands of lesser craft. The greatest army ever to strike at a hostile shore—that vast force of men and machines, tens of thousands of men increasing to hundreds of thousands, millions before it is over. And the greatest air assault ever delivered.

President Roosevelt says that the decision to launch today's blow was made last December, at the Roosevelt-Churchill-Stalin conference in Teheran.

In Soviet Russia the D-day invasion news was announced with all the military fanfare that attends the proclamation of a great Red Army victory.

*June 7, 1944*—General Eisenhower paid his first visit to the embattled Norman coast, making the trip aboard a British warship. He made a tour of all the beachheads, without, however, going ashore.

The news emphasizes heavy fighting—increasingly heavy. The Allied troops have cleared the Norman beaches which they seized, and have linked up the beachheads.

In Italy the Allied advance is continuing at lightning speed.

The Japs in invaded India appear to be in a state of collapse tonight.

*June 8, 1944*—We know definitely that the first phase of the great invasion is a success. This is stated at supreme invasion headquarters, and the reports from there are consistently conservative.

The people of the old Norman town of Bayeux almost went wild with joy today as Allied troops poured into their town.

All indications are that the Germans are bringing up forces from many directions for a concentration against the Allied beachheads.

Today the Allies captured the important railroad town of Viterbo—on the main line from Rome to Florence.

*June 12, 1944*—At the end of the day British troops are having a fierce battle with Nazi units near Caen.

One of the big events of the seventh day of the invasion was the capture of Carentan, the anchor point of the German defense line across the neck of the Cherbourg peninsula.

General Eisenhower visited the front in Normandy today, and with him were General Marshall, Chief of Staff, General Hap Arnold, chief of the Air Forces, and Admiral King, commander-in-chief of the United States Navy. In another part of the line was Prime Minister Winston Churchill, visiting the British end of the front.

*June 13, 1944*—The news from that battle front in Normandy indicates that the Nazi command is throwing into the fight now one fourth of all its forces available in France and the Low Countries.

*June 14, 1944*—Tonight the Allied column is placed twenty miles inside of France.

Tonight on an Allied beachhead in France there is a French general—De Gaulle.
It is a striking development—De Gaulle setting foot on French soil for the first time in almost exactly four years.

The new Nazi line of defense in Italy has already been broken.

The storm of war is pushing and roaring into Finland. The news tonight tells of Red Army forces smashing their way steadily through the Karelian Isthmus.

*June 15, 1944*—Word from Admiral Nimitz at Pearl Harbor of a landing, in force, on the island of Saipan in the Marianas, not far from Guam and less than fifteen hundred miles from Tokyo.

The Allied high command announces that our bridgehead on the French beaches tonight is secure and Montgomery's armies are now in the build-up stage.

*June 16, 1944*—Tonight those new strange things of menace are flashing over the English countryside—the Nazi robot planes. Late accounts picture fantastic scenes as the flame-shooting rockets go streaking through the sky.

We find ourselves on the verge of breaking diplomatic relations with Finland, and maybe declaring war.

American troops are pushing forward on the island of Saipan.

*June 19, 1944*—A task force off Saipan in the Marianas, destroyed more than three hundred Japanese planes at one clip. The biggest air battle of the entire Pacific war.

The Russians have completely smashed the celebrated Mannerheim line in Finland.

The Allies tonight have a stranglehold on the Cherbourg peninsula.

Everybody in Europe tonight is talking about that new weapon of the Nazis, the robot plane. It turns out to be a flying torpedo, propelled by a jet and launched from ramps in the area round Calais, in northern France.

*June 20, 1944*—There was mention today of a new army, the name of which was puzzling at first—the French Army of the Interior.
It turns out to be the underground, the partisan French patriots who are fighting the Nazis behind the invasion line.

American Flying Fortresses and Liberators bombed the bases for the robot planes this evening.

*June 21, 1944*—American troops are not only in Cherbourg—but are smashing their way to the area of the docks.

The Allies have captured several robot launching platforms in their drive against Cherbourg.

*June 22, 1944*—At this moment General Omar Bradley's flying columns are locked in battle with the Nazis in an all-out attack on Cherbourg.

London is still being hammered by the robot planes.

The much discussed "G.I. Bill of Rights" is an accomplished fact tonight. Became law this afternoon when President Roosevelt signed it.

*June 23, 1944*—The buzz-bomb attack against southern England continued today.

*June 26, 1944*—On Saipan Island the American forces have captured the biggest obstacle that confronted them—the tall peak, Mount Tapotchau.

We are told what the Germans think about the equipment of the American troops fighting on the Cherbourg peninsula. The Nazis there call our big invasion units "divisions de luxe" because they are so superbly equipped for their tasks of war.

*June 27, 1944*—"American business and American labor," declared Stalin today, "have done a remarkable job of production for war. American machines of war and American food," said Stalin, "have contributed to the successes of the Red Army in its victories."

The battle for the great port of Cherbourg is now over, save for two isolated nests where die-hard Nazis are still fighting.

A flash from Finland this afternoon announces that the northern republic has decided to remain in the war and has asked for German help.

*June 28, 1944*—At the Republican National Convention we had been told that, in spite of the overwhelming majority in favor of Dewey, the convention would stick to the routine of nominating all the other candidates.

But after the Governor of Nebraska had finished nominating Tom Dewey there followed the scene almost without precedent.

Governor Bricker gallantly seconded the nomination of his successful rival.

British armored forces have won the biggest tank battle of the Normandy invasion.

*June 30, 1944*—The advance of Soviet troops over the Berezina River is a historic spectacle. It was there that the Russians 132 years ago devasted the grand army of Napoleon.

Copenhagen, capital of Denmark, is paralyzed tonight by a general strike. The Danes have revolted against the Nazi suppressors and have hamstrung the Germans in Denmark.

*July 3, 1944*—At Minsk the Soviet legions are now 588 miles from Berlin. In Normandy the British and Americans are 640 miles away. General Clark's Fifth Army, pushing up the west coast of Italy, is 760 miles from Berlin.

*July 5, 1944*—In southern England the buzz-bomb terror campaign was in full blast today—with robots coming across the Channel in steady streams.

*July 6, 1944*—Hitler has fired Field Marshal von Rundstedt and appointed a new commander-in-chief for the forces in the west. The new man is Field Marshal von Kluge.

*July 7, 1944*—British today blasted those buzz-bomb nests with 6-ton superbombs—12,000-pounders.

Tonight's late bulletin from invasion headquarters states that American troops driving ahead are having a difficult time. The Germans are putting up a stubborn fight, and rain has turned the country into a sea of mud.

*July 10, 1944*—Over the entire island of Saipan tonight flies the American flag.

The Soviet armies tonight are pouring through gaps in the German defenses, rolling ahead on a three-hundred-mile front.

The Nazis are keeping up the robot-bomb attacks on London and on other points in southern England.

General de Gaulle left Washington for New York this afternoon, after a visit which appears to have been a complete success.

*July 11, 1944*—President Roosevelt announced today that De Gaulle's committee is now recognized by the United States as the working authority for civil administration in France.

There was a great exodus from London today, 41,000 people leaving, mothers and children. They are fugitives from what Londoners are calling the "ersatz blitz." That is, the buzz-bomb assault.

*July 12, 1944*—Partisan bands in France have been joined by parties of Allied Commandos.

*July 13, 1944*—Tonight Vilno, the key city in Lithuania, is in Russian hands.

A task force is throwing a terrific bombardment of shells and explosives into Guam.

General Mikhailovitch has announced his decision to form an independent government in Yugoslavia. He refuses to recognize or have anything to do with the partisans under Marshal Tito.

*July 14, 1944*—The battle in Italy is raging around two historic places, Leghorn and Arezzo.

*July 17, 1944*—The armies of Soviet Russia have now reached what is called the Curzon line, the Polish frontier as suggested by former British Foreign Secretary Lord Curzon.

House-to-house fighting in the streets of St.-Lô tonight.

*July 18, 1944*—Tojo has been removed as Chief of Staff of the Japanese Army. Apparently he still remains Premier. Three things occurred in swift and dramatic succession, the ousting of the navy chief, the removal of Tojo as Army Chief of Staff, and the announcement of the loss of Saipan. The logic is only too evident.

*July 21, 1944*—It is a foregone conclusion that the President will be nominated tonight on the first ballot.

In Chicago today one topic of conversation overshadowed even the convention, even the bitter fight for the vice-presidential nomination. The most exciting news, for delegates and spectators alike, was the bulletin telling of the latest attempt to blow up Adolf Hitler. This time the Fuehrer escaped by a far narrower margin. However, he did escape, with slight burns and bruises. The official Nazi news agency announced that the singed Fuehrer then went back to work and had a conference with Mussolini, the now much befuddled Duce.

In Normandy, Nazi Marshal Rommel threw an army of fifty thousand men into the breach to stem the advance of the British beyond Caen. All of which did not prevent Montgomery's men from capturing Vimont, on the main railroad to Paris.

Tojo and his entire Cabinet resigned after confessing they could not win the war.

Tonight's event at the Democratic Convention in Chicago is a classic example of the band wagon rolling to triumph. This time a Truman band wagon—so the ticket will be Roosevelt and Truman.

Today's news from Naziland began by identifying Colonel General Ludwig Beck as the leader of the plot to kill Hitler and seize control. Then later came the announcement that Beck had been executed for his part in what Nazi propaganda is calling the "general's *Putsch*."

The latest from Guam is—American advances from the beachheads. Army troops and Marines are pushing inland and are encountering increased resistance.

*July 24, 1944*—In Germany, Gestapo executioners are combing the country for leaders in the conspiracy.

*July 25, 1944*—The news from Guam tells of a junction of forces, a linking up of two beachheads.

On Tinian Island, nearby, the Japs have been making wild counterattacks.

Moscow announced today that the Red Army has begun what Moscow calls "the liberation of the brotherly Polish people." This liberation takes the form of establishing the authority of the Polish group in Moscow, the newly formed Polish Committee of Liberation, which supports the policies of Stalin.

*July 26, 1944*—The American drive on the invasion front of France has broken through the German lines and plunged out into open country.

*July 28, 1944*—In the far Pacific the battle of Guam is turning into a deadly affair for the Japs.

The American offensive in Normandy has cracked the German line wide open.

This evening Stalin announces the capture of Brest-Litovsk, the mighty stronghold of central Poland.

*July 31, 1944*—A spokesman at MacArthur's headquarters announced that the move had virtually completed the plan of campaign for New Guinea and has brought that entire great island under Allied control.

The British and the Yanks between them have now conquered the entire peninsula of Normandy except for a few scattered pockets of Nazi resisters.

For all the publicity about our superb military equipment, the equipment of our men in Normandy, we hear now that American tanks are not as good as German tanks.

*August 2, 1944*—The invasion drive today was a rush for the Americans, who swept on for startling gains of more than thirty miles in twenty-four hours.

Today's account from Berlin states: No, Rommel was not killed, but he was injured. He was banged and battered and suffered concussions, but has recovered. So say the Germans. The Nazis explain that it happened in what they call an "accident." But they add that the accident occurred during an air attack. Apparently it was an automobile wreck, caused by an Allied strafing assault.

The battle of Florence has reached the peak of violent fighting.

The Red Army is pouring like a flood through Lithuania.

Words of high hope were spoken today in London, with Churchill doing the talking. "I fear greatly to raise false hopes," said Winston Churchill, "but I no longer feel bound to deny that victory may perhaps come soon."

*August 4, 1944*—The Russians have driven twenty-two miles beyond the river Vistula, and are thundering across the plains of Poland.

*August 7, 1944*—London today reports that the First Canadian Army, under the command of Lieutenant General H. D. G. Crerar, is now in France. This means that at least three Allied armies are in action on that western front.

The Nazi attack on England with robot bombs was resumed today, and the Nazis have added a new twist to it. Many of the latest buzz bombs, as they exploded, scattered quantities of small incendiary bombs in all directions.

*August 8, 1944*—The Soviet advance is rolling on beyond the Vistula—though against increased opposition. The Germans are rallying bitterly to defend the soil of Germany, and have orders from Hitler to stand or die.

Twenty thousand Polish patriots are defending parts of Warsaw against ferocious Nazi attacks. And a Polish warning is given that the insurrection cannot continue to hold out unless direct help is given by the Russian Army, which has reached the outskirts of the city.

In Moscow tonight skepticism was expressed in Soviet circles—skepticism about the uprising in Warsaw, doubt that there was any such thing.

Here is testimony from still another quarter—the Nazis. There was an official Nazi announcement today that the Poles in Warsaw had staged an uprising—a large-scale affair. But the revolt of the patriots has been suppressed, say the Nazis.

In Nazi Germany today they hanged a field marshal, a colonel general, a lieutenant general, a major general, and four other officers—including a count of ancient noble family. Proud aristocrats of the Prussian military caste, all put to death as the commonest malefactors might be—by hanging, condemned for their part in the plot to kill Hitler.

*August 9, 1944*—On the eastern front the Germans are launching last-ditch attacks to defend East Prussia.

*August 10, 1944*—Today the news was released for the first time that Mr. Roosevelt passed three days at Honolulu, his first man-to-man inspection of the war against Japan. He had conferences with both General Douglas MacArthur and Admiral Chester Nimitz.

One of the thrilling incidents of the fall of Guam was the rescue of George Ray Tweed, born at Portland, Oregon. He was chief radioman on Guam when the Japs landed. He escaped and managed to live hidden on that small island for thirty-one months. When the American task force finally attacked the island, Tweed swam from shore out to one of our ships, and now he's in San Diego with his family.

*August 11, 1944*—The insurrection in Warsaw is likely to lead to new bitterness between the Poles and the Russians. Today's word is that the Polish patriots who, in their capital, rose against the Nazis are in a desperate plight. Their commander, the mysterious General Bor, sends wireless word that his partisan forces cannot hold out much longer against the powerful German drive to crush the revolt.

*August 14, 1944*—Today's reports indicate that the stories of the destruction of ancient buildings in Florence were exaggerated. It now appears the most important of the classical monuments have been spared.

*August 15, 1944*—Tonight American troops landed in southern France—a 120-mile stretch of the coast between Marseilles and Nice.

*August 16, 1944*—In southern France, American and British forces have captured that famous resort town on the Riviera—Cannes.

A savage battle is raging along the borders of East Prussia.

The battle for the city of Warsaw takes a new turn with the arrival of supplies for the patriot Poles who are fighting the Nazis—supplies from the sky. A force of British planes flew nine hundred miles to Warsaw, and there dropped guns and ammunition into the section of the city which the Poles are defending.

This brings wireless word of gratitude from the Polish commander, the mysterious General Bor.

The news from London is that the buzz bombs hit hard today.

*August 18, 1944*—German propaganda is preparing the German people for the fall of the capital of France.

Stories from southern France grow more spectacular every hour.
Americans and veterans of the Free French are now fighting on a front 150 miles wide.
A considerable part of the Spanish frontier is now in the hands of the Free French.

The Russians admit a definite defeat for the first time since their latest big offensive began. The evacuation of a section of Latvia thirty-three miles east of Riga.

The long-heralded three-power conference at Dumbarton Oaks began today, the conference to outline preliminary drafts of a world organization to keep the peace.

In Paris tonight the partisan forces inside the capital are now battling the German garrison.

*August 22, 1944*—Nazis arrested the aged head of the Vichy government, Marshal Pétain, on Sunday, together with a number of his officials, and took them to Germany.

*August 23, 1944*—While Paris rejoiced over liberation today, London had a grim time of it. For today brought a climax of the buzz-bomb assault.

*August 24, 1944*—French columns driving to the relief of the patriots in Paris are under the personal command of General Charles de Gaulle himself and General Jacques LeClerc, the man who led a division from Lake Tchad in the heart of the Sahara all the way to Tunisia last year.

*August 25, 1944*—Tonight Allied forces are in complete control of the capital of France, not a German soldier left in the historic city save as a prisoner of war.

Rumania has declared war on Nazi Germany!

There is important news about Winston Churchill in Rome. It tells of a long conference the British Prime Minister had today with Pope Pius XII.

Pope Pius is said to have urged that in the framing of peace terms the principle of nationalities be maintained, the pontiff arguing that nationalities do not die. And among the nationalities foremost in the Pope's mind was Poland.

*August 28, 1944*—French patriots today announced that they have arrested nine celebrated Frenchmen on charges of having collaborated with the Nazis. One of them is well known to the American theater, the playwright and actor, Sasha Guitry.

There is fierce fighting in the streets of Warsaw between Polish patriots and Nazi troops.

*August 29, 1944*—Tonight the news features such nostalgic names as Chateau-Thierry, Soissons, Reims, the Aisne, the Marne, and the Somme, and the Hindenburg line.

The ground that Pershing's doughboys on foot had to gain yard by yard in slow and bitter trench fighting Patton's armor is eating up in great rolling strides of battle.

This was a day of days in Paris. The American Army made its formal entrance.

Moscow announces the capture of the great Rumanian port of Constanta, which the Nazis used as a basis for what warships they had in the Black Sea.

*August 30, 1944*—It was stated in London today that the American and British have already drawn up long lists of Nazi war criminals.

The chairman of the commission was asked whether Hitler's name was at the head of the list. To which he replied dryly: "The list is alphabetical."

*August 31, 1944*—The British and Canadians, our own troops, and the Fighting French, are on the rampage all over France.

Eisenhower tells us that his troops have destroyed the cream of the German Army.

*September 4, 1944*—Tonight the Allies are across the border of Holland.

British troops made their formal entrance into Brussels today—an entrance amid cheers and acclamation.

Finland is out of the war—the Helsinki government has surrendered to Soviet Russia.

The Russians took the offensive again today in Poland. The Germans are putting up a savage battle.

The Poles today made the bitter charge that the Warsaw patriots have been abandoned by their Allies and left to their fate.

*September 5, 1944*—Red Army troops are moving for a junction with the Yugoslav partisans commanded by Marshal Tito.

*September 6, 1944*—The Bulgars have asked for an armistice.

*September 7, 1944*—The presidential campaign began in earnest tonight. Dewey started with a direct frontal attack on the New Deal.

From General Omar Bradley's headquarters we have the definite report that Hitler's battered armies of the west are in headlong flight for the fatherland.

*September 8, 1944*—Today Soviet troops crossed into Bulgaria.

The great Belgian fortress of Liége was captured today by the American First Army.

*September 11, 1944*—Today American troops crossed the German frontier and are tonight fighting on the soil of Hitler land.

The British tonight are in Holland.

General Patch's men have occupied Dijon.

Advanced guards of the Third White Russian Army have crossed the river separating Poland and East Prussia, home of the German *Junkers*.

Admiral Halsey has launched our first naval attack on the Philippines. He sank eighty-nine Jap vessels.

President Roosevelt and Prime Minister Winston Churchill are now in Quebec, engaged in what they call their "victory conference."

*September 12, 1944*—Today's dispatch declares that five thousand planes were in action over Germany, assailing everything in sight—from the fortifications of the Siegfried line on back to war plants in central Germany.

American and British planes have brought new supplies to the patriot forces fighting in the Polish capital.

*September 13, 1944*—Today American troops crashed into the Siegfried line.

The German big guns near Calais are hurling streams of shells across the Channel.

This was the sixth day of the sustained knockout air offensive against Germany, and once again Allied air power was out in stupendous force.

Governor Dewey tonight declared that MacArthur should be given what Dewey called "greater recognition and adequate supplies."

*September 14, 1944*—Planes of Admiral Halsey's Third Fleet are still attacking the Philippines.

American troops are now eleven miles over the German border.

Italian partisans announce that they have begun a general offensive in northern Italy.

In Warsaw, Polish patriots are still fighting the German garrison.

*September 15, 1944*—The Siegfried line has been cracked open.

The Finns are now fighting the Nazis.

Tonight a savage battle is on at Palau, the Marines having landed on the key island—Peleliu.
For weeks we've been hearing how army bombers based on New Guinea were smashing Halmahera, and this is now followed by a landing on the key island of Morotai.

*September 18, 1944*—The toughest of all the tough battles fought so far in the Pacific is now going on, on the island of Peleliu.

*September 19, 1944*—Tonight in Copenhagen a battle is on between the Danish police and German troops.

British troops have reached the Rhine.

*September 20, 1944*—Late news tonight places the most critical point of battle at the northern tip of the line, near the Dutch city of Arnhem. That's where air-borne forces landed—on the other side of the Rhine.

Soviet troops today entered Finland in accordance with yesterday's armistice, and are now fighting against Nazi forces in the northern republic.

*September 21, 1944*—Our air-borne troops are completely surrounded by the Germans at Arnhem.

The Red armies have begun the big battle for East Prussia.

*September 22, 1944*—On Peleliu Island, so close to the Philippines, the battle for the caves continues.

In Holland the air-borne force beyond the Rhine is in a more critical position than ever.

Stalin tonight announces the capture of Tallinn, the capital of Estonia.

*September 25, 1944*—When the history of this war is written, one of its epic chapters will be the story of the battle of Arnhem, the stand of those air-borne divisions encircled by the Nazis north of the river Rhine.

*September 26, 1944*—A mystery commander was identified today—General Bor, the legended leader of the Polish insurrection in Warsaw. A forty-six-year-old Polish officer named Komorowski.

In Italy, Allied troops have crossed the Rubicon.

*September 27, 1944*—The remnants of the British paratroop force beyond the Rhine in Holland have been evacuated.

American forces are now in complete control of Peleliu Island.

*September 28, 1944*—The Russians are in Czechoslovakia.

The invasion of Hungary, plus the defeat of Hungarian troops in the Carpathians, has thrown that country into a panic.

Warnings to neutral nations: If you give shelter to Adolf Hitler, Ribbentrop, Goebbels, Goering, Himmler, or any other Nazi criminals, you are no friends of ours. And that's official: announced today by Secretary Hull.

Winston Churchill announced what amounted to the approval of the British Government of the proposition that Soviet Russia take over certain Polish territory.

*October 2, 1944*—There is a much oversung song called "The St. Louis Blues," but there are no blues in St. Louis tonight. The slogan is the St. Louis Browns. Yes, they are the pennant winners of the American League for the first time in the history of the club.

*October 3, 1944*—The patriot uprising in Warsaw has ended, the partisan forces fighting the Germans have had to yield, surrender.

Tonight Moscow, in telling of the surrender of the patriot forces in Warsaw, continues its angry tone against them, saying that General Bor gave up without consulting the Allies.

*October 5, 1944*—In Greece tonight the German garrisons are retreating as fast as they can all over the entire peninsula, the historic Peloponnesus.

Co-operating with the British, the partisans under Tito are attacking the Germans all over Yugoslavia.

*October 6, 1944*—The latest tells of Allied invasions of half a dozen Grecian isles—historic bits of land in the Aegean Sea.

*October 9, 1944*—General Hodges' army today sealed the fate of the Nazi garrison at Aachen—Aix-la-Chapelle.

The name of the new organization to police the world and enforce peace is to be the United Nations.

Winston Churchill is in Moscow.

*October 10, 1944*—British and Greek patriot forces today occupied the legended city of Corinth.

New York is paying a great tribute to Wendell Willkie, whose death was an unexpected shock. Tens of thousands thronging for a last farewell.

*October 11, 1944*—The Russians are continuing their sweep across the flat Hungarian plains.

*October 13, 1944*—The big Russian bulletin tonight is: Riga captured!

The flag of Greece flew triumphantly from the Acropolis today. Meaning, Athens liberated.

Here is a statement on the health of the President made by the White House physician, Admiral McIntire. He describes the Roosevelt physical condition in these words: "He is in good shape."

*October 18, 1944*—The United States has two major fleets in the Pacific, each of which is powerful enough to defeat the entire navy of Japan. Secretary Forrestal mentioned the Third Fleet, commanded by Admiral Halsey, and the Fifth Fleet, commanded by Admiral Spruance.

Hitler today ordered the mobilization of every German boy and man from sixteen to sixty years old for a fight to the finish inside of Germany.

Russian forces today drove clear across Czechoslovakia.

*October 20, 1944*—Tonight's picture of the invasion of the Philippines shows our troops driving inland from beachheads on Leyte.
"I am particularly anxious," said MacArthur, "to get at the division which is on Leyte. It is the 15th, the outfit that did the dirty work at Bataan."
An intensely dramatic phase of the Philippine invasion is the degree to which it is a personal MacArthur affair.

In France today a sentence of death was pronounced against Laval, *in absentia*.

Belgrade captured today! The capital of Yugoslavia taken by Russian troops and Yugoslav partisans.

*October 23, 1944*—The reconquest of Leyte is so rapid that civil units have followed close behind the Army. Osmeña, President of the Philippines, arrived in Leyte along with MacArthur.
The front on Leyte now extends along a continuous line of about twenty miles, and at all points is more than five miles inland.

*October 24, 1944*—An organized Philippine guerrilla army of four thousand men is fighting to join forces with the Americans.

From the fighting front in Europe we have a statement that the fanatical bitter-end resistance of the Germans is being inspired by talk back in the

United States—talk of a harsh and relentless peace to be inflicted on defeated Germany.

German prisoners speak constantly of that much talked about "Morgenthau Plan," which would reduce Germany to a pastoral economy.

*October 25, 1944*—The story of the great naval victory off the Philippines becomes clearer as the hours pass, as the dispatches pour in.

It's a surprising picture—that of Japanese fleet units coming out through narrow channels between islands and engaging the American warships.

Early in the engagement one of the enemy battleships was sunk. Carrier planes hit hard, and several cruisers and destroyers were sunk, three battleships and three cruisers were heavily damaged. The Japanese force, beaten up like that, turned and fled.

The MacArthur dispatch states that for long months a vast network of agents in all of the islands have been working on behalf of the United States.

*October 26, 1944*—And now for the score of yesterday's big naval battle of the Philippines: ten enemy warships definitely sunk, including one 29,000-ton battleship, two aircraft carriers, four cruisers, and at least three destroyers.

*October 27, 1944*—The Japs today made a candid admission that their fleet had taken a heavy blow.

Churchill, in a report to the House of Commons on his recent talks with Stalin in Moscow, devoted the most attention to the Russian-Polish dispute, which was discussed in Moscow by himself, Stalin, and the Premier of the Polish Government in Exile. "I wish," said he to the Commons, "that I could tell the House that we had reached a solution of these problems. It was certainly not for the want of trying," he added.

*October 30, 1944*—Military observers point out that the Russian armies now are fighting on the longest front ever recorded in military history.

In Washington congressmen today declared that the Political Action Committee of the C.I.O. and the National Citizens Political Action Committee were instruments with which Communists are fighting for control of a major political party.

*November 2, 1944*—MacArthur's men have fought their way to the north coast of Leyte.

*November 3, 1944*—The great seaport of Antwerp is now ours.

Says dictator Franco: His country has never been either Fascist or Nazi, and has never been allied in any fashion, secret or otherwise, with any Axis power.

*November 6, 1944*—Tonight the whole world wonders whether Joseph Stalin is going to throw the might and power of the Soviet Union against the Japanese. For today he threw aside his hitherto literal neutrality and described Japan as an aggressor nation.

In the Japanese homeland the jittery inhabitants continue to talk about reconnaissance flights over the Tokyo end of the main island, reconnaissance flights by the B-29s.

Tomorrow war news will be of secondary importance for the first time since the Japanese attacked us at Pearl Harbor. Both sides agree that it will be one of the most important election days in the history of the United States.

*November 7, 1944*—In the election today early figures favor Roosevelt.

General MacArthur now announces that the enemy succeeded in landing reinforcements on Leyte and heavy fighting is going on.

The new enemy boss has a name of sinister meaning for Americans—Yamashita. He commanded the Japanese Army in the overwhelming of the outnumbered Americans at Bataan and Corregidor.

*November 8, 1944*—The Roosevelt presidential victory had its effect on the races for Congress—the Republican hope of winning the Lower House was not fulfilled.

Today in Cairo two killers said: "Yes, we are members of the Fighters for the Freedom of Israel organization, and what we have done we did on instructions of the organization." They assassinated British High Commissioner Lord Moyne.

*November 9, 1944*—In case it's any consolation to the Republicans, Mr. Roosevelt wins this time with the smallest plurality of any President since 1916.

*November 10, 1944*—Japanese commander Yamashita is committing all his forces to the battle on Leyte, trying to drive MacArthur's men into the sea.

During the weeks of secrecy British scientists were studying the V-2, and today they present an alarming picture for the future—a prospect fantastic and inhuman for future wars, if any.

British scientists today are foreseeing a new kind of war—with giant rockets as one of the most formidable of weapons.

*November 15, 1944*—The conflict on Leyte is mounting, and casualties are growing in what is described as the bitterest fighting of the Philippine campaign.

*November 20, 1944*—General de Tassigny, leading the First French Army in a record overnight march of twenty-eight miles, has blasted loose the entire left flank of the Germans and driven through the Belfort Gap, right up to the river Rhine.

The Soviets have launched their big winter offensive on the Baltic front.

News from Norway. The Nazis are in full retreat from Lapland.

*November 22, 1944*—New word comes of disturbances inside of Germany. In Cologne the Nazis machine-gunned a peace demonstration.

*November 24, 1944*—The story of the B-29 attack on Tokyo is almost twenty-four hours old, but it remains the exciting news of the day.

American infantry have begun the "watch on the Rhine." They joined up today with the 2nd French Armored Division, under General Jacques LeClerc, at Strasbourg.

Estonia now is completely freed of the German yoke.
The battle is now on for Latvia.

*November 27, 1944*—On the western front the Allied offensive has definitely slowed down.

*November 29, 1944*—Late news tonight tells of still more B-29s over Tokyo.

*December 1, 1944*—It was announced late this afternoon that there will be no court-martial for either General Short or Admiral Kimmel, the army and navy commanders at Pearl Harbor on December 7.

*December 4, 1944*—With martial law proclaimed in Athens, the British commanding general ordered all armed forces of the Elas, the left-wing party, to leave Athens and the port of Piraeus within seventy-two hours.

*December 5, 1944*—In London, Prime Minister Winston Churchill today reaffirmed British support of the present Cabinet in Athens. He stated that the purpose of the leftist organizations was to set up a Communist dictatorship—this with weapons provided by the Allies.

The main forward action on the western front was in the Saar today—Patton's Third Army storming ahead.

*December 6, 1944*—This afternoon British warplanes went into action against the leftist rebels in Athens.

*December 7, 1944*—Admiral Nimitz, by way of commemorating the Pearl Harbor attack, tells us today that all the six Jap aircraft carriers which attacked on December 7, 1941, are now at the bottom of the sea.

In Greece the British today were using warships as well as artillery and planes to fight the discontented Elas Greeks.

*December 8, 1944*—A record-breaking sea and air raid has hit the Japs on the island of Iwo Jima, in the Volcano group.

The Japs are abandoning the northern half of Burma.

More bridgeheads across the Saar River—that's the news from the western front today.

The civil strife in Greece went on unabated today.

Churchill today agreed that the liberated peoples should have the choice, but he said he wanted to be sure that it was the people and not some gang trying to seize power by violence.

Late today the House of Representatives voted to create new and higher ranks for our American Army and Navy commanders—the ranks of general of the army and admiral of the fleet—these to be on the level of the highest European ranks.

Four army commanders are to have that lofty status of general of the army. They are Chief of Staff General Marshall, air force commander General Arnold, supreme allied commander in Western Europe General Eisenhower, and supreme allied commander in the Southwest Pacific General MacArthur. And four navy commanders are to have the rank of admiral of the fleet: navy commander Admiral King, Presidential Chief of Staff Admiral Leahy, Pacific Fleet commander Admiral Nimitz, and Third Fleet commander Admiral Halsey.

*December 11, 1944*—De Gaulle is on his way back to Paris after signing a treaty of alliance with Soviet Russia.

Tonight, Budapest in flames. With the Nazis getting out as fast as they can, under a rain of bombs and shells from Soviet guns.

On Leyte the Yanks of the 77th Division have wiped out the entire garrison at Ormoc.

There is a virtual state of war between the British and the Greek Elas.

*December 12, 1944*—Tokyo is being evacuated, millions moving out of the enemy capital that is now under the bombs of the Superfortresses.

*December 14, 1944*—British labor leaders are still indignant about the goings on in Greece, but Churchill stands pat.

H. G. Wells said: "Mr. Churchill has served his purpose and it is high time he retire. In the midst of a still uncertain war," continued Wells, "this ineffable Prime Minister of ours has precipitated us into a class war and on the wrong side."

*December 15, 1944*—In the Philippines the invasion of Mindoro—just announced.

Today's crossing of the border now places the Allied armies either inside Germany or along the frontier, all the way from Switzerland to southern Holland.

In the House of Commons, Prime Minister Winston Churchill today came out flatly in favor of the Moscow demand for pre-war Polish territory —about half of pre-war Poland.

The civil war in Greece is not only continuing, but is spreading.

*December 18, 1944*—The big story tonight is that counterattack the Nazis mounted over the weekend.

Little by little, we learn how far the great German counterattack has smashed the lines of the American First Army.

Reports that filter in give an alarming picture of the depth of the German penetration.

*December 19, 1944*—The word from the western front continues to be ominous—great battles raging, with the German offensive still in progress.

American planes report masses of German tanks and armored vehicles moving westward, the roads choked with motorized equipment on its way to the front.

Ring the gong! Make it forty for Dick Bong! Our No. 1 ace has shot down another Jap in air battle over Mindoro, boosting his total to a record-breaking forty!

*December 20, 1944*—The news of the general German offensive has featured the fact that the Nazis are using robot bombs in their drive forward—sending swarms of the robot planes against the American lines.

*December 21, 1944*—The Germans have now driven thirty miles into Belgium.

*December 22, 1944*—Since the last report the Nazis have gained from nine to twenty miles.

They have surrounded Bastogne, which is only thirty-seven miles from the historic fortress of Sedan, and they are still advancing.

*December 25, 1944*—Here's a Christmas present for the American people—a gift from MacArthur. In a dispatch this afternoon he announces: "The Leyte campaign has been closed."

Tonight's MacArthur bulletin states: "General Yamashita has sustained perhaps the greatest defeat in the annals of the Japanese Army."

The latest picture from the western front is one of American drives to cut into the flank of the salient that the Germans have thrust forward—while Nazi forces continue to advance at the tip of the bulge.

*December 26, 1944*—Von Rundstedt's offensive rolls on.

This afternoon's word from Athens indicates that there was indeed a conspiracy to blow up British Prime Minister Winston Churchill. The dynamite plot discovered was meant definitely to get Churchill—together with Foreign Secretary Anthony Eden, British commander in Greece General Scobie, and officials of the legal Greek Government.

*December 27, 1944*—The American troops pocketed at Bastogne have been relieved.

*December 28, 1944*—The B-29s over Tokyo again today.

Today we have an official confirmation of previous reports that the German commander in the invasion battle of Normandy committed suicide because of the Nazi defeat: Field Marshal Guenther von Kluge.

*December 29, 1944*—The fighting in Greece today became hotter than ever.

# 1945

This is a year of great events in quick succession. Germany and Japan both surrender unconditionally. Hitler commits suicide in his Berlin bunker as Marshal Zhukov's troops storm through the wreckage of the city. Mussolini is captured and executed by Italian Communists. MacArthur assumes control of Japan and begins a process of democratization.

President Roosevelt dies, and is succeeded by Vice-President Truman. In England, Winston Churchill suffers a staggering defeat in the elections. He is succeeded by Socialist Clement Attlee, who starts to nationalize British industry.

As the year ends, two great problems are formidable—one caused by science, the other by politics. The atom bomb has knocked Japan out of the war, but it also raises the fear of a new and more horrible kind of conflict. Men and women everywhere begin to be tormented by the question of whether this new destructive force can be controlled and harnessed for peace instead of war.

The political problem follows from the Yalta Conference between Roosevelt, Churchill, and Stalin. Roosevelt tells the country that peace and freedom have now been secured, but some critics question the wisdom of trusting Stalin, a feeling that will become general as he breaks his promises, foments civil war in China, imposes Communist tyranny on the nations of Eastern Europe, and shows the first signs of disrupting the new United Nations.

*January 1, 1945*—Today the exiled Polish Government denounced the Lublin Committee, declaring that the Soviet-sponsored group was abolishing democratic liberties. London refuses to recognize the Lublin Committee as the government of Poland.

*January 2, 1945*—The American air forces based on the Philippines and in China now overlap in the territory they cover.

The crisis has passed on the front of the Belgian salient. The Nazis are in retreat.

*January 3, 1945*—The estimate from Allied headquarters is that Von Rundstedt has thrown in two hundred thousand troops—units of infantry and armor—to hold the bulge.

*January 4, 1945*—Yesterday large formations of our carrier-based planes attacked not only Formosa, but also the island of Okinawa, which is even closer to Tokyo.

*January 5, 1945*—The most ferocious battle of the western front campaign is being fought along the northern side of the German salient in Belgium.

Moscow today recognized the Soviet-sponsored Lublin Committee as the official government of Poland, and this causes a split between the United States and Britain on one side and Russia on the other.

*January 9, 1945*—By this time American troops have pushed inland for deep advances in the invasion of Luzon.

General MacArthur himself went ashore with his troops. He is described as having been in high spirits as he set foot on the soil of Luzon—on the road to Manila. Yes, and on the road to Bataan, where he commanded the heroic defense.

*January 10, 1945*—The Germans are pulling out as fast as they can from the western tip of the salient in Belgium.

*January 11, 1945*—The Lublin provisional government of Poland has already commenced the job of splitting up the big Polish estates among the small farmers.

The civil war in Greece is over. Leaders of the Elas, the left-wing Greek rebels, signed a truce with the British Army.

*January 12, 1945*—Field Marshal von Rundstedt has succeeded in getting the bulk of his armor and infantry out of the trap.

*January 16, 1945*—For three days Halsey's planes have been smashing at the Japs, along 350 miles of the China coast.

*January 17, 1945*—In Poland the whole German line is receding, following the Russian capture of Warsaw.

MacArthur's men are pushing down the Luzon coast in the direction of a peninsula, the one with the famous name—Bataan.

*January 23, 1945*—Tonight Soviet troops are in Germany, along the Oder River.

The Germans, before withdrawing from the city of Tannenberg, blew up the famous Hindenberg monument. At Tannenberg, Germany's military hero of the last war, the formidable Von Hindenberg, won his reputation by inflicting a disastrous defeat upon the Russians of the Czar.

On the western front today they were battering in what remains of the German salient.

*January 25, 1945*—The Russians have cut off the province of East Prussia.

*January 26, 1945*—The new Ledo Road, successor to that famous Burma Road, has begun operations—the way cleared by the recent reconquest of northern Burma from the Japs.

On the western front the battle of the salient has ended.

*January 30, 1945*—The fall of Berlin to Zhukov's army might not be many days away. And that's a name to remember—Zhukov. It seems likely that he is the Soviet leader scheduled to command the Russian capture of the capital of the Nazis.

Hitler's harangue tonight, if it means anything at all, another indication of Nazi determination to make Germany fight it out to the bitter end, a ruthless blood-mad resistance.

*February 1, 1945*—Huge Soviet armies are spreading terror and devastation in Pomerania, Brandenburg, and Silesia. Their battle cry is: "Remember Stalingrad!"

*February 5, 1945*—Europe is agog with rumors about the place where President Roosevelt, Prime Minister Churchill, and Marshal Stalin are holding their conference.

*February 6, 1945*—There is house-to-house fighting in Manila tonight.

While the conference of the Big Three is trying to harmonize possible points of disagreement, the exiled Polish Government in London issues a pronouncement emphasizing the bitterness of the Polish-Soviet dispute.

It excoriates the Red Army refusal to help the uprising of the patriots in Warsaw and to permit American bombers to use Russian air bases in bringing supplies to the patriots.

The Japs have set fire to the downtown business district of Manila.

The Russians have forced their way across the Oder.

*February 7, 1945*—General MacArthur made his official entrance into Manila today, receiving a fervid ovation—MacArthur, who had said he would return.

Marshal Zhukov's army is now on the highway that leads to Berlin.

American forces have smashed completely through the Siegfried line.

President Roosevelt, Prime Minister Churchill, and Premier Stalin have concluded their discussion of war measures for the final defeat of Nazi Germany.

The huge fires set by the Japs in Manila caused hardly any loss of life, but thousands of Filipinos are homeless, and today they are shouting a vengeful slogan—"Burn Tokyo!"

*February 9, 1945*—The bitterest kind of fighting is going on in south Manila.

*February 12, 1945*—As many people guessed, President Roosevelt, Winston Churchill, and Stalin met in the summer palace of the Russian Czars at Yalta, the beautiful watering place east of Sevastopol. Before Roosevelt went to the Crimea, he had a consultation with Churchill on the island of Malta in the Mediterranean.

This is the decision on Poland: a Polish provisional government to be set up. And "This Polish provisional government of national unity shall be pledged to the holding of free and unfettered elections."

This means that Washington and Downing Street have thrown overboard the Polish Government in Exile in London.

Another raid by B-29s, at a place with a now familiar name, Iwo Jima.

*February 13, 1945*—The London Polish attitude is reflected in the United States, where Polish-American groups today spoke up in protest. In Washington, Congressman John Lesinski of Michigan, who is of Polish descent, stated that the decision should not be allowed to stand—the Yalta decision depriving Poland of so much of its pre-war territory.

*February 14, 1945*—Today's hint from Tokyo is that the Japs are willing to make peace. The only trouble, from the Tokyo point of view, is that instead of a hand offering peace the American hand is offering unconditional surrender.

At Cairo today the Foreign Ministers of six Arab nations met to form an Arab union.

*February 16, 1945*—The reconquest of Bataan, announced a few hours ago, has an emotional meaning for every American—Bataan, the scene of the heroic defense.

*February 19, 1945*—One American newspaperman, who saw the landing on Iwo Jima from a bomber, describes the island as smoking from end to end as our battleships, cruisers, and bombers continued the bombardment. From only a thousand feet up he saw marines dashing ashore, wave after wave of them, on the southeastern beach.

*February 20, 1945*—On Iwo Jima, Japanese resistance increases with every hour. And tonight's dispatch states: "Iwo has become a hell on earth" —a Pacific isle turned into an inferno of war.

Now comes the turn of exotic romance, the Roosevelt meeting with three kings, three kings of the East. Farouk of Egypt, Haile Selassie of Ethiopia, and Ibn Saud of Saudi Arabia. Their talks obviously emphasized the situation in the Middle East.

*February 21, 1945*—Savage fighting continues on Iwo Jima, on Corregidor, and in Manila.

*February 22, 1945*—The terror of Iwo is disclosed today in the somber tones of casualties, a dispatch from Pacific Fleet headquarters stating that the Marines were now incurring casualties that have risen from seventy-seven an hour to ninety casualties an hour.

*February 23, 1945*—On the western front the big Allied push began today.

On Iwo Jima the Marines have captured that volcano, the mountain called Suribachi, at the southern tip of the island. They raised the American flag on the dominating summit today.

*February 27, 1945*—The news tells of shattering melodrama on Corregidor. The subterranean Japs have been blowing themselves up.

Winston Churchill in Parliament today upheld the Polish settlement agreed upon by the Big Three at the Yalta Conference.

"The Poles," he said, "will have their future in their own hand, with the single limitation that they must honestly follow, in harmony with their allies, a policy friendly toward Russia."

*February 28, 1945*—The battle for Corregidor is over.

*March 1, 1945*—President Roosevelt set another precedent when he appeared before both Houses of the Congress today and made his personal report of the Yalta Conference.

One important sentence contained these words: "It spells the end of the system of unilateral action and exclusive alliances and spheres of influence and balances of power and all other expedients which have been tried for centuries—and have failed."

Henry Wallace is the new Secretary of Commerce.

*March 2, 1945*—There is no letup in the ferocity of the battle on Iwo Jima.

*March 5, 1945*—American troops are in the city of Cologne, fourth largest in Germany.

We learn today from Washington about the rules to be followed by the Security Council of the new United Nations in settling international disputes. The first rule is that any one member of the Big Five, the United States, Britain, Russia, China, or France, can veto the use of force or sanctions either against itself or against any other country involved in the dispute. That means that the new league will be impotent to stop an aggressor nation by either force or sanctions if the aggressor nation happens to be one of the Big Five.

*March 6, 1945*—The battle on Iwo Jima is playing out to a nightmare conclusion. Mad attacks made by Japs who are crazed by thirst.

*March 8, 1945*—Apparently the advance units of the First Army achieved a complete surprise, a surprise not only to the enemy but even to our own forces. They rolled so fast that they arrived at the Ludendorff Bridge, at Remagen, south of Cologne. There they found that the Germans had not had time either to organize a defense or to destroy the bridge. An advance patrol doubled across the Ludendorff Bridge, found no opposition, and established a bridgehead.

*March 9, 1945*—That slugging, bitter fight for Iwo Jima is still on.

*March 12, 1945*—The First Army now has a bridgehead on the east side of the Rhine that is ten miles wide and five miles deep.

Tonight the news that Kustrin has fallen to the First White Russian Army of Marshal Zhukov.

*March 13, 1945*—The latest giant rain of fire from the sky has hit Japan's No. 2 city—Osaka.

News from the western front is still focused on that bridgehead across the Rhine.

*March 14, 1945*—The American flag was formally raised on Iwo Jima today, signalizing the conquest of the island.

*March 15, 1945*—Six huge Allied armies are attacking the Germans simultaneously in the Saar and Ruhr valleys.

Zhukov is throwing reinforcements into the battle for Berlin. The Germans will soon be swamped, overwhelmed.

*March 20, 1945*—Tokyo admitted today that the B-29 raids were causing heavier damage than bombing ever did to Nazi Germany.

The status of Hitler as a war criminal was announced officially in London today.

*March 22, 1945*—Hitler has fired Field Marshal von Rundstedt as commander-in-chief on the Rhine, replacing him with Field Marshal Kesselring, who proved such a tough nut to crack in Italy.

Goebbels continues to hold the great illusion before his people, the idea that the Allies are quarreling and will split if only the German people will hold out long enough. That seems to be the secret weapon that Hitler dangles before his unfortunate followers.

*March 26, 1945*—While Winston Churchill was returning to London from the front, his famous predecessor, Lloyd George, died at his home in Wales, bringing to an end one of the most spectacular careers in British history.

*March 27, 1945*—Seven giant Allied armies are pouring swiftly into the heart of Nazi Germany.

*March 28, 1945*—American troops beyond the Rhine have reached the first prison hospital to be captured by the Allies, and what they found enraged them. The hospital is described as "a living hell of starvation, filth and medical neglect."

*March 30, 1945*—The news from the western front pictures a wildly surging advance, with Allied columns driving ahead at breakneck speed.

All dispatches indicate that one of the greatest mass surrenders in history is in progress on the First and Third Army fronts.

The Russians have captured the city that was the Nazi pretext for starting the war—Danzig.

*April 2, 1945*—Thrilling news from Okinawa tonight! The American infantrymen of the XXIV Army Corps have cut all the way across the island.

The British are now one hundred miles east of the Rhine, tearing ahead at a pace literally terrific.

*April 4, 1945*—The Russians are storming Vienna tonight.

Late news from Okinawa states that the battle for that island has begun —the violent clash that has been expected.

*April 5, 1945*—By the manner in which Stalin denounced the neutrality pact with Japan he leaves the door open for an immediate attack upon the Mikado's empire from the maritime provinces of Siberia.

By a decision of the Joint Chiefs of Staff of the United States, MacArthur becomes commander-in-chief of all American Army forces in the Pacific; and Nimitz, of all the naval resources.

*April 6, 1945*—American troops today captured a trainload of V-2 rockets—the first of the stratosphere missiles that the Allies have been able to lay their hands on.

Sarajevo—the capital of Bosnia in Yugoslavia—was taken today by the forces of Yugoslav Marshal Tito. Sarajevo, where the fateful shots were fired in 1914, the shots that touched off World War I.

The battle on Okinawa is developing into a savage struggle.

*April 9, 1945*—The battle of southern Okinawa has reached the phase of hand-to-hand fighting.

Tonight the First and Third armies of the United States are together east of the Weser River on a hundred-mile front.

*April 10, 1945*—Today American scout planes flew over the German capital, and they report that Berlin appears to be a deserted city.

Word has just come in that General Eisenhower announces: "German resistance in the West has collapsed."

*April 11, 1945*—On Okinawa savage fighting continued today.

*April 12, 1945*—The city often referred to as the Athens of Germany, the city of Weimar, home of Goethe and Schiller, and birthplace of the German Republic, in 1919, fell today—captured by General George Patton's onrushing tanks.

Four hours have now elapsed since the nation, and for that matter the world, was stunned by the news of the death of President Roosevelt.

He was posing for his portrait as he sat in front of the fireplace in his cottage at Warm Springs, Georgia, while he was going over a big stack of state papers. At one o'clock he suddenly exclaimed: "I have a terrific headache!" A quarter of an hour later he fainted. A Filipino attendant picked him up bodily and carried him into a small bedroom in the cottage, which was known as the "Little White House." Mr. Roosevelt never regained consciousness.

On Okinawa the fighting has become as grim as it was on Iwo Jima.

*April 13, 1945*—It has been noted that Harry Truman is a plain and modest Midwesterner, whom surprising circumstance has carried from ward politics back in Missouri to the presidency of the United States. And today with the newsmen he certainly was in character.

Talking to them, he said: "Boys, when they told me yesterday what had happened, I felt like the moon and stars and all the planets had fallen on me."

The race for Berlin goes on, with five American armored columns on their way to the Nazi capital.

Vienna fell today.

*April 16, 1945*—East of Berlin tonight are long lines of Russian heavy guns, wheel to wheel, letting loose a thundering bombardment upon the capital of the German Reich.

*April 17, 1945*—President Truman held his first news conference to-day. He said he would be happy to meet Churchill and Stalin.

The Allied drive in Italy is making progress.

*April 18, 1945*—There was justice indeed in General Patton's order compelling German civilians to make a sight-seeing tour of the Nazi prison camp near the city of Weimar. There have been endless rumors about the horrors of Hitler prison camps, rumors that now become reality as those places of Nazi ferocity are captured by American forces. One of the worst was at Weimar, the city so famous in the annals of German liberalism and enlightenment—Weimar, with its shrines dedicated to the poets Goethe and Schiller. There is no need of trying to describe the ghastly scenes, but there was justice in compelling the citizens of Weimar to behold them.

On Okinawa bitter fighting raged today.

The story of the death of Ernie Pyle, killed by a Japanese bullet, shows that he lost his life in the line of duty—duty specifically as Ernie Pyle said it. He was the poet laureate of the common soldier in the foxhole, and he met his end with the infantry.

*April 20, 1945*—The Russian drive on Berlin is in full swing.

General Eisenhower stated today that the meeting of the Americans and Russians would soon take place.

*April 23, 1945*—The most dramatic and popular part of the news tonight concerns the battle of Berlin. Soviet Marshals Zhukov and Konev, between them, already have two thirds of the German capital.

*April 24, 1945*—Two Russian columns have joined forces in the heart of Berlin.
Hitler is in Berlin—directing the final convulsions of Nazi power.

At San Francisco the leaders of the United Nations are ready for the beginning of the conference tomorrow.

*April 25, 1945*—Tonight Berlin is encircled.

*April 26, 1945*—Benito Mussolini has been captured again. A group of Italian patriots found him at the town of Pallanza, on the west shore of Lake Maggiore.

Better news from Okinawa tonight. The Yanks have smashed the first Japanese defense line.

*April 27, 1945*—Genoa fell today; Genoa, the home town of Christopher Columbus, captured by the American Army.

Today at San Francisco, Molotov demanded that the conference admit the Soviet-sponsored provisional government of Poland. To this, American Secretary of State Stettinius replied with an immediate no, polite but firm. And others of the United Nations rallied to his support.

The long-awaited meeting of the troops of the Western Allies with the Russians is announced with formal precision in statements issued simultaneously in Washington, London, and Moscow.

The official meeting of the forces occurred today at the town of Torgau, on the river Elbe.

*April 30, 1945*—When I talked to General Mark Clark, word had come from Italian partisans that Mussolini had been picked up. That was all, at first. But as we sat at lunch a penciled note was handed to the general. It read: "Mussolini, his mistress, and a group of his close associates —eighteen in all—have been shot, and their bodies are now on exhibition in a public square in Milan."

The Red flag of victory flies tonight over the Reichstag Building, once the home of the parliament of the Reich.

*May 1, 1945*—At press headquarters here in Paris there is much excitement tonight; that is, during the last few minutes. All caused by Admiral Doenitz's broadcast telling the Germans, and the rest of the world, that Hitler is dead, that he died yesterday defending the Reichschancellery in Berlin; and that he, Admiral Doenitz, is stepping into his place to lead the German forces and fight on.

*May 2, 1945*—Mussolini dead, and the war officially coming to an end in Italy; Hitler dead, so it appears if we can believe Admiral Doenitz, and Berlin tonight entirely in the hands of the Russians; German forces everywhere trying to give themselves up; our airmen given orders not to fire on horse-drawn transport along roads for fear of killing refugees; it all adds up to one thing: that the Nazis have little, if any, fight left in them.

The Russians announce that the Nazi Fuehrer killed himself.

*May 3, 1945*—Among the places that have fallen to the Americans

is Braunau. In case you don't remember, it is the place where Adolf Hitler
was born.

The confusion in Germany is quite indescribable.

From Munich tonight comes a story that plump little Eva Braun, the
Fuehrer's lady friend, died with him.

*May 4, 1945*—The surrender of the German armies in the northwestern part of Germany, in Holland, and in Denmark leaves the situation generally as follows: There are only two areas now in which formidable enemy forces are still holding out—in Norway and in Czechoslovakia.

One minor headline today is the capture of Berchtesgaden.

Today the French government of De Gaulle joined the United States
and Great Britain in protesting against the establishment, under Soviet
auspices, of an Austrian provisional government.

A late story tonight gives us an interview with Nazi Field Marshal von
Rundstedt, now a prisoner of war. Von Rundstedt, telling of the victorious drive of the Western Allies into the heart of Germany, cited a
reason that will surprise nobody—Allied air power. He said the tremendous
American-British air superiority paralyzed the German war machine.

The Burma campaign is at an end.

*May 7, 1945*—Following yesterday's announcement of Germany's surrender, Admiral Doenitz has ordered all U-boats to return to port immediately.

*May 8, 1945*—Well, the Great Russian V-day mystery was solved
this evening when Moscow, for the first time during the day, made mention of the end of the European war.

There is, we note, no mention of the Western Allies, no mention of the
British or American armies, only the Red Army.

*May 9, 1945*—Things were quiet in Norway. The archcollaborationist,
Quisling, is a prisoner tonight.

Goering surrendered today.

Today Tokyo propaganda, having to tell about the end of the European
war, retained as much face as it could—stating that the Japs will fight on,
no matter.

*May 10, 1945*—Investigators of four nations are combing the Continent looking for thousands of Nazi war criminals. The hunt includes

the dead as well as the living. They want to be quite sure that they are dead. Number one among those, of course, they want Adolf Hitler.

The German fleet began surrendering today.

*May 11, 1945*—We have a new story about the end of Rommel, the old Fox of the Desert, who won the top reputation among German commanders. Today his widow stated that he was put to death by the Nazis, on orders from Hitler.

Internecine quarrels among the Yugoslavs were sharpened today by an announcement that General Mikhailovitch, once so famous as the leader of the Chetniks, will be tried as a traitor and shot.

*May 15, 1945*—The battle on Okinawa raged with wild fury today.

The Russians announce that they have found the body of Goebbels.

*May 21, 1945*—The fighting on Okinawa continues to be more ferocious than anything ever seen or imagined before.

*May 22, 1945*—American and British troops moved today into the province of Istria—which is in dispute between the Western Allies and Marshal Tito's Yugoslav regime.

Here's a new name for Hitler—"a unique natural catastrophe." This term is applied to der Fuehrer by his personal physician, Dr. Theodor Morell.
The doctor states that Hitler was so strangely unbalanced that his type of abnormality did not fit into any of the usual psychological patterns.
He denies a lot of legends. For example—that Hitler was a rug chewer who flew into uncontrollable rages and bit the carpet. On the contrary, the Nazi dictator was most dangerous and made his most important decisions when he was in a cold and silent rage.

*May 23, 1945*—All the suppositions that President Truman would drastically revise the Cabinet left to him by President Roosevelt were confirmed today—with the White House acceptance of three resignations. The departing Cabinet members are Attorney General Biddle, Secretary of Labor Frances Perkins, and Secretary of Agriculture Wickard.

Tokyo took its heaviest air battering today.

The final vestige of the Nazi regime was eliminated in Germany today with the abolition of the acting German government headed by Admiral Doenitz.

One of the most notorious of Nazi leaders has been captured in south Germany, Julius Streicher. This No. 1 Jew-baiter among the Nazis was found today at a farm and turned over to American troops.

*May 24, 1945*—Heinrich Himmler is dead. The infamous Gestapo chief killed himself last night by poison. He was being held in a villa at Lueneburg in northwestern Germany by the British.

*May 28, 1945*—On Okinawa the Yanks are killing the Japs at a rate of almost one thousand a day.

*May 29, 1945*—New gains on Okinawa.

The British have captured Lord Haw-Haw—the Nazi propaganda voice with the cultured Oxford accent—who was long a favorite joke in England.
Lord Haw-Haw is William Joyce, who was born in New York of Irish parents.

*May 30, 1945*—Japan reports that most of Yokohama lies in ruins. After yesterday's great fire attack by B-29s sixty thousand houses were destroyed by the tempest of flames. Two hundred and fifty thousand persons are homeless.

*June 4, 1945*—Tokyo announced today that the entire aviation corps of the Mikado's navy has become a suicide force for attacks on American and British warships.

The Congress of the Arab League convened at Cairo today. The Arab leaders hope and believe that this means the beginning of Pan-Arab unity for the first time since the capture of Baghdad by the Mongols.

*June 5, 1945*—One of the important events in post-war Europe occurred today—the organization of the Allied Supreme Control Commission for the government of the conquered Germany.
The commission met for the first time in Berlin, Marshal Zhukov representing Soviet Russia, General Eisenhower the United States, Field Marshal Sir Bernard Montgomery Great Britain, General de Tassigny France.

*June 6, 1945*—Russia repeats its charge that the Western Allies are mistreating Soviet prisoners of war. This accusation was made previously, and has been officially denied by Great Britain.

*June 7, 1945*—In Turin military police arrested the American woman who used to broadcast Fascist propaganda. The doughboys christened her "Axis Sally."

Her name, Rita Louisa Zucca. She was born in New York City.

King Haakon, tall, slender, smiling, seventy-two years old, returned to Oslo after five years of exile.

There was only one secret agreement made at Yalta. That's what Winston Churchill told the House of Commons today. That one agreement was the two extra votes for Russia at the San Francisco Conference.

*June 8, 1945*—The indications are that President Truman's policy is having an effect in Japan—his policy of assuring the Japanese people that unconditional surrender does not mean that they will be destroyed or enslaved. The Truman Declaration in pamphlet form has been showered on Japan by American planes.

*June 15, 1945*—The capture of Von Ribbentrop is now official.

*June 20, 1945*—Another story about the end of Hitler. It comes from the personal chauffeur of the Nazi Fuehrer. At Berchtesgaden today Hitler's automobile driver stated that both the Fuehrer and his sweetheart, Eva Braun, committed suicide. This, he says, was on April 30—and they had been married two days before. They shot themselves, he declares, in the underground shelter of the Chancellery in Berlin.

What happened to the bodies? They were burned, says the chauffeur. This had been ordered by Hitler to keep the bodies of himself and his newly married wife from falling into the hands of the Russians.

*June 21, 1945*—All of the major cities of Japan have been knocked out by the B-29s.

On Okinawa the battle is all over.

*June 22, 1945*—The Japs appear to be afflicted with the same kind of nervous apprehension that the Germans displayed just before the D-day invasion of Normandy. They are doing all sorts of agitated guessing about the place where the next blow will fall.

From Okinawa a scene that is certainly surprising—the first mass capitulation of Japanese troops.

The Polish Government in Exile announced today that it is going to lodge an international protest against the conviction of twelve of the sixteen Polish leaders who were tried in Moscow.

*June 26, 1945*–Today was signature day out here in San Francisco. Delegates one after another have been putting their names on the Charter of the United Nations.

*July 2, 1945*–The Senate today confirmed the nomination of James F. Byrnes as Secretary of State.

*July 3, 1945*–The Americans marched into Berlin today.

The Polish provisional government in Warsaw has accepted the principle of free and unfettered elections.

Harry Hopkins retires. He has been in bad health for some time.

*July 5, 1945*–Great Britain recognized the new Polish Government.

Henry Morgenthau is out as Secretary of the Treasury.

*July 6, 1945*–The new Secretary of the Treasury will be Fred M. Vinson.

*July 9, 1945*–President Truman tonight is on the high seas. He sailed from the naval base at Norfolk late Saturday, accompanied by a large staff.

*July 10, 1945*–The Russians, Americans, and British have finally got together in conquered Berlin, and have set up an Inter-Allied Commission to govern the city.

*July 11, 1945*–From the cruiser *Augusta*, aboard which President Truman is crossing the Atlantic:
"Today President Truman held a conference with Secretary of State Byrnes and Presidential Chief of Staff Admiral Leahy. They talked over American positions to be taken in negotiations with Soviet Premier Stalin and British Prime Minister Churchill in the meeting of the Big Three at Potsdam."

*July 13, 1945*–A sweeping decree was issued in Berlin today–a decree that sounds like an economic revolution. The city government ordered the confiscation of the property of all Nazis and of everybody who supported or profited by the Nazi regime.

*July 16, 1945*—The Russians have already removed at least half of all heavy machinery in the big industrial plants of Berlin.

Out there in the Far Pacific, "Toohy" Spaatz took over today. From now on the air war out there will be run by the man who headed up our strategic air forces in the air war on Germany.

*July 17, 1945*—The headline of the day—the Big Three conference gets under way.

The tremendous airplane and warship assault against Japan continued today.

*July 18, 1945*—Great American and British air fleets are still smashing at Tokyo.

A subcommittee of the House of Representatives gives a list of thirteen army officers who are charged either with being Communists or having a Communist background.

In the list of names given by the committee today, one immediately catches the eye. Lieutenant Joe Lash. Time was when that name was rather familiar, when Joe Lash, heading a youth movement, was a guest at the White House, a protégé of Mrs. Roosevelt.

*July 23, 1945*—A historic trial began today, the trial of Marshal Henri Pétain, former head of the Vichy government.

*July 25, 1945*—The Big Three conference is marking time while Prime Minister Churchill is in London awaiting the election returns.

*July 26, 1945*—It's difficult to speak of the big news of this day without a feeling of sadness. For today's news has brought us the story of the fall of a titan. And he went down as great men usually go down, engulfed by a landslide—the landslide that sweeps Winston Churchill and his Conservative government out of office in Britain.

Major Clement Attlee now becomes King George's First Minister. The first time in history for Labour to go into office in England with a clear majority.

Japan's plea for more lenient surrender terms was answered today in a spectacular proclamation issued from Potsdam by President Truman and Prime Minister Winston Churchill, also signed by Generalissimo Chiang Kai-shek. It stated the terms of the Allies in no uncertain language. The terms are: unconditional surrender.

*July 30, 1945*—Winston Churchill has refused the highest honor which can be bestowed on a British subject. King George VI asked him to become a Knight of the Garter, an order usually reserved for the highest nobles of the kingdom, and for members of the royal family. Churchill replied that he wanted to continue in politics without any title.

*July 31, 1945*—Another string of Jap cities is on the death list. Today American B-29s dropped three quarters of a million pamphlets on twelve more Japanese war centers, notifying them that they are marked for destruction.

Laval arrived in Austria today, and was made a prisoner by American forces there. He is being turned over to the French as a war criminal.

*August 1, 1945*—The meeting of the Big Three has ended—Generalissimo Stalin, President Truman, and Prime Minister Attlee bringing the Potsdam Conference to a close.

The archcollaborationist, Pierre Laval, was brought to Paris today, a prisoner charged with treason.

*August 3, 1945*—On an American cruiser steaming westward across the Atlantic a blunt and outright statement was made today—made with a Midwestern accent, Missouri. President Truman stated that at recent meeting of the Big Three there had been what he called "no secret agreements of any kind."

It will be recalled that after the previous Big Three meeting, the one at Yalta, President Roosevelt subsequently told of agreements that had not been mentioned in the announcement of the Yalta decisions.

*August 6, 1945*—That news about the atomic bomb overshadows everything else today; and the story of dropping the first one on Japan.

The way the Japanese describe last night's raid on Hiroshima indicates that this one bomb was so destructive that the Japs thought they had been blasted by squadrons of B-29s all loaded with bombs.

*August 7, 1945*—The American-British-Chinese warning to Japan was deliberately given in advance of the atomic bomb, the Japs warned in time. They did not yield, and then, according to schedule, elemental devastation hit them.

*August 8, 1945*—Russia declared war ahead of schedule.

The Washington information is that when Stalin learned of the cataclysmic destruction wrought by the atomic bomb dropped on Hiroshima he decided on war against Japan right away.

*August 9, 1945*—The Far Eastern legions of the Soviet Union have struck at the famous Kwantung army of the Mikado in Manchuria.

Planes based on Guam flew over the Japanese home islands today, scattering some three million leaflets; urging the people to petition Emperor Hirohito to surrender at once, unconditionally. Also notifying them that two of their cities, Hiroshima and Nagasaki, had been almost wiped off the face of the earth; that unless they give in all their cities will get the same fate.

*August 10, 1945*—Discussions by radiotelephone are being held, discussions of Japan's offer of surrender.

As the Japs decided to give up, the Russians were driving into Manchuria.

*August 13, 1945*—More than two days have elapsed since that Allied reply was sent on its way to Japan.
Washington believes that Japan may be stalling.
Of course, all sources acknowledge that Tokyo may be in turmoil.
The air war in the Pacific is raging with full fury.

*August 14, 1945*—The Japanese reply is now at the White House—and President Truman is considering it.

Today a series of hot headlines came blazing across the wire, taking up a lot of space, and the echo was: so what! Moscow sent a whole batch of detailed war bulletins about sensational Red Army advances into Manchuria.

*August 15, 1945*—The Chinese Reds are on the move, trying to take as much as they can under the surrender. They have rebuffed a Chiang Kai-shek order to stay put, and are hurrying to take over from the Japs.

In London, King George today delivered his royal address to the new Parliament, with its Socialist majority. The sovereign of Britain announced a beginning in the establishment of socialism in Britain.

*August 16, 1945*—Winston Churchill today cut loose in his battle against communism, his first move as leader of His Majesty's loyal opposition. In so doing he made the broad statement that dictatorial Communist forces are trying to dominate Europe "by terroristic methods." And he demanded that the secret of the atomic bomb be restricted to the United States and Britain.

*August 17, 1945*—Tokyo informed General MacArthur today that the surrender envoy will proceed to Manila on Sunday.

The death sentence imposed on Marshal Pétain has been commuted—as was expected. Today General de Gaulle followed the recommendation made by the court that condemned the aged marshal for treason. He commuted the death sentence to life imprisonment—which is not likely to last long, considering the great age of the one-time hero of Verdun, condemned for treason as the head of the Vichy government.

*August 20, 1945*—MacArthur issued a formal statement today that the Japanese emissaries have imparted to general headquarters all the information requested. And they are conveying the instructions of the United Nations to the Government of Japan and to Japanese imperial headquarters.

*August 21, 1945*—The surrender of Japanese forces in various parts of Asia and the Pacific is proceeding.

*August 22, 1945*—Japan gives its first detailed report on the atomic bomb, stating that the blast of elemental havoc at Hiroshima and Nagasaki killed 70,000 persons, injured 120,000, and made 290,000 homeless.

And Tokyo accentuates the unearthly terror of the atomic bomb by stating: "The number of dead is mounting, as many of those who received burns cannot survive their wounds because of effects of the bomb on the human body."

The official Soviet paper, *Izvestia*, states that an Allied supervision of elections would constitute an infringement of the sovereignty of the liberated states.

*August 24, 1945*—Here's another Arab statement that President Roosevelt promised that the United States would not support any move to establish Jewish control in Palestine, a dramatic repetition of the story that the late President gave that pledge to the Arab King, Ibn Saud, when the two met during the time of the Yalta Conference.

*August 27, 1945*—What a sight it must have been out there at Sagami Bay today! One of the spectacles of all time! The mighty Third Fleet, some four hundred ships, steaming up the bay and dropping anchor just off Tokyo.

In the Philippines, meanwhile, our forces at last have received an offer of surrender from none other than General Yamashita, the "Butcher of Bataan."

*August 28, 1945*—The conferences between the Chinese Nationalists and the Communists have begun.

*August 30, 1945*—There was a great moment today when Douglas MacArthur stepped out of his transport plane—the plane named *Bataan* —onto the imperial soil of Japan. As he set foot on the ground, MacArthur said: "Well, we got here, didn't we?"

*September 3, 1945*—Today's news palls before yesterday's historic event in Tokyo Harbor—when General MacArthur presided over the formal Japanese surrender aboard our great battlewagon, the *Missouri*.

*September 5, 1945*—American soldiers rolled into Tokyo today.

Lieutenant General Wainwright has been promoted. He becomes a four-star general. A fitting reward for the commander who stuck with his troops, went through three years of Japanese imprisonment and, upon being liberated, was present at the formal surrender of Japan.

*September 7, 1945*—The formal entrance into Tokyo will soon be staged, but Admiral Halsey will not ride Hirohito's white horse down the Tokyo Broadway—the Ginza.

Today's news dispatch from the admiral's flagship states that Halsey's cabin looks right now like what the dispatch calls "a supply dump for a cavalry regiment." That is, after all the saddles and bridles and stirrups and spurs that were sent to Halsey as a result of his announcement that he intended to ride the imperial white horse.

Having talked so grandly about riding Hirohito's white steed, Admiral Halsey now admits that he has never been on a horse in his life.

*September 10, 1945*—General MacArthur abolished Japanese imperial general headquarters, and he clamped down a strict censorship on Japanese newspapers and broadcasters.

*September 11, 1945*—The Pearl Harbor Premier of Japan is in a critical condition after shooting himself.

With Tojo's name at the head of the list, General MacArthur today ordered the arrest of all of the members of the Tojo Cabinet, which launched the war in the Pacific.

*September 12, 1945*—General MacArthur today took one of the most important steps for the elimination of militarism and fanatic nationalism in Japan. He ordered the abolition of the Black Dragon Society and the arrest of seven of its leaders, these to be tried as war criminals.

Tojo is getting better. American doctors report that he will probably survive, to face the court as a war criminal.

*September 19, 1945*—Today Lord Haw-Haw, the British traitor who did Nazi propaganda during the war, was found guilty of treason, and sentenced to hang.

*September 20, 1945*—Korean leaders are complaining that Korea has been divided into two zones without any consideration for either the interests or the wishes of the Koreans. One, the industrial zone occupied by the Russians; the other, the agricultural part of the country occupied by us.

For our soldiers in Europe, the lid is off on hobnobbing with the enemy.

*September 21, 1945*—From Trieste come charges made by American and British military authorities. They declare that in the country surrounding the city the Yugoslavs are conducting a reign of terror against the Italian inhabitants.

Today Henry Ford retired as head of the giant Ford Motor Company and turned that office over to his grandson, Henry Ford II.

*September 24, 1945*—It became known in London today that the British Government has offered to issue 1,500 permits a month for Jewish immigration into Palestine. But the World Zionist Organization and the Jewish Agency turned that down.

*September 27, 1945*—MacArthur has not disclosed a word of what passed between him and the Emperor during the thirty-eight minutes in which they talked.
Hirohito unquestionably humiliated himself in the eyes of his subjects and his ancestors. In two thousand years of recorded Japanese history no Emperor ever called upon a foreigner.

*October 2, 1945*—The official announcement is that Marshal Zhukov has been compelled to postpone his American visit because of illness.

Great Britain has rejected President Truman's proposal for greater Jewish immigration into Palestine.

In Japan, General MacArthur continues the task of liquidating the Japanese war machine.

*October 3, 1945*—Soviet Russia today renewed its demand that General MacArthur be removed from his post and be replaced by an international council.

*October 4, 1945*—MacArthur today ordered complete and widespread freedom of speech, and even abolished the law by which the Japs hitherto had been forbidden to discuss their Emperor.

*October 5, 1945*—French courtroom dramatics had another big day today as Laval fought for his life.

Laval put all the blame on Marshal Pétain—the old story of offenders trying to shift the guilt onto each other.

*October 9, 1945*—Laval is guilty of treason, and sentenced to death.

In Argentina, Perón has resigned. The No. 1 figure in the government of the colonels.

*October 11, 1945*—General MacArthur has informed the new Japanese Premier, Baron Shidehara, that Japan is to have woman suffrage, religion henceforth shall be free, education liberalized, and industry conducted on a democratic basis.

Workers in Japan are to organize unions.

There is more trouble in the Holy Land. An armed force, reported to be Jewish, raided a British Army training depot near Tel Aviv.

*October 15, 1945*—The courtyard of the French prison today was the scene of the most memorable execution of our time in France. A squad of a dozen French soldiers fired a volley into the body of Pierre Laval, the man of Vichy.

*October 17, 1945*—Soviet Russia has again demanded that General MacArthur be ousted.

The labor disturbances in Argentina increased today—strikes and demonstrations by workers in favor of Colonel Perón.

*October 18, 1945*—The military tribunal representing four Allied powers today received an indictment charging twenty-four leading Nazis with having plotted and started the second world war.

A copy of the indictment, in German, was sent today to Nuremberg, to be served on the leading defendants: Hermann Goering, Rudolf Hess, Von Ribbentrop, Field Marshal Keitel, and Grand Admirals Karl Doenitz and Erich Raeder.

All of central and eastern Java is seething: Nationalists versus the Dutch.

*October 22, 1945*—General MacArthur today tackled the problem of educating the Japanese. He published a proclamation ordering immediate and stringent reform of their entire school system. No more military drill at schools, and no teaching of ultra-nationalist ideas.

Mao Tse-tung's Communist troops are reported battling the Generalissimo's in Shantung.

*October 24, 1945*—In Norway today complete secrecy concealed the execution of Quisling.

The self-styled Indonesian Republic announces that it has created a regular army.

There are contradictory reactions to the advent of a Negro player into regular league baseball—the signing of Jackie Robinson. If Jackie Robinson shows he's of major league ability, he'll become a member of the Dodgers.

*October 29, 1945*—The trial of General Yamashita, the "Tiger of Malaya," began at Manila today.

The fighting in China now amounts almost to a full-fledged war.

Fighting in the streets of Soerabaja, the big seaport at the eastern end of Java. British and Dutch troops were battling Indonesians.

*November 1, 1945*—Molotov today turned down scornfully and abruptly an appeal from the Anglo-American Press Association in Moscow to mitigate the strictness of Soviet censorship.

British troops are now seriously engaged in the task of crushing the natives of Java for the benefit of the Dutch.

The story from Palestine today is one of explosions, destruction, sabotage, and shootings.

*November 5, 1945*—General MacArthur ordered the Tokyo Cabinet to break off diplomatic relations with the agents of neutral countries in Japan. All foreign diplomats are to make contacts with the Japanese through MacArthur's headquarters.

*November 6, 1945*—Holland offers home rule to the revolting Indonesians in Java.

*November 7, 1945*—The Dutch offer of home rule has been turned down by the Indonesian leader, Dr. Soekarno.

*November 8, 1945*—President Truman today opened the doors on all Pearl Harbor information in the possession of the United States Government.

*November 12, 1945*—Today the Indonesian Republic, turned down by the United States and Great Britain, appealed to Stalin.

*November 13, 1945*—General de Gaulle was elected Chief of the Government of France today.

President Truman has accepted the British compromise plan for dealing with the question of Palestine.

*November 14, 1945*—The Jewish general strike in Palestine flared with violence tonight, with wild fighting in Tel Aviv.

The fighting is still going on in Java.

*November 15, 1945*—Tonight it's an investigation of Pearl Harbor! The committee room was jammed as Senator Alben Barkley called the meeting to order this morning. Among the deeply interested spectators were Admiral Kimmel and General Short, both in civilian clothes, accompanied by their counsel.

Uncle Sam is not going to share his hard-won information about the release of atomic energy with Russia or any one particular nation.

*November 19, 1945*—Socialization in Great Britain seems to be steaming along in high.

Admiral J. O. Richardson told the Pearl Harbor investigating committee today that President Roosevelt ordered Uncle Sam's Pacific Fleet concentrated in Hawaii in May 1940 against his, Admiral Richardson's, advice.

*November 20, 1945*—Chief of Staff General Marshall steps out. His place taken by General Eisenhower.

Admiral Richardson said the fleet at Pearl Harbor was not ready for war.

At the Palace of Justice in the old city of Nuremberg, today, a British Lord Chief Justice opened the trial of the Nazi war criminals.

*November 26, 1945*—The proceedings of the Pearl Harbor investigating committee today became, in effect, an inquiry into the foreign policy of President Roosevelt and Secretary Hull.

*November 27, 1945*—General Marshall becomes Ambassador to China.

*November 29, 1945*—Yugoslavia today proclaimed a "people's republic"! The regime of Communist Marshal Tito takes over—with King Peter ousted.

*December 3, 1945*—Major General Sherman Miles today admitted to the Pearl Harbor investigating committee that the Japanese attack on December 7, 1941, succeeded because the army forces there were not properly alerted or prepared.

The war crimes trial at Nuremberg today heard that Adolf Hitler had ordered the destruction of Czechoslovakia as early as May 30, 1938. That was four months before the fateful day at Munich when Neville Chamberlain gave way to Hitler.

*December 4, 1945*—It was disclosed today that secrets which we gained by breaking the Japanese code were transmitted to General MacArthur in the Philippines—but not to General Short, our army commander at Pearl Harbor.

*December 12, 1945*—In Manila today arrived Lieutenant General Masaharu Homma, brought to the Philippine capital to stand trial as a war criminal.

*December 14, 1945*—At the Nuremberg trial an American prosecutor today brought forward the record of the Nazi extermination of the Jews, a record derived from written evidence left by the Nazis themselves.
A total of six million lives were taken.

*December 18, 1945*—The Tokyo parliament was dissolved today to make way for a new democratic house of representatives that is to be elected.

*December 21, 1945*—In Tokyo there is a common saying nowadays that if Japan were a republic and if MacArthur were to run for President he would be elected by a landslide vote.

The death of General Patton brings to mind inevitably the trite old story of the soldier who comes home from the wars and many perils and is killed by a fall down the stairs. He died after an automobile accident.

In Washington today Ezra Pound, the modernist poet, was found to be insane—mentally unfit to stand trial for treason.
He was accused of giving wartime broadcasts for Fascist Italy, where he lived for many years.

*December 31, 1945*—The Emperor of Japan, worshiped by a nation of eighty million as a god, issued a proclamation today stating that there is nothing divine about him at all.

# 1946

The war is over, but there isn't much peace. The Russians are stirring up trouble wherever they can, with their greatest success in China. In the United Nations they use the veto to hamstring the organization. They turn down the Baruch Plan for controlling atomic energy. In Moscow, Stalin unleashes a cultural purge against writers, artists, and scientists. In Fulton, Missouri, Churchill describes the dividing line between the Communist countries and the democracies as an "iron curtain"—a phrase that quickly becomes famous.

Violence breaks out in many places. India, as independence nears, sees Moslems fighting Hindus. In Yugoslavia, Tito executes Mikhailovitch, and claims Trieste. In Argentina, Colonel Perón seizes power. In Italy the house of Savoy falls before the new republic. In Palestine more terrorism as the Jews fight both the Arabs and the British.

At home President Truman ousts Henry Wallace as Secretary of Commerce for an unauthorized speech calling for a new pro-Soviet policy.

---

*January 3, 1946*—The voice of Lord Haw-Haw will be heard no more. William Joyce, born in Brooklyn but a British subject, has paid the penalty for his treason. Hanged.

*January 7, 1946*—The first conference between representatives of the Chiang Kai-shek government and the Chinese Communists and our own Ambassador, General Marshall, was held today.

*January 8, 1946*—President Truman says that we have no reason to believe that Soviet Russia possesses an atomic bomb.

*January 15, 1946*—China announces a complete settlement of the civil war. The new government is to be headed by Chiang Kai-shek—this the Chinese Reds concede.

*January 16, 1946*—Admiral Kimmel stated today that he had protested personally to President Roosevelt against the weakening of the fleet in the Pacific to build up naval power in the Atlantic.

The admiral said that at the time of the Pearl Harbor disaster he was so short of planes he couldn't maintain a long-range patrol all the time and at the same time do other things that he was ordered to do.

*January 21, 1946*—General de Gaulle is out of the French Government. French independence is firmly established, and the French hold the Rhine. So he considers his job is done.

*January 22, 1946*—General Short's defense is along the line of the argument that Admiral Kimmel presented—the contention that Washington did not provide the vital information. Like the admiral, the general stated today that he had not been given the intercepted Japanese messages that indicated an attack on Hawaii.

*January 25, 1946*—The U.N.O. is going to investigate Greece, Indonesia—and Iran too.

*January 29, 1946*—In London the Security Council of the U.N.O. has voted its choice for a Secretary-General. He is Trygve Lie of Norway.

In 1937, in Catholic churches throughout Germany, a papal encyclical was read—an encyclical denouncing nazism. The Hitler people were enraged by this church attack.

How had the encyclical got *into* Germany? The document had been smuggled in. By whom? The answer comes today. The papal encyclical was taken secretly into Germany by the present cardinal-designate, Cardinal Spellman of New York, who was then an official in the office of the papal Secretary of State.

The death of Harry Hopkins ends a career as singular as it was eminent, a career connected from beginning to end with that man of destiny Franklin Delano Roosevelt.

*January 31, 1946*—In Jerusalem today the sounds of a ram's horn was heard—and an outcry of wailing. This because of the British decision to permit only 1,500 Jews to enter Palestine each month.

*February 1, 1946*—Fireworks at the U.N.O. in London continued today, and again it was Vishinsky versus Bevin.

Bevin stated that Vishinsky's story about terrorism in Greece was Moscow propaganda.

*February 11, 1946*—Anti-British riots broke out in the ancient land of the Pharaohs for the third day in succession.

*February 13, 1946*—In his long letter of resignation Secretary Ickes leaves no room for doubt that he is quitting because he and President Truman do not see eye to eye.

The exit of Ickes leaves Henry Wallace the only out-and-out New Dealer in the Truman Cabinet.

*February 20, 1946*—Joseph E. Davies, former American Ambassador to Moscow, declares that Soviet Russia had a moral right to resort to espionage to procure the atomic secret. Davies argued that our refusal to give the bomb to the Soviets was, as he expressed it, hostile.

*February 22, 1946*—The Chinese view is that at the Big Three conference at Yalta, China was sold out to the Soviets. The late President Roosevelt is blamed for this, for conceding everything to Stalin.

*February 25, 1946*—Disorders in India are spreading. All across the subcontinent of Hindustan discontent with the British raj has caused strikes and riots.

*February 27, 1946*—One of the historic transformations of Britain under socialism is occurring this week—the nationalization of the Bank of England.

*March 1, 1946*—The Soviets have taken out of Manchuria tens of thousands of pieces of machinery from over twenty plants.

*March 6, 1946*—The whole world is aware tonight of the strong dark picture Churchill painted in his Fulton, Missouri, address of the doings and apparent aims of Soviet Russia and communism—the former Prime Minister speaking somberly of the world peril of tyranny, which already exists behind what he called the "iron curtain."

*March 7, 1946*—Uncle Sam today sent a note to Moscow asking Russia immediately to withdraw every Soviet soldier in Iran.

*March 11, 1946*—Soviet Russia charges Britain's war Prime Minister—Winston Churchill—with being a warmonger, trying to stir up a conflict against Russia.

Chinese Communist forces are spreading over a large section of Manchuria as fast as the Russians are withdrawing.

*March 15, 1946*—Today's British declaration of independence for India may well be one of the turning points of history.

Four Canadian scientists and the only Communist member of the Canadian Parliament arrested for doing spy work at the behest of Soviet Russia.

*March 19, 1946*—Iran has taken a fateful step in placing its dispute with Soviet Russia before the Security Council of the U.N.O.

Dr. Alan Nunn May, the British scientist, admits that he disclosed confidential atomic information.

*March 25, 1946*—The responsibility for the execution of Jimmy Doolittle's flyers in his raid on Tokyo belongs to none other than Tojo, ex-Premier of Japan. This came to light in the trial at Shanghai today.

*March 26, 1946*—This afternoon Soviet delegate Gromyko said he would boycott the Security Council so far as the affair of Iran was concerned.

*March 27, 1946*—Gromyko has walked out.
The Iranian delegate is asked to state his country's complaint against Soviet Russia.

Civil war is raging in Manchuria.

*March 28, 1946*—The returns are all in from the election in Argentina, and the result is a victory for Colonel Juan Domingo Perón, the so-called strong man of the Argentine Republic.

*April 2, 1946*—General Homma has been executed at Manila. Homma found guilty for that monumental atrocity—the death march of Bataan.

*April 3, 1946*—It's official now that it's the U.N., not the U.N.O. "United Nations," and not "United Nations Organization."

*April 4, 1946*—Iran's troops have occupied Karau, a city twenty-five miles northwest of Teheran, keeping a safe distance between themselves and the Soviet forces.

*April 8, 1946*—It was Hermann Goering himself who ordered the execution of those fifty recaptured officers of the R.A.F., the airmen who got away from a Nazi prison camp. This was testimony given at the Nuremberg trial of Nazi war criminals.

*April 9, 1946*—Red Army troops are speeding up their evacuation of Iran.

*April 11, 1946*—The Communists are attacking cities in Manchuria and north China by the tens of thousands.

*April 12, 1946*—Yugoslavia turns down the proposal that American soldiers be permitted to testify in behalf of General Mikhailovitch, famed as the leader of the Chetniks.

*April 18, 1946*—As the clock strikes twelve tonight, the League of Nations dies.

At the Nuremberg trial Hans Frank, who became internationally infamous as the Nazi Governor General of Poland, confessed today that he felt terribly guilty over 6,500,000 Poles who died while he was Governor General.

*April 24, 1946*—Still another U. S. Army transport plane has been shot at by Soviet fighters in Austria.

*May 1, 1946*—The joint Anglo-American Committee recommends that the Holy Land be neither an Arab nor a Jewish nation, both Arabs and Jews to be treated alike—which is a middle-of-the-road compromise.

*May 3, 1946*—In Tokyo somber and imposing proceedings have begun—the trial of Tojo.

*May 7, 1946*—The Red Army has completed its evacuation of Iran.

*May 8, 1946*—The Soviet delegate continued his boycott of the Security Council on the subject of Iran.

*May 9, 1946*—King Victor Emmanuel is no longer King of Italy. He abdicated in favor of his son.
This may be the end of the historic house of Savoy.

Without radar we never would have won the battle of the Atlantic.
That statement comes from someone who ought to know, Grand Admiral Karl Doenitz of the Nazi navy.

*May 10, 1946*—The Italian Cabinet has accepted Crown Prince Humbert as King of Italy, pending an election to decide the fate of the crown.

*May 21, 1946*—In Czechoslovakia one of the arch war criminals sentenced to death today—Karl Hermann Frank, the destroyer of Lidice.

*May 28, 1946*—In London the House of Commons tonight nationalized the British steel and iron industry.

*June 3, 1946*—The Supreme Court of the United States today decided, 6 to 1, that the Virginia statutes providing for segregation of Negroes on buses is unconstitutional so far as buses cross state lines.

The spy trial in Montreal shows that the Russians paid for information about the atomic bomb while we were allies of the Soviets.

*June 5, 1946*—Italy has voted for a republic, and the election sends the royal family into exile.

The fall of the house of Savoy traces, of course, to fascism and the war. The old King, Victor Emmanuel, was blamed for letting Mussolini seize power. He himself was anti-Nazi, but he yielded to Mussolini's determination to get into the war.

*June 7, 1946*—There were violent monarchist disturbances in Italy today.

*June 11, 1946*—The trial of General Mikhailovitch began today in Belgrade.

*June 24, 1946*—Today in Moscow, *Pravda* assailed the Baruch plan for control of the atomic bomb as an American attempt to establish what *Pravda* called "world domination."

*June 26, 1946*—A bulletin of historic drama comes from Soviet Russia —the wiping out of Crimean Tartars, uprooted and transported to some other part of Russia.

The reason for the elimination of the Crimean Tartars and the Circassian communities in the Caucasus was disloyalty in the war.

*June 28, 1946*—Today's meeting in Paris is described as the angriest that the Foreign Ministers have held thus far, and tempers have not been too good any time. Molotov, for Soviet Russia, objected to nearly everything that came up. He agreed to nothing.

The University of California announces the first triumph of atomic science in the healing of that mortal malady, the dread of the human race—cancer. Skin cancers cured by radioactive isotopes.

*July 1, 1946*—Trieste for the third day was the scene of riots. Mobs of Italians fighting mobs of Slovenes.

The Holy Land tonight is in the throes of a conflict which recalls the days when the Irish were fighting the British Black and Tans.

*July 2, 1946*—Today's news discloses one bit of evidence, vivid and weird, of the effect of the radioactivity of the atomic-test explosion at Bikini. Aboard one of the target ships a folding metal chair was leaning against a gun turret when the atomic flames were let loose, and the radiation was so powerful that it photographed the shadow of the chair on the gun turret—like a sort of X-ray picture.

*July 3, 1946*—Here's the full official score from Operation Crossroads. Fifty-nine out of seventy-three ships were affected by the heat and force of the atom bomb.

*July 4, 1946*—The independence of the Philippines was made formal and complete here in Washington today by President Truman, who proclaimed the Philippine Islands to be a free and sovereign nation—after nearly half a century under the American flag.

*July 8, 1946*—The Arabs demand the stopping of all Jewish immigration into Palestine.

*July 11, 1946*—Another riot at Trieste, with the business of that seaport paralyzed and the railroad blown up.

*July 12, 1946*—The Big Four conference ended in Paris tonight with a new note of acrimony and ill feeling.

*July 15, 1946*—Tito's military court today found a verdict of guilty against General Mikhailovitch.

*July 17, 1946*—The bitterest personal drama of the war came to its tragic end today with the execution of General Mikhailovitch.

The Moscow wire flashes a report that Marshal Zhukov has been named commander of the Odessa military district.
On the surface it would look as if Russia's No. 1 war commander had fallen out of favor at the Kremlin.

*July 22, 1946*—There were nearly a hundred casualties in Jerusalem today when land mines exploded in British Army headquarters.
The mines destroyed the whole west wing of the King David Ho-

tel, and virtually wrecked the building next door, Jerusalem's famous Y.M.C.A.

*July 24, 1946*—Today makes it definite about the Soviet rejection of the American plan for the atomic bomb.

*July 25, 1946*—The underwater atomic bomb apparently has left the Bikini lagoon resembling a naval junk yard.

*August 13, 1946*—One of the great writers of the world died today—H. G. Wells, seventy-nine years old. He foresaw many of our later-day miracles.

There was enacted today the first large episode in the carrying out of the new British policy on illegal immigration in Palestine.

The illegal immigrants were forced aboard two transports, which thereupon put out to sea—bound for Cyprus.

*August 15, 1946*—As Jewish immigrants were unloaded today at Cyprus, they started a battle with the British troops.

*August 19, 1946*—Today the Communists in China openly declared war on the Nationalist government of Chiang Kai-shek.

*August 23, 1946*—It's official now. All five United States Army fliers in the unarmed American transport shot down by Yugoslav fighter planes on Monday are dead.

*August 26, 1946*—Marshal Tito has promised there will be no more incidents, no more American planes shot down, no more Americans shot to death. We are taking him at his word, but from now on heavily armed Flying Fortresses will make that run from Vienna to Udine.

Armies are on the march in China tonight, with warfare in nine provinces.

*August 30, 1946*—Greece charges that Communist bands are being armed in Yugoslavia and then sent over the mountains to stir up trouble in Greece.

*September 2, 1946*—The King of Greece will return home. The monarchists swept the election, and were doing a lot of celebrating today.

The new interim government of India took office today. The new regime is headed by Hindus—the Moslem party refusing to have anything to do with it.

*September 5, 1946*—In Bombay, rioting for the fifth day in succession.

*September 6, 1946*—Workers at a New York dock have gone on strike to protest against being made to load a cargo of UNRRA supplies for Yugoslavia.

As for Tito, he is strictly on the receiving end, accepting charity while shooting down American planes.

*September 9, 1946*—The latest from Jerusalem, more savage violence.

Jewish terrorists have blown up the British headquarters in Tel Aviv.

*September 11, 1946*—At the Round Table Conference in London the Arabs today rejected all idea of a Jewish state in Palestine.

*September 13, 1946*—Last night in New York's Madison Square Garden, Henry Wallace proposed a new and different foreign policy for the United States. He said, in effect, let's ease up on our tough talk toward Russia, and let's break our close ties with Great Britain.

*September 17, 1946*—Tonight Secretary of Commerce Henry Wallace, contrary to President Truman's wishes, made public a long letter which he said he wrote to the Chief Executive nearly two months ago—a letter containing Wallace's views on current American foreign policy, especially his belief that the United States should ease up on Russia. He says President Truman read and okayed his Madison Square Garden speech.

*September 18, 1946*—The threat of a struggle within the ranks of the Jewish underground in Palestine has become more serious. Today, Hagana, the official secret army of Zionism, issued a declaration that it would fight against what it called "purposeless terrorism."

*September 19, 1946*—Navy Secretary Forrestal and Secretary of War Patterson deny categorically Henry Wallace's accusation that there are high officers in our military establishment who are in favor of our having a war with Russia now, before the Soviets get that atomic bomb.

*September 20, 1946*—From tonight on the former Vice-President speaks as private citizen Wallace. He's out of the Cabinet, President Truman demanding his resignation. This settlement should make Secretary Byrnes stronger than ever in his dealings with the Soviets.

*September 23, 1946*—President Truman has selected Averell Harriman as Wallace's successor. Harriman is now Secretary of Commerce.

*September 25, 1946*—Tito's government today formally indicted Archbishop Aloysius Stepinac, head of the Roman Catholic Church in Yugoslavia, on six charges, including those of war crimes.

*September 26, 1946*—Tonight a prominent Russian paper, carrying Moscow's present cultural purge to its final depth of absurdity, lashes out at Sherlock Holmes, the favorite fiction character created by Conan Doyle.

Says the Soviet journal: "Sherlock Holmes is dangerous to Soviet morals and ideologies." It charges that the adventures of this detective of fiction are poisoning the minds of Russian readers with false beliefs concerning the strength of the foundations of private property.

*September 30, 1946*—At Nuremberg, after one of the great trials of all time, all of the twenty-one defendants have been found guilty.

*October 1, 1946*—Twelve of the Nazi war criminals have been sentenced to hang—including Goering. The Nuremberg court gave the others prison sentences.

*October 2, 1946*—Bernard Baruch, America's elder statesman, angrily charges tonight that Henry Wallace has, in effect, sabotaged the American atomic control plan.

The Russians oppose the American plan, and Wallace, in his letter of resignation to President Truman, backed the Russian objection.

*October 7, 1946*—The latest from the trial of Archbishop Stepinac. Tito's government lawyers object to any testimony in behalf of the archbishop.

*October 10, 1946*—The appeal of the Nazis from the sentences of the war crimes tribunal at Nuremberg rejected.

Generalissimo Chiang Kai-shek issued an order today again putting his part of China on a full war basis.

The vote from Alaska is in. Two to one in favor of immediate statehood.

*October 14, 1946*—The Paris Peace Conference today wound up in a storm of anger and recrimination.

*October 16, 1946*—It is a mystery how Goering procured the cyanide that enabled him to cheat the gallows. Shortly before the hour set for the hangings, he was found dead in his cell, a suicide. The other eleven were hanged.

*October 17, 1946*—The name of the Soviet secret agent who commands and directs the activities of all Communists in the United States? Gerhart Eisler.

The activities of Eisler were first revealed by Louis F. Budenz.

*October 18, 1946*—Refugee Hindus are pouring into Calcutta, fleeing the Moslems.

*October 21, 1946*—The British today intercepted another ship with eight hundred Jewish refugees trying to run the blockade into Palestine.

*October 23, 1946*—The United Nations Assembly met for the first time at Flushing Meadows today.

*October 24, 1946*—In the Assembly of the United Nations, Mexico today added its voice to those of John Bull and Uncle Sam—calling for the abolition of the veto.

Many of the Germans whom the Soviet officials are taking to Russia are scientists and workers trained in atomic research, rocket and jet propulsion.

*October 28, 1946*—President Truman today appointed the head of Uncle Sam's Atomic Energy Commission.

The new chairman is a lawyer, David E. Lilienthal, for thirteen years chairman of the Tennessee Valley Authority.

In the Bulgarian elections the Reds have 55 per cent of the ballots.

*October 29, 1946*—The United States has joined Great Britain in a new protest to Rumania—a complaint against the way elections are being prepared in that Soviet satellite.

*November 6, 1946*—We intend to keep the Japanese island possessions that we conquered during the war. This was announced by President Truman today.

*November 8, 1946*—We're withdrawing our political mission from Albania, that Balkan country which has become a Soviet puppet.

*November 11, 1946*—Today Bevin tried in vain to open the old question of withdrawal of Russian troops from Balkan countries.

Molotov's answer was a resounding "No."

In London, British officials are on the extreme alert because of threats from the Jewish underground. Threats even to kill Field Marshal Montgomery.

*November 15, 1946*—In a vote tonight the C.I.O. gave President Philip Murray the power to expel Communists.

*November 18, 1946*—Jimmy Walker, Mayor of New York during the fabulous 1920s, died this evening. Sixty-five. But he didn't seem that old.

The dapper and witty Jimmy was more than just New York City's mayor. He was a national figure, the symbol of an era.

Russia is holding out against all efforts to restrict the use of the veto in the Security Council.

*November 20, 1946*—Man is now able to see this earth from the farthest point away—sixty-five miles.

This new view of mother earth comes by means of photography and a rocket—one of those German V-2s launched into the remotest atmosphere at the White Sands Proving Grounds in the New Mexican desert.

*November 26, 1946*—The State Department has sent a biting note to the Communist puppet government in Rumania—a note charging that the recent elections in that country were fraudulent.

*November 29, 1946*—John L. Lewis is now on trial. His plea is "not guilty."

*December 3, 1946*—The Lewis court speech today indicated clearly that he will not call off the strike even if he is sent to jail.

*December 4, 1946*—The result of the hearing of John L. Lewis was conclusive, 100 per cent. The judge took the government's figure for a fine and imposed a penalty of $3,500,000 on the United Mine Workers union.

*December 6, 1946*—The London Conference on India has failed.

The Chinese Communists today turned down all ideas of further negotiation.

A German prisoner of war has arrived in Stockholm to receive a Nobel

Prize. He is Professor Otto Hahn, famed for his discoveries that played a large part in the development of the atomic bomb.

*December 13, 1946*—The leaders of the leftist rebels in northern Iran have fled across the border to Soviet Russia.

*December 18, 1946*—From Palestine there is more news of terrorism, but this time it's a different kind—Arab terrorism.

That New Mexico rocket of last night broke all records for altitude, soaring 114 miles into the outer atmosphere of the earth.

*December 20, 1946*—War is on in Indochina.

*December 25, 1946*—The French situation in Indochina is so serious that a second world war hero of France is flying out to take military charge —General Jacques LeClerc.

*December 30, 1946*—The Atomic Energy Commission of the United Nations has gone overboard for the Baruch Plan. The vote, 10 to 0. Sounds unanimous, but it wasn't. Russia and Poland refused to vote.

Television sets will be on the market in large numbers next year.

# 1947

By now it is clear that Stalin doesn't want a settlement of the international situation. His henchmen—Vishinsky, Gromyko, Molotov —continue to use the veto at the U.N. and stymie every Big Four meeting on peace treaties for Germany and Austria. The Communist grip on Eastern Europe grows tighter. Stalin sets up a new Communist organ—the Cominform—to co-ordinate conspiracy throughout the world.

But the West answers with the Marshall Plan. And America states at the U.N. that our atomic bombs will not be destroyed.

The British withdraw from the subcontinent of Hindustan—leaving it to be partitioned between India and Pakistan. In Palestine, Jews and Arabs gird for war over the coming partition. There is fighting in Indonesia, Greece, Trieste. Britain plunges into austerity under the impact of the dollar crisis—cheered only by the gaiety surrounding the wedding of Princess Elizabeth and the Duke of Edinburgh.

At home Henry Wallace says he will head a third party in revolt against the anti-Communist policy of President Truman. Congress passes the Taft-Hartley law over the President's veto. John L. Lewis withdraws from the A.F. of L. Henry Ford dies—the genius who transformed daily life by means of the mass production of automobiles.

January 7, 1947—The resignation of Secretary Byrnes came as a rather sudden shock to the country. As you may have heard by now, the White House announcement of the Byrnes resignation came tonight and with it word that General George C. Marshall, former Army Chief of Staff, until now our special presidential envoy to China, would succeed him.

January 15, 1947—Soviet Russia has rejected an American demand. This was another protest about the forthcoming election in Poland—which will not be a fair and democratic election, according to our government. The Soviets had guaranteed that Poland would have free elections.

Molotov says that the election in Poland is okay, free, democratic.

*January 20, 1947*—Poland's elections ran according to form. A government spokesman in Warsaw now says that the government's Communist-dominated party—they call it "democratic"—will have 390 out of the 424 seats in the next Polish parliament.

*January 24, 1947*—We are given an outline of a report our Ambassador to Poland is making on the Polish election.

It tells of terror and intimidation by the Communist government—an election of fraud and violence.

The voting was public for the most part, no secret ballot, and the people were afraid to vote publicly against the Reds.

*January 30, 1947*—Admiral Byrd is in command again at Little America, landing there today after an unprecedented flight in a plane that took off from an aircraft carrier in the Bay of Whales.

*February 4, 1947*—Out at Lake Success, Long Island, today, where the United Nations Security Council is meeting, Russia and the United States both agreed that it is their fervent wish to disarm. Then they disagreed violently on how to go about it—especially what to do about the atomic bomb.

*February 10, 1947*—Italy is at peace today with the rest of the world, at peace officially and finally, just forty-one months after she surrendered to the Allied armies.

The treaty cuts Italy down to a third-rate power, cuts the Italian Army and Navy to virtually nothing but token military forces, takes away her colonies, and gives a chunk of Venezia Giulia to Yugoslavia.

Finland continued to pay interest on the money she owed to the United States, although the fact was not made public until after the war, since President Roosevelt considered it bad policy to reveal it.

*February 14, 1947*—Before the Security Council of the United Nations this afternoon Gromyko demanded that we destroy our atomic bombs without waiting for a system of atomic control.

*February 18, 1947*—The polar sky voyage turns out to have been, in fact, only one of a concerted series of exploration flights made at the same time—a fleet of planes covering vast areas of the Antarctic solitude.

Admiral Byrd had stated that he wanted to go beyond the Pole and have a look at a region utterly unknown.

All he saw was a flat expanse of unbroken ice.

*February 19, 1947*—The Russians in Austria seized a great deal of property in violation of the Potsdam Agreement, property which they alleged to be German but which actually was not. That's what General Mark Clark told the Conference of Deputies of Foreign Ministers in London today.

*February 21, 1947*—Six times in the past year our government has called upon the Soviets to enter negotiations for a settlement of the huge Lend-Lease bill—American wartime aid to the Soviets.

So what does Molotov promise? Soviet Russia will, in his words, "look into the matter," which certainly is a magnificent concession.

British newspapers today were almost unanimous in assailing yesterday's announcement on India, Prime Minister Attlee stating that the British would pull out of India by June of next year.

*February 24, 1947*—The Soviets, in Korea, are conscripting the Koreans for military service. This was stated today by Lieutenant General Hodge, our commander out there. He said that behind the Soviet iron curtain in Korea the Russians are building up a military force—a Soviet army of Koreans.

*February 28, 1947*—The hope for peace in China came to a formal end today—civil war now an open and acknowledged thing.

*March 3, 1947*—Stalin has given up one of his many jobs. He has resigned as Minister for the Armed Forces. In his place is General Nikolai Bulganin, who has been his No. 2 man in the Soviet War Department.

This was a historic day in Mexico, the first official visit of an American President to our neighbor south of the Rio Grande.

Two chiefs of state, President Truman and Mexican President Miguel Alemán, sat down together at a sumptuous state dinner.

*March 6, 1947*—The Supreme Court has decided against John L. Lewis and the United Mine Workers.

The decision upholds completely the injunction issued by Judge Goldsborough of the Federal District Court—the injunction ordering Lewis to call off the coal mine strike toward the end of last year.

Margaret Truman is making her debut with the Detroit Symphony Orchestra Sunday night. She has studied voice for seven years, a coloratura soprano, and is a serious artist.

*March 7, 1947*—Rioting in the Punjab, the great northwest province of Hindustan, has become so sanguinary that British civilians are leaving as fast as they can. This is the fourth day of virtual rebellion. Sikhs fighting Moslems and both fighting Hindus.

Jewish extremists battled British troops in Jerusalem and Haifa again today.

*March 17, 1947*—Ten billion dollars to be paid in twenty years. That's the stupendous burden the Soviets want to place on conquered Germany —for Russia alone.

*March 18, 1947*—At the Moscow Conference Molotov declared that at Yalta the late President agreed that the reparations to be exacted from defeated Germany should be based on a general figure of twenty billion dollars and of this Russia was entitled to half—ten billion.

So what had our Secretary of State, General Marshall, to say to that? He replied that the Roosevelt-Stalin agreement at Yalta was merely preliminary, tentative, not a definite thing.

*March 21, 1947*—It almost takes away one's breath to tell it—airplane flights daily to the North Pole. A weather-service routine of a flight per day to the ultimate north of this earth.

Such is the disclosure that follows the news of an army B-29 winging to the Pole and back.

*March 24, 1947*—The publication late today of the official agreements made at the Big Three conferences at Teheran, Yalta, and Potsdam verifies two recent disclosures made of clauses that have been kept secret.

It shows the Molotov version of the agreement at Yalta to have been entirely correct.

President Roosevelt did concede to Stalin half of the reparations to be paid by Germany, ten billion out of a staggering total of twenty billion— with British Prime Minister Churchill dissenting.

The Big Three at Yalta made a secret agreement that part of the reparations to Soviet Russia would be forced labor by Germans—in effect, slave labor.

*March 27, 1947*—Henry Wallace, former Vice-President, is dead against the Truman policy of trying to check the advance of communism in the Near East. This might be expected of that same Henry Wallace who was ousted from the Truman Cabinet after he raised an uproar with that famous Madison Square Garden address advocating a policy of go easy with the Soviets.

*March 31, 1947*—At midnight tonight this nation will bid farewell to the draft—good-by to Selective Service.

*April 2, 1947*—At Lake Success today the British Government dumped the Zionist baby in the lap of the United Nations.

Uncle Sam is going to keep permanent possession of the islands he conquered from the Japanese in the Pacific. That's the word just in from Lake Success, Long Island, where the Security Council of the United Nations is holding a night meeting. The council has approved, unanimously, America's request for permanent control.

*April 8, 1947*—Henry Ford always lived in unpretentious fashion. His residence—a quiet house in Dearborn.

Apparently he was in good health, considering his eighty-three years.

His end was sudden and unexpected. Shortly before midnight, a cerebral hemorrhage.

*April 9, 1947*—Over in Greece an army of sixty thousand men, trained by British officers, equipped with tanks, artillery, and planes, began a spring campaign at dawn this morning. The objective is to wipe out Red guerrillas in northern Thessaly, also in western Macedonia.

*April 11, 1947*—In London today Henry Wallace launched his campaign to rally Europe against the Truman policy of checking communism.

*April 14, 1947*—A federal grand jury has again indicted Gerhart Eisler, described as the No. 1 American Communist.

*April 18, 1947*—Uncle Sam scores a major victory at a Security Council meeting. The council today rejected a Russian resolution giving the United Nations supervision over American aid to Greece, which virtually amounts to United Nations approval of President Truman's four-hundred-million-dollar loan to Greece and Turkey.

Wallace late today announced that he's going to attack the Truman anti-Communist policy at home as well as abroad.

Henry Ford's will was offered for probate today, and it shows the fabulous motor magnate leaving his immense fortune in two parts: one, consisting of the voting stock of the Ford Motor Company, goes to his family, chiefly his grandchildren. Motor Company control is vested in Henry Ford II; the other part of the fortune, consisting of non-voting stock, is bequeathed to a fund for scientific, educational, and charitable purposes.

*April 23, 1947*—The epitaph of the Moscow Conference can be written with virtual certainty tonight—complete failure. News dispatches from the Soviet capital stated today that the American delegation had abandoned the hope of an Austrian treaty.

Hope of a German treaty has been given up for some days now—and those two peace pacts were what the Foreign Ministers met to negotiate in the first place.

*April 24, 1947*—The Foreign Ministers had only one thing left to do in Moscow tonight—survive an official banquet at the Kremlin.

*April 30, 1947*—President Truman signed today the resolution for restoring to Boulder Dam its original name—Hoover Dam.

*May 5, 1947*—Socialism on the march again in England, with the House of Commons now voting to nationalize all of Britain's railroads, long-distance bus and truck lines, and all inland waterways.

*May 9, 1947*—The congressmen whooped through a rousing okay for the President's bill to give four hundred million dollars' worth of aid to Greece and Turkey to combat communism—the Truman policy.

*May 19, 1947*—Gromyko said that Russia will not submit to unlimited inspection of her atomic resources.

*May 30, 1947*—Events in Hungary are moving to an inevitable conclusion—Red dictatorship.

In Budapest today the place of resigning Premier Nagy was immediately taken by Vice-Premier Rakosi, head of the Hungarian Communist party, who is forming a new Cabinet—all Red.

*June 2, 1947*—Uncle Sam will send neither food nor any other kind of relief to a Communist Hungary.

*June 13, 1947*—In London there's enthusiastic support for the Marshall Plan. The British Government is hugely interested in the proposals made by the Secretary of State in his address at Harvard last week—proposals for the nations of Europe to get together and estimate their critical needs for the next four years, the United States then to underwrite the job of supplying those critical needs at a cost of six billion dollars the first year.

*June 16, 1947*—Henry Wallace threatens to lead a third party in 1948 —the first time he's openly come out and said so.

*June 18, 1947*—Great Britain and France have issued an appeal to Soviet Russia—please come in and join the Marshall Plan!

*June 19, 1947*—There has been keen speculation in New York and in university circles about the successor to Nicholas Murray Butler as president of Columbia University.

Today it came to light that the trustees offered the job to none other than the Chief of Staff of Uncle Sam's Army, yes, General Dwight D. Eisenhower.

*June 23, 1947*—Never before was a presidential veto overridden in such circumstances as accompanied the final and definite enactment of the Taft-Hartley Bill this afternoon, the labor bill that is now law. Never before had there been so much agitation and pressure from both sides.

*June 25, 1947*—Soviet blasts against the Marshall Plan continued today.

*June 27, 1947*—The Chinese Government charges that the Communist armies have been given huge supplies of weapons and ammunition by the Soviets.

Now about the airman at Pendleton, Oregon, who yesterday told of seeing "flying saucers"—a strange, unheard of type of airplane—whizzing over southern Washington at 1,200 miles an hour.

That aviator, Kenneth Arnold, has been having his troubles today, phone ringing constantly, people coming around to stare at him and shake their heads.

*June 30, 1947*—Soviet Russia will have nothing to do with Secretary Marshall's plan for bringing the European countries out of their condition of want and hardship.

*July 3, 1947*—Great Britain and France lost no time in sending invitations to twenty-two nations of Europe for a get-together on the Marshall Plan.

The mystery of the flying saucers is becoming fantastic, with a whole string of witnesses in eight states all over the country and in Canada declaring that they have seen the weird objects speeding through the air.

*July 7, 1947*—Rumania, Poland, and Yugoslavia will not participate in the forthcoming Paris conference for European economic recovery. Where does that announcement come from? From Moscow!

As late as this weekend the Poles announced that they were still "definitely interested." Then the Kremlin spoke—and Poland was interested no longer. The Government of Czechoslovakia has accepted the invitation.

*July 9, 1947*—The world's No. 1 marriage has just been announced, the British royal wedding that has been rumored for some time.

Elizabeth marries a distant cousin, who was Prince Philip of Greece, but whose Germanic ancestry is much like that of the British royal family. He has become a British citizen.

*July 10, 1947*—The Czechs late today made an about-face—withdrawing their acceptance of an invitation to the Paris conference. An emergency meeting was held in Moscow today between three Czechoslovak officials and Premier Stalin. Then came the Czech refusal.

*July 15, 1947*—Greek Regular Army units have encircled two thousand Communist guerrillas who attacked last Sunday, with a battle of annihilation now on.

It seems hard to believe that the Paris conference on the Marshall Plan has completed the task for which it assembled. The delegates met only four days ago, but they've already done their jobs.

*July 17, 1947*—Greek troops, reinforced by Lend-Lease tanks and planes, have the invading guerrillas on the run.

*July 18, 1947*—Out in the Marquesas Islands, in mid-Pacific, a raft arrived today—a raft made of South American balsa wood and bamboo. Aboard the raft were six young Norwegian scientists, who had made the voyage from the coast of South America, 3,500 miles.

The leader of the scientific voyage on a raft is Thor Heyerdahl, a Norwegian ethnologist and archaeologist.

They will continue their voyage and proceed by raft to Tahiti, another 1,200 miles—sailing the way they think prehistoric navigators did thousands of years ago.

*July 31, 1947*—The Government of Greece today laid a formal complaint before the Security Council of the United Nations—a complaint against the Soviet stooges, Albania, Bulgaria, and Yugoslavia. The Greek Foreign Minister declared that the governments of those three countries were practicing bold aggression.

*August 4, 1947*—In Indonesia the war is over, for the time being at least. The Dutch high command flashed a cease-fire order by radio to all its units.

*August 5, 1947*—The crisis in Britain is said to be the most serious ever faced by that nation.

It looks as if the winter ahead will be grim indeed for the average Briton.

Anti-Semitic riots in the English industrial city of Manchester today, the fourth day of such demonstrations in widely scattered parts of England. All an aftermath of the hanging by the Jewish underground of the two British sergeants in Palestine last week.

*August 6, 1947*—From Britain a correspondent sends a grim picture of life in darkened London. No gaiety. Restaurants and bars closing at ten o'clock. Meals limited, dirty tablecloths, no napkins. He describes the atmosphere as one of grim silence. A baffled people fighting an enemy they can't see, reading news they don't understand—about the dollar exchange and export markets.

Prime Minister Attlee stood up in the House of Commons today and called on the British to put their hearts into what he calls a "new battle of Britain"—economic restrictions to help Britain back on its industrial feet. A bitter program: more work and less food. Privations to avert national bankruptcy.

*August 11, 1947*—The first President of the India-Moslem state of Pakistan is Mohammed Ali Jinnah, head of the Moslem League.

*August 13, 1947*—One of Gandhi's followers states tonight that he is, in the words of the follower, "the most despondent man in India," so despondent that he is issuing no message to acclaim the independence for which he toiled—he, Gandhi, the very soul and symbol of India.

*August 14, 1947*—Exit British India.

*August 15, 1947*—The formalities of Indian independence were concluded today when Lord Louis Mountbatten, Britain's last Viceroy in India, handed the seals of office to the Government of the Dominion of Hindustan at New Delhi. Yesterday Mountbatten did the same in the case of the Mohammedan dominion—Pakistan.

*August 21, 1947*—The string of Soviet vetoes at Lake Success went up. Yes, sixteen and seventeen. They were for the purpose of keeping Italy and Austria out of the United Nations.

*August 22, 1947*—Soviet Russia rejects the American protest about the death sentence decreed against Petkov in Bulgaria. Petkov, in Bulgaria, represents democratic liberalism—so he is doomed to be executed.

*August 25, 1947*—In India the state of affairs on the Punjab frontier between Pakistan and Hindustan is described tonight as civil war.

*August 26, 1947*—The Indonesian Republic today accepted the proposal for mediation by the Security Council of the United Nations.

*August 27, 1947*—London announces the British "master plan for economic survival." It is austerity plus!

*August 29, 1947*—Today the United States broke off those futile two-year negotiations with the Soviet for the creation of an independent Korea.

*September 1, 1947*—The Communists didn't do nearly as well as they should have in a rigged election; but just the same, they come out in control of Hungary, as expected.

*September 2, 1947*—At Petropolis, Brazil, today President Truman addressed the representatives of nineteen American nations. He pledged an all-out attempt to maintain world peace.

The President described the post-war era as a bitter disappointment to this country.

In Calcutta today Mahatma Gandhi began another fast. Again fasting for peace in strife-torn India.

Elsewhere in India savagery and massacre go on between Moslems and Hindus.

*September 3, 1947*—President Truman has just made a historic disclosure. The United States is ready to share the peacetime medical benefits of atomic energy with other nations.

*September 10, 1947*—Mahatma Gandhi began what he calls his crusade for peace and moderation. He visited the refugee camps in Old and New Delhi, moving fearlessly among the hate-inflamed people.

*September 15, 1947*—The city of Trieste celebrated its initiation as free territory today with a full-dress riot. Yugoslavs and Italians went at it with fists and clubs and other more lethal weapons.

*September 16, 1947*—Man traveled at a rate of over four hundred miles an hour—in an automobile—today.

At Bonneville Salt Flats, Utah, this afternoon, John Cobb, the British racing driver, broke the world's land speed record—his own record.

*September 19, 1947*—Today Vishinsky offered a sweet idea in formal fashion to the United Nations—filing a resolution to condemn the United States for fomenting war.

*September 24, 1947*—Our government has issued a warning to the Red dictatorship of Communist Marshal Tito—a warning that the Yugoslavs had better behave in the disturbed area of Trieste.

*September 29, 1947*—The Soviets refuse to take back the Moscow insult—calling President Truman a Hitler.

*September 30, 1947*—News from China tells of large Communist forces striking a major blow in what a Chinese-language news dispatch describes as the "battle for Manchuria."

*October 2, 1947*—The Jewish Agency for Palestine announced that it accepts the United Nations plan for dividing the Holy Land into separate Arab and Jewish states.

The Arabs have announced their intention to drench the entire Middle East in blood before permitting the partitioning of Palestine.

In Italy that left-wing movement of squatters onto farms, which didn't seem so serious a couple of days ago, has become a crucial issue. There are thirty thousand of them now, clamoring to be allowed to remain on what they call unoccupied, uncultivated lands.

*October 3, 1947*—This afternoon was staged the most extraordinary ninth inning in the history of baseball.

Yankee pitcher Floyd Bevens had not allowed a hit.

But he was wild. Allowing no hits, he had given a lot of bases on balls— eight in eight innings. And that was approaching the record for wildness. The Dodgers scoring a run without a hit because of the way Bevens issued those passes.

It was 2–1 as the ninth inning began.

Bevens with only three outs to go for a no-hit game, the only one in World Series history.

The first Brooklyn batter up with the ninth was catcher Edwards. Edwards fouled out—the crowd roaring.

The next batter up, Carl Furillo. Bevens couldn't get the ball over the plate. He walked Furillo and that tied the record, the World Series record for bases on balls.

Then Jorgensen fouled out—and Bevens had only one out to go for his no-hitter. But he passed the next man up, Reiser—the Yankees not wanting to take a chance with a dangerous hitter like Pistol Pete. That broke the record for *bases on balls!* And now two men were on base, the *tying and winning* runs for Brooklyn.

Next man up.

Lavagetto—old Cookie Lavagetto, pinch-hitting.

Well, the incredible happened. Bevens got two strikes on Lavagetto! *Just one more to go! But it happened. The last man up in the ninth got the only hit off Bevens!* And it was a double that won the game for Brooklyn.

They say anything can happen in Brooklyn, but that ninth inning couldn't happen in Brooklyn—or anyplace else. Only it did.

*October 15, 1947*—The agitation of the Arabs against the United States continues because of American support of the plan to partition.

*October 17, 1947*—In London today signatures were appended to a document that makes history. The treaty of Burmese independence was signed today.

The British Empire relinquishes another of its most resplendent possessions.

*October 22, 1947*—The Government of Iran rejects all Soviet demands for an oil concession.

*October 23, 1947*—The organization of a bureau representing the Communists of nine countries—that is not a revival of the old Comintern, says Stalin.

Its proper name is the Cominform—Communist Information Bureau—and it's not directed from the Kremlin, added the Red Premier.

*October 28, 1947*—The military situation in that beautiful Vale of Kashmir shows an army of fanatical Moslems in the process of being surrounded by soldiers of the Delhi Hindu government of India and troops of the Kashmir Maharajah. The trouble, of course, stems from the fact that the Maharajah is a Hindu, while the majority of the people of Kashmir are Moslems—a paradoxical situation.

Hollywood film writers refusing to answer the question of whether or not they are Communists. Yesterday it was Hollywood scenarist John Howard Lawson. Today, film writers Dalton Trombo, Alvah Bessie, and Albert Maltz.

*October 29, 1947*—Mahatma Gandhi came out today in favor of the Delhi government's support for Kashmir.

After the war the painter Hans van Meegeren was accused of having dealt with the Nazis, of having aided them in looting art treasures of Holland. Nazi No. 2 man Goering, for example, acquired masterpieces of the

Dutch school. Van Meegeren stated today that the old masters he had enabled the Nazis to procure were really fakes. He himself had painted them. This confession put him in a class with the greatest art fakers of history.

*November 3, 1947*—The Polish leader Stanislaw Mikolajczyk is safe in London. We hear today how he got away from Poland just in time to escape a Communist purge trial, which for him would have meant execution.

*November 4, 1947*—At Lexington, Kentucky, Man o' War, the most famous race horse in the world, was buried with full honors.

*November 6, 1947*—There was excitement all over the world today over that speech made by Molotov in Moscow, the speech in which he hinted the Soviet Union was in a position to make the atomic bomb.

Uncle Sam has been called lots of names at Lake Success—today a new one. Yes, by Vishinsky. He compared Uncle Sam and John Bull to a boa constrictor.

*November 7, 1947*—Rumania has a new Foreign Minister, an interesting Foreign Minister—Mrs. Ana Pauker.
She is the chief of the Rumanian Reds and is reported to be the only one who can get Stalin on the telephone at any time.

*November 12, 1947*—Reds on the rampage in the great industrial city of Milan. All over Italy during the past few days there have been clashes and killings.

The United Nations has passed a resolution condemning Franco Spain. This was done today in spite of objections by the United States.

*November 14, 1947*—In Milwaukee they're launching the MacArthur-for-President boom.

The United Nations has again defied a Soviet boycott—today voting to set up a special U.N. commission for Korea. The purpose is to establish a free government in that Far Eastern country—a liberal regime to take control when forces of occupation are withdrawn.

*November 19, 1947*—In London tonight, shortly after the final rehearsal for tomorrow's royal wedding, King George created Lieutenant Philip Mountbatten His Royal Highness, the Duke of Edinburgh, Earl of

Merioneth and Baron Greenwich. At the same time investing him with the British Empire's highest honor—the Order of the Garter.

*November 20, 1947*—The word from London tonight is that there were at least a million lining the streets, cheering the new Duke and his Princess.

After all of King George's widely heralded intentions to preserve simplicity and austerity, the wedding represented old English pageantry at its best.

*November 21, 1947*—General Omar Bradley was named to succeed General Eisenhower as Chief of Staff.

*November 24, 1947*—In Palestine the Jews are reported to be at work night and day getting ready in case the Arabs resist partition by force.

In China the situation has grown so menacing that the Communist armies have already conquered nine tenths of all Manchuria, a region larger than France and Germany.

*November 25, 1947*—The meeting of the Foreign Ministers of the Big Four got off to not such an auspicious start today, Molotov immediately saying no. Secretary of State Marshall, backed by Great Britain and France, suggested that the conference should first take up a peace treaty with Austria—do that, and then go on to a German peace treaty. Molotov immediately refused with a charge of "American imperialism."

American motion pictures have made an official decision not to employ Communists.

*November 28, 1947*—From Rome came an order putting Milan, the second largest city in Italy, under military control in charge of the army, the generals in command.

That's the state of things in the great city of Milan tonight. It may be the beginning of the Communist revolution.

*December 1, 1947*—The Premier of Lebanon, who is at Baghdad this week, announced today that he has called a meeting of the Arab League to be held in Cairo, Saturday. The avowed purpose is "to safeguard Palestine for the Arabs."

*December 2, 1947*—In Cairo the faculty of the largest Moslem university in the world—the Alazhar Council of Ulemas—issued a call to all Moslems to a holy war, to prevent the partition of Palestine.

*December 3, 1947*—The government at Paris today called eighty thousand new soldiers to reinforce the police and mobile guards in crushing the Communist campaign of strikes and sabotage.

*December 4, 1947*—In Washington tonight the Justice Department issued a list of seventy-eight organizations it had branded as subversive groups, including the Communist party and the Ku Klux Klan and also a number of schools which Attorney General Tom Clark says appear to be adjuncts of the Communist party.

*December 9, 1947*—The Communists in France have sustained an all-around defeat. Today they called off the general strike and ordered nearly a million workers to return to their jobs.

*December 10, 1947*—The ancient city of Rome is in the grip of a general strike. Opinion in Rome is that the real purpose of the Communists is to overthrow the government.

*December 11, 1947*—The Big Four Foreign Ministers concur in a decision to raise the limit of German steel production some 7,500,000 tons a year—to 11,500,000.

The obstacle to this one has not been the Russians, but the French. Reds or no Reds, the people of old Gaul cannot overcome their perpetual consciousness of the German menace.

*December 12, 1947*—A telegram consisting of four words, a message scrawled with a blue crayon in the big handwriting of John L. Lewis, was addressed to President Green of the American Federation of Labor:

"Green—we disaffiliate—Lewis."

Years ago Lewis seceded from the A.F. of L. to form the C.I.O.; then he seceded from the C.I.O. and later rejoined the A.F. of L. The reunion hasn't lasted long, Lewis and his union seceding again.

Lewis demanded that the A.F. of L. defy that clause of the Taft-Hartley Act which requires union leaders to file affidavits that they are not Communists. A majority at the A.F. of L. convention disagreed—so now Lewis explains that he's taking a walk because the A.F. of L. is not fighting the Taft-Hartley law vigorously enough to suit him.

The general strike in Rome has collapsed.

*December 15, 1947*—The London Conference of the Big Four Foreign Ministers ends—a complete failure.

All possibility of agreement blocked by Molotov's attitude on one issue after another—reparations, German frontiers, the economic unity of Germany.

*December 24, 1947*—The Navy announces that the population of Eniwetok has been evacuated. The atoll in the far Pacific is to become a great atomic station.

*December 25, 1947*—Thousands of homeless, hungry Germans are moving across the frontier separating the British and Russian zones.

*December 26, 1947*—In Greece, a new Red offensive, following quickly upon the formation of a Communist guerrilla government.

*December 29, 1947*—Henry Wallace announced that he will head a third-party ticket for President in 1948. Wallace to run on a platform whose main planks will be "a people's peace and economic and social rights for the common man."

He is fighting the Truman Doctrine and the Marshall Plan.

*December 30, 1947*—King Michael, the twenty-six-year-old sovereign of Rumania, today announced that he was quitting his royal job.

Rumania now becomes a republic.

# 1948

For Americans, the story of the year is the election—President Truman winning in spite of the Dixiecrat revolt, the Wallace Progressive party movement, and the almost universal prediction of a Dewey victory by the pollsters.

Abroad the big story is the establishment of the Jewish state of Israel—the re-emergence of a people whose national life had been submerged for two millennia. The Jewish-Arab conflict develops into war.

In India, more violence, and the assassination of Gandhi. Communist conspiracy goes on. There is war in China and Indochina and Greece, a Red coup in Czechoslovakia, the arrest of Cardinal Mindszenty in Hungary. In Yugoslavia, Marshal Tito rebels successfully against Soviet domination—the first big split in the Communist ranks. In Germany, Stalin throws a blockade around Berlin, only to be beaten by the Allied airlift.

America is horrified by the revelation of Red espionage in Washington, with emphasis on the accusations against Alger Hiss. Scientists are amused and then outraged by the theories of Stalin's pet biologist, Lysenko.

At home there is mourning for the passing of three famous Americans—General Pershing, Charles Evans Hughes, and Babe Ruth.

January 1, 1948—In Great Britain the new year began with new phases of socialism going into effect—the Labour government taking over the railroads, for example, and other properties connected with transport.

January 5, 1948—The United States has given Britain blanket authority to transfer any Lend-Lease military equipment held by British forces in Greece to the hard-pressed Greek Army battling the Communist guerrillas.

President William Green of the American Federation of Labor declares against Henry Wallace.

In New York the American Labor party today endorsed Henry Wallace and his third party.
But this was accompanied by a major walkout from the A.L.P.

At Frankfurt the United States and Great Britain handed to a conference of German political leaders a sweeping proposal for the establishment of a legislature, a cabinet, a high court, and a central bank. The word "government" was not used; but that's what it means, West Germany offered a plan for setting up its own legislative, administrative, judicial, and financial administration.
This follows directly from the breakdown of the London Conference of Foreign Ministers, which failed to agree on a unified German government.

*January 8, 1948*—The Greek Army will have the benefit of the advice of a corps of American officers in its fight to wipe out the guerrillas.

The C.I.O. already has expressed itself as opposed to the support of a third party. Its principal goal in the election being to defeat every member of Congress who voted for the Taft-Hartley law.

*January 9, 1948*—The British coal board announces that during the six months of government ownership the coal mines of Britain lost more than one million, seven hundred and forty-five thousand pounds sterling.
During the same period in 1946, under private ownership, the British coal mines made a profit. They earned a net of more than sixteen million pounds, nearly sixty-seven million dollars.

*January 14, 1948*—The Americans are not going to get out of Berlin—that was made official in Washington today.

In India the news of Mahatma Gandhi's new fast is accompanied by a story of horror. Gandhi is undergoing his Hindu penance as a protest against the violence between Hindus and Moslems. And now comes word of the massacre of 1,300 Hindus and Sikh refugees.

They're evacuating missionaries in China, taking them out of the upper Yangtze Valley, away from the threat of the Communists.

*January 15, 1948*—In China the Communists have blasted themselves a corridor six hundred miles long, all the way from Peiping to the Yangtze River near Hankow.

*January 16, 1948*—The Jews stormed into Haifa today in a regular military assault.

*January 19, 1948*—The leaders of Indonesia and the Netherlands today signed an agreement at Batavia.

*January 20, 1948*—In India, Gandhi was bombed today, a small homemade grenade bursting as he presided at a prayer meeting in his garden. The Mahatma was unscathed, though nine of his followers were injured.

*January 21, 1948*—At last we have the publication of Nazi documents that were seized by the American Army in the war, secret papers giving an official account of the relations between Nazi Germany and Soviet Russia during the time when Hitler and Stalin were pals.

Hitler, then at the height of his victories in the European war, offered a scheme whereby Nazi Germany would get European conquests and Central Africa; Fascist Italy would acquire North Africa; Soviet Russia would get what the document calls "the territory south of the Soviet Union in the direction of the Indian Ocean," which pointed toward Iraq, Persia, and India.

Molotov, in behalf of Stalin, agreed to this division of the world. So what happened? Why didn't they go ahead with the scheme? Because Molotov also demanded an immediate Soviet grab in the Balkans—those same Balkans which today are Soviet puppet dictatorships. The Nazis themselves had Balkan ideas, and Hitler never replied to the Molotov demand. Instead, the documents show that he gave a secret order to the German Army command, an order to be prepared "to crush Soviet Russia in a quick campaign."

Mahatma Gandhi was going from Birla House to a prayer meeting in the garden. The seventy-eight-year-old Mahatma walked feebly after the fast, leaning on a long cane. He stopped to speak to a friend. Beside this friend was a tall, heavily built man wearing a uniform of military khaki. His hands were folded together in the Hindu gesture of greeting. But between his hands was a pistol. He raised it and shot Gandhi three times.

The assassin was about to be torn to pieces when police intervened and took him off to prison. He is a Hindu opposer to Gandhi's policy of peace with the Moslems.

Thus passes Mahatma Gandhi, the great soul. To all of India he was the Mahatma, which means "great soul."

*February 2, 1948*—Uncle Sam today arrested Gerhart Eisler, described as the most dangerous Communist in the U.S.A.

The government headed by Pandit Nehru at New Delhi is being blamed for failure to take measures to protect the Mahatma, to which the government replies it was Gandhi's own doing. The police wanted to search people who attended his prayer meetings, but this Gandhi refused to allow. He would not consider his own safety.

*February 3, 1948*—Tonight begins the independence of Ceylon—the Crown Colony of Ceylon now becomes a dominion within the British Commonwealth.

*February 6, 1948*—At White Sands, New Mexico, today American scientists succeeded in controlling the flight of the German V-2 rocket. A tremendous forward step in the science of guided missiles, a giant rocket shot aloft and successfully guided on its flight by radio control.

The United States has named a new director to head the American Mission to Greece. He's an officer with a great war record, Major General van Fleet, who commanded the American division that finally broke the German drive in the Battle of the Bulge.

*February 11, 1948*—The Russian composers are accused of turning out symphonies and operas with a wrong political slant.

The offending composers are named, a whole string of them. At the top of the list are the famous names of Shostakovich and Prokofiev.

*February 12, 1948*—Two and a half million weeping people took part in the final service for Mahatma Gandhi. Cabinet Ministers, princes, and untouchables were there. Landowners, bejeweled rajahs, pundits, sadhus, and peasants crowded the banks of the Ganges, where the two holy rivers converge—the Jumna and the Ganges. They watched while Gandhi's sons consigned into the sacred waters the ashes of the little brown man in the loincloth.

*February 13, 1948*—In Germany the Soviets have set up a German administration of their own—thus countering the policy of the British and Americans in their unified zone.

*February 16, 1948*—Northern Korea today proclaimed, by radio, an independent republic. At the same time it was publicly announced that this new Asiatic state has a strong army, equipped with Russian arms, commanded and trained by Soviet officers.

*February 19, 1948*—In China the Communist armies are pushing farther and farther south.

*February 23, 1948*—Henry Wallace today received a Washington's Birthday present. He obtained the services of a candidate to run for Vice-

President on his ticket. His candidate, the Honorable Glen H. Taylor, United States Senator from Idaho, popularly known as the "Singing Cowboy."

*February 24, 1948*—It's all over in Czechoslovakia. Or about that. The Communists grabbed everything today, complete control.

The Red authorities at Prague sent an edict to all the mayors and town councils, commanding them to take orders from local action committees of the Communists.

A new Constitution for ancient India. A bill of rights promising justice, liberty, equality, and fraternity to 333,000,000 people, regardless of caste, race, religion, or sex. Freedom of conscience, freedom of worship—even abolition of the caste system.

*February 25, 1948*—What now about Benes?

Today he yielded. Benes gave his presidential assent to the Red dictatorship of Communist Premier Gottwald. President Benes going through the formality that completes the transformation of Czechoslovakia into a police state behind the iron curtain.

*March 4, 1948*—Secretary of Commerce Averell Harriman has refused to turn over to the House Un-American Activities Committee his department's file on the loyalty investigation of Dr. Condon of the Bureau of Standards.

*March 5, 1948*—Dramatic news from Damascus, the ancient capital of ancient Syria. Fawzi el Kawkji, commander-in-chief of the Arab anti-partition forces, entered Palestine late this evening at the head of a column of troops.

*March 8, 1948*—It is not lawful to teach religion in the public schools of the United States even though the parents of the pupils consent. This from no less an authority than the Supreme Court of the United States.

*March 10, 1948*—Now the announcement made by the Red government in Prague that Foreign Minister Jan Masaryk threw himself from a window to his death, and that the Red regime is paying him solemn funeral honors.

*March 11, 1948*—Uncle Sam made a plea to Britain today, asking that the evacuation of troops from the Holy Land be postponed. Britain's answer was a polite "No!"

*March 15, 1948*—Today the President issued a formal order to officials of the executive branch of our federal government to ignore subpoenas from congressional committees—subpoenas asking for reports on loyalties of employees.

Our State Department today issued a warning to the people of Italy. That if the Communists win the elections on April 18 no more help from Uncle Sam.

*March 17, 1948*—The tone of the President's message was not unexpected—the somber picture that he painted of the threat of Red aggression, the fall of Czechoslovakia, the Soviet demands on Finland, the peril of this to neighboring Scandinavia, the danger of a Red seizure in Italy.

What could be more dramatic in the situation than to call for a renewal of Selective Service—the draft?

*March 19, 1948*—The United States proposes that the partition plan for Palestine be abandoned! Washington reverses itself and offers an alternative—the establishment of a United Nations trusteeship over Palestine.

In Paris today it was stated that the atomic physicist Madame Joliot-Curie was invited to the United States by Professor Einstein—as well as by the anti-Fascist organization she came over here to address. That organization is described by the Department of Justice as disloyal and subversive.

On this side of the ocean Madame Joliot-Curie has been released—after having been detained by the immigration authorities overnight.

*March 23, 1948*—In Jerusalem today the Jewish provisional government rejected the American proposal for a U.N. trusteeship instead of partition and decided to proceed according to the original plan—as if there had been no reversal.

*March 26, 1948*—Two sons of the late President Roosevelt come out for Eisenhower—Franklin D., Jr., and Elliott. They oppose the nomination of President Truman on the Democratic ticket.

All of which brings a new climax in the Democratic revolt—discard Truman and draft Eisenhower.

*March 31, 1948*—In Italy today the Reds let out a scream—and their wails of anguish are of a kind to interest us Americans in particular. They are howling because of letters written by Italian Americans and Americans of Italian descent to families and relatives in Italy. Letters giving sound advice about freedom and civil rights here in America as compared with the totalitarianism of Soviet Russia. All of which has its meaning for the critical Italian election less than two weeks from now.

A good deal of attention is being given to a Soviet move in the Berlin area—the Reds tightening suddenly on travel controls.

*April 1, 1948*—The present situation arose last night when the Soviets halted all rail traffic between Berlin and the American, British, and French zones by insisting on the right to board and search any Allied rolling stock crossing their territory. The roads were also blocked.

The United States Army is now running supplies into the American zone by airplane. We have some two million German civilians and ten thousand army and civilian personnel to feed.

*April 2, 1948*—All that is needed now for the foreign relief program to become a law is President Truman's signature.

The bill provides for the European Recovery Program, together with aid to China. The version that becomes a law excludes Franco Spain. That was inevitable after the way the liberal countries of Western Europe protested against the vote by the House of Representatives to put Franco into the Marshall Plan.

The princes of India are being dispossessed, their territories incorporated into the new nation of India. Maharajahs, hereditary rulers of rich domains with many palaces and golden revenues, and rajahs of lesser states are permitted to retain their titles, and each is allowed to keep one palace, and is granted one tenth of the revenue of his former principality.

*April 5, 1948*—In Berlin today General Lucius Clay announces that fighter planes will escort all American transport planes flying through the Russian zone from now on.

*April 8, 1948*—After four days of fierce fighting two thousand fully equipped Arab soldiers stormed and captured the fortified village of Kastel, on that historic and vital highway between the Holy City and the coast. By capturing the village the Arabs gain strategic control of the life line between the Jews in Jerusalem and on the coast.

*April 12, 1948*—In London the unveiling of the statue to Franklin Delano Roosevelt in Grosvenor Square—"Eisenhower Platz" the G.I.s used to call it. Grosvenor Square being where the general had his headquarters.

Mrs. Roosevelt unveiled the ten-foot bronze statue which depicts our wartime President.

*April 13, 1948*—The Moscow radio announces a flat turndown on the suggestion by the Western powers that Trieste be restored to Italy.

*April 16, 1948*—From Palestine the word is Armageddon. It's a great symbolical word, Biblical, for the culminating clash. But there's nothing symbolical about it today—Jewish and Arab armies locked in battle, on the plain of Jezreel, and that's Armageddon.

The latest tells of trained Arab troops entering Palestine from Transjordan—as announced by an Arab military spokesman. Abdullah's kingdom has a well-trained army, and now we hear that five thousand soldiers have crossed the river Jordan with modern equipment, including heavy artillery—reinforcements for the Arabs. At the same time the Jewish militia, Haganah, is reported to be rushing armored cars with a thousand troops and artillery to the scene where Jewish and Arab forces are locked in a desperate battle.

*April 19, 1948*—The news in Washington indicates we have tried out an improved atom bomb. Tested it in secrecy at Eniwetok atoll, in the remote Pacific.

*April 20, 1948*—A late bulletin tonight tells of the shooting of Walter Reuther, president of the auto workers' union. A gunman fired at him through a window of his Detroit home!

Reuther was standing in his kitchen when a shotgun blast nearly tore off his arm.

*April 21, 1948*—All day the figures have been rolling in from Italy and telling the same story—the Communist front beaten by two to one. The Christian Democratic party, led by Premier de Gasperi, has almost an absolute majority over all other parties.

A new marvel in the field of radioactivity—an artificial substitute for radium.

It is the metal cobalt, which is common and inexpensive, cobalt made radioactive.

*April 22, 1948*—The Jews tonight are in possession of a rich prize—Palestine's most modern port, the city of Haifa. The Arabs quitting the captured city in every available craft.

*April 30, 1948*—The Jewish forces won what appears to have been a signal victory in Jerusalem today. Opening a showdown battle for the Holy City, they seized the General Post Office Building and stormed an Arab section called the Katamon quarter.

*May 3, 1948*—General Ike is now officially a "military elder statesman." Today he became President Eisenhower, president of Columbia University.

*May 7, 1948*—Today the representatives of the Western powers in the United Nations announced that all atomic negotiations have been abandoned because Soviet Russia has blocked the establishment of any international machinery that could be effective for world atomic control.

*May 10, 1948*—The Reds took a sound shellacking at the polls as the Koreans voted for the first time in four thousand years.

The Communists had no candidates, but tried to stop the election by violence.

The score in this first Korean election? Six million people voted; over a hundred were killed, scores were injured, and two hundred arrested.

A truce in Jerusalem! Under this the Holy City will become a hospital zone, completely demilitarized.

*May 11, 1948*—The truce at Jerusalem was endangered today when a ferocious battle between Jews and Arabs on the Tel Aviv highway surged near to the suburbs of the Holy City.

*May 14, 1948*—A little less than an hour ago the minute hand of the clock came around to a point that marked a decision in history.

The Jewish state began its formal existence after having been proclaimed a little earlier this afternoon. The British mandate ended. The British are pulling out.

Everybody waits to see what the various Moslem states will do. Push into Palestine—they will. But what are their ultimate plans? Will they be content with merely occupying the so-called Arab areas of the Holy Land? Or will they invade Jewish sections—thereby bringing about immediate war with the new Jewish state?

Rabbi Abba Hillel Silver, leader of the Jewish group that has been fighting for Palestine before the United Nations, tells me that the Jews are not fearful of the outcome even if full-scale war does develop, that the fighting power of the Moslems, of Syria and Transjordan, has been overrated. That the Jews have a modern army and the Arabs' army is not so modern.

A few minutes after the six o'clock deadline President Truman had taken action, the White House announcing that the United States recognizes the new nation, Israel.

*May 17, 1948*—The Soviet Government today recognized the state of Israel. British recognition of Israel is withheld purely for legal reasons, says the London Foreign Office.

*May 18, 1948*—Troops of the Arab Legion have entered the old walled city of Jerusalem, and are taking part in the Moslem attack on the Jewish quarter.

*May 19, 1948*—The Arabs claim to have won control of all of the ancient walled city in Jerusalem, beating down resistance in the Jewish quarter.

*May 20, 1948*—The United Nations has appointed Count Folke Bernadotte, vice-president of the Swedish Red Cross, to act as its mediator in Palestine.

A desperate battle is being fought in the old city of Jerusalem tonight.

*May 21, 1948*—Cairo tells of a lightning-fast Egyptian drive for forty miles which seized Beersheba and then Hebron on the road to Jerusalem.

Today the defenders of the Jewish quarter in the old walled city were blasted hour after hour by the guns of the Arab Legion.

*May 26, 1948*—The Arabs turned down the demand by the U.N. that they stop fighting.

They will agree to quit fighting on three conditions: that the new Jewish state of Israel be dissolved, Jewish immigration into Palestine be stopped during the period of the armistice, the importation of weapons be halted.

The battle for Jerusalem shifted westward today. The focus of savage fighting was on the highway to the coast, a Jewish life line. There the troops of Haganah are making a desperate attempt to break through an Arab roadblock and open the way to the Holy City—where defenders of Israel have been battling so stubbornly.

*May 27, 1948*—The fighting in Jerusalem appears to be almost over. Five hundred Jewish soldiers reported to be left in this last-ditch stand.

Heavy fighting along that northern border, the Arabs attacking daily from the north and the east with tanks. Although some of the frontier villages have changed hands several times, the Jews are holding their own.

A surprise from South Africa: Field Marshal Jan Christiaan Smuts, Prime Minister, has been defeated at the polls. This means that Smuts must resign as Prime Minister. A position he has held since 1939.

*May 28, 1948*—The Jews in the Holy City have surrendered. The soldiers of Haganah—the four hundred still alive—laying down their arms. In the burning ruins and the face of the blistering fire of Glubb Pasha's mechanized Arab Legion, they at last gave up.

*May 31, 1948*—A new national leader appears upon the stage of world politics tonight—a Korean. Today at Seoul the newly elected Korean legislature named a chairman, which was only the first measure in making him the head of the Korean Republic. He is Syngman Rhee, seventy-three years old, and an anti-Communist.

*June 3, 1948*—Eisenhower says he will never run for President on the Democratic ticket because he is a Republican.

Count Bernadotte of Sweden is busy in the Middle East today trying to arrange a truce between the Arabs and the Jews.

*June 4, 1948*—The biggest battle of the Palestine war still continues at Jenin.

*June 7, 1948*—The story in Prague today is that Benes has quit because he is disgusted with the new Communist Constitution of the country he helped found.

West Germany is to have home rule under a federal government. So announced today in Berlin, and in five European capitals—announced by the United States and the five nations of the European Western union.

*June 9, 1948*—The Palestine truce agreed upon today was, in surprisingly large part, the personal doing of the nephew of the King of Sweden, Count Bernadotte.

Today President Truman, in the Pacific Northwest, continued his verbal bombardment against the Republican Congress. Throughout his cross-country trip he has been assailing the G.O.P. lawmakers on one point after another, and today he summarized in thirteen words. "This," said he, "is the worst Congress we have had since the first one met!"

*June 10, 1948*—Tel Aviv dispatches speak of anger and hostility to the truce terms, the Jews alleging that Bernadotte has favored the Arabs.

An American Air Force pilot has flown faster than the speed of sound. That is, more than seven hundred and sixty miles an hour, sea level. The first man to break through the supersonic wall! Air Secretary Symington announced the news today, although the flight was made by twenty-five-

year-old Captain Charles Yeager at Muroc Air Base, California, as long
ago as last October.

*June 21, 1948*—The Supreme Court today ruled that unions are permitted to use their newspapers in behalf of political candidates. This
negates one clause of the Taft-Hartley law.

*June 23, 1948*—I'm at the Republican National Convention tonight.
The dominant event today was the formation of a stop-Dewey coalition.

*June 24, 1948*—The Dewey band wagon never stopped rolling. All
through the balloting Dewey ran consistently ahead of the estimates made,
not only by his opponents, but also by neutral newsmen. So now Thomas
E. Dewey is the Republican candidate for President.

It is feared the Soviets may now be launching a decisive attempt to
get the Western Allies out of the German capital.
Cutting of all railroad and highway traffic to and from the American,
British, and French areas—the Russians blocking all the supply lines on
the ground.

*June 25, 1948*—The Soviets have called off their ban on railroad and
highway transportation for the Western Allies in Berlin. This being the
latest in the puzzling game that the Russians are playing.

President Truman today signed the bill to admit 205,000 displaced
Europeans into the United States, but he signed with an angry rebuke for
Congress. He said the bill to bring in the D.P.s included restrictions that
discriminate against Jews and Catholics.

*June 28, 1948*—Here's amazing news: a dispatch from Yugoslavia says
that Marshal Tito has been read out of the Cominform by the Soviet
Government.
Tito charged with deserting the tradition of communism. Tito said to
fear that the Soviet Union threatens the independence of Yugoslavia. He
is charged with seeking to gain favor with the "imperialist states." Meaning us, of course, and the British.

In Berlin the Soviets are trying to starve us out by stopping the shipment of all food by rail and road.
American and British planes are flying food into Berlin on a shuttle
run.

*June 29, 1948*—The regime of Red Marshal Tito answered back with defiance. The Yugoslav declaration states: "The Cominform has abandoned the principle on which it was founded."

*June 30, 1948*—The biggest air operation since the end of the second world war is in full swing tonight—western Berlin being provisioned by air.

All day long, great transports landed on the flying field of the Western Allies in Berlin, giant planes loaded with supplies.

*July 1, 1948*—The Arab League political committee has turned down Count Bernadotte's proposals for a Palestine peace.

In Berlin today Russia ended all four-power co-operation for Germany. The Russian delegation walked out of the Kommandantura, the four-power council which governs Berlin.

*July 5, 1948*—General Ike himself has burst the Eisenhower boom, and the band wagon which was rolling so fast today now comes to a complete stop. The general says no, once and for all.

In that greatest airlift in all history American planes alone have flown 1,115 cargo flights in nine days. The mileage comes to nearly seven hundred thousand, enough miles to circle the world twenty-eight times.

*July 7, 1948*—In far off Malaya a total war has been declared against Red terrorists.

*July 9, 1948*—In Palestine today the renewal of the war was widespread. Clashes between Israelis and Arabs are reported all the way from Galilee in the north to Gaza in the south.

*July 13, 1948*—I'm at the Democratic National Convention, where the big noise is the Dixiecrat revolt.

*July 15, 1948*—Around the convention everybody supposed that President Truman, in his address, would seek to appease the bitterness of the Southern revolt.

He virtually ignored the revolt, and gave the South no mention. He lashed at the Republican Congress with telling phrases and biting sarcasm. The ticket—Truman and Barkley.

*July 16, 1948*—The first transatlantic flight by jet planes has just been completed—six British Vampire jets landing late this afternoon at Montreal.

*July 19, 1948*—Washington announces that we have backed Marshal Tito's hand against Russia by freeing the forty-seven million dollars in gold and other Yugoslav assets frozen here since the war.

General Pershing was buried today at Arlington in the National Cemetery. His body lowered into the grave that he himself chose years ago—among his comrades of World War I, not far from the tomb of the Unknown Soldier, the unknown warrior who was one of his men.

*July 21, 1948*—The Berlin aerial supply line, jumping over the land blockade, is carrying on in great style—aided by good weather. .

The FBI today was arresting or looking for big-time Communists. The federal grand jury indicted twelve yesterday, the list of what is being called the twelve-man politburo of American communism. Six were arrested in New York last night, headed by William Z. Foster, Communist party chairman and several times Red candidate for President.

*July 23, 1948*—The third-party convention got going in Philadelphia tonight with the slogan "Wallace or war." The left-wing political oratory is thundering.

*August 3, 1948*—Whittaker Chambers, a former Communist member of the Red underground, told the House Un-American Activities Committee how in 1939 he sought to warn the White House, the late President Franklin D. Roosevelt, of the way Communist conspirators were infiltrating into the government—Reds holding high federal offices.

What happened? Nothing.

Chambers named a new series of names of Communists who were high in the government—including Alger Hiss, a high-ranking official of the State Department, who helped in the founding of the United Nations, who accompanied President Franklin D. Roosevelt to the Yalta Conference, and who is now head of the Carnegie Endowment for International Peace.

*August 4, 1948*—In Washington today Nathan Gregory Silvermaster denounced the charges made against him by Elizabeth Bentley. She, having confessed that she did Red spy work during wartime, has accused Silvermaster of having been the head of a Communist underground group in the government.

But he refused to say whether he is or has been a Communist. He refused on constitutional privilege, on the ground that by answering he might incriminate himself.

This afternoon Mrs. Roosevelt gives her opinion of the Red spy revelations. She describes Elizabeth Bentley's testimony in the following words: "the fantastic story of this evidently neurotic lady."

*August 5, 1948*—President Truman at a press conference authorized the following direct quotation: "They are using these hearings simply as a red herring, to keep from doing what they ought to do."

The House committee, meanwhile, questioned Alger Hiss. About Whittaker Chambers he said: "Why, I don't know Chambers." Then he added: "As far as I know, I have never laid eyes on him."

*August 6, 1948*—One of the greatest exploits in the history of athletics was completed tonight at the Olympic games in London. A seventeen-year-old American schoolboy won the decathlon, the most grueling event in Olympic competition. Bob Mathias of California.

*August 11, 1948*—Houston, Texas, is having a Dixiecrat celebration tonight—with Governor Strom Thurmond of South Carolina accepting the nomination.

*August 12, 1948*—The Russians are making frantic, but so far futile, efforts to see Mrs. Kasenkina, the Soviet schoolteacher who fell or jumped from a third-story window of the Soviet consulate this afternoon.

The United States today gave diplomatic recognition to the new government of Korea, which the Russians are boycotting.

The United States considers the Korean Government in Seoul as the government of all Korea—including the northern Russian zone.

*August 13, 1948*—The Red government at Moscow is charging the State Department in Washington with full responsibility for what Moscow calls the "kidnaping" of the Russian woman teacher, Mrs. Kasenkina.

Lauchlin Currie, as administrative aide to the late Franklin D. Roosevelt, took part in the formation of the United Nations, and was on the presidential staff at the Yalta Conference. Today he denied he had ever given out secret information, rejecting especially the charge that he had tipped the Silvermaster spy ring off to the fact that American Intelligence had broken the Soviet code.

*August 17, 1948*—Alger Hiss admits that he did know Whittaker Chambers. He declared that he was acquainted with Chambers under the name of George Crosley.

A new turn of drama enters the espionage with the sudden death from a heart attack of Harry Dexter White, former Assistant Secretary of the

Treasury, who was accused by both Elizabeth Bentley and Whittaker Chambers.

Tonight Babe Ruth lies in state at the Yankee Stadium—the house that Ruth built. This evening the gates were opened, and throngs of people poured in, mourners passing for a last look at the home-run king whom the baseball fans knew so well a few years ago.

*August 19, 1948*—Alger Hiss, former State Department official, has refused to take the lie detector test.

*August 25, 1948*—Today Mrs. Kasenkina, the Russian schoolteacher, spoke out. For the first time the doctors at Roosevelt Hospital permitted her to be interviewed by newsmen. She said the Soviet Government had killed her husband and her son, and that she had decided to escape from the Reds even before she left Russia.

*August 27, 1948*—Former Chief Justice Charles Evans Hughes died tonight at the age of eighty-six.

*August 31, 1948*—Zhdanov, whose death at fifty-one is announced by Moscow, was long regarded as the No. 1 candidate to take the place of the Soviet dictator when Stalin disappears from the scene.

*September 2, 1948*—The Democratic National Committee read the Dixiecrat revolters out of the Democratic party. From now on, says the committee, it recognizes only Southern Democrats who support the regular Democratic Truman-Barkley political ticket.

*September 3, 1948*—In Czechoslovakia tonight they are mourning former President Benes, who died today at the age of sixty-four—the people remembering him as a representative of their lost freedom.

*September 6, 1948*—At Amsterdam, in the old, old church called New Church, they crowned Juliana as Queen of the Netherlands.

*September 7, 1948*—The Red riots in Berlin have produced a logical conclusion. Berlin tonight has two administrations, the legal non-Communist majority and the Red factions setting up a rump assembly.

*September 8, 1948*—The Central Committee of the Communist party of Soviet Russia hurls furious denunciation at Red Marshal Tito. His government is described in the following words: "a brutal terrorist regime, with repressions, mass arrests and murders."
The Yugoslav Communists are urged to overthrow Tito and his nationalist policy.

*September 9, 1948*—Today's Roper poll announcement is the subject of much comment from coast to coast. Roper sums it up as follows: "I am not going to stop gathering facts about this presidential election. But I am going to stop reporting them unless something really interesting happens. My silence on this point," he adds, "can be construed as an indication that Mr. Dewey is still so clearly ahead that we might just as well get ready to listen to his inaugural."

A Talmadge is head man in Georgia again today. Herman Talmadge, son of the late Governor Gene Talmadge, being elected governor in the Democratic primary.

*September 16, 1948*—A report from Tel Aviv—more heavy fighting in Jerusalem.

*September 17, 1948*—The news tonight brings an account of the assassination of Count Bernadotte, nephew of the King of Sweden, mediator for the United Nations.

The crime occurred while he was driving through the Jewish Katamon quarter of Jerusalem. The assassins were in Jewish Army uniforms, riding in a jeep of the Jewish Army type.

The road was blocked by the jeep. Two men armed with machine guns looked in. When they saw the Count they poked a gun through a window and opened fire.

The word is that the assassins were members of the Stern gang of the Jewish underground. During recent weeks the extremist group conducted a violent campaign demanding that Bernadotte, the United Nations mediator, get out of Palestine.

Late news tells us that a temporary successor to Count Bernadotte has been named. He is Dr. Ralph Bunche, an American Negro who was Bernadotte's chief assistant in Palestine.

*September 20, 1948*—A dispatch from Seoul, capital of South Korea, says that the Red regime in North Korea has a Russian-trained army of five hundred thousand fully equipped men, enough for a full-scale invasion if our troops were withdrawn.

*September 21, 1948*—In Palestine, news that the extremist organization, Irgun Zvai Leumi, has ended its underground existence, yielding to a twenty-four-hour ultimatum issued by the government of Israel. The other group is the Stern gang, which assassinated Count Bernadotte. Those terrorists are still a problem for the government of Israel, which now has made hundreds of arrests.

*September 22, 1948*—En route to San Francisco and Oakland for major speeches, the President today continued his embittered remarks, calling Republican leaders in Congress "a bunch of old mossbacks living back in 1890."

*September 23, 1948*—In Tel Aviv the Israeli Government offers a reward of twenty thousand dollars for information leading to the arrest of the assassin of Count Bernadotte and his French aide.

*September 24, 1948*—The Dewey address tonight had to do with communism. "The head of our own government," said Dewey, "called the exposure of Communists in our government a red herring."

*October 1, 1948*—Tonight's headline, all over the nation, is Vishinsky's hint that Soviet Russia has the atomic bomb.

*October 4, 1948*—In London today Field Marshal Viscount Montgomery, Monty of El Alamein, was officially named supreme commander of the Western union defense countries.

*October 8, 1948*—The United Mine Workers took official action today in declaring against President Truman and giving implied endorsement to Governor Dewey. At the convention in Cincinnati, John L. Lewis repeated his violent attack upon the President-candidate, calling him an enemy of the miners.

*October 12, 1948*—The Red command informed the airlift authorities that they were going to hold blind-flying practice in the corridors through which the food planes are flying to Berlin. Which sounds like a ghoulish idea, sending pilots without vision along a busy line of air traffic.

*October 14, 1948*—In Paris today before the U. N. Security Council, Dr. Ralph Bunche, acting mediator for Palestine, charged the state of Israel with negligence in regard to the assassination of Count Bernadotte.

*October 19, 1948*—Fighting between soldiers in the southern part of the Holy Land, the Negeb, the desert—Israeli and Egyptians. Today the conflict burst into a new fury.

*October 21, 1948*—The Israeli forces announce the capture of the ancient town of Beersheba, the oasis of the southern Palestine desert— ancient home of Abraham and Lot.

*October 22, 1948*—There're peace and quiet tonight in the Negeb, the desert of southern Palestine—both sides obeying the cease-fire order issued by the United Nations.

*October 25, 1948*—In Paris today Russia formally vetoed the Security Council plan to end the Berlin blockade.

France now has more than one hundred thousand soldiers in Indochina. They are fighting the Communist-led Vietnam nationalists.

The guerrilla war is being led by a Moscow-trained Communist, Ho Chi Minh.

*October 26, 1948*—The Government of Israel declares that not one inch of captured territory will be given up.

President Truman tonight continued his battle against the public opinion polls. At Cleveland he charged that there is a conspiracy—which accounts for the fact that the polls are unanimous in predicting the election of Governor Dewey.

*October 28, 1948*—The Western powers' reactions to Soviet Premier Stalin's charge that they repudiated a solution of the Berlin crisis—after such a solution had been agreed upon in private—are scathing.

Across the other side of the world, in China, Chiang Kai-shek's Manchurian expeditionary force is facing disaster.

*November 1, 1948*—In London today the British people were told by their newspapers that "to all purposes" Governor Dewey has already won.

*November 2, 1948*—The latest total for scattered votes shows Truman 83,000, Dewey 76,000.

*November 3, 1948*—Our nation today may well salute the greatest political gladiator in American presidential history. The classic formula is this: to go in against great odds, wage a singlehanded battle, keep on fighting when everybody else thinks it is hopeless, never yield an inch, and then win out in the end. Which classic formula pretty much tells the story of President Truman in the election.

Looking back on it all, it would seem to me that Governor Dewey was the No. 1 victim of the polls and the experts.

In the face of the universal verdict he could only be convinced that victory was sure. So therefore he felt he could keep his political argument on a lofty plane and avoid anger and enmity, feuds and rancor.

*November 4, 1948*—Figures today confirm the magnitude of the Truman victory. The popular vote—a little short of a majority of two million.

The World parliament, the General Assembly of the United Nations, has adopted the American program for the control of atomic energy.

The Security Council of the United Nations voted tonight to order the Jewish state to withdraw from territory captured in the southern desert of Palestine, the Negeb.

*November 9, 1948*—The latest from Palestine pictures a new flare-up of war in the southern desert, the Negeb.

*November 10, 1948*—From Shanghai tonight comes the news that Generalissimo Chiang has placed all China under martial law.

*November 15, 1948*—In London tonight the police had to check the noisy demonstrations of the happy crowd outside Buckingham Palace. Celebrating the birth of a royal prince, son of Princess Elizabeth and the Duke of Edinburgh.

*November 16, 1948*—The news tonight confirms the decision of Ireland to withdraw entirely from all connection with Great Britain. Ireland is virtually independent, but hitherto has kept a vague shadowy sort of tie with the British Commonwealth. But now even that is to end.

*November 17, 1948*—We hear that India intends to *remain* within the British Empire—or, as they now say, the Commonwealth of Nations. Yet India will become an *independent* republic.

The scheme, we hear, is for King George VI to represent the President of the Indian Republic in certain circumstances.

*November 18, 1948*—President Truman today reaffirmed his faith in the idea of a bipartisan foreign policy. He did this by appointing John Foster Dulles to fill the role of acting chairman of our delegation to the U.N. in Paris.

*November 19, 1948*—The Soviet arms proposal was rejected today by the General Assembly of the United Nations. The Moscow plan called for the big powers to reduce armament by one third. Also the outlawing of the atomic bomb—the United States to give up the bomb before the establishment of any world system for atomic control.

*November 22, 1948*—In the capital of Nationalist China foreign embassies are packing—getting ready to leave.

*November 23, 1948*—In Tokyo, General Douglas MacArthur has passed on the death sentences decreed against six Japanese war criminals —headed by Tojo, the Pearl Harbor Premier.

MacArthur upholds the death sentences, and orders them to be carried out.

*November 29, 1948*—Today sixty million untouchables, those age-old social outcasts, officially became men and women. A law passed in the Indian parliament gave them civil rights.

Thanks to twenty years of campaigning by Gandhi, the untouchables are free.

*December 1, 1948*—The Moscow Academy of Sciences has severed all contact with the British Royal Society. The reason—Communist party action in the field of biology.

Lysenko is Stalin's favorite scientist. He propounds a theory which discounts the importance of heredity—thereby going against world biological opinion, which emphasizes heredity.

Last night three top British scientists denounced Lysenko as an ignorant swindler who has used terror and suppression to force his ideas on genuine Russian scientists.

*December 2, 1948*—In China the Communist radio announces the fall of strategic Suchow.

East and West parted in Berlin today. The United States, Great Britain, and France ordered their liaison officers to quit city hall in the Soviet sector. Leave the offices where the German Communists have set up that rump Berlin City regime.

A report from Seoul tells of South Korean armies in action against the Communists in the north. With the Reds trying to capture a power plant fifty miles inside the border of South Korea.

*December 3, 1948*—Committee investigator Robert Stribling tells how Whittaker Chambers took him to the farmhouse where he lives and led him to a dried pumpkin. He lifted the cap off the pumpkin and took from the hollow space inside rolls of microfilm.

The microfilm is shown to include all sorts of secret documents of the State Department.

*December 6, 1948*—Our State Department today has praise for the Berlin citizens because they turned out in such large numbers to vote in the face of Communist threats of violence.

An overwhelming anti-Communist vote in spite of Red threats to their safety.

Whittaker Chambers has formally accused Alger Hiss of stealing confidential State Department documents. These to be delivered to Russia's top secret police agent in the United States.

*December 9, 1948*—President Truman today delivered another blast at the House Un-American Activities Committee. He told the reporters that the Washington spy hunt is all a search for headlines.

*December 13, 1948*—In his capital at Amman, Transjordan, today King Abdullah was formally proclaimed King of Transjordan and Arab Palestine.

Alger Hiss has temporarily given up his twenty-thousand-dollar-a-year job as president of the Carnegie Endowment for International Peace.

*December 14, 1948*—The infant son of Princess Elizabeth, heiress to the crown, will be baptized tomorrow, and the names were announced today—Charles Philip Arthur George.

Maybe some romantic reminiscence of Bonnie Prince Charlie.

*December 15, 1948*—The indictment of Alger Hiss for perjury is to be interpreted in the light of the fact that he cannot be indicted for espionage. This because of the Statute of Limitations—three years. He is accused of having given secret State Department documents to Whittaker Chambers back in 1938, ten years ago. So the grand jury in New York could indict only on the perjury charge, that Hiss lied under oath when he denied he had given secret State Department material to Whittaker Chambers for transmission to Soviet espionage.

*December 17, 1948*—At the Smithsonian Institution they placed formally on exhibition the Wright brothers' original plane. This on the forty-fifth anniversary of man's first flight.

*December 22, 1948*—The United States has taken strong action in the case of the Dutch attack on the Indonesian Republic. In the Security Council of the United Nations today American delegate Philip Jessup called the invasion a threat to the world peace.

The progress of the Dutch offensive in Java continues to be rapid.

The condemned Japanese war lords received the last rites of religion—Buddhism.

The seven were executed in two groups.

In the first group, of four, was Tojo, the Tokyo Premier who ordered the Pearl Harbor surprise and launched the war in the Pacific.

*December 23, 1948*—In Palestine war has broken out again, a Jewish offensive launched in the Negeb.

*December 28, 1948*—In Budapest tonight the charge of treason against Cardinal Mindszenty was made public, with gaudy details. Documents are said to prove that the Primate of Hungary was engaged in a royalist plot to make Otto of Hapsburg the King of Hungary—that same Otto who is the heir of the old-time Austro-Hungarian emperors.

*December 29, 1948*—These days are becoming fantastic, with all those new ideas of science. So fantastic that now we have Secretary Forrestal announcing an "earth satellite vehicle program."

The rocket, according to theory, would circle the earth as a satellite.

*December 31, 1948*—Israel gives a report of sweeping victories in the battle of the Negeb, which now has died down.

# 1949

This is the year in which the balance of power between East and West becomes generally stabilized. China falls to the Communists and East Germany becomes a new Soviet satellite. But the North Atlantic Treaty Organization is formed to protect Europe, and the West German Federal Republic gains its independence. One hopeful sign is the widening split between Tito and the other Communist countries.

The tide turns against the Greek Reds, their rebellion is a failure. Peace comes to Indonesia and the Middle East.

At home Shostakovitch stars at the Waldorf "peace conference" of Reds and their dupes. Our top Communists are convicted of conspiracy. In Washington the "revolt of the Admirals" fails with the dismissal of Admiral Denfeld.

*January 5, 1949*—Tel Aviv lifts the veil of censorship far enough to show that forces of Israel penetrated sixty miles into Egyptian territory, the Sinai Peninsula.

*January 7, 1949*—President Truman has just named Dean Acheson Secretary of State.

*January 10, 1949*—Generalissimo Chiang Kai-shek is getting ready to leave China.

*January 13, 1949*—On the island of Rhodes today United Nations mediator Ralph Bunche opened the armistice talks between Israel and Egypt.

Chiang's army, navy, and air force already have established headquarters on Formosa.

*January 17, 1949*—King Abdullah of Transjordan has entered into what he calls "a gentlemen's non-aggression agreement" with Israel.

The trial of twelve of our top-ranking Communists began in New York today.

*January 21, 1949*—What next for the Generalissimo? The Communists have put a price on his head as the No. 1 war criminal.

*January 25, 1949*—Moscow announces a new Red line-up of the Soviets and the puppet countries. This in answer to the alliance of Western democracies that is forming—a North Atlantic security system.

Marshal Tito, in revolt against the Soviets and the Cominform, is left out.

*January 26, 1949*—The votes in Israel's first general election give a strong lead to Mapai, the labor party of provisional Premier David Ben Gurion.

*January 28, 1949*—In New York today Federal Judge Harold Medina, who is presiding over the trial of those eleven Communists, revealed that he has been getting threatening communications.

*February 3, 1949*—President Truman repeats the official statement of yesterday, that he will not go into any two-way meeting with Stalin.

In Red Hungary, at Budapest, Josef Cardinal Mindszenty, the Primate of Hungary, went on trial today.

*February 7, 1949*—The government of Red Hungary has rejected the British protest against the way the Communists are conducting the trial of Cardinal Mindszenty.

The news tells how five wealthy women of San Francisco have put up one hundred thousand dollars to restore a shrine. Sounds like an echo out of a vanished past, but the sanctuary is dedicated to Rudolph Valentino, the movie sheik of yesteryear.

*February 8, 1949*—The scene in a Budapest courtroom today was grim. The Red tribunal was packed by guards with Tommy guns as prison sentences of various lengths were pronounced on the defendants, a life sentence for the Primate of Hungary.

*February 10, 1949*—The Red government of Bulgaria announces that it is bringing to trial fifteen ministers of the United Evangelical Church.

A dispatch from Washington states that a loyalty board has cleared William Remington, the employee of the Department of Commerce who was accused by Elizabeth Bentley.

*February 11, 1949*—In Northern Ireland, Belfast, an almost complete count of votes tonight shows an overwhelming majority for continued union with Great Britain.

In Red Bulgaria, same old story—the Protestant pastors have confessed.

*February 14, 1949*—Today the first Jewish parliament went into session.

Today's papal consistory was the most solemn way in which the pontiff of Rome, according to medieval ritual, could present a protest to the world, addressing the cardinals in Rome.

In a measured address he denounced the Red trial and denied the charges made by the Communists.

*February 17, 1949*—Selden Chapin, our Minister to Hungary, states that the Red charges accusing him of conspiring with Cardinal Mindszenty are "nonsense and pure fantasy."

He said he didn't know just how the Reds were able to wring a partial confession from the cardinal. But he added: "All kinds of pressures were used."

The first President of Israel was inaugurated today, Dr. Chaim Weizmann, taking the oath of office.

*February 22, 1949*—In France the Communist party is on record that if the Soviet Army occupied France the French people would co-operate with the invaders. That is, the Communists would.

*February 24, 1949*—The agreement between Israel and Egypt was formally signed.

Israel remains in possession of the Negeb. Egypt acquires a strip of Palestine coast from the Egypt-Sinai border to Gaza.

*February 25, 1949*—For the first time something made by man went outside the atmosphere of the earth. The missile they sent aloft from the New Mexico desert soared to an altitude of 250 miles.

*March 2, 1949*—The American Communist party follows the lead of the Reds in France and Italy. In case of war our Reds would co-operate with the Soviets too.

*March 3, 1949*—Secretary of Defense Forrestal has resigned. He is succeeded by Louis A. Johnson.

*March 4, 1949*—Molotov removed from the post of Foreign Minister of Soviet Russia, succeeded by Vishinsky.

*March 7, 1949*—Today Judge Medina rejected the demand that the case against the Communist leaders be thrown out of court because the President called those Red leaders traitors.

*March 8, 1949*—The Bulgarian trial of Protestant pastors ends with prison sentences.

Should Soviet forces invade the land down under, they would be welcomed and aided by the Australian Communists. So say the Australian Communists.

*March 11, 1949*—Israel and Transjordan signed a cease-fire order today.

*March 16, 1949*—The Southern Democrats today called off their long-distance oratory as the result of a deal with the Republicans.
Which means that the Truman racial program goes into the discard.

*March 18, 1949*—When the Soviet composer Shostakovich arrives in this country, he will not be greeted by Russian composer Stravinsky. The great exile refusing to meet Stalin's musical yes-man.

*March 23, 1949*—An armistice has been signed between Israel and Lebanon.

*March 25, 1949*—New York is having peculiar scenes tonight in connection with that world peace conference staged by the leftists. The Waldorf-Astoria picketed by marchers, who chanted slogans and waved placards championing human liberty.
Meanwhile, inside, a news conference was being held—the iron curtain delegations introduced to reporters. Introductions by Dr. Harlow Shapley, the Harvard astronomer. He's a top leader of the Council of the Arts, Sciences and Professions, the leftist outfit which has sponsored this Red peace conference.

The Academy Awards were made last night, those Hollywood Oscars, and the lion's share went to nobody less than the Bard of Avon.
For the best motion picture of the year—*Hamlet*. For the best acting of the year the winner is Sir Laurence Olivier, for playing the role of

Hamlet. There were other honors, too, for the British film production of the tragedy of the melancholy Dane.

*March 28, 1949*—Shostakovich at Madison Square Garden provided the unique spectacle of a musician confessing before an audience in America. He admitted that he had committed what he called "decadent bourgeois faults."

*March 31, 1949*—Winston Churchill addressed a convocation of the Massachusetts Institute of Technology today.

Churchill said the Russians are more afraid of our friendship than of our enmity.

*April 4, 1949*—This afternoon, the signing of the North Atlantic security pact. The nations that signed represent 332,000,000 people of the Atlantic powers.

*April 5, 1949*—The Red government of Bulgaria announces the ousting of the Communist Vice-Premier, Kostov. He failed to obey Moscow abjectly enough.

In England they were saying that the mishap to American Ambassador Douglas was an accident in a million. Which would seem to be an apt description of an expert fly-casting fisherman hooking his own left eye.

*April 6, 1949*—In the New York Red trial a Communist party member testifying that he has been in continuous touch with the FBI. He is Herbert Philbrick of Melrose, Massachusetts.

*April 8, 1949*—Great Britain, France, and the United States have okayed a plan for the formation of a West German republic.

*April 11, 1949*—The Nuremberg trials are ending at last. Today verdicts of guilty were handed down against eight more of the top officials of Hitler's Nazi regime.

*April 15, 1949*—Secretary of State Dean Acheson says that further military aid to Nationalist China would do more harm than good.

Israeli Premier David Ben Gurion says that Israel will never agree to the internationalization of the Holy City of Jerusalem.

*April 19, 1949*—The Western powers have rejected a Soviet approach for ending the Berlin blockade. They will not cancel their plans for a West German government.

Three former professors charge that Boston College is teaching heresy. This heresy, they say, consists of teaching the students that there is salvation outside the Catholic Church. The suspended Jesuit priest, Father Feeney, spoke up in the defense of the ousted professors.

*April 22, 1949*—The Chinese Communists are storming across the Yangtze.

The British sloop *Amethyst* is still trapped up the Yangtze. Today the crew of the *Amethyst* buried their dead, seventeen, in the gray waters of the river.

Today brings an official answer in the Roman Catholic controversy at Boston.

A new catechism clearly upholds the view of the Jesuit College and the archbishop that salvation is possible outside the Catholic Church.

*April 25, 1949*—General Chennault says the Communist sweep in China is due to blundering American Far Eastern policy.

*April 26, 1949*—Prime Minister Attlee indicates that Britain will do nothing violent about the Red Chinese attack on the British warships.

*May 4, 1949*—One of the most spectacular and tragic of air crashes occurred in Italy today when a big airliner crashed into the steeple of the cathedral in the city of Turin. At least twenty-nine persons killed—including the members of the champion football team of Italy.

*May 6, 1949*—The Dutch Government and the Indonesian Republic have agreed on a cease-fire.

*May 9, 1949*—Chiang Kai-shek is personally directing the defense of Shanghai.

*May 10, 1949*—The Frank Hague machine has lost the election in Jersey City.

The provisional capital of the new government of West Germany will be the old city of Bonn.

The Berlin blockade is over.

Princess Margaret was received by Pope Pius XII today.

*May 11, 1949*—Israel has been voted into the United Nations.

Gerhart Eisler has been discovered as a stowaway aboard a Polish steamship bound for Europe. The Department of Justice announces that Scotland Yard has been asked to seize Eisler when the Polish steamship docks at Southampton.

*May 12, 1949*—In London tonight the House of Commons ratified the Atlantic pact.

General Clay is the hero of the airlift to the German population.

*May 16, 1949*—Gerhart Eisler, the Communist spy chief, has been taken to a London jail.

*May 17, 1949*—In Berlin today the Communists finally made public the result of the vote in the Soviet zone last weekend.

Without any opposition candidates to vote for, nearly a third of the Germans in the Soviet zone voted no.

The name of Roosevelt is back in the Washington scene, Franklin D. Jr., going to Congress. The district, the Twentieth of New York.

*May 18, 1949*—President Truman names the first American civilian High Commissioner for Germany. He is John J. McCloy.

*May 19, 1949*—Great Britain won't extradite Communist Eisler if the British Government decides that Eisler is a bona fide political refugee.

The Senate Appropriations Subcommittee was told today that all future applicants for government fellowships in atomic science will be required to sign non-Communist affidavits.

*May 23, 1949*—A new flag is flying in Europe today—the banner of the Federal Republic of Germany.

The new federal Germany includes all the German states in the U.S., British, and French occupation zones.

The psychiatrist's opinion is that James Forrestal jumped to his death during a sudden fit of despondency. The tragedy happened at Bethesda Naval Hospital.

*May 24, 1949*—The news of the fall of Shanghai came with an abrupt suddenness tonight.

*May 27, 1949*—America's No. 1 Communist, Gerhart Eisler, is walking the streets of London, a free man. He'll go to East Germany instead of back to America.

*May 30, 1949*—The new Soviet-sponsored government of East Germany started in business today.

*May 31, 1949*—The reason for Eisler's presence in Prague is being kept a dark secret, but the guessing is he's attending a meeting of the Red Cominform.

*June 2, 1949*—Today the jury heard Whittaker Chambers tell of Hiss, in 1935, producing official documents on U.S. munitions to be sent to Russia.

Lysenko, at that meeting of biologists in Moscow, announced that his report had been okayed by the Central Committee of the Communist party.

Lysenko's antagonists at once confessed they had been wrong, and agreed with Lysenko on all points.

The Soviet Government is now enforcing a doctrine called "the inheritance of acquired characteristics."

*June 14, 1949*—There are savage goings on in the Balkans, the Reds having a ferocious purge. Today we are told why—Titoism.

Dr. Frank Oppenheimer, a brother of Dr. Robert Oppenheimer, today admitted that he had been a member of the Communist party—and so was his wife. He refused to comment about why he denied it two years ago. Today his resignation was accepted at the University of Minnesota.

*June 16, 1949*—In New York today Henry Julian Wadleigh, a former State Department economist, admitted that he did turn over some of our secret government documents to the Russians.

*June 17, 1949*—Tonight the blame is placed on Israel for rejecting proposals on behalf of the tens of thousands of Arab refugees.

Now Red prosecution of a Jewish group. The trial goes on in Hungary before the same Red court that condemned Cardinal Mindszenty. The defendants now are Zionists, accused of smuggling Jews out of Communist Hungary.

*June 20, 1949*—The Vatican announces that all members of the Czechoslovakian Catholic Action group are excommunicated.

*June 23, 1949*—Alger Hiss today denied, under oath, that he had ever been a Communist, or that he ever turned over any government secrets to any unauthorized person.

*September 5, 1949*—The longest championship tennis match was played today—Pancho Gonzales beating Ted Schroeder in three out of five sets. Gonzales and Schroeder went to sixty-seven games.

In the Cleveland air races Bill Odom, the round-the-world flyer, was killed.

*September 7, 1949*—The British-American conference in Washington began this afternoon. The British want to earn more of the dollars they need so badly.

*September 8, 1949*—The United States Export-Import Bank has loaned twenty million dollars to Red Marshal Tito.

Today a giant passed from the world of melody—the creator of *Don Juan, Salome,* and *Der Rosenkavalier.* In Germany the composer, Richard Strauss, after a long illness, died at the age of eighty-five.

*September 12, 1949*—The British, American, and Canadian representatives have formulated a program to bolster up the shaky British economy.

The West German Government elected its President today—Dr. Theodor Heuss.

*September 13, 1949*—Today, at the Security Council of the United Nations, Soviet Russia cast seven vetoes in rapid succession, banning the admission of seven countries into the U.N.—Portugal, Transjordan, Ireland, Austria, Italy, Finland, and Ceylon.

*September 14, 1949*—Belgrade was flooded with pamphlets and posters today, calling for the overthrow of Red Marshal Tito.

*September 16, 1949*—Red Hungary had its big confession today—from Laszlo Rajk, as his trial began.

*September 23, 1949*—President Truman's announcement today is taken to mean that Soviet Russia has the atomic bomb.

*September 26, 1949*—Tonight the state of Israel rejected all proposals to internationalize Jerusalem.

Hungary has flatly rejected the Yugoslav protest against the latest Red trial, which doomed the former No. 2 Communist of Hungary and was, as well, a bitter indictment of Marshal Tito.

*September 29, 1949*—The Kremlin today renounced its treaty with Yugoslavia.

*September 30, 1949*—Red Hungary has renounced its treaty with Yugoslavia, and so has Red Poland. The rush of the satellites is on!

*October 5, 1949*—The Chinese Communist regime was recognized today by Yugoslavia.

*October 6, 1949*—A new satellite was born today, not in the sky, but in Berlin. The German Communists in the Soviet zone proclaimed an East German state.

*October 11, 1949*—Today brought a climax of terror to Red Czechoslovakia—with hundreds of arrests. This is known in polite Marxist language as the liquidation of the bourgeoisie.

*October 13, 1949*—In Washington the admirals completed their case today with Admiral Denfeld, Chief of Naval Operations. He declared that the Air Force and the Army have been ganging up on the Navy.

*October 14, 1949*—The news tonight is dominated by the conviction of the eleven Communist leaders, members of the American politburo.

*October 17, 1949*—In Washington today the Marines had their say. General Vandegrift said an attempt is being made to cripple the Marines.

King Leopold of Belgium speaks about the surrender of his army in the second world war. He says he did notify his allies, and that it was the British who failed to notify the Belgian command when they started withdrawing their troops for the Dunkirk evacuation.

*October 21, 1949*—Secretary of Defense Louis Johnson denies that he is out to scuttle the Navy. But he won't revive the plan for that supercarrier on which the Navy had set its heart.

In Britain they are calling the new Attlee plan superausterity.

*October 25, 1949*—The Soviet Government demands the recall of the Yugoslav Ambassador to Moscow.

*October 27, 1949*—Admiral Denfeld is out. The Chief of Naval Operations removed from his post without ceremony.

Congress is angry because when Admiral Denfeld testified before the

House Armed Services Committee, Secretary of Defense Johnson promised that there would be no reprisals.

*October 28, 1949*—At the Pentagon Building in Washington today a crowd of 250 sailors and Waves jammed into the office of the Chief of Naval Operations. They were there conveying sympathy and loyalty of the rank and file to Admiral Denfeld. The admiral addressed them, and told them: "Nobody can stop the Navy from coming out on top."

*November 1, 1949*—The C.I.O. has tossed out the Reds.

We have a new Chief of Naval Operations—Admiral Forrest Sherman. Admiral Sherman favors unification.

*November 2, 1949*—At The Hague they signed a formal proclamation establishing the sovereign state of Indonesia.

*November 7, 1949*—Soviet Marshal Rokossovsky becomes Defense Minister of Poland. Warsaw has surrendered the control of its army to Soviet Russia.

*November 10, 1949*—At the United Nations late this afternoon Vishinsky talked atomic. His version is that the Soviets are using atomic energy at a great rate for peacetime purposes.

*November 15, 1949*—In Atlanta they're holding the trial of the automobile driver who ran down and killed Margaret Mitchell, author of *Gone with the Wind*.

*November 17, 1949*—The President joins the chorus of indignation over the arrest and imprisonment of American Consul General Angus Ward in Red Manchuria.

*November 18, 1949*—The United Nations has just imposed an arms embargo on Albania and Red Bulgaria until they stop helping Communist guerrillas in Greece.

The Vice-President got married today. Mrs. Carlton Hadley became Mrs. Alben Barkley.

*November 22, 1949*—The United States has developed a small atom bomb to support the infantry.

In the Philippines the government is fighting the Huks, peasant rebels led by Communists.

In Hungary the Reds announce the American, Robert Vogeler, has "confessed."

*November 23, 1949*—Consul General Angus Ward has been sentenced to deportation from Red China.

*November 25, 1949*—At the U.N. tonight Vishinsky took a walk. He paraded out of the General Assembly as the delegate from China began a bitter accusation, charging Soviet Russia with giving aid to the Chinese Reds.

The Chinese Communist radio quoted the Panchen Lama as calling for a Red "liberation" of Tibet.

*November 28, 1949*—The Chinese Red radio confirms the creation of a Far Eastern Cominform.

*November 30, 1949*—Tonight Chungking is in the hands of Communists.

*December 1, 1949*—The big Yugoslav trial began today, with eleven defendants accused of doing spy work for Stalin.

Here's the gist of a dispatch from Moscow: The Soviet weekly, *New Times,* says that American radio commentator Lowell Thomas was sent to Tibet by the U. S. Government to try to tear that country away from China and turn it into an Anglo-American colony.
Do I have to say that this is an utter falsehood—that when I left for Tibet I had no preliminary consultation whatever with the government in Washington?

*December 2, 1949*—The U.N. has just voted a fifty-five-million-dollar program to aid the Arab refugees in Palestine.

*December 5, 1949*—An admission by the State Department that atomic materials for the Soviets were cleared by the State Department in 1943.
A former air force major asserts that shipments of blueprints were jammed through by the late Harry Hopkins, No. 1 aide to the late President Franklin D. Roosevelt.

*December 7, 1949*—At Houston, Texas, tonight General Eisenhower again declared himself out of politics.

General Groves denies that either Harry Hopkins or Henry Wallace ever put pressure on him to clear atomic shipments to Soviet Russia.

Today's news from China continues the picture of debacle and disaster for the Nationalists.

A dispatch from China tells of a new blast of Red propaganda calling for a Communist invasion of Tibet.

*December 8, 1949*—Former Deputy Premier Kostov, No. 2 Bulgarian Communist, retracts and denies the confession he made to the police.

General Groves declares that he did withhold atomic secrets from the former Vice-President. Asked the reason why, he said: "My decisions were based on what I thought the best interests of the United States. I decided I wasn't going to show any more reports to Mr. Wallace."

*December 9, 1949*—The U.N. decrees that Jerusalem shall be internationalized.

Prison sentences were imposed today in the Yugoslav Red trial—which presented the unusual spectacle of Soviet agents being tried before a Communist court.

*December 13, 1949*—Israel's Premier Ben Gurion proclaims Jerusalem capital of Israel. Such is Israel's answer to the decision of the United Nations to internationalize the Holy City.

Kostov, once the virtual Red ruler of Communist Bulgaria, listened with impassive calm today as his own lawyer damned him, loudly and at length. Then he himself arose to have his say. He again insisted on his innocence.

*December 14, 1949*—The Premier of Israel set up headquarters in Jerusalem today.

*December 16, 1949*—China's Communist President, Mao Tse-tung, is in Moscow.

In Bulgaria, Kostov was executed today.

*December 19, 1949*—The victory for the Communist government of Bulgaria is by a majority so overwhelming you can hardly find any minority at all—97.66 per cent.

*December 21, 1949*—Israel stands pat on Jerusalem as its capital—rejecting a remonstrance from the United Nations.

*December 27, 1949*–Queen Juliana has signed the official document creating the United States of Indonesia.

*December 29, 1949*–Today a petition arrived in London, with nearly one million Scottish signatures, calling for a separate Scottish Parliament, home rule!

*December 30, 1949*–Today signatures were appended to a document that makes French Indochina a sovereign state–though in union with France.

The break to recognize Communist China by countries of the British Commonwealth began today–India leading off, as expected.

# 1950

North Korean troops invade South Korea in the most brazen Communist aggression of the post-war period. At first successful, they drive all the way to the Pusan perimeter, only to be hurled back by MacArthur's Inchon landing. Then the Chinese Reds enter the fighting, helped by the fact that MacArthur is forbidden to attack their "Manchurian sanctuary." The result is stalemate roughly along the line of the 38th parallel.

For once the United Nations have been helped by Soviet tactics — the Security Council acting promptly to deal with the Korean crisis because the Russian delegate is boycotting it.

The new outbreak of fighting emphasizes President Truman's decision to push work on the hydrogen bomb. It also aids Senator McCarthy in his charges of Communist activity in America. The magnitude of Soviet espionage becomes clearer with the conviction of Alger Hiss.

Abroad, two old men pass from the scene where they have long been central figures — Jan Christiaan Smuts and George Bernard Shaw.

January 5, 1950—The President declared that the United States will not do anything to help the Chinese Nationalists defend Formosa.

Senator Taft of Ohio says the White House declaration is contrary to our anti-Communist policy everywhere else in the world.

The British will continue to deal with the present regime at Formosa—while recognizing the Communists as the government of China.

January 10, 1950—Secretary of State Acheson has begun his testimony on Formosa—appearing today before the Foreign Relations Committee of the Senate. He stated that the island refuge of the Chinese Nationalists is not necessary to the American line of defense in the Pacific.

*January 17, 1950*—President Truman is faced by one of the greatest decisions of history. Whether or not to develop a hydrogen bomb.

The biggest profit in the history of business was announced today—more than half a billion in a year. That record was established by General Motors for 1949.

*January 18, 1950*—Tonight rewards of $150,000 have been posted for the capture of the nine bandits who staged last night's record-breaking holdup in Boston—and for the recovery of money they stole. The total loot—$1,500,000, stolen from Brink's armored car service, which handles bank and commercial funds.

*January 23, 1950*—Reverberations in Congress following the conviction of Alger Hiss over the weekend. Today Republican Senator Capehart of Indiana called on President Truman to apologize for the remark he made during the 1948 campaign when the President called the charges against Hiss a "red herring." Alger Hiss, now found guilty of committing perjury when he swore he never handed documents of the State Department for delivery to Communist espionage.

It is becoming monotonous—but the Soviets took another walk today. At Lake Success they are boycotting every committee on which the Chinese Nationalist delegation is represented.

*January 25, 1950*—Secretary of State Acheson says that he will not turn his back on Alger Hiss. In a news conference today he made a gravely spoken statement, explaining that he once called Hiss his friend, and that his Christian principles do not permit him to go back on this—even in the face of conviction for perjury and an accusation of Red espionage.
Alger Hiss was calm and stoical today when sentenced to five years in prison.
Alger Hiss, being sentenced, put the emphasis on the testimony of the typewriter—declaring that Whittaker Chambers had used it for forgery.

*January 26, 1950*—Our American chiefs of defense give the opinion that the island of Formosa does have "strategic significance" for the United States if in enemy hands. Secretary of State Acheson declared that the island, held by the Chinese Nationalists, is of no consequence for American strategy in the Pacific.

*January 27, 1950*—Elder statesman Bernard Baruch today gave some strong advice—urging this country to go right ahead and make what is being called the "hell bomb."

*January 30, 1950*—Soviet Russia has recognized the Communist rebels in French Indochina.

The Chinese Reds make their demand on Tibet—calling upon that isolated Himalayan country to negotiate with Communist Peking for "a peaceful liberation of Tibet."

*January 31, 1950*—President Truman says: "I have directed the Atomic Energy Commission to continue its work on all forms of atomic weapons—including the so-called hydrogen or superbomb."

He says that we'll go ahead with the hell bomb until a sound system of atomic control is established.

*February 3, 1950*—FBI Director J. Edgar Hoover is quoted as saying that Dr. Klaus Fuchs, a top-ranking atomic scientist in Britain, was planted by the Soviets as a spy.

He worked for the Manhattan Project, so famous in the creation of the bomb, and was at Los Alamos, New Mexico, when the first atomic missile was put together.

Dr. Karl Fuchs transmitted atomic secrets to foreign agents, according to the indictment in a London court today.

*February 6, 1950*—Late dispatches from the coal fields picture the miners in defiant mood tonight after President Truman invoked the Taft-Hartley law today.

*February 7, 1950*—The British Government has recognized the French-sponsored government of Indochina. This puts Britain directly on the side of France in the quarrel with Soviet Russia. Moscow having recognized the Indochina Communists as the legal government.

*February 10, 1950*—The confession of Dr. Klaus Emil Julius Fuchs is as remarkable a document as was ever transmitted on a new wire.

Dr. Fuchs declares that he divided himself into two separate persons. One—the honorable British scientist. The other—the agent of Red espionage. Which, of course, suggests immediately the old figure of Dr. Jekyll and Mr. Hyde.

*February 14, 1950*—A treaty has been signed between Red China and Soviet Russia.

The Chinese won important concessions in Manchuria—and thus have entered into a Far Eastern alliance with Soviet Russia.

*February 24, 1950*—In the previous election in the post-war year of 1945, when Winston Churchill was tossed out, the Labour party won a huge majority of two hundred seats in Parliament. In the House of Commons elected yesterday, they will have a majority that you can almost count on your fingers.

*February 27, 1950*—Tonight an account is given to explain why Stalin got many concessions in those Roosevelt-Churchill-Stalin conferences—as at Teheran and Yalta. The Soviet war leader, we are told, had a trump card up his sleeve—offers from Hitler. This is stated by Dr. Robert Kempner, who was a prosecutor at the Nuremberg trial of the Nazi war criminals.

*March 2, 1950*—In London the Labour government has announced: no new schemes of socialism to be introduced into the new Parliament. Not with a mere majority of seven.

Red Rumania tells the U.S. and Great Britain to close their information office in Bucharest.

*March 3, 1950*—The coal strike has been settled by agreement between the companies and the union.

*March 8, 1950*—Before a committee today Senator McCarthy of Wisconsin expanded his charge that right now there are fifty-seven Communists in the State Department. He declared that U. S. Ambassador at Large Philip C. Jessup has what the senator called "an unusual affinity" for Communist causes.

*March 13, 1950*—Senator McCarthy says that Far Eastern expert Owen Lattimore has a long pro-Communist record and, in McCarthy's words, "may have done this nation incalculable and irreparable harm."

*March 14, 1950*—A further naming of names by Senator McCarthy—including John Stewart Service, State Department diplomat now in India, and Dr. Harlow Shapley, the Harvard astronomer. These accusations are countered by immediate denials from all concerned.

*March 16, 1950*—The State Department issues a blast—the angriest thus far—against the charges of Red infiltration into the department.

*March 20, 1950*—President Truman comes to the defense of Secretary of State Acheson—and in the strongest terms: "The President has complete confidence in the Secretary of State, and believes he is running the department admirably."

Before a congressional committee today American Ambassador at Large

Philip Jessup gave his answer to an accusation made by Senator McCarthy of Wisconsin—the charge that Jessup has what McCarthy calls an "unusual affinity" for Red causes. The reply is blazing. "False and irresponsible," cries the Ambassador at Large.

*March 24, 1950*—In the ornate city of Brussels today mounted police, with naked sabers, charged mobs of rioters. Workers on strike against the proposal to return exiled King Leopold to his throne.

*March 27, 1950*—In the Communist uproar the angriest denials thus far are aroused by the disclosure of the identity of the personage accused by Senator McCarthy of Wisconsin as the top Soviet spy. Owen Lattimore, expert on Far Eastern affairs, is the one whose name has been kept so closely concealed that we've been having to speak of the case of the "unknown Red."

*March 28, 1950*—A dispatch from Pakistan, where Owen Lattimore made a statement today. He called those charges "complete moonshine" and "pure hallucinations."

*April 3, 1950*—Today President Truman ordered the FBI and other government agencies to ignore the subpoena issued by the Senate committee demanding the loyalty files.

*April 6, 1950*—In Washington, Owen Lattimore declared that McCarthy is a "willing tool" of a Chinese Nationalist cabal in Washington.

The hearing ended with a committee statement exonerating Owen Lattimore. Chairman Senator Tydings of Maryland told the Far Eastern expert that a summary of his loyalty file put him "completely in the clear."

*April 13, 1950*—The first shipment of Atlantic pact armament arrived in France today.

*April 20, 1950*—Louis Budenz declared today that he knew of Owen Lattimore as a Communist because of what he was told by the top leaders of the American Red party.

The Politburo, he said, agreed that Lattimore should be given the assignment of picturing the Reds of China as "agrarian reformers."

In the Institute of Pacific Relations, said Budenz, a Red "cell" was formed, one member of which was Owen Lattimore.

Brigadier General Edward Thorpe, retired, former chief of counterintelligence for General Douglas MacArthur in Tokyo, gave his opinion of Owen Lattimore in the following words: "a loyal American citizen and in no way an agent of the Communist party."

*April 25, 1950*—Bella Dodd, former prominent Communist, who was expelled from the Party last June, denied that the leadership of the Communist party ever regarded Far Eastern expert Lattimore as a Communist. She stated, moreover, that Budenz, although managing editor of the *Daily Worker*, was not high enough in the Party to know what went on in the local politburo.

At Sydney the Red dean, the Reverend Hewlett Johnson, was making a speech to students, and had a few remarks to make about the British House of Commons. During which he mentioned "the leader of the opposition."

Whereupon a student spoke up mildly and asked: "Mr. Dean, can you tell us, please, the name of the leader of the opposition in Soviet Russia?"

That was when the Red dean was stumped for an answer—no reply at all.

*April 27, 1950*—The London government granted full diplomatic recognition to the state of Israel. And similarly recognized the annexation of Arab Palestine by the Hashimite Kingdom of Jordan.

An appearance by Frank Costello before a Senate committee investigating nationwide crime. Costello—often called the big boss of the cross-country rackets.

He admitted to the committee that he had once engaged in illegal bookmaking and slot machine business, but he claimed that for the last five or six years he has been merely a businessman with investments.

*April 28, 1950*—France today dismissed the chief of the French atomic energy program—Professor Joliot-Curie, scientist and Communist. He is, of course, the husband of the daughter of the famous Madame Curie—who, with her own husband, discovered radium.

*May 2, 1950*—Lattimore replies to Budenz—and exhausts the vocabulary of opprobrious epithets. He calls the former editor of the Communist *Daily Worker* a "paid informer and unscrupulous finger man."

*May 4, 1950*—The President today agreed to give the Senate committee the loyalty files in the State Department on eighty-one officials named by McCarthy.

*May 8, 1950*—The Supreme Court upholds the non-Communist oath required by the Taft-Hartley law, saying that the anti-Red affidavit required of union officials is constitutional.

*May 10, 1950*—The United States has rejected an offer from Moscow —an offer to settle Soviet Lend-Lease for two cents on the dollar.

At Oakland, California, testimony continues—placing atomic scientist Dr. Robert Oppenheimer at a Communist meeting back in 1941. To which Robert Oppenheimer replies by denying that he ever attended a closed Communist meeting. That is, an official session of the Red party. But he says he has never denied that he has known plenty of left-wingers and associated with them.

*May 23, 1950*—The FBI announces the first arrest in this country in connection with the case of Dr. Fuchs. In Philadelphia a man named Harry Gold is in custody tonight. J. Edgar Hoover states: "Fuchs turned over secrets of the atomic bomb to Harry Gold in the United States."

*May 24, 1950*—A dispatch from Washington states that Harry Gold was recruited for Red spy work by Jacob Golos, then head of a Soviet espionage ring in the United States.

*June 5, 1950*—General Douglas MacArthur has ordered the Japanese Government to ban the Central Committee of the Communist party from public life.

*June 6, 1950*—In the Senate today McCarthy of Wisconsin hurled another charge—stating that in 1947 twenty officials of the State Department were tagged by the FBI as possibly being agents of Soviet Russia, with three of these still in the State Department.
The State Department issues an immediate denial, calling the charges "absolutely false."

*June 7, 1950*—The puppet government of East Germany has recognized the Polish annexation of East German territory.
The Western powers declare that they will not recognize the Polish annexations.

*June 8, 1950*—A federal grand jury has indicted William Remington, the official of the Department of Commerce who was named when the Red spy sensations began a couple of years ago. At that time he denied everything—stating under oath that he had never been a Communist. Which is the basis of the grand jury indictment today—a charge of perjury.

A new government took office in Belgium today—pledged to bring King Leopold back to the throne.

*June 15, 1950*—The FBI announces another arrest in the atomic spy case of the Philadelphia biochemist, Harry Gold. The prisoner, in custody tonight, is Alfred Dean Slack of Syracuse, New York—also a chemist. J. Edgar Hoover says that Slack turned over to Gold secret information about a wartime explosive—the information to be handed over to Red espionage.

The Western powers ask Soviet Russia to sign an Austrian treaty right away.

*June 16, 1950*—Another arrest today—on the charge of turning over atomic secrets to Red spies. The latest prisoner—David Greenglass of New York.

*June 19, 1950*—The Government of Israel makes an outright confession of having been at fault in the assassination of Count Bernadotte of Sweden, the United Nations mediator. No proper precautions to safeguard Count Bernadotte against attack by terrorists. And negligence in the effort to detect and arrest the murderers.

*June 23, 1950*—The Board of Regents of the University of California voted today to dismiss 157 university employees, both faculty and non-faculty, for refusing to sign declarations that they are not Communists.

*June 26, 1950*—It is always a portentous event of war when the capital of a nation is captured by invaders—and in this case it will signalize the brutal, blatant surprise of the latest Red aggression.

It is apparent now that the assault begun on Saturday was launched with overwhelming power—like a Hitler blitzkrieg. Seoul has been captured, and the South Korean Government is in flight.

President Truman takes the lead in calling the invasion by the Red puppet unprovoked aggression. In Japan, General Douglas MacArthur is responding with quick planeloads of ammunition and light artillery.

From the Korean side, an old echo—too little and too late. They received light weapons and equipment, whereas the Red satellite is driving with masses of Russian artillery and Soviet-made tanks.

*June 27, 1950*—MacArthur is in command of this new war.

If it were not for the fact that we so suddenly find ourselves in a shooting war, the big headline today would be the Truman decision ordering the American Seventh Fleet to protect the island of Formosa from Red invasion.

*June 29, 1950*—MacArthur conferred today with Korean President Syngman Rhee—and everywhere he went he was cheered by Korean soldiers.

President Truman says: "We are not at war." At a news conference today he took the position that the American Air Force and Navy in Korea are merely carrying out a mandate given by the United Nations.

Moscow replies to our note with the propaganda charge that the war in Korea was started by the free Koreans and places upon them the responsibility—also on the governments that are supporting free Korea.

*June 30, 1950*—The latest from Korea states that the Reds have captured the town of Suwon. American headquarters moved south to Taejon, ninety-three miles away. This represents a considerable success for the Korean Reds.

News that after the capture of Seoul the Communists began a reign of Red terror, with mass executions.

There was a reading of the replies by the members of the United Nations, answering the call to support the United States in military measures against the Red invasion of Korea. One after another, from around the globe, the many governments respond—yes.

*July 7, 1950*—General Douglas MacArthur today became the United Nations commander-in-chief, military chief for the world organization in the battle against Red aggression in Korea. This afternoon the Security Council of the United Nations authorized our government to name MacArthur to that post. The Security Council was able to act so quickly because the Soviet delegate, Jacob Malik, is still boycotting it.

All along the fighting front there was little change today—the Reds massing for new attacks after the retirement of advanced American forces.

A fleet of Superfortresses, B-29s, opened a thundering offensive.

For the first time jet planes are being used in actual war. The Germans did have a few in World War II. But Korea begins the big-time use of jet aviation in battle.

President Truman asked Congress today to put up $260,000,000 for hydrogen superbombs.

NOTE: *There is a gap in the broadcasts between July 7 and August 28. During those seven weeks I was away because my sponsor at that time, Procter & Gamble, took the program off the air.*

*During those seven weeks the situation in Korea became worse for the United Nations. The Communist North Koreans pushed us back down the peninsula. And when I returned to the air, the United Nations were grimly trying to stop the Red drive.*

*There were other important news stories during the same period. The arrest of Julius Rosenberg broke the Soviet Washington spy ring wide open. Henry Wallace resigned from the Progressive party. In Belgium, King Leopold returned after six years of exile—and that touched off anti-*

*monarchial rioting, which finally overthrew him, and Crown Prince Baudouin succeeded him.*

*August 29, 1950*—The whole Korean front was ablaze as the day began in the Far East. All along the line the Communists lunged forward in a series of attacks.

*August 31, 1950*—The North Korean Communists have driven a wedge five miles deep into the American line, a menacing thrust.

*September 5, 1950*—The state of affairs in Korea is critical. The entire United Nations line is being rolled back.

*September 7, 1950*—American troops in Korea today captured 120 rounds of Russian mortar bombs dated 1950. This supports the charge that the Soviets are supplying the Korean Reds right now.

*September 11, 1950*—The world loses one of its historic figures— Field Marshal Jan Smuts of South Africa. He was the world's elder statesman—a South African soldier who fought against the British in the Boer War, and then took the lead in the reconciliation between the Boers and the British.

*September 12, 1950*—From the battle fronts of Korea the news is good all along the perimeter. The fifty-mile northern front reports enemy withdrawals everywhere—the U.N. troops advancing.

*September 15, 1950*—Morning in Korea brought another landing in MacArthur's latest offensive. This time tanks. At Inchon, the port of Seoul, the mechanized equipment for the Marines has just gone ashore, turning the amphibious forces into an armored column—for a drive to the Korean capital.

We can now get a glimpse of what the MacArthur plan really was during those long weeks of critical, desperate fighting around the perimeter. It looks as if he were holding the South Korean beachhead with minimum forces while building up a war machine to strike by sea and carry the offensive to the area behind the Red Army.

*September 18, 1950*—Two Marine Corps spearheads in the Inchon landings have reached the outskirts of Seoul.

The Senate confirms the nomination of former Mayor William O'Dwyer of New York as American Ambassador to Mexico.

*September 19, 1950*—U.S. marines from the Inchon beachhead have stormed across the Han River for the seizure of the capital city of Seoul.

Our troops, having broken out of the perimeter, are now driving after the columns of Reds, hurrying north toward Seoul. The picture is one of the mass of the Reds caught between the 7th Division, pushing south from the capital city, and the 1st Cavalry, thrusting north from the perimeter.

*September 20, 1950*—The Senate has confirmed General Marshall as the new Secretary of Defense.

*September 21, 1950*—How about that now famous 38th parallel? Will the Americans, when they defeat the Korean Reds, completely chase them beyond that boundary line?

In Korea the President of the free republic, Syngman Rhee, says that he expects to preside over a united Korea—north as well as south.

*September 22, 1950*—The Marines have driven five miles into Seoul. Down at the perimeter the big break-through turns into a dash forward—a race between the 1st Cavalry and the 24th Division. The South Koreans are on a wild rampage—scoring their biggest gains of the war.

The Nobel Peace Prize goes to Dr. Ralph Bunche, the American Negro educator who presided over the settlement of the war in Palestine.

*September 25, 1950*—The jaws of the nutcracker offensive tonight are only thirty-eight miles apart in that drive to link up with the Inchon-Seoul area.

*September 26, 1950*—In Korea, south of Suwon, two tanks today met patrols from the U. S. 7th Division. Those two pincers, which we have watched coming closer and closer together, finally joined.

General MacArthur announced the liberation of Seoul today.

The twelve-nation Atlantic pact council agreed tonight to the earliest possible establishment of an integrated European army.

*September 27, 1950*—Masses of Reds fleeing from Seoul, as the Marines and G.I.s move rapidly to clean out remaining pockets of resistance. Once again American prisoners of war have been found murdered.

*September 28, 1950*—The war news from Korea pictures the Marines driving north from Seoul. Commander of the U. S. Eighth Army said he was waiting for orders—whether or not to drive across the 38th parallel.

The Korean capital had a big parade tonight when General Douglas

MacArthur escorted Syngman Rhee, President of the Korean Republic, back to the legal seat of his government.

*September 29, 1950*—Free Koreans pushed up to that 38th parallel—and, at last reports, were hurling artillery fire at the Reds on the other side. The American command sent orders to them, stern orders—don't cross that 38th parallel.

The question of whether or not the forces under General MacArthur will be permitted to strike into the home grounds of the Reds—that still remains for the United Nations to decide.

*October 2, 1950*—We now have the first official recognition of the movement of troops across the 38th parallel. Apparently only South Koreans.

At the U.N. tonight the Soviet bloc put forward that expected Korean peace proposal. The resolution called for an immediate cease-fire in Korea, withdrawal of United Nations forces, and nationwide elections conducted by a joint commission representing the North and South Korean governments. A United Nations on-the-spot team of observers to watch, see to it that the elections are fair—both Communist China and Russia to be members of the United Nations team.

*October 4, 1950*—Tonight's bulletin from Tokyo tells of Red reinforcements rolling into the Communist capital at Pyongyang.

The free Koreans are still pushing across the 38th parallel.

*October 9, 1950*—In Korea today the American 1st Cavalry, in tanks, swept across the 38th parallel. By tonight they were several miles farther along the road to the North Korean capital, Pyongyang.

*October 10, 1950*—The situation in Indochina tonight is described as "serious." Near the northern frontier, in a disastrous defeat, almost three thousand crack Foreign Legion and Moroccan troops were wiped out yesterday by the Reds.

*October 11, 1950*—The G.I.s were fourteen miles north of the 38th parallel today—slow going through a difficult rugged valley, with heavy Red resistance in places.

*October 12, 1950*—Tonight President Truman is flying to his meeting with MacArthur—somewhere west of Hawaii.

*October 16, 1950*—Two hundred and thirty-eight miles of the border between Indochina and China tonight is in Communist hands. The Reds are now within ninety miles of the large city of Hanoi.

General Eisenhower responds to Governor Dewey, who sprang a weekend political sensation by coming out in favor of Eisenhower for President. Today General Ike replied by referring to his former refusal to seek a presidential nomination. Harking back to those opinions, he said: "They have not changed."

*October 19, 1950*—The President talked about his Wake Island meeting with General MacArthur, from which he has just returned. At a White House news conference today he was asked—had he and General MacArthur discussed Formosa? The President said there was no Formosa question to be considered—American policy having been settled four or five weeks before the conference on Wake. Which would go back to the time when the White House intervened and suppressed a MacArthur statement that this country should make sure the Reds don't get Formosa.

*October 20, 1950*—Today's announcement that the Korean War is about over came from top authority, General Douglas MacArthur.

All along the line the soldiers of the U.N. are obeying General MacArthur's latest command—to drive at full speed through the remainder of North Korea all the way to the border of Communist Manchuria and Siberia.

*October 23, 1950*—In North Korea, U.N. forces today threw land and air blockades across every rail and highway escape route remaining to the Reds.

Spearheads are now only forty-eight miles from Manchuria, and fifty miles from the Soviet Siberian frontier.

President Syngman Rhee of South Korea confirmed today that he is taking over control of North Korea—against the orders of the U.N.

*October 24, 1950*—In Korea tonight the Allies are still driving north —meeting no opposition.

*October 25, 1950*—Tibet has surrendered. This follows news of a Chinese Communist army mobilized on the frontier of the roof of the world ready to invade. The Chinese Red government sent a final demand—and the ministers of the living Buddha at Lhasa yielded. They acknowledge the sovereignty of China, and only hope to retain some degree of local autonomy for Tibet.

*October 26, 1950*—This was another day of history in the Korean War—troops of the United Nations reaching the border of Red Manchuria, the Yalu River. There are reports of the capture of Chinese Reds, fighting along with the Korean Communists—and one rumor is that the Chinese have sent a powerful force into Korea.

*October 27, 1950*—General Eisenhower—named as the supreme commander of the united defense forces of Western Europe.

*October 30, 1950*—The news from Korea takes a turn tonight—word that the Chinese Reds have thrown three divisions against Hamhung, and that the troops of the Republic of Korea have fallen back fifteen miles.

*November 1, 1950*—The would-be assassination in Washington this afternoon was a mad-dog affair.

A White House uniformed policeman, Donald Birdzell, was standing on guard when one of the assailants, Torresola, walked up and opened fire. Birdzell fell, seriously wounded. Whereupon a secret service man and another uniformed guard dashed out of the sentry box on the sidewalk, shooting as they ran. The Puerto Rican dropped, shot dead.

At the same time the other assailant, Collazo, came forward, shooting—and making a dash to the Blair House entrance. The two guards returned the fire and cut Collazo down at the foot of the Blair House doorstep. He was wounded, not critically. In the Blair House shooting Leslie Coffelt of the White House police was fatally wounded.

*November 2, 1950*—Near the Yalu, Chinese and Korean Reds drove a deep wedge into the American line and forced a general withdrawal.

The world is saying farewell to George Bernard Shaw at ninety-four—and recalling his amazing career. We know how he became the world's most famous writer—a prodigy of success. Yet he began as a prodigy of failure. It was not until middle age that he plunged into the medium which was to make him famous—the stage.

*November 6, 1950*—Air reconnaissance tonight reports Chinese Communist troops and supplies still pouring across the Yalu River.

In London the House of Commons learned today that "without doubt" Professor Bruno Pontecorvo, Britain's cosmic ray specialist, is now in the Soviet Union. During the war he worked in Canada with Dr. Allan May and Dr. Fuchs—both of whom gave atomic secrets to Russia.

*November 7, 1950*—In Korea today U.N. planes were ordered to bomb right up to the Manchurian border. Up to now U.N. airmen have been under orders to halt three miles south of the frontier.

*November 8, 1950*—News from Korea tells how history was made when the first air battle was fought with jets.

*November 9, 1950*—Today General MacArthur's headquarters declared there were sixty thousand Chinese now inside North Korea and half a million massed north of the border.

*November 10, 1950*—William Faulkner was chopping wood today at Oxford, Mississippi, when he was informed that he had won the Nobel Prize for Literature.

*November 16, 1950*—As day broke in Korea, the 7th Division was in sight of the mountains of Manchuria.

The Red government of China gives an outright rejection to a second protest from India against the invasion of Tibet.

*November 20, 1950*—General MacArthur's spokesman in Tokyo said today that all Chinese prisoners interviewed so far said they were ordered into Korea. Moscow and Peking claim that all Chinese forces fighting in Korea are "volunteers."

*November 27, 1950*—All along the line tonight's reports tell of U.N. forces falling back, between three and four miles, under the savage assaults of more than a hundred and twenty-five thousand Red Chinese troops.

*November 28, 1950*—Red China's delegate took the floor at Lake Success late today and charged the United States with building a military encirclement of China. General Wu demanded the withdrawal of the United States forces from both Formosa and Korea.

In Tokyo, General MacArthur met with his two top commanders, who had flown from Korea, General Walker and General Almond.

While the generals talked far into the night, drawing up new plans to stem the Red offensive, two hundred thousand Red Chinese continued the drive against the U.N. defenses. An attack which General MacArthur calls an "entirely new war."

The Chinese are taking full military advantage of the fact that MacArthur's army and air force are forbidden to strike north of the border into Red Manchuria—forbidden by the U.N.

*November 29, 1950*—Northwest Korea is a scene of stupendous retreat. Everywhere the roads are crowded with streams of vehicles, rolling bumper to bumper, as the soldiers, armament, and supplies of an army of one hundred thousand press on by every avenue of escape.

Hordes of Reds are swarming down the central range of mountains— trying to sweep around to the west and cut off the retreat of the American forces.

The American command is trying to establish a line of defense across the narrow waist of the Korean peninsula, about thirty miles north of Pyongyang, the captured Red capital.

*November 30, 1950*—Is General MacArthur authorized to use the atomic bomb whenever he sees fit? The answer is no. He would have to receive specific orders from the President.

In the Security Council of the U.N. tonight Soviet Russia cast three vetoes, not one, against the Western power resolution ordering the Chinese Reds out of Korea.

In Korea the battle to hold the line has begun. The huge forces of Communists are trying to cut around behind the line that is being established north of Pyongyang.

The marines holding the strategic Choshin reservoir are threatened with encirclement.

*December 4, 1950*—The big war question tonight is—where will the U.N. forces try to establish a new defense line? The front in northwestern Korea was outflanked by the horde of Chinese Reds, and Pyongyang, the capital of the Korean Communists, was hastily evacuated.

General MacArthur now says the Chinese offensive is backed by a force of a million.

Suspense continues for the division of marines and two regiments of infantry at the Choshin reservoir.

*December 5, 1950*—Tonight India and thirteen other countries asked Red China to stop the invasion of Korea at the 38th parallel.

*December 6, 1950*—The latest in the breakout of the marines from the Choshin reservoir trap pictures a drive of ten miles. They reached the town of Koto, where five thousand American troops were encircled. These, upon being relieved, joined in the push southward.

*December 8, 1950*—Contact has been made with the column of marines and infantry units that made the break-through from the Choshin reservoir. An advance party of the U. S. X Army Corps fought its way to the escaped column for a meeting at a point about twenty-five miles from Hamhung.

Singer Margaret Truman had a concert in Washington on Tuesday, and critic Paul Hume wrote things like this:

"She cannot sing very well. She is flat a good deal of the time."

Later he received a handwritten letter on White House stationery signed "H.S.T." The letter said: "I have just read your lousy review buried in the back pages. You sound like a frustrated old man on a four-ulcer job, and all four ulcers working. I never met you, but if I do you'll need a new nose and plenty of beefsteak."

*December 11, 1950*—The Eighth Army has fallen back fifty miles down the west coast—has dug in just north of Seoul.

*December 13, 1950*—The North Atlantic Treaty powers announce full agreement on the inclusion of German troops in the West European army.

In the minor Dunkirk of the Korean east coast sixty thousand soldiers are being taken out with mountains of equipment. The Marines, who made the great battle march of escape from the Choshin reservoir, for example, brought out nearly all their armament.

*December 15, 1950*—The state of emergency was pretty well spelled out by President Truman tonight in his radio address. He called for the mobilization of this country—man power and industrial power.

President Truman, in the bluntest of words, blamed Soviet Russia for pushing the world to what he called the brink of a general war.

*December 25, 1950*—The merriest Christmas in all the world was at the Korean seaport of Pusan—where today the final ship of the evacuation landed the last of the troops and equipment from the Hungnam beach-head.

London was in a state of astonishment and confusion this Christmas Day—after the most sensational theft in English history. Robbers broke into Westminster Abbey and plundered the royal throne. They took away that venerated historic treasure the Stone of Scone.

In the dim past the kings of Scotland were crowned on the Stone of Scone. They also called it the Stone of Destiny.

There's a faction of Scottish Nationalists, who have long been demanding independence, and today in London, while Englishmen were aghast, the Scottish Nationalists were celebrating in open jubilation.

*December 29, 1950*—News from French Indochina tells of a huge Communist offensive.

Lieutenant General Matthew Ridgway, the new commander of the U. S. Eighth Army, expresses complete confidence that his forces will be able to beat off the expected offensive of the Chinese Communists. So stated at a news conference held by the commander, who succeeds Lieutenant General Walker, killed in a jeep accident.

# 1951

*The most dramatic moment of the year is President Truman's dismissal of General MacArthur.*

*In Korea truce talks begin amid a barrage of abuse, accusations, and propaganda from the Communist side of the tent. In Hungary an anti-Semitic purge of the Communist party begins. In Iran, Premier Mossadegh nationalizes the Abadan oil refinery and starts his country down the road to bankruptcy. In the Suez Canal zone, anti-British rioting. In Britain two top diplomats suddenly disappear.*

*There are hopeful developments in Europe. The Schuman Plan for an international pool of coal and steel is established; Winston Churchill returns to power.*

*At home unpleasant things demand attention. The Rosenbergs are caught and convicted. A scandal involving influence peddlers and five-percenters breaks out in Washington. The televised crime investigations keep the public spellbound—and make Senator Kefauver of Tennessee a power in national politics.*

*January 2, 1951*—In Korea tonight two major enemy drives are converging on the South Korean capital of Seoul—from the north and northwest.

South Korean President Syngman Rhee and his Cabinet have decided to evacuate their capital.

*January 4, 1951*—The Chinese Reds have occupied Seoul, and some have crossed the Han River on the ice. The U.N. withdrawal southward is being made in orderly fashion.

President Truman says the United States has no intention of bombing Communist China—not now, anyway.

*January 9, 1951*—The Red advance has rolled forward some fifteen miles in the last twenty-four hours. There is still no word of the expected new defense line for General Ridgway's Eighth Army.

*January 10, 1951*—In Korea the counterattack that recaptured Wonju has been forced back.

Cannon hurled a rain of steel and fire into the ranks of the Communists. But they kept coming on, only to run into a cross fire of machine guns—but that didn't stop them.

The battle was fought in a blizzard—a great snowfall in some of the wildest mountains of Korea.

*January 12, 1951*—In the Korean battle of Wonju the U.N. forces lashed back at the Reds today. They stormed hills and ridges overlooking the town.

This infantry action followed a stupendous air bombardment.

*January 16, 1951*—For the second day in Korea the limited U.N. offensive—that "reconnaissance in force"—rolled forward unopposed below Seoul.

In Indochina today the Vietminh rebels threw thousands of fresh troops into the battle for the Red River rice bowl.

*January 17, 1951*—The recapture of Wonju is just another sign of a strange state of affairs. The town was taken by a mere patrol thrust, a party of G.I.s driving in and finding Wonju deserted.

This reconnaissance activity pictures a strange vacuum—the G.I.s unable to find any Chinese forces in front of them.

*January 18, 1951*—Governor Dewey of New York still supports General Eisenhower for the Republican nomination. In Albany today he stated that he did not change his opinion—that General Ike is the one to name for the presidency in 1952.

*January 19, 1951*—In Korea a violent battle is being fought southeast of Wonju—where a division of Korean Reds has been surrounded, and is being wiped out.

*January 24, 1951*—In Korea the Communists have made a withdrawal on a broad front. That's the explanation of the news we've been having for several days, telling how American patrol thrusts have been driving deeply without being able to find the Red enemy.

*January 29, 1951*—Along a ninety-mile front in Korea the Eighth Army's full-scale offensive drove forward today. The enemy holding on to their snowy foxholes ridge by ridge and mile by mile.

*January 30, 1951*—One hour ago at Lake Success the United Nations Political Committee approved by an overwhelming majority the U.S. resolution branding China an aggressor.

*January 31, 1951*—On the Korean battle front, a heavy Red offensive at the center of the line. After a day of virtual stalemate along the front, the U.N. offensive halted by bitter enemy resistance.

*February 1, 1951*—This is an offer to Red China—we'll stop at the 38th parallel if they will accept the cease-fire terms proposed by the United States.

*February 2, 1951*—The Chinese Reds give a defiant reply to the U.N. resolution condemning them as aggressors.

Today's fourth atomic explosion in Nevada is described as the most powerful of the series. The blast shook Las Vegas one hundred miles away, and the blazing glow was witnessed in places as far off as Los Angeles and San Francisco.

*February 5, 1951*—Today was the day of the tanks in Korea. All along the Eighth Army battle front U.S. armor drove in fast-moving columns and struck deep into the territory of the Reds.

*February 7, 1951*—United Nations artillery once more looks down from the hills around Seoul; the Korean capital within easy range.

*February 9, 1951*—An American patrol has pushed into Inchon, harbor of Seoul. That famous Inchon, where the amphibious invasion was made, now retaken from the Reds.

*February 14, 1951*—Four hours ago, at midnight in Britain, the British steel industry passed under the ownership of the government, nationalized.

*February 15, 1951*—Everywhere the Reds took a beating today, incurring murderous losses, as the U.N. forces went at them with counter-attacks on the ground and assaults from the air.

*February 19, 1951*—U.N. forces in Korea today swept forward on the heels of a general Communist withdrawal.

*February 22, 1951*—Washington's Birthday was celebrated in Korea with a major U.N. offensive on the central front.

*February 26, 1951*—Tonight three divisions of Korean Reds, battered and shattered, are withdrawing into mountain wilderness.

*February 27, 1951*—The anti-third-term amendment, now written into the Constitution with Nevada, the thirty-sixth state to ratify, providing the necessary three fourths.

The investigation of the RFC brings forward a sumptuous, magnificent mink coat. Described as "natural royal pastel mink." Worn by Mrs. Loretta Young, assistant to President Truman's private secretary at the White House. Her husband, Merl Young, was an official of the Reconstruction Finance Corporation.

Today the testimony was that the money for the fur was loaned to Merl Young by Joseph Rosenbaum, a lawyer who has represented various firms getting RFC loans.

*February 28, 1951*—The Senate crime investigating committee issued a report today stating that the underworld is dominated by two major crime syndicates.

One based on New York and Miami. Directed by Frank Costello and Joe Adonis.

*March 1, 1951*—Another air battle between jets is reported in the war news—and this might seem to tie in with stories that the Chinese Reds are prepared to throw in a considerable force of the Russian-built MIG-15s.

*March 7, 1951*—In Washington late this afternoon the jury found Collazo guilty of murder in the first degree. That means the death penalty.

He is condemned for the murder of White House guard Leslie Coffelt, who was killed in the shooting affray. Actually, the fatal shot was fired by Torresola. But under the law Collazo is equally responsible.

The assassination of the Premier of Iran was the doing of grim fanaticism, religious and political.

The Premier, Ali Razmara, was going to the mosque, traversing the courtyard, when the reader of the Koran approached him and fired three pistol shots, killing him instantly.

The battle for Seoul is on. Strong American forces went storming across the Han River today and drove into the hills in a move that would outflank the Korean capital.

The MacArthur statement is that the Korean War will settle into a stalemate unless he receives large reinforcements and is permitted to strike by air at the Red bases in Manchuria, Chinese territory.

*March 8, 1951*—In Teheran tonight a parliamentary committee voted unanimously for the nationalization of Iran's immensely rich oil industry.

Tonight's vote came only a few hours after the funeral of Premier Ali Razmara, who was assassinated by a fanatic yesterday for opposing the nationalization measure.

*March 9, 1951*—Britain's redoubtable Foreign Secretary, Ernest Bevin, sent in his resignation today on his seventieth birthday because of ill health. Deputy Prime Minister Herbert Morrison will step into the post of Foreign Secretary.

A dispatch from India states that a settlement between Tibet and Red China has been made. Tibet to have internal autonomy and continue its theocratic way of life. The Chinese Communists to take over Tibetan frontiers and have control of Tibet's foreign policy.

*March 12, 1951*—The Supreme Court has rejected the appeal of Alger Hiss—which means that the former State Department official will have to go to jail for the five-year sentence imposed on him.

*March 13, 1951*—The spy trial in New York brought out a dramatic story today—featuring the name of Dr. Klaus Fuchs, the top-ranking British atomic scientist convicted of Red espionage, now in prison in England. Former Army Sergeant David Greenglass, who has confessed, testified that his brother-in-law, Julius Rosenberg, reminded him that Harry Gold had been the Red contact man in transmitting atomic data provided by Dr. Klaus Fuchs.

*March 14, 1951*—The recapture of Seoul only dramatizes the puzzle in Korea—why are the Reds retreating all over the place? The capital city was taken by a small force of South Koreans who crossed the Han River in fishing boats and didn't fire a shot.

It was a rough time today for the alleged gambling czar, Frank Costello, who was on the televised witness stand in New York. Costello kept twisting his hands and feet—as they wrung testimony from him.

*March 15, 1951*—In a New York television extravaganza today Frank Costello, alleged to be the big boss of the gambling racket, stalked out of the hearing with the statement that "under no condition" would he give further testimony.

*March 19, 1951*—In Paris the Schuman plan was signed today—the long-debated program for the pooling of the coal and steel resources by six Western European nations. The countries that signed were France, West Germany, Italy, Belgium, Luxembourg, and the Netherlands.

In the Senate crime investigation the star witness appeared today—Ambassador to Mexico William O'Dwyer, former Mayor of New York. He testified in a long and stormy hearing, denying that, as Mayor of New York, he had had any political connection with the underworld.

*March 21, 1951*—In Korea the Reds have pulled back behind the parallel.

*March 22, 1951*—The reappearance of the famous name of Krupp on the roll call of German industry. It is announced that permission has been given for Krupp at Essen to build a new foundry and a steel plant.

Word from London is the authorities know who swiped the Stone of Scone. They've learned, likewise, that the historic slab of rock is in Scotland.

*March 26, 1951*—The State Department has put in a complaint against General Douglas MacArthur as a result of the statement by the supreme commander that he was willing to go into battlefield negotiations with the Communist commander. This invitation to a parley was made without consultation—the State Department knowing nothing about it. Which has irked a number of diplomatic officials, who are working at their own plans for bringing an end to the war in Korea.

*March 27, 1951*—A dispatch from Tokyo states that General MacArthur offered to negotiate with the Chinese Reds because he considered it a military affair.

*March 30, 1951*—The Senate voted a whole series of citations for contempt this afternoon. All as a result of the crime investigation. The list of those accused begins with Frank Costello, sometimes called the prime minister of the underworld.

*April 2, 1951*—The Allied command in Europe, headed by General Eisenhower, today began its formal existence. Activated—as the military men say.

"Supreme Headquarters Allied Powers Europe"—the initials spell "SHAPE."

*April 5, 1951*—A London newspaper prints an interview with General MacArthur in which the supreme commander is quoted as saying that his army could easily defeat the Chinese Reds if the U.N. would "take the wraps off." That is, permit American air power to hit the Chinese Red air bases in Manchuria.

The spy trial in New York brought a grim verdict today—the death penalty imposed on Julius Rosenberg and his wife, Ethel. They were convicted of having transmitted atomic secrets to Soviet Russia.

A third defendant, Morton Sobell, was let off with a lighter sentence—thirty years in prison.

*April 6, 1951*—The latest in Korea pictures a general advance. The Communists fighting it out bitterly in their powerful fortifications. But they are being driven out, the advance continuing above the 38th parallel.

*April 9, 1951*—We hear that the President's party leaders in Congress have assured him of full Democratic backing if he should decide to curb the supreme commander in the Far East.

Great Britain and France are described as much annoyed by the Mac-Arthur declarations. Particularly his latest—that he favors the use of the Chinese Nationalist soldiers of Chiang Kai-shek against the Reds in Korea.

*April 11, 1951*—I suppose that nearly everybody listened to President Truman's address tonight by radio and television—his defense of the dismissal of General Douglas MacArthur as our supreme commander in the Far East.

He declares that General MacArthur did not agree with the administration foreign policy of trying to keep the Korean War isolated.

Republican leaders are planning a congressional investigation of the firing of MacArthur. Nearly all the Democrats have rallied to the President.

Headquarters in Tokyo was stunned by the news, as were the Japanese—among whom MacArthur has been like a god. Similarly in Korea, where the G.I.s gaped in amazement.

London predicts that the removal of MacArthur will be followed by a new attempt to end the Korean War by diplomatic negotiations.

The Stone of Scone has been recovered, handed back.

The scene—Abroath Abbey, Scotland. Two men carried in the coronation stone and left two letters. These missives declared that the Stone of Scone was taken as a way of calling attention to demands for Scotland's self-government.

*April 12, 1951*—General MacArthur does not believe he violated instructions from Washington, as President Truman charged.

His statement points to the fact that President Truman, in a news conference in January, denied there was any curb on MacArthur—the general being free "to speak freely on the Korean War."

*April 13, 1951*—The story that Soviet Russia has given the Chinese Communists a large air force is being borne out in spectacular fashion. Today jet armadas of one hundred on each side flashing in swiftest maneuvers in the battle of the sky.

The Stone of Scone is back in Westminster Abbey tonight. It was brought from Scotland by the police and placed in the abbey, from which it was stolen on Christmas.

*April 16, 1951*—The parliament of Japan, the Diet, voted a resolution reading as follows: "The general of the army, Douglas MacArthur, former supreme commander for the Allied powers, helped our country out of the confusion and poverty prevailing at the time the war ended."

*April 19, 1951*—The MacArthur speech before Congress today had an enormous audience on radio and television—probably the greatest ever. The MacArthur style of eloquence was one of restraint, no shouting, no thunder. He got some of his best effects by lowering, not raising, the voice—as at the end of the address, so tensely emotional with the line from the old barrack room ballad: "Old soldiers never die, they just fade away."

President Truman states that in dismissing General Douglas MacArthur he acted on "the unanimous recommendation of his principal civilian and military advisers, including the Joint Chiefs of Staff."

*April 20, 1951*—All records were broken in New York today—7,500,000 people turning out to see MacArthur. Scores of thousands from the suburbs poured in.

*April 26, 1951*—In Korea a rigid security blackout obscures details of the battle above Seoul.

*April 27, 1951*—Denmark agrees to let the United States maintain bases in Greenland—that vast island northeast of Canada, so strategic with reference to America in the Arctic. The agreement was signed in Copenhagen today.

*April 30, 1951*—In Korea the tremendous Chinese build-up north of Seoul goes on.

*May 1, 1951*—The final report made by the Kefauver crime investigating committee presents a drastic indictment of O'Dwyer's conduct when he was Mayor of New York—also, previously, when he was Brooklyn District Attorney.

"Neither he nor his appointees," declares the committee, "took any effective action against the top echelons of the gambling, narcotics, waterfront, murder, or bookmaking rackets."

The committee says Costello's testimony "reeks of perjury" and recommends that he be prosecuted—and, if possible, deported.

In Korea the vast Chinese army around Seoul vanished. The hordes which yesterday were laying siege to the very gates of the South Korean capital "disappeared."

*May 2, 1951*—The document released tonight gives the formal White House answer to speculation about what really transpired between the President and the supreme commander at that mid-Pacific conference last October. The dialogue is quoted as follows:

The President asked: "What are the chances for Chinese or Soviet interference?"

"Very little," MacArthur is said to have replied. "Had they interfered in the first or second month, it would have been decisive. We are no longer fearful of their intervention."

Today the Shah of Iran signed a bill nationalizing Iranian oil—and immediately ordered the Premier to take over the Anglo-Iranian oil fields, operated by the British.

*May 3, 1951*—Did MacArthur expect Red China to enter the Korean War? To a congressional committee today he replied that he knew the Chinese had collected large forces north of the Korean border, the Yalu River. But in November our Central Intelligence Agency in Washington said they felt there was little chance of any large intervention by the Chinese.

Why did we sustain so large a reverse when the Chinese hordes did come surging into Korea?

MacArthur's reply is that his orders were to occupy northern Korea, and he had only a limited force to do that. So he had to spread it thin.

The trouble was, he argued, that he was not able to bomb the huge concentrations of troops and supplies north of the Yalu after the Reds attacked.

He said he never for a moment questioned the right of the President to recall him. But he said he resented the implication that he had been insubordinate.

While the MacArthur hearing was going on, President Truman held a news conference this afternoon. He said that at the Wake Island conference the supreme commander persuaded him that Red China would not intervene in Korea.

*May 4, 1951*—At the Senate hearing today General Douglas MacArthur took direct issue with President Truman. The claim that MacArthur had barred the Central Intelligence Agency from operating in Japan until recently.

MacArthur snapped: "That statement is all tommyrot." He said that in Japan he had given the Central Intelligence Agency all possible aid.

*May 8, 1951*—All along the hundred-mile Korean front the enemy appeared to be withdrawing tonight behind that 38th parallel.

*May 15, 1951*—"The wrong war, at the wrong place, at the wrong time, and with the wrong enemy." Those were the words of General Omar Bradley, chairman of the Joint Chiefs of Staff, who today began his testimony before the Senate investigating committee. General Bradley was referring to General MacArthur's strategy for expanding the war against Communist China.

The chairman of the Joint Chiefs of Staff said bluntly that Russia is the real enemy.

*May 17, 1951*—President Truman today said he had considered dismissing MacArthur before the Korean War began, months before.

The President said that even then the supreme commander in Tokyo was not giving his wholehearted support to the policies of the government in Washington.

The general was critical of the administration policy toward Formosa and the Chinese Nationalists.

The British note rejects all idea that Iran has the right to cancel the treaty which grants oil concessions to the Anglo-Iranian Company. It proposes that Britain send a mission to Teheran to negotiate a settlement.

*May 18, 1951*—The Security Council of the U.N. tonight called on Israel to suspend the swamp-draining project, which is the real key to the border dispute with Syria.

*May 21, 1951*—James Jabara of Wichita, Kansas, the first jet ace in history. Yesterday Captain Jabara shot down two enemy jets—his fifth and sixth. It takes five kills to qualify as an ace.

General Omar Bradley, in his third day of testimony, said that the Joint Chiefs of Staff unanimously endorsed the dismissal of General

Douglas MacArthur because they feared he might take action on his own which would ignite a major Far East war.

*May 22, 1951*—While the enemy withdrawal all along the central and western fronts went on, the new Chinese break-through in the east drove southward more than twenty-five miles below the 38th parallel.

*May 24, 1951*—At Teheran the Iranian Government has given the Anglo-Iranian Oil Company an ultimatum—demanding that the company start co-operating on nationalization by next Wednesday. Either that or the great oil fields will be taken over without further ado.

*May 25, 1951*—In Washington a report on the recent atomic tests at Eniwetok says: "The test program included experiments contributing to thermonuclear weapons research." Translated, that means the hydrogen bomb. Hydrogen turned into helium by means of intense heat.

*June 1, 1951*—In London, King George has a slight inflammation of the lung. So announce the royal physicians, who have ordered His Majesty to cancel all appointments for some time to come.

The health of George VI has never been too robust. A couple of years ago he was found to be suffering from Buerger's disease, a malady that causes a congealing of the blood in the arteries.

*June 4, 1951*—Secretary of State Acheson, testifying before a Senate committee, defended the Yalta agreements, which made so many concessions to Soviet Russia. He said that at the time of Yalta we did not know we had the atomic bomb and thought we would have to invade the main islands of Japan in savage battle.

Moreover, the Secretary contended that the concessions to Stalin at Yalta would have been taken by the Soviets anyway upon the defeat of Japan.

*June 7, 1951*—The disappearance of two diplomats of the British Foreign Office has all the elements of a first-class mystery. Have they fled to Soviet Russia?

Donald MacLean, thirty-eight years old, was the head of the American Department of the London Foreign Office. Guy Francis de Moncy Burgess, forty years old, was a Foreign Office specialist in Far Eastern affairs.

*June 8, 1951*—The mystery of the missing British diplomats is only deepened by telegrams from them to their families. A telegram to Donald MacLean's American-born wife says: "Had to leave unexpectedly. Sorry, darling."

*June 11, 1951*—From Korea front dispatches speak of "the fleeing Communist Army."

Three of Britain's Sunday newspapers discuss the likelihood of King George VI's relinquishing the throne in favor of Princess Elizabeth. This because of the King's serious illness.

*June 13, 1951*—The Prime Minister of Ireland—De Valera! Following the recent election that most famous of all living Irishmen won back his old-time position by a mere two votes, independents giving him their support to assure that narrow margin.

The news from Korea indicates the capture of the last angle of the "Iron Triangle."

*June 19, 1951*—Negotiations broke down in Teheran today, negotiations between Britain and Iran over the nationalization of Anglo-Iranian oil. So the stage seems to be set for Iran to seize the oil installations at dawn tomorrow.

*June 21, 1951*—Patrick J. Hurley, former U. S. Ambassador to China, said that soon after the Yalta conference he went to the White House to protest vehemently against the concessions to the Soviets, giving them virtual control of Manchuria.

But when he saw the President, "all the fight I had in me went out." The President's hand was "a very loose bag of bones." "The skin seemed to be pasted down to his cheekbones." Which illustrates Hurley's contention that F.D.R. was not to blame for Yalta because he was "a very sick man."

*June 25, 1951*—Bitter hand-to-hand fighting marked the opening of the second year of the Korean War today. All along the front Communist attacks were beaten back.

Iran stepped up the pressure on the British Anglo-Iranian Oil Company today. In Teheran, Eric Drake, manager of the world's greatest oil refinery at Abadan, is being accused of sabotage.

At four-thirty this afternoon the first color television program was put on the air. CBS began televising in all the hues of the rainbow—the program lasting from four-thirty to five-thirty.

*June 28, 1951*—The Iranians ousted the British company staff from the headquarters of the great refineries at Abadan today, seizing their offices and compelling them to leave.

*June 29, 1951*—All the way across Korea the Reds are digging in north of the 38th parallel, with deep trenches and fortified bunkers—establishing a front to hold when and if negotiations get going.

The Anglo-Iranian Oil Company is closing down all its operations. To-day in London, Basil Jackson, general manager of Anglo-Iranian, said: "We shall never reach an agreement with Iran so long as Mohammed Mossadegh is Premier."

NOTE: *At this point I was off the air again for another seven weeks. During that period negotiations about a possible truce in Korea began at Kaesong. The Anglo-Iranian oil dispute reached a deadlock—and the great Abadan refinery was shut down. Here at home an unusual story came out of West Point when ninety cadets were dismissed for cheating at examinations.*

*August 27, 1951*—Back on the air tonight, I suppose I ought to give some account of things I noted while away on a vacation for a few weeks.

In England the topic was the Festival of Britain. That country-wide celebration over there has brought in myriads of visitors, which helps the home economy. Everybody has something to say, most of it unkind, about the Labour government.

In France local politics again and the swarming Americans. In Spain, Franco, the monarchy, will it return and when?

Argentina—the spectacular maneuvering to get another term for Perón as President, with Evita for Vice-President. That's of prevailing interest all over Latin America—especially Evita, the woman who seems to have imperial ambition.

People abroad fail to display any feverish interest in communism, danger of war, and the truce talks in Korea.

In Korea today the Reds made their reply to General Ridgway. They keep the door open for further negotiations if something is done about the alleged American air attack in the neutral Kaesong area. We deny any such air attack.

The latest from the war front pictures a new series of violent assaults by the Reds—against South Koreans.

*August 28, 1951*—Tonight's note from General Ridgway confirms the strong belief armistice talks may resume. Tokyo rumors are that General Ridgway may propose a new meeting place—away from Kaesong.

*September 5, 1951*—General Ridgway's new proposal is that liaison officers from both sides meet immediately at the village of Panmunjom, five miles south of Kaesong, to select a new site for further peace talks.

*September 5, 1951*—King George is returning to London—interrupting his vacation in Scotland. The purpose—a thorough medical examination.

*September 12, 1951*—Congress unites in praise of retiring Secretary of Defense George Marshall. He accepted office during the Korean crisis with the proviso that he would step out at the end of this June, but stayed on these extra months under a sense of duty.

The Persian monarch, Reza Pahlevi, is known to be a moderate in the oil dispute—but he is helpless in the face of wild fanaticism. Today he warned the Premier against a "hasty act." But Mossadegh went ahead and sent the ultimatum—demanding that Britain resume negotiations on Iranian terms within fifteen days or the British oil technicians remaining in Iran will be expelled.

*September 13, 1951*—In Korea the talk of the truce is drowned out by the roar of battle. Today the conflict rose to a greater violence than at any time since the armistice negotiations began.

*September 14, 1951*—Red occupation troops have entered Lhasa, the capital of Tibet.

*September 19, 1951*—In Korea the Communists are ready to start peace talks again. They have left it up to the U.N. supreme commander to set a time for the next meeting.

*September 20, 1951*—The latest—a powerful armored assault on the central front. U.N. forces launching the biggest tank drive in the Korean War thus far. American officers explain the armored offensive is just intended to beat up the Reds.

In Britain the election campaign is getting off to a fast beginning. The odds favor Churchill and the Conservatives.

*September 21, 1951*—King George VI will undergo an operation. A bulletin issued by seven physicians declares: "The condition of the King's lung gives cause for concern."

*September 24, 1951*—Tonight King George is described as in a "semi-comatose state," under the influence of drugs administered to ease the great pain following the chest operation.

The Allied liaison team has left for Kaesong by helicopter with instructions to "tell the Communists they must agree to a new site for any future truce talks."

U.N. headquarters explained why Kaesong is considered unsuitable. "It is plain that partisan groups, responsible to neither command, are active in that area."

*September 25, 1951*—"Mig Alley" was the scene of the longest aerial battle of the Korean War. For more than half an hour thirty-seven Sabre jets fought a swirling battle with eighty Red MIG-15s. Five of the enemy jets are down, with five more damaged.

*September 27, 1951*—The Iranians have seized the great oil refineries at Abadan. Ten top-ranking British technicians were permitted to enter, but the rest of the three hundred were kept out.

A sudden explosion of Red attacks across the entire Korean battle front, enemy assaults along a line of sixty miles.

West Germany accepts responsibility for the crime and injury inflicted by Hitler and the Nazis on the Jewish people.

Chancellor Adenauer expressed the will of his government to make reparation for Jewish losses.

King George VI has appointed a Council of State to carry out the royal duties while he recuperates from the lung operation. The council consists of members of the royal family.

*September 28, 1951*—In Argentina, Perón announces—revolt suppressed. During the day dispatches came through heavy censorship—telling, in fragmentary fashion, of an army insurrection.

Perón claims that the revolt included a plot to assassinate him and his wife, Evita.

The Red offensive in Korea was beaten off today, with hardly any enemy gain.

Before a subcommittee on elections Senator Benton of Connecticut pressed his demand that McCarthy be expelled from the Senate. He presented a full list of charges—alleging smear tactics, as in the defeat of Tydings of Maryland and in the McCarthy talk about Communists in the State Department.

*October 3, 1951*—A news dispatch stating: "United Nations tanks, infantry, hundreds of big guns, and deadly flame throwers ripped and seared Communist lines today as blazing action erupted along the entire Korean battle front."

The British are getting out by order of the Iranian Government, leaving the greatest oil refinery in the world.

Soviet Russia has exploded another atomic bomb. The announcement comes from President Truman. This one, the second—the President having announced a previous atomic explosion in Russia more than two years ago.

*October 5, 1951*—American soldiers have ripped through the "winter line" which the Communists had built as a snug bulwark against the severe Korean winter.

*October 8, 1951*—Today General Ridgway accepted an enemy proposal for a resumption of negotiations at the village of Panmunjom, just inside the Red lines.

Winston Churchill calls for a Big Four conference. In Washington, Harry Truman has shown little enthusiasm for another palaver with Stalin.

Iranian Premier Mossadegh is in a New York hospital tonight, to which he went immediately after arriving by plane. He is in feeble health, and faints from time to time. Mossadegh will stay in the hospital until his appearance before the United Nations on Thursday.

*October 9, 1951*—Foreign Secretary Herbert Morrison states that the move in Cairo to scrap the Anglo-Egyptian Treaty is illegal. He declares that British troops will remain at the Suez Canal—and in the Sudan.

London announces the cancellation of the trip of the King and Queen to Australia and New Zealand. Because of the illness of King George the sovereigns will not go. Instead, their places will be taken by Princess Elizabeth and the Duke of Edinburgh—following their Canadian and American tour.

Today tens of thousands of people were jammed in dense crowds along the miles of Quebec streets—hailing the royal visitors as they toured the old capital of French Canada.

*October 10, 1951*—The reception the Princess and the Duke got at Ottawa today was a record-breaker.

*October 11, 1951*—American and French troops have captured the last summit of Heartbreak Ridge—ending the bitterest battle of the Korean War.

*October 12, 1951*—The truce talks take a sudden turn for the worse—with Red charges of two new violations of the neutral zone. They charged that a few hours after the liaison officers had ended their session three Americans flew over the neutralized Kaesong area and made two strafing attacks, swooping down and blazing away with machine guns. Two children hit, one killed—said the Reds.

Canada's greeting came to a climax in Toronto today. There were wild scenes of cheering and singing—acclaim for Princess Elizabeth and the Duke of Edinburgh.

*October 15, 1951*—Drama supplied by the personality of the Teheran Premier. Feeble and fainting—most of the time ill in bed, falling into a swoon on almost any occasion at the U.N.

He spoke only fifteen minutes—then turned his manuscript over to an aide to finish.

The contents were according to schedule—insistence that the oil dispute was purely an Iranian internal affair, therefore was out of the jurisdiction of the United Nations.

The Egyptian parliament voted unanimously to go ahead with plans for throwing the British out of the Suez Canal zone and taking over the Anglo-Egyptian Sudan.

*October 16, 1951*—News of the assassination of Prime Minister Liaquat Ali Khan of Pakistan. Late word from Karachi describes the assassin as a member of a fanatical Moslem group which has long been clamoring for a "holy war" with India over Kashmir.

There was rioting along the Suez Canal.

Egyptian mobs set fire to six British buses, a British Army canteen, and a British Army post exchange store. At Ismailia two of the British and twelve Egyptians were killed, with more than a hundred others injured.

*October 17, 1951*—Tonight in Korea the remnants of five Chinese battalions are in a trap—the jaws of which closed on them today.

*October 18, 1951*—The British have seized all communications across the zone of the Suez Canal—including the one bridge across that strip of water. Egypt proper is cut off from its territory on the other side of the Suez, the peninsula of Sinai, Biblical Sinai.

*October 22, 1951*—The White House has just disclosed that the Soviets have touched off their third "atomic explosion."

The Atomic Energy Commission announces that "the seventh atomic explosion within the continental United States took place at 9 A.M. today."

The appointment of an Ambassador to the Vatican. President Truman naming General Mark Clark—in a stunning weekend surprise. A storm of criticism from top-ranking Protestant churchmen everywhere.

*October 23, 1951*—At Blair House today President Truman welcomed that surprisingly healthy invalid Mohammed Mossadegh.

Britain is willing to negotiate with Iran, with the United States acting as mediator. This message was passed on to the Persian Premier by the American President. But there will be no developments until after the British elections.

A dispatch from Washington about the Eisenhower boom. We hear that Eisenhower has told his backers that he will not declare himself while he is in uniform. Meaning not while he is in command of the Western European army.

*October 24, 1951*—The truce talks are on again—in a tent city at the mud village of Panmunjom. Today tents were put up by G.I.s, who operated like an old-time circus gang.

*October 25, 1951*—President Truman insists that the nomination of an Ambassador to the Vatican does not, in any way, conflict with the basic American principle of separation of church and state.

So when Congress convenes he will press the nomination of General Mark Clark.

*October 26, 1951*—Churchill arrived at Buckingham Palace amid the cheers of the waiting crowd—and was received by the King, who asked him to form a Cabinet.

Tonight the figures show 319 seats in Parliament for the Conservatives. Two hundred and ninety-four for Labour. Liberals—five. Miscellaneous—two.

Another of the great ones went the way of oblivion tonight when Joe Louis was knocked out. In the eighth round Rocky Marciano flattened the one-time invincible Brown Bomber.

*October 31, 1951*—Today the Red negotiators came forward with a counterproposal yielding so much that hope for a truce rose to high optimism.

The heiress to the British crown and her husband in Washington for a three-day visit.

Half a million people shouted an ovation as the procession of automobiles rolled through Washington streets.

*November 1, 1951*—The first atomic war games were held—at Frenchman Flat on the Nevada desert. Fifteen hundred troops were in the area, and there were maneuvers in conjunction with the giant atomic blast. The explosion was so powerful it broke plate-glass windows in Las Vegas, ninety miles away.

*November 6, 1951*—Señora Perón, wife of the Argentine President, has just undergone an operation. Perón himself waited at the hospital all day, together with Ministers of his Cabinet—all in homage to the famous Evita, so influential in Argentine politics.

*November 7, 1951*—The Red proposal is for the armistice line to be the present battle line—and not the one at the time when the armistice is signed. Which, in effect, would freeze the battle front where it is right now, no change. The Reds' own position on the war front would be safeguarded.

*November 12, 1951*—The United Nations was the scene of a familiar wrangle today. Once again over the question of a seat in the U.N. for Red China. Vishinsky swinging at Acheson. When it came to a ballot, the Soviets were voted down.

*November 14, 1951*—The United States and Yugoslavia have signed a military aid agreement. Under which the United States will ship large quantities of armament to Marshal Tito, the Communist in a bitter feud with Soviet Russia.

*November 15, 1951*—President Truman told newsmen today that he does not want to go to any face-to-face meeting with the heads of state, including Stalin.

*November 16, 1951*—The Soviets come forward with a plan for atomic disarmament—and it's the same old thing. At the U.N. General Assembly in Paris, Vishinsky called for the prohibition of atomic weapons and the establishment of atomic control. But he skated around the question of inspection.

*November 23, 1951*—The long wrangle about an armistice line is over, and it now remains to be seen if it can be settled on other terms—like prisoners of war.

Today President Klement Gottwald went on the air and announced the arrest of Rudolf Slansky, Czechoslovak Vice-Premier. Slansky, former Secretary-General of the Czech Communist party, is charted with "leading a conspiracy against the Republic" and with "anti-state activities."

*November 28, 1951*—Paris buzzed with the rumor today that General Eisenhower will soon retire as Atlantic Treaty Organization commander. Purpose—to seek a nomination for President.

Today brought the largest purge of government employees in the recent history of the United States—a list of thirty-one, belonging to the income tax bureau. All dismissed from their jobs in the scandals that have been shaking the Bureau of Internal Revenue.

*December 3, 1951*—There was violent fighting along the Suez Canal today—three clashes between British troops and Egyptian police and civilians. As many as twenty-four killed.

*December 4, 1951*—In Korea the truce talks are tangled up. The Reds want an end to the rotation system, whereby we take battle-weary soldiers out of Korea and replace them with fresh troops.

*December 11, 1951*—In the Iranian parliament an oil debate was on. There are opposition deputies—and they have their courage. They are living right in the parliament building, which is guarded by soldiers. They don't dare to venture out for fear of the mob.

Today a huge crowd was gathered in front of the Teheran parliament, yelling and chanting: "Long live Mossadegh, death to the traitors."

Fights broke out in parliament—deputies punching each other. Shouts of the brawling legislators were combined with the howls of the mob.

*December 13, 1951*—In the truce talks the U.N. delegates are pressing their demand for information about Allied prisoners of war. They tell the Reds they will not consider any Communist proposal concerning prisoners until they get the figures.

Egypt has called its Ambassador from London—bringing the quarrel over Suez and the Sudan to a new crisis.

From Jerusalem a report of an address by Premier Ben Gurion to the parliament of Israel.

Ben Gurion is reported by the New York *Times* as declaring that the problem is how to induce American Jews to immigrate to Israel. "There were not," he added, "five leaders who got up to go to Israel after the state was established."

The State Department announces that John Stewart Service has been dismissed—one of the diplomats prominently mentioned in charges of communism. Service was high on the list of Senator McCarthy of Wisconsin—the senator hurling charges at him.

*December 18, 1951*—The number of the American prisoners of war—3,198. That many out of more than twelve thousand missing in the Korean War. The figure, two thousand lower than had been expected.

The U.N. truce team handed over to the Communists a list of Red prisoners, a huge number, more than a hundred and thirty-two thousand—of whom nearly twenty-one thousand are Chinese. The question is now whether we should hand over such large numbers for such small numbers.

*December 19, 1951*—Today brings confirmation of reports that the Czech Red purge is largely anti-Semitic. The evidence is a speech made by the Premier, which is printed in the Communist party newspaper at Prague. He attacks what he calls "Jewish capitalists," and "interference from Jerusalem!" Apparently a reference to Slansky and other Jewish politicians.

*December 21, 1951*—A Republic of Italy today scrapped the peace treaty. Rome repudiates the clauses of armament limitation. This is done with the full consent of the United States, Great Britain, France, and other Western allies.

*December 24, 1951*—Senator Kefauver for President! The Tennessean's boom is building up, and may have possibilities if President Truman decides not to run again.

Today the Communists made a concession—proposing that prisoners of war be permitted to write letters to their families. In token of which they presented to the American delegation a letter from General Dean to his wife—word from the Congressional Medal of Honor commander of the 24th Division, who was captured early in the war.

*December 26, 1951*—Today's developments in the talks at Panmunjom were grim. The Reds declared that 571 prisoners of war were killed by Allied air attack or gunfire, or perished from disease. Our negotiators retorted immediately with bitter suspicion of murder committed by Reds guarding prisoners.

*December 28, 1951*—The Reds intimate that *they* will break off the talks rather than yield on the question of rebuilding air bases. Which would, in effect, permit them to use a truce as a means of providing bases for their jet planes.

The U.N. command charged that 450 American prisoners are known to have reached Communist camps and are now missing. The implication is atrocity.

# 1952

General Eisenhower becomes President of the United States after a landslide victory over Adlai Stevenson.

In Korea the truce talks go on, the big problem being what to do with the prisoners who refuse to go back to communism.

France begins to have trouble with the empire. Rebellion flares in North Africa. In Indochina, French troops are forced to retreat before the Communist hordes.

In the Suez Canal zone there is anti-British rioting. King Farouk falls after a violent outburst in Cairo, and is replaced by a military junta. In South Africa new segregation laws cause unrest among the colored people of the Cape.

The year sees four important deaths: King George VI of Britain (who is succeeded by his daughter, Elizabeth II); William Green, long-time head of the A.F. of L.; Chaim Weizmann, first President of Israel; and Eva Perón, wife of the Argentine dictator and one of the world's most scintillating and powerful women.

---

*January 1, 1952*—Reports that the Reds have been trying to indoctrinate American prisoners of war with communism. Trying to overwhelm them with arguments to prove the correctness of Marxian theory and the doctrine of Stalin.

*January 2, 1952*—The White House announces a crackdown on the Bureau of Internal Revenue to clean up the income tax corruption, "a sweeping reorganization."

The entire income tax bureau will be put under Civil Service, as long ago recommended by the Hoover Commission.

*January 3, 1952*—In the Korean truce talks the main question is now out in the open, plain for all to see. Numbers of Red prisoners of war do not want to be sent back to the Communist Army.

The Reds want their prisoners back whether the prisoners like it or not.

*January 7, 1952*—Today's Eisenhower statement pictures a general in a dilemma. He is willing to accept the G.O.P. nomination, would welcome the offer. But he wants to make it clear that he does not put political advancement above his duty as commander of the Western European army.

In Jerusalem today rioters were demonstrating against the decision to negotiate with West Germany on the subject of reparations to be paid for injury done to the Jewish people by the Hitler persecutions.

Extreme conservatives are against any dealings whatever with Germany— even for the purpose of getting reparations.

*January 9, 1952*—Senator Paul Douglas of Illinois called for the nomination of Eisenhower by the Democrats. The general has, of course, declared for the G.O.P.—but the senator wants him to have the Democratic nomination. Have both parties name Eisenhower.

The President and Prime Minister Churchill have been conferring in Washington.

They agree that American atomic bombers based in Britain will not make any attack except by "joint decision." Britain to have a veto over any action based on British flying fields.

Messrs. Truman and Churchill have put aside any notion of a top-level conference with Stalin—a thing advocated previously by Churchill.

*January 10, 1952*—The President told the newsmen that if General Eisenhower wants to return home to campaign for the Republican nomination he is perfectly free to do so.

Today began the seventh month of the truce talks in Korea—all tied up in a deadlock.

*January 11, 1952*—The West German parliament has okayed the Schuman Plan. The vote overwhelmingly in favor of the international scheme for the pooling of coal and steel.

*January 14, 1952*—General Mark Clark has withdrawn from the nomination as Ambassador to the Holy See. The Vatican is not surprised, declares a news dispatch from Rome.

Today Protestant Church leaders declared against any future appointment the President might make.

*January 22, 1952*—There are 177,000 prisoners on Koje Island. Of these, about twenty-six hundred are fanatical Communists, dominated by

Red officers trained in Moscow. They form an inner circle and run a reign of terror.

Nevertheless, six thousand North Koreans have made a formal protest against being sent back to Red Korea during any prisoner exchange—and more than twelve thousand Chinese have done the same, signing petitions in blood.

*January 24, 1952*—Alger Hiss has appealed for a third trial.

Hiss insisted that Chambers had committed forgery—by typewriter. So now his lawyers say that a New York typewriter expert has built them a machine with type that no expert could tell from the typing of the Woodstock machine in the trial. Which, they intimate, indicates that Whittaker Chambers could have planted the typewriter. If you can make machines with identical type, forgery by typewriter is possible!

*January 25, 1952*—Today brought the deadliest, most violent battle thus far in the trouble along the Suez Canal. It began as a result of an order from London—disarm the Egyptian police at Ismailia.

When the police were told to surrender their weapons, they refused. They fought like fanatics, and sixty were killed in the battle, which lasted for five hours.

*January 28, 1952*—More than one hundred and fifty fires were set by the frenzied crowd in Cairo. Night clubs, theaters, and bars—the haunts of foreigners—were the first to go up in smoke. Including a hotel renowned in Shanghai, in Kansas City, everywhere—Shepheard's.

*January 31, 1952*—In London today Princess Elizabeth and Prince Philip started off on their trip to Australia and New Zealand. Their first stop will be at a wedding present. When they were married more than three years ago, the gifts they got made a long list. One item—a lodge in Kenya. They've never seen it—a royal bungalow in an African valley.

*February 5, 1952*—The New Hampshire primary, on the Democratic side, now becomes a sort of popularity contest between Truman and Kefauver.

*February 6, 1952*—Elizabeth II is flying to London tonight. Immediately upon the news of the death of her father she took a plane at an airport in East Africa—where the royal couple were making a stay.

From all over the world messages of condolence are pouring into Buckingham Palace—the heads of the nations expressing their sorrow over the death of King George VI.

*February 7, 1952*—In London this afternoon the new Queen performed her first act of state. For the first time she signed her name in royal style—Elizabeth Regina. It was a mournful duty issuing a decree for her father's funeral—to be held on Friday, February 15.

*February 15, 1952*—On the islands of Britain—at two o'clock this afternoon—all activity stopped for two minutes of silence and prayer.

That was at the moment when the coffin of George VI came to the door of St. George's Chapel at Windsor, traditional home of the royal family.

*February 18, 1952*—Washington announces a new series of atomic explosions at Eniwetok atoll. So immediately the surmise is hydrogen bomb.

*February 19, 1952*—General MacArthur is at it busily withdrawing from primaries.

*February 21, 1952*—Bitter rioting broke out tonight in the ill-famed U.N. prisoner-of-war camp on Koje Island. First word from the stockade is of one American soldier and sixty-nine Korean prisoners dead. Fifteen hundred Koreans attacked security guards with steel picks, spiked wooden clubs, barbed-wire flails, blackjacks, and knives.

*February 25, 1952*—A serious setback reported for the French in Indochina. In what is described as a "strategic withdrawal," the French high command has pulled back its forces defending the beleaguered city of Hanoi.

*February 27, 1952*—Today the U.N. delegation served what sounds like an ultimatum. They told the Reds that they would never agree to force prisoners of war to go back to the Communists—any prisoner exchange would have to be on a voluntary basis.

*March 3, 1952*—The Supreme Court throws out a protest against the reading of the Bible and reciting the Lord's Prayer in New Jersey public schools.

The verdict is of nationwide importance because the Bible is either required or permitted in schools of many states.

*March 4, 1952*—At Panmunjom today the arguments echoed back and forth. The Allies insisting that no prisoners should be forced to go back to Communist territory against their will, while the Reds insist that all prisoners must be returned.

*March 10, 1952*—New and rigid restrictions clamped on Soviet officials in Washington and New York. Retaliation for the severe limitations of travel which the Reds have long placed on foreign diplomats in Moscow.

Colonel Fulgencio Batista, the one-time army sergeant, set a record by overthrowing three Cuban presidents. Now he has deposed a fourth—President Carlos Prio Socarras.

He went to the chief military camp at Havana and assumed command of the troops. Just made a speech and marched the soldiers against the presidential palace.

*March 12, 1952*—The New Hampshire primary. The final count giving Eisenhower 46,000, Senator Taft 35,000. Of delegates to go to the Chicago Republican Convention, General Ike takes every one of the fourteen.

On the Democratic side the surprise, of course, is Kefauver. The Tennessee senator beating out President Truman by 20,000 to 16,000.

*March 13, 1952*—Independent India has abolished the sovereign power of the traditional potentates—the princes of India. Many of these have gone into the new parliamentary government, and you'll find more than one a provincial governor of his former realm.

Today the Nizam of Hyderabad arrived at New Delhi for the conference of governors with a princely retinue of seventy-three rolling through New Delhi in forty limousines.

*March 14, 1952*—The strategy of the "big lie" was on today at the United Nations. Soviet Russia demanding that the United States be condemned for practicing germ warfare in Korea and China. Which, of course, only repeats the fantastic accusations made by the Chinese Red radio.

*March 19, 1952*—In the Minnesota primary Stassen ahead by about eleven thousand. He takes 42 per cent as against Eisenhower's 38 per cent. It was a write-in vote for Ike.

*March 20, 1952*—General Eisenhower says those Minnesota results are making him reconsider. Which goes back to his declaration in January that he would not campaign unless there was "a clear-cut call to political duty." Apparently Minnesota might be that "clear-cut call."

*March 26, 1952*—France takes drastic measures in Tunisia, declaring a state of siege and arresting the Tunisian Premier, together with a whole string of other leaders. This incited by a move to place a demand for Tunisian independence before the United Nations in New York.

A two-million-dollar suit between a couple of United States senators. McCarthy of Wisconsin going to the law against Benton of Connecticut, charging slander and libel, and a conspiracy to oust McCarthy from the Senate.

*March 27, 1952*—Indochina reports a big offensive against the Communists. Thousands of French troops in a drive against an enemy division thrusting to within twenty miles of the vital seaport of Hanoi.

*March 28, 1952*—The Bey of Tunis has bowed to the French, yielding to their demand that he name a Ministry of moderates. He was told if he didn't knuckle under he'd be deposed.

The big lie caused an uproar in the United Nations tonight. Soviet delegate Malik had to be silenced—he was so loud with charges of American germ warfare.

The Republicans in the State of Maine held their convention today, naming delegates to the G.O.P. National Convention. General Eisenhower gets nine, Senator Taft five.

*March 31, 1952*—That weekend sensation—President Truman declaring himself out. The Democratic side of the presidential picture is thrown into dizzy confusion.

One thing became evident immediately—the rise of favorite sons. Vice-President Barkley is being boomed as Kentucky's favorite son. Michigan presents Governor Mennen Williams. Connecticut—Senator Brian McMahon.

Illinois, of course, has Governor Adlai Stevenson, who continues to say he's not a candidate. Today he conferred with President Truman.

Tonight Senator Kefauver of Tennessee and Governor Kerr of Oklahoma both predict victory for themselves in the Nebraska primary tomorrow.

*April 2, 1952*—Wisconsin and Nebraska present the same picture—victory for Taft, but with a vote smaller than the totals for Warren and Stassen, both of whom are on record as being favorable to Eisenhower.

Both campaigned for Eisenhower votes—the general not being on the ballot.

Actually, it means a big boost for the Taft campaign. He wins his first primary successes.

How about the Democratic side? Both Wisconsin and Nebraska provided victories for Senator Kefauver.

*April 4, 1952*—General Ike wins a victory in Iowa—where the Republicans held their convention today.

Eisenhower gets fourteen, Taft eight. Four delegates uncommitted.

*April 10, 1952*—General Eisenhower today won twenty of his home state's twenty-two G.O.P. delegates. The other two in Kansas go to Taft.

*April 11, 1952*—The announcement of General Eisenhower's resignation from his command in Europe. General Ike now goes on the inactive list of the Army—enabling him to campaign with virtually the status of a civilian.

*April 16, 1952*—Adlai Stevenson's answer: "I have repeatedly said that I was a candidate for the Governor of Illinois and had no other ambition. To this I must add that I could not accept the nomination for any other office this summer."

With the New Jersey count nearly all in, it is Eisenhower, 380,000; Taft, 223,000.

*April 17, 1952*—Here is the latest: Governor Adlai Stevenson comes out in support of Averell Harriman, the administration diplomat who ranks as a New York favorite son.

*April 22, 1952*—After I witnessed today's atomic explosion here in the Nevada desert, my impressions are still almost as badly scrambled as that desert floor, which we saw rise up before our eyes.

By far the most spectacular part was the atomic mushroom in the heavens—rolling and boiling. Within ten minutes the atomic cloud was at an altitude somewhere between forty and fifty thousand feet.

*April 23, 1952*—Today's tally for New York shows that General Eisenhower will have virtually the entire delegation. It looks as though Taft wins only one delegate.

But then New York State always was an Eisenhower stronghold. Governor Dewey started the Eisenhower boom rolling months ago—first to come out for General Ike.

In Pennsylvania, General Ike polled around eight hundred thousand. But Senator Taft received a strong write-in, about a hundred and fifty thousand.

*April 25, 1952*—When our people investigated and made lists of prisoners willing to go back to communism, they found that, out of the total of 170,000 only 70,000 were willing to return to Red territory.

*April 28, 1952*—Our war with Japan ended formally today when Secretary of State Acheson deposited the peace treaty in the government archives at Washington.

*April 29, 1952*—This afternoon Federal Judge David Pine found that presidential seizure of the steel industry unconstitutional. He rejects the claim that the President has unlimited powers in an emergency. The president of the steel workers issued a strike order a half hour after the decision was announced.

*April 30, 1952*—Of thirty-eight Massachusetts delegates Eisenhower gets twenty-nine, Taft three. The United Press gives the national score as: Taft, 271; Eisenhower, 271. Even Steven.

*May 2, 1952*—Union president Philip Murray calls off the steel strike. He does so in deference to an urgent plea from President Truman.

*May 8, 1952*—We can only gape with amazement at the news from Korea about General Dodd. The commandant of the prison camp on Koje Island seized by Red captives and held as a hostage.

At the gate of the barbed-wire enclosure in which the prisoners are kept, the general was talking with some Communists when the Reds broke into violence and General Dodd was pulled into the enclosure, a prisoner of the prisoners.

Meanwhile it would appear that the general has been negotiating for his own release. A message from General Dodd was passed along by the Red prisoners of war.

The seizure of the general happened two days ago, kept secret until now.

*May 9, 1952*—General Dodd is still held as a hostage by Red prisoners of war in the camp he commanded. He has passed along demands made by the Communist prisoners, who insist that they be given the right to have telephone communication with other compounds where prisoners are kept and the privilege of organizing those other captives.

*May 12, 1952*—General Dodd was released after Communist terms were accepted. First the Reds were given an ultimatum that troops would move in unless they yielded. They told the general that if this threat of armed force were carried out he would be killed and the prisoners would stage a mass break for freedom. The deadline went by, and the general was not turned loose until eleven hours later—following an acceptance of terms by camp commander General Colson.

General Mark Clark, our new commander-in-chief in the Far East, declares that Colson conceded the terms "under duress." And intimates that they will not necessarily be kept.

*May 13, 1952*—The truce talks at Panmunjom have degenerated into a poisonous lather of Red propaganda. The usual propaganda charges, with new ones weaving around that fantasy of the prison camp and the capture of General Dodd.

*May 15, 1952*—General MacArthur comes out against General Eisenhower. He says the election of a military man as President would be a national tragedy.

We hear that the repudiation of those concessions to Red prisoners was on direct orders from Washington. General Mark Clark instructed to reject the terms as blackmail, extorted under menace to the life of General Dodd.

On Koje Island the new camp commandant, General Boatner, announces a stern regime. No negotiations with prisoners of war, no concessions to Red propaganda.

*May 16, 1952*—Governor Byrnes, former Secretary of State to President Truman, is a leader of the Dixiecrat revolt. He called upon the South to bolt—vote Republican—if they cannot get a reasonable compromise on the civil rights issue.

*May 22, 1952*—News from that tough, turbulent prisoner camp on Koje Island pictures Communist prisoners on guard. Inside the barbed wire of the notorious Compound 76 today sentries appeared standing on duty wearing uniforms with red bands on their arms. Outside the barbed-wire barricade American G.I.s also stand on sentry duty.

The Senate this afternoon passed the McCarran immigration bill after beating down attempts to modify the measure. One amendment aimed to eliminate a provision restricting Asiatic immigration, which opponents denounced as racial discrimination.

The railroads will be returned immediately to their owners. So stated by President Truman today—following the settlement of the wage dispute last night. The federal government took over the railroads back in 1950 to avert a strike—and has been operating them nominally ever since.

*May 23, 1952*—Military penalties for Brigadier Generals Dodd and Colson. Both demoted, reduced to the rank of colonel. This as punishment for their parts in that farcical prison-camp travesty on Koje Island.

*May 26, 1952*—Today the war with Germany ended officially, at least so far as the western part of that country is concerned.

At Bonn, the old city on the Rhine, the Foreign Ministers of the Western Big Three put their signatures on the treaty, making peace with West Germany on the condition that twelve divisions of German troops be mobilized for the army of the Atlantic Treaty Organization.

Details are now disclosed of brutalities inflicted by fanatical Reds at Koje Island on captives out of sympathy with communism. Torture and mutilation. Murderous executions ordered by Red kangaroo courts. Now as the camp command moves to put a stop to this, the Reds are organizing armed resistance. They have been able to turn out quantities of primitive weapons—knives, tomahawks, steel-tipped spears.

*May 29, 1952*—In France today the acting head of the French Communist party was jailed.

Yesterday Duclos was in command of the Red mobs that staged a furious demonstration against the arrival in Paris of American General Ridgway, new military commander of the North Atlantic Treaty Organization.

President Truman has vetoed the tidelands oil bill. Sending the measure back to Congress, he said it would give away a "precious national heritage," which belongs to the whole country and not to a few lucky states situated fortunately along our coasts.

*May 30, 1952*—In Paris today General Eisenhower gave up his command, handing it over to General Ridgway. General Ike is flying to Washington.

*June 2, 1952*—General Ike, as a five-star general, would be entitled, under the law, to draw his high-ranking pay while in retirement. More than nineteen thousand dollars a year. But he relinquishes the military money as he becomes a civilian—in politics.

Today a Republican seeking the presidency, he was decorated by the Democratic President. At the White House, President Truman presented the Distinguished Service Medal. Third occasion on which Mr. Truman has bestowed that military honor on Ike.

*June 3, 1952*—The downfall of the world's No. 1 woman Communist is confirmed. Today the Rumanian Communist party announced that Mrs. Ana Pauker has been removed from the Rumanian Politburo and from the Secretariat of the Central Committee of the Party.

*June 4, 1952*—It was sure wet in Abilene, Kansas—raining on the parade and then drenching General Ike's address at the stadium. But he stuck it out—bareheaded and wearing a raincoat. Forty-five hundred people braved the downpour to hear the speech.

The general plunged into domestic political issues, decrying inflation, excessive taxation, and bureaucracy.

There was action on those Koje Island prison camps today.

Troops in gas masks, armed with flame throwers and tear gas, pushed into compounds dominated by Communists. Turning flame throwers on Communist flags and banners, also shooting fiery streams into special tents the Red bosses had used as headquarters.

The soldiers found seventeen prisoners, their hands bound at the wrists.

They were awaiting death, having been sentenced by the Red kangaroo courts.

During all this the Red captives gave no sign of resistance—looking on meekly.

*June 5, 1952*—At his first news conference as a candidate he said he'd be delighted if they'd stop calling him "General." He'd like to be just "Mister."

So there was Mr. Eisenhower, in a natty gray suit, light blue shirt and a dark blue tie—100 per cent civilian.

In truce talks the Reds today making things awkward by invoking the Geneva convention. The Geneva convention, framed years ago, requires all prisoners of war to be repatriated upon the conclusion of peace. But we refuse to send back to the Reds prisoners who don't want to go. The Geneva convention never foresaw anything like that. Never foresaw ideological war.

*June 9, 1952*—On Koje Island today American soldiers forced their way into notorious Compound No. 76. That's the nest of Red fanatics where prison-camp commander General Dodd was held a hostage.

The Reds jeered and howled, and a bitter fight was on. One paratrooper was killed—and twenty-four Communists.

The battle lasted for ninety minutes before the Reds could be subdued. Then the work proceeded—cutting notorious Compound No. 76 into smaller sections.

*June 13, 1952*—Candidate Averell Harriman comes out in full support of civil rights, backing up President Truman. He is the only prominent presidential candidate to take that stand.

*June 16, 1952*—General Matthew Ridgway was in Rome today.

The Communist party in Italy had threatened a wild outbreak against the new commander of the Atlantic Treaty Organization. To which the Italian Government responded by mobilizing fifty thousand soldiers and police.

Scores of Reds arrested—the others chased away.

*June 17, 1952*—The West German Government offers to pay the state of Israel three billion marks—$714,000,000. In restitution for Nazi crimes against the Jewish people. Israel demands about a billion dollars. World Jewish organizations ask for five hundred million.

*June 18, 1952*—Today in the ancient city of Teheran the Finance Minister said: "Let us pray to Allah."

The Minister of the public purse declares he hasn't the funds to meet the current bills. No money to pay the salaries of government employees.

The reason, of course, the cutting off of revenues from Anglo-Iranian oil.

*June 23, 1952*—The tremendous air strike in Korea today devastated targets of vital importance. The system of mighty dams on the Yalu River —source of immense hydroelectric power for industries in Red Manchuria.

*June 25, 1952*—President Truman today vetoed the McCarran immigration bill on the grounds of racial discrimination—particularly against the peoples of Asia. He criticized, likewise, a continuance of our immigration quota system, which favors English, German, and Irish immigrants.

*June 26, 1952*—In South Africa a "civil disobedience" campaign began today. Protesting against the racial segregation laws imposed recently.

An organized mass move to violate the segregation laws. Same tactics as Mahatma Gandhi used to use in India.

Senator Taft let out a blast, simply blazing, today. He said that the campaign for General Ike has been taken over by Governor Dewey's organization in New York. With a spreading of propaganda that Taft can't win!

*June 27, 1952*—The Senate overrides the veto of the immigration bill. Which makes it a law.

NOTE: *At this point there was another summer hiatus. However, I could not ignore the big story just about to break—the presidential conventions. So my stories of the nominations of Dwight D. Eisenhower by the G.O.P. and of Adlai Stevenson by the Democrats are below. Elsewhere the King of Egypt fell—Farouk replaced by a junta led by General Mohammed Naguib. In Argentina, Eva Perón died of cancer—she had once been the most powerful woman in the world. And here at home President Truman commuted to life imprisonment the death sentence of Oscar Collazo, one of the Puerto Rican terrorists who had tried to assassinate him.*

*July 7, 1952*—Here in Chicago, General Eisenhower has just won the first victory at the Republican National Convention of 1952.

The Eisenhower people proposed that all delegations in dispute be kept from voting on whether or not other disputed delegations should be seated.

The Eisenhower contention was that, under the old rules, the Taft forces were out to steal Southern delegations. The Taft argument was that the rules should not be changed in the middle of the game.

Then the vote—and an Eisenhower compromise was adopted.

*July 10, 1952*—Senator Taft is holding out grimly, saying that his forces will stand firm and that he'll win enough support to give him the nomination. But late reports picture something like a panic in the ranks of the Taft followers. This follows the vote on the convention floor seating the Eisenhower delegation from Texas, which set the pattern for action on disputed Southern delegations.

*July 11, 1952*—The bitterness on the Taft side was concentrated on Governor Dewey of New York—who became a target for booing and jeering. I thought at the time they were going too far—bad strategy. Illinois Senator Dirksen, a Taft leader, pointing his finger at Dewey and singling him out for the bitter charge that Dewey had led the Republican party to defeat twice.

Then came the roll call at the convention today. The states giving their votes, on down the alphabet, until they came to the Ns.

The chairman of the New York delegation arose. Tom Dewey—the focus of dramatic interest. What he said was plenty impressive. "New York gives ninety-two votes for Eisenhower, four for Taft!"

Eisenhower was going to have it on the first ballot.

Here at the convention we're all set for the acceptance speech. We heard MacArthur's keynote speech—which sounded a lofty tone but did not stampede the convention, as many thought it would. Then there was former President Hoover's address, high-minded and stately in wisdom. And now, in about an hour, General Eisenhower's acceptance of the Republican nomination for President.

The vice-presidential candidate, Senator Richard Nixon of California—that decision was made this afternoon by a conference of top-ranking Republican leaders.

There's political importance in the warm cordiality with which Senator Taft greeted Eisenhower when the general dashed over to Taft headquarters.

*July 23, 1952*—At the Democratic National Convention today the Credentials Committee's report okayed the delegations from Virginia, South Carolina, and Louisiana. Although they refused to take the new version of the loyalty pledge. Which has been watered down with compromise and reservation.

Nevertheless, top Southern leaders are still rejecting the pledge. Headed by Senator Harry Byrd of Virginia, whose influential Virginia delegation has decided, unanimously, to ignore the loyalty business.

All day Chicago had rumors about a "stop Stevenson" combination. The Illinois governor, though reluctant, had been persuaded to enter the competition for the nomination.

Senator Kefauver issued a blazing attack on the Stevenson partisans. He said: "They are trying to engineer a synthetic draft."

*July 25, 1952*—South Carolina won the right of staying in the convention—so did Louisiana. Virginia had been granted that same privilege a couple of hours before. Although none of those three Southern states took the loyalty pledge—their delegations defiantly refusing to do so.

Stevenson was against the whole business of kicking the Southerners around and running them out of the party. One report was that he would not accept the nomination if the Dixiecrats were driven to bolt.

The first ballot took nearly four hours—and when it was over, Kefauver was in the lead.

*The convention ended on July 26, Saturday, with the nominations of Stevenson and Sparkman.*

*August 26, 1952*—In Argentina there were dramatic scenes today—commemorating the first month since the death of Eva Perón, wife of the Argentine strong man.

Labor stoppages throughout the country—ordered by the Federation of Unions. Workers paying honor to the woman who rallied what she called the Decamisados, those without shirts.

Well, she made a mark in history. She knew how to play the game of power, and was the most loved and hated woman in the world—the blonde one-time actress whom they called Evita.

*August 27, 1952*—Governor Stevenson's address to the American Legion had its turn of courage and boldness.

He said: "Too often sinister threats to the Bill of Rights, to freedom of the mind, are concealed under the patriotic cloak of anti-communism." He excoriated the attacks on the wartime Chief of Staff, General Marshall. "To me," declared Stevenson, "this is the type of patriotism which is, in Dr. Johnson's phrase, 'the last refuge of scoundrels.'"

*August 28, 1952*—Governor Stevenson is concentrating his fire on McCarthyism—the McCarthy charges of communism in our federal government. He summons General Ike to get rid of what Stevenson calls "middle of the gutter" advisers.

*September 2, 1952*—General Ike has begun his fighting campaign—hitting hard. He's touring the South, and in Atlanta cut loose with verbal haymakers. "This Washington mess," he cried, "is not a one-agency mess, or a one-bureau mess, or a one-department mess. It's a top-to-bottom mess."

*September 3, 1952*—At Birmingham, Alabama, forty thousand people jammed a park to hear General Ike.

One striking development is the appearance of "Independent slates" on ballots in the South. That is, lists of Eisenhower electors labeled "Independent," not Republican.

*September 4, 1952*—At Stevenson headquarters in Springfield, Illinois, the word is that the candidate will "treat the American people as the adults they are." This in response to comment that Adlai Stevenson may be talking over the heads of the people.

*September 9, 1952*—Texas Governor Shivers is the second Southern governor to turn against the national ticket. Governor Kennon of Louisiana having made the formal announcement over the weekend that he would support Eisenhower.

The Texas state convention has voted—calling upon Governor Shivers and all other state officials to campaign for General Ike.

*September 12, 1952*—Senator Taft today announced his unconditional support of the Republican ticket—this after a two-hour discussion with the general.

*September 15, 1952*—General Ike was out on the whistle stop trail today, and made a lashing attack. The target—the Stevenson quips and wisecracks. The general said the great questions before the nation "are not laughing matters." And added, "I see nothing funny about them."

"The great crusade," declared Stevenson, "has turned to the great surrender."

That's the campaign line the Democrats are taking, following the conference after which Taft pledged support and promised to campaign for General Ike.

*September 18, 1952*—Governor Byrnes of South Carolina says he will vote for General Ike. Byrnes was once President Truman's Secretary of State.

At Los Angeles the statement is that a group of Californians put up sums of money for paying the expenses of Senator Nixon in Washington.

At Senator Nixon's campaign headquarters in Washington the statement is confirmed that the senator has used "a private fund" to "take care of expenses" not covered by government allowances.

Democratic headquarters launches an attack at once, challenging General Eisenhower to demand the resignation of the vice-presidential candidate from the Republican ticket.

*September 19, 1952*—Today Attorney General James McGranery

ordered Immigration authorities to bar Charlie Chaplin from re-entering the United States until he has been investigated.

Last Wednesday, Chaplin, who has always remained a British subject, sailed for Europe. His wife and children with him.

Chaplin has often been accused of extreme left-wing sympathy.

*September 22, 1952*—Here's the latest in this whirling political storm, a charge that Governor Stevenson "promoted" a private fund to supplement the pay of his own Illinois state employees. That is, a fund similar to the one put up in California for Senator Nixon.

In New York tonight Stevenson admitted that, as Governor of Illinois, he had a fund, and there were contributions from private sources. He says: "I have tried to reduce the financial sacrifices of a number of men whom I induced to leave private employment and work for the state."

Last night, at St. Louis, General Eisenhower put in a telephone call to his running mate in Oregon for the first talk the general has had with Senator Nixon since the disclosure of that eighteen-thousand-dollar fund. Its effect on the young senator was tense. He said he was going immediately to Los Angeles for a nationwide television and radio appearance tomorrow night to explain his financial affairs.

*September 23, 1952*—On radio-television in Los Angeles, Senator Nixon's financial explanation was persuasive, showing a young man in political life, without any resources of wealth, trying to make a go of it, accepting help from people backing his cause. His tone was simple, affecting.

In Cleveland, Ike delayed his own speech until his running mate had had his say. During the Nixon explanation he was in a nearby room, watching and listening at a television set. A dispatch from Los Angeles stated that, while more than fifty million Americans would be listening, Senator Nixon would be really talking to one man—General Dwight Eisenhower.

Meanwhile the audience in Cleveland was waiting; they heard a broadcast of the Nixon address.

After the Nixon explanation was over, General Ike came out for his own speech. He told the crowd: "I have seen many brave men in tough situations but I have never seen any come through in better fashion than Senator Nixon did tonight."

*September 24, 1952*—General Eisenhower announced that he is for Senator Nixon, and that the Republican National Committee is for him. The flood of pro-Nixon telegrams from all over the country shows no sign of abating.

The attack on Nixon may turn out to be a boomerang. A United Press dispatch from Washington states: "For the moment, the Democrats were speechless."

*September 26, 1952*—The Moscow newspaper *Pravda* has published a bitter attack on American Ambassador George Kennan. In Berlin, Kennan said that the Soviet Government was still carrying on its "hate America" campaign. He compared his experience in Moscow with his internment in Nazi Germany during the war.

*September 29, 1952*—The Stevenson accounting of income is just about what you'd expect. The governor is known to be wealthy.

But his accounting of the much debated Illinois "fund" is being criticized. On the list of contributors are donations marked "anonymous." Other donations are by individuals who have been named in scandals in Chicago gambling affairs.

*September 30, 1952*—In the Stevenson camp they are hailing the Truman whistle stop technique—that blasting style. It's a contrast to Stevenson's own style.

The Democratic nominee travels mostly by air, and believes it's the correct way for him, considering the advantages enjoyed by General Ike.

For every voter who would recognize Stevenson on sight, it is reasonable to believe there are thousands who would instantly know the general.

*October 1, 1952*—The Truman whistle stop campaign is really rough. Statements like this one at the Hungry Horse Dam: "I can't think of a worse combination than an uninformed military man fronting for the big lobbies."

General Ike was whistle-stopping in Michigan today, greeted by large enthusiastic crowds at every stop.

*October 2, 1952*—At Wenatchee, Mr. Truman told a crowd of four thousand: "I like Ike so well I'd send him back to the Army if I get the chance—and that's what I am going to do."

*October 3, 1952*—The Russians have expelled our Ambassador to Moscow, George Kennan. The Kremlin has formally demanded Kennan's immediate recall. The reason given is the Ambassador's Berlin statement.

General Eisenhower today, in Wisconsin, shared his train platform with Senator Joe McCarthy. Ike called on voters to support all Republican candidates, including McCarthy. He referred to the differences between him and the senator from Wisconsin, and said these are minor compared to their agreement that Communists must be driven from our government.

*October 8, 1952*—The Korea truce talks may be considered as having ended. Today the Western Allies called an indefinite recess. Announcing they saw no hope of breaking the deadlock over prisoner exchange.

*October 10, 1952*—The decision to withdraw U.S. forces from Korea in 1948 has become a major campaign issue.

President Truman says General Eisenhower, then Chief of Staff, agreed with him at the time. General Ike denies this, and says the decision was made by civilian officials.

*October 14, 1952*—Here is the financial statement from General Ike. The only real point of interest concerns that Eisenhower book, *Crusade in Europe.*

The publishers paid the general $635,000. He sold the book outright, as an amateur author, and his tax came under the heading of capital gains. Amounting to nearly one hundred and fifty-nine thousand dollars.

*October 17, 1952*—One of the most familiar and sinister words in our political vocabulary will be heard no more. The word "Politburo." The Russians, instead of the Politburo, now have a Presidium.

*October 22, 1952*—Iran broke diplomatic relations with Great Britain today—carrying out the threat made by Iranian Premier Mossadegh.

The campaign grows rougher and rougher—President Truman ran into a heckling session today, while Governor Stevenson had an egg thrown at him.

*October 23, 1952*—Governor Stevenson declares that in his testimony at the Hiss trial all he did was report what he had heard from others—namely, that Alger Hiss had a good reputation.

*October 24, 1952*—General Eisenhower will visit Korea if he wins the election. He promised this tonight in his speech in Detroit. He said he would go to Korea in order to examine every possible way of ending the fighting.

Senator Wayne Morse of Oregon has resigned from the Republican party. He says General Eisenhower has allied himself with reactionaries.

Republican political expert John Foster Dulles declares that both he and Stevenson, like many others, were deceived by Hiss. But Dulles then went on to say that he himself refused to testify to the good character of Alger Hiss while Stevenson did so voluntarily.

*October 27, 1952*—General Ike explains his promise to make a trip to Korea if elected. He said it would allow him to "consult with people on the ground." Purpose—to use more South Korean troops to replace Americans.

*October 29, 1952*—Today General Ike stated: "I'm the same man

I was in 1948." Referring to the fact that Harry Truman offered to support him for President in 1948—and a series of top-ranking Democratic leaders urged him to run.

*October 30, 1952*—General Eisenhower today visited New York's garment district, which is traditionally a Democratic stronghold. A crowd estimated at a quarter of a million gathered to hear him blast the Democrats.

Governor Stevenson today resumed his campaign after taking time out to visit that state prison at Menard, Illinois, where rioting convicts have been holding seven guards as hostages. As governor of the state, Stevenson thought it was his duty to visit the scene.

*November 4, 1952*—All afternoon General Ike has been in the lead. But here's how small the figures were: Eisenhower, 11,005; Stevenson, 6,548.

Here's a later total, 26,000 to 18,000—in favor of Eisenhower. The figures are still exceedingly small.

New England always gives us early figures in a presidential election, and the ones today ran strongly for General Eisenhower. He was doing a good deal better than Governor Dewey four years ago. Stevenson—not so well as Truman four years ago.

First returns from Virginia looked favorable for the Republicans.

*November 5, 1952*—Eisenhower has carried thirty-eight states with 431 electoral votes. Stevenson is ahead in ten states, with one hundred electoral votes. The only states that Adlai carried are in the South. So far three lost down in Dixieland: Virginia, Florida, Texas.

The Republicans win control of Congress, and congressional victory is the final measure of the landslide.

General Ike will fly to Korea after a ten-day rest at Augusta, Georgia —where he'll play some golf.

Today at Springfield, Illinois, Adlai Stevenson was the governor again. He took his defeat with smiling acceptance.

*November 6, 1952*—Tennessee for Eisenhower. This means that Ike has broken into the Solid South by taking four states—Virginia, Florida, Texas, and Tennessee.

*November 10, 1952*—Reports grow more insistent that a hydrogen bomb was exploded at Eniwetok atoll.

In South Africa a general strike by native workers adds to the tenseness— following a weekend of savage rioting. The Negro population in outbreaks against the racial policy of the South African Government.

A dispatch from Tel Aviv tells of the last words of Chaim Weizmann,

President of the state of Israel. He was told that General Eisenhower had won. Hearing this, Dr. Chaim Weizmann whispered: "He is a fine man." Then lapsed back into unconsciousness, from which he never emerged again.

*November 14, 1952*—New York's Governor Dewey has conferred with General Eisenhower in Augusta, Georgia. Afterward the general issued a statement that the governor does not want a job in the new Cabinet. He wants to finish out his term as Governor of New York.

In Korea, R.O.K. forces have captured Pin Point Hill once again. The South Koreans had been pushed off the hill during a fierce hand-to-hand battle in the fog. Now, for the fifteenth time, the South Koreans are back on the summit of Pin Point Hill.

*November 17, 1952*—A compromise on Korea was placed before the United Nations today—India offering a plan for an armistice. The significant part of the suggestion is this: prisoners of war who refuse to be repatriated would have their status decided by a conference later on.

*November 18, 1952*—The dramatic meeting occurred today. How did they greet each other, the President and the general, after the slam-bang of electioneering? They smiled as they talked. No sign, anywhere, of any lingering resentment.

Senator Taft says he has made some recommendations for an Eisenhower Cabinet. The general asked him for suggestions.

Today the government opened the biggest anti-trust case in the history of American courts—against the Du Ponts.
The government claims that the Du Pont family and company control both General Motors and U. S. Rubber.

The Eisenhower-Taft meeting today.
Senator Taft calls the discussion "very harmonious."

*November 20, 1952*—John Foster Dulles to be Secretary of State; Charles E. Wilson of General Motors to be Defense Secretary.
John Foster Dulles is an old friend and adviser of Governor Dewey, and in 1948 it was known that if the Republicans won Dewey would appoint him Secretary of State.

Czechoslovakia is having the biggest Communist mass trial since Stalin carried out his purge in the thirties. Rudolf Slansky, who was Secretary-General of the Czech Communist party, accuses himself of being "an enemy of the people," in the pay of "Anglo-American imperialists."

*November 21, 1952*—George Humphrey, Secretary of the Treasury; and Herbert Brownell, Attorney General.

Humphrey is a newcomer to politics. But he is a particular friend of Senator Taft.

Herbert Brownell was one of General Eisenhower's closest advisers on political strategy. Before that, of course, he played a top role in helping Governor Dewey win the nomination in 1948.

*November 24, 1952*—The name of Ezra T. Benson will be unfamiliar to most—but not in Utah. The coming Secretary of Agriculture is one of the twelve apostles of the Church of Latter-Day Saints. He's the first Mormon ever to be named to a presidential Cabinet.

*November 25, 1952*—The A.F. of L. elects a new president—George Meany, secretary-treasurer of the federation. He succeeds William Green, who died last week.

The city of Seoul, battered by war, was a scene of military preparations today—thousands of troops moving in. Joining some six thousand South Korean police in precautions for the visit of President-elect Eisenhower.

*November 26, 1952*—The United States has okayed that India compromise for a truce in Korea. Under the plan the U.N. would have authority for the disposal of prisoners of war who refused to go home to the Reds.

So it's all agreed—on our side! The only trouble being that Vishinsky today rejected the whole thing—for a second time.

*December 1, 1952*—The Cabinet is complete, with two final appointments today. One—a real surprise. Secretary of Labor—a union leader. Martin P. Durkin, president of the plumbers' union of the A.F. of L. He's a registered Democrat, and says he did not support Eisenhower in the November election.

*December 2, 1952*—Senator Taft does not approve of yesterday's nomination—Martin Durkin to be Secretary of Labor. He says the job should not go to a Democratic union leader who supported Stevenson. He calls the selection "incredible."

A New York grand jury accuses the State Department in connection with Reds in the U.N. The statement is that American Reds were cleared for important posts in the U.N.

*December 3, 1952*—The General Assembly of the United Nations this afternoon passed that Indian compromise for a truce in Korea.

Today was hanging day at Prague—capital of Czechoslovakia, a land that once was free. The sentences pronounced at that monstrosity of a trial were executed—eleven one-time big shots of the Reds, headed by former Foreign Minister Clementis and Rudolf Slansky, former Secretary-General of the Czech Communist party, were hanged.

*December 4, 1952*—The new president of the C.I.O. is Walter Reuther! He will continue as leader of his own union, the United Auto Workers.

*December 5, 1952*—General Eisenhower has landed at Guam, homeward bound.

As soon as he was safely away from the war area, the veil of censorship was lifted.

He visited American, British, and South Korean troops, watched our planes as they blasted enemy positions only five miles away. He saw the wounded just back from the front. And he looked over the South Korean trainees preparing to go to the front.

General Eisenhower warns that there is no easy way to victory. He has —here are his own words—"no panaceas, no trick ways of settling any problems."

*December 8, 1952*—In Morocco the seaport of Casablanca was the scene of savagery and insane violence. Mobs of Moroccans went storming through the streets in an orgy of destruction and murder. They killed seven Europeans with revolting barbarity.

The new President of Israel is Itzhak Ben Zvi, a sixty-eight-year-old scholar.

Israel offered its presidency to Professor Einstein, scientist of world-wide renown. But Einstein declined.

*December 16, 1952*—Tito of Yugoslavia denounces the naming of Archbishop Stepinac as a cardinal.

Archbishop Stepinac is, of course, the prelate who served five years in a Communist prison. Released last year—but confined to a Yugoslav village ever since.

*December 22, 1952*—A congressional report on the Katyn forest massacre charges that there was, in this country, a deliberate suppression of evidence that the Soviet Reds were guilty of the atrocity.

That the Roosevelt and Truman administrations deliberately covered up evidence that the Reds perpetrated the mass murder of some fourteen thousand Poles.

# 1953

This year is memorable for the disappearance of one of the most repulsive tyrants of all time—Joseph Stalin. His death touches off a brutal struggle for power inside the Kremlin, and Beria loses out to Malenkov. Beria's execution is followed by a purge of his henchmen throughout the Communist apparatus.

In Korea the exchange of prisoners gets under way, and America is shocked when twenty-three brain-washed G.I.s decide to stay with Communism. In Iran, Mossadegh falls in time for Iran to avoid bankruptcy. Trouble continues in Indochina, in the Suez Canal zone, and in Kenya, where the Mau Maus are becoming a deadly menace. In East Germany there is rioting against Communist control.

At home President Eisenhower signs the tidelands oil bill. The Communist issue is still important, with the Rosenbergs executed, the late Harry Dexter White accused, and Fort Monmouth under investigation. The death of Senator Taft removes the man who for years has been known as "Mr. Republican."

The pleasantest story of the year comes from Britain, where young Queen Elizabeth is solemnly crowned with all the pomp and ceremony of age-old tradition. Across the world Hillary and Tensing reach the top of Mount Everest just in time to present their achievement to the Queen as a coronation gift.

---

January 5, 1953—Winston Churchill and Dwight Eisenhower met today at the apartment of still another old friend, Bernard Baruch, elder statesman.

In the capitals of Western Europe—anti-American demonstrations, charging that the Rosenbergs were falsely convicted, victims of anti-Semitism.

January 7, 1953—The news wires are calling today's Truman message a proclamation of the hydrogen bomb era.

Strongest of all was a passage of warning to Stalin: "You claim belief in Lenin's prophecy—that one stage in the development of Communist society would be a war between your world and ours. But Lenin was a pre-atomic man who viewed society and history with pre-atomic eyes. War has changed its shape and its dimension. It cannot now be a 'stage' in the development of anything save the ruin of your regime and your homeland."

There was a pilgrimage in Brooklyn today. British Prime Minister Winston Churchill went on a visit to the house where his mother was born. She was Jennie Jerome—of an old New York family.

*January 13, 1953*—Tonight's dispatch from Moscow says the Soviet press and radio are going all out in the case of the nine eminent physicians charged with sensational murders. Called agents of U. S. Intelligence and of Jewish nationalism, Zionism. The charges include the murder of Zhdanov, once regarded as a probable successor to Stalin.

The Republican Senate has ousted Wayne Morse of Oregon from the Armed Services Committee—he is the Oregon Republican who bolted the Eisenhower ticket in the election campaign.

*January 15, 1953*—Speaking in a relaxed, homespun way, President Truman spent half an hour reminiscing about the last seven years.
He thinks the decision to intervene in Korea was the most important he ever made.
A fitting valedictory by the man from Independence, who now makes way for the man from Abilene.

*January 20, 1953*—The reaction to the inaugural address seems to be favorable everywhere. In Congress, Democrats join Republicans in applauding.
President Eisenhower made it immensely clear that this country will seek safety through strength—and there will be no appeasement.

*January 21, 1953*—The Senate has okayed the Cabinet. The list, of course, does not include Charles E. Wilson, named Secretary of Defense. His case held up by the fact that he owns that $2,500,000 in General Motors stock. G.M.—which does an enormous business with the Department of Defense.

President Eisenhower is withholding decision in the case of the Rosenbergs. Retiring President Truman left him with the question.

*January 22, 1953*—Charles E. Wilson has agreed to dispose of all his stock in General Motors—all $2,500,000 worth—and at a loss to him of $500,000.

*January 26, 1953*—The Senate has confirmed Charles E. Wilson as Secretary of Defense.

*February 2, 1953*—The repercussions are world-wide following President Eisenhower's declaration on Formosa—the decision to stop shielding Red China from attack by Chiang Kai-shek's forces.

*February 10, 1953*—Today was historic for Western Europe. Just a freight train hauling coke a few miles. But the train started in the German Ruhr and ended in French Lorraine, as if there were no border between France and Germany. This was the practical beginning of the Schuman Plan for a pooling of steel production.

General Naguib declares himself dictator of Egypt. The strong man, who drove ex-King Farouk into exile, taking over absolute authority in the land of the Pyramids.

In Israel suspects are being rounded up following the bombing of the Soviet legation in retaliation for the anti-Semitism which has been growing behind the iron curtain.

*February 11, 1953*—Soviet Russia has broken diplomatic relations with Israel. The Soviets reject Israel's apology for the bombing of the Russian legation in Jerusalem.

President Eisenhower today rejected clemency for the Rosenbergs—stating he does not feel justified in interfering to save the two atomic spies.

*February 20, 1953*—President Eisenhower this afternoon sent Congress the resolution for a repudiation of wartime agreements that have led to the enslavement of free peoples. Which, of course, might apply first of all to that famous Yalta pact negotiated by Roosevelt-Churchill-Stalin.

*February 24, 1953*—In Korea ground fighting has erupted all along the line. The Allies and the Reds striking at one another right across Korea.

President Eisenhower is for a division of the oil on the continental shelf between the national government and the individual states.

*February 25, 1953*—President Eisenhower would be willing to meet Stalin. He says he'll go halfway to confer with anybody *if* it would increase the chance of world peace—and world freedom.

*March 2, 1953*—In Iran, Mossadegh seems to have won out in his contest with the Shah—a contest of raging mobs. Today Mossadegh rioters were out, howling through Teheran.

The Senate has confirmed the appointment of Ambassador to Italy Clare Boothe Luce with a unanimous vote. This action followed renewed assurance that Mrs. Luce, a convert to Catholicism, will not engage in diplomatic relations with the Vatican.

*March 4, 1953*—The latest from Moscow is a radio announcement that Stalin's condition continues to be "serious."

Stalin was stricken in the Kremlin on Sunday night. But this was not made public until two days later—Tuesday night.

*March 5, 1953*—Tonight's Moscow dispatch begins: "Premier Joseph Stalin lay near death tonight after his heart had begun to fail. He grew steadily worse during the day."

There's a supposition that, in Soviet Russia, a triumvirate may be formed. Malenkov, Molotov, and Beria sharing power.

*March 6, 1953*—The Red czar is dead. And Malenkov succeeds Stalin.

The two other members of the triumvirate, Molotov and Beria, are named as Deputy Premiers. At the same time Beria, who heads the Soviet police, also becomes Interior Minister. And Molotov again becomes Foreign Minister.

*March 9, 1953*—Today top leaders of the Soviet Union, headed by Malenkov, were pallbearers as the mortal remains of Stalin were carried to Red Square to be placed beside Lenin in that tomb which is a sort of holy shrine for Communist worship.

*March 16, 1953*—Malenkov repeated today what he had said at Stalin's funeral—that there were no differences between Soviet Russia and the Western powers that could not be settled amicably.

*April 1, 1953*—President Eisenhower has set up a new department of government, to be called the Department of Health, Education and Welfare. The head of the agency, Mrs. Oveta Culp Hobby, will become a member of the Cabinet.

*April 3, 1953*—The nine Moscow doctors go free! They were accused, among other things, of murdering Andrei Zhdanov, a leading member of the Politburo. But now we hear that the whole thing was a matter of fraudulent evidence and false arrest.

*April 7, 1953*—The Panmunjom discussions go on. And so does the war—the Reds attacking all along the line on the ground. The fighting was heavy, but the enemy was beaten off.

In Iran, Mossadegh is moving openly against the supporters of the Shah. His police raiding two political clubs and arresting six monarchists.

*April 8, 1953*—Today a Kenya court sentenced Jomo Kenyatta, leader of the Mau Mau murder ring, known to his followers as "Burning Spear," to ten years in prison.

*April 13, 1953*—While the Korean War goes on and the armistice negotiations continue, the return of the prisoners began today. At camps near the Yalu River six hundred captives, including 120 Americans, started out on a journey to the truce tents at Panmunjom.

*April 15, 1953*—Charles Chaplin is not going to return to the United States. At Geneva today he handed over to U.S. officials his re-entry permit.

*April 16, 1953*—In the South African election the Nationalist party, headed by Premier Daniel Malan, has won a sweeping victory. They, of course, are extreme advocates of racial segregation—white supremacy.

*April 20, 1953*—The second day of prisoner exchange has begun in Korea. The scene at Panmunjom is much the same as yesterday. Liberated captives laughing and joking, some weeping with happiness, others in solemn mood as they pass through "Freedom Gate."

*April 21, 1953*—News dispatches from Panmunjom emphasize the clock-like precision of the exchange of prisoners. They hand over so many, we hand over so many.

*April 24, 1953*—In Korea today returned American prisoners were telling of "Death Valley" in North Korea, where prisoners of war were held in such frightful conditions that they died by the score.

At Panmunjom, scene of the exchange of prisoners, the truce talks have been resumed.

President Eisenhower has ordered new security tests for all government employees. He signed an executive order today abolishing the old loyalty program begun by President Truman in 1947.

*April 30, 1953*—Today in the city of Luxembourg a blast furnace flamed and molten metal poured out. Pig iron was drawn—and that was historic. The first to be produced under the Schuman Plan.

*May 1, 1953*—The Moscow May Day celebration today featured the new Soviet line—conciliation. The address was delivered by Marshal Bulganin, Minister of Defense—who, together with Malenkov, Beria, and Molotov, reviewed the usual May Day parade.

*May 6, 1953*—Today De Gaulle dissolved the R.P.F., his "Rally of the French People." This follows heavy reverses in recent municipal elections.

*May 7, 1953*—London has a report that Stalin's son is in trouble with the new Malenkov regime. General Vassily Stalin demoted, leaving Moscow secretly.

*May 11, 1953*—Prime Minister Winston Churchill wants a meeting of himself and President Eisenhower with Soviet Premier Malenkov.

*May 13, 1953*—The Suez Canal is taking on a warlike aspect again. Today the British garrison of eighty thousand was in readiness for possible violence. The reason—the breakdown of British-Egyptian negotiations.

*May 14, 1953*—President Eisenhower today spoke his mind on the Winston Churchill proposal for a top-level conference. He said he had no objection whatever—if he thought it would be of any real service to world peace. But he wants good faith all around.

*May 15, 1953*—The West German parliament has given final approval to the European army pact—under which the West Germans will recover full sovereignty and contribute half a million soldiers to the international army.

*May 19, 1953*—Freezing temperatures and blinding snowstorms high up on Mount Everest. That's the latest word as this year's British expedition prepares for its final assault on the world's highest mountain.

*May 21, 1953*—An invitation has been sent to Prime Minister Winston Churchill and the Premier of France to meet with President Eisenhower. The invitations were immediately accepted.

The time—next month. The place—Bermuda.

*May 22, 1953*—President Eisenhower signed the tidelands oil bill today. The President declared against any further concession to states interested in oil resources. Under the bill they get the mineral rights as far out as their historic boundaries.

*May 25, 1953*—Soviet Russia rejects the invitations to resume conferences on an Austrian peace treaty. An Austrian treaty has been named by President Eisenhower as one of the evidences of good faith Russia could give in advance of a top-level four-power conference suggested by Prime Minister Winston Churchill.

Once again the Supreme Court rejects an appeal by the convicted atomic spies Julius and Ethel Rosenberg.

Over the weekend there were two attempts to make the final dash to the summit of Mount Everest. Both failed.

The Indian Weather Bureau promises good weather for the next twenty-four hours—giving the British another chance for a coronation exploit.

*May 28, 1953*—News from the British expedition, high up on the slopes of Mount Everest, is that they made another attempt to reach the summit and failed.

In London, Queen Elizabeth has approved of a change in her coronation titles. She'll have the traditional string of them, with something new—"Head of the Commonwealth." The change reflects the political development in the association that once was called the British Empire.

*May 29, 1953*—The Korean war front is aflame tonight—violent battles in two sectors.

The Rosenbergs, in the death house at Sing Sing, have been informed that they may receive clemency if they will tell about Soviet spy rings in this country, with which they were accused of having worked.

*June 1, 1953*—Tonight London was cheering the conquest of Mount Everest.

The final victory over Everest was won by a thirty-four-year-old New Zealand beekeeper—Edmund Hillary. He was accompanied by a fabulous native guide named Tensing.

*June 2, 1953*—In Westminster Abbey a new Queen was crowned today. After the anointing the Queen was handed the symbols of majesty—the spurs, the sword, the royal robes, the orb, the scepter, the rod.

Then the great moment—the crowning. The Archbishop of Canterbury placing the ornate and bejeweled crown of St. Edward upon the head of the Queen.

And so Elizabeth officially became the Queen.

*June 8, 1953*—South Korean opposition to the truce terms was modified today in a statement by Syngman Rhee. The South Koreans refuse to accept the armistice terms, but will confine themselves to verbal protest.

*June 9, 1953*—The French commander in Indochina, General Henri Navarre, arrived in Hanoi today. French observers anticipate a major counterattack against the Reds.

*June 10, 1953*—The Korean Ambassador to Washington has just made the statement that his country will refuse to sign the armistice terms.

*June 15, 1953*—At Panmunjom bulldozers were at work today leveling the ground for additional truce tents. The whole picture giving all the impression that the signing of an armistice is at hand.

*June 17, 1953*—The revolt of East Berlin has been crushed. The violent anti-Communist outbreak put down by Russian troops and tanks after one hundred thousand East Berlin workers went storming in what began to look like a full-scale anti-Communist revolution.

Masses of workers burned Red flags, ripped up pictures of Stalin, and yelled curses at the Soviet puppet government of East Germany.

At last reports the Soviet Army had clamped on martial law.

South Korea has revolted against the truce terms. The rebellion taking the form of a mass release of anti-Communist prisoners from the camps. The U.N. commanders are reported shocked. This could impede the truce negotiations—which are just about concluded.

*June 18, 1953*—Egypt is a republic. The ancient land of the Pharaohs abolishes the monarchy. Strong man General Mohammed Naguib becomes the first President of Egypt.

President Eisenhower today sent a sharply worded protest to Syngman Rhee—rebuking Rhee for ordering South Korean guards to release anti-Communist prisoners of war.

East Berlin was quiet today. The riots were over—which doesn't mean that things go back to normal. The quietude was ominous—a general strike —work stoppage almost complete.

*June 19, 1953*—Julius and Ethel Rosenberg were executed tonight at Sing Sing. The two Communist spies paying the penalty for gathering atomic information to be handed over to the Soviets.

*June 22, 1953*—That armistice is waiting—after having been concluded. The next thing will be our answer to the Red protest against the Syngman Rhee release of prisoners.

Moscow announces the lifting of travel restrictions imposed on foreign diplomats and news correspondents. Still another symptom of the new policy since the death of Stalin.

*June 23, 1953*—The Soviets announce that they will relax the martial law imposed on East Germany.

*June 29, 1953*—In Korea the Allied reply has been handed to the Communist representatives at Panmunjom. U.N. commander General

Mark Clark tells them that there is no chance of recapturing the twenty-seven thousand anti-Communist prisoners of war released by Syngman Rhee.

*June 30, 1953*—East German workers still rampage. Reports of mass arrests continue. The estimate is that fifty thousand have been thrown into Communist prisons.

*July 1, 1953*—At East Berlin today the Red regime announced that food supplies are being rushed in. They are trying to quiet the popular discontent.

*July 3, 1953*—A dispatch from London reveals that Captain Peter Townsend is about to leave his job as equerry to Queen Elizabeth.

The captain's departure is causing much talk in the British capital. For Captain Townsend has been linked romantically with Princess Margaret.

*July 9, 1953*—A world-important headline broke tonight from Soviet Russia. The downfall of Beria—who has been deposed from power and expelled from the Communist party as an enemy of the state. Specifically he is charged with anti-state and anti-Party activities in Berlin—in connection, obviously, with the workers' revolt in the Soviet sector. The Communist party in Moscow says that Beria will be "handed over for examination to the supreme court of the U.S.S.R."

Senator McCarthy denounces the new policy for U. S. Information libraries abroad. The new directive permits the circulation of books by Communists—if they serve "the ends of democracy."

*July 10, 1953*—In the downfall of Beria, Malenkov spoke the formal indictment—charging treason. Malenkov—dooming his partner in the triumvirate that assumed power after the death of Stalin only four months ago.

President Eisenhower tonight made a move to take advantage of the Soviet crisis. He asked Russia to accept fifteen million dollars' worth of American food—to be distributed among the hungry people in East Germany.

The three Democrats have resigned from the subcommittee headed by Senator McCarthy of Wisconsin after the dispute over investigator J. B. Matthews, who made charges of communism against the Protestant clergy.

*July 13, 1953*—The United States told East Germans that food relief will be on its way in spite of the scornful rejection from Soviet Russia and the Communist government of East Germany. The suggestion is that shipments will be sent to the border—where East Germans, in one way or another, will be able to get at them.

*July 14, 1953*—In Korea the fighting grows fiercer all the time. This Red attack the biggest in two years.

The Communist attack is tied in with the truce talks at Panmunjom. The Reds hope to drive Syngman Rhee to accept the truce.

*July 15, 1953*—In Korea a powerful Allied counterattack is stopping the Reds and hurling them back.

The purge is on in a big way behind the iron curtain. News from Moscow tells of three top-ranking officials deposed—in East Germany, in Estonia, and in the Soviet province of Georgia. All followers of Beria, the fallen member of the Kremlin triumvirate.

*July 20, 1953*—Diplomatic relations were patched up today between Soviet Russia and Israel.

*July 22, 1953*—President Eisenhower rejects the Soviet protest against the shipment of American food intended for the East Germans.

The Committee on Un-American Activities today cleared Methodist Bishop G. Bromley Oxnam of all suspicion that he might be a Communist or a sympathizer with communism. The committee vote was unanimous. But some members think he may have aided Communist-front organizations unwittingly.

*July 23, 1953*—The armistice agreement has been completed, the documents forwarded for confirmation to Washington, Peiping, and Pyongyang.

*July 27, 1953*—The truce in Korea has been signed. Along the battle front the shooting continued right down to the deadline.

Today one hundred thousand East Germans flocked into West Berlin to get American food.

*July 28, 1953*—In Korea the picture is one of incessant movement. Thousands of prisoners of war are being transported toward exchange points.

*July 29, 1953*—The food rush in Berlin is becoming a fantastic stampede. The East Germans, with sullen defiance, continue streaming into West Berlin to get those "Eisenhower food packages."

*July 30, 1953*—In East Berlin the Reds are confiscating "Eisenhower food packages" by the thousands.

*July 31, 1953*—Senator Taft died in a New York hospital today, a victim of cancer. The passing of "Mr. Republican" breaks up the famous team of Bob and Jean. Senator and Mrs. Taft were almost always together during his great political campaigns. Mrs. Taft was not with her husband at the end. She is an invalid, confined to a wheel chair, and was in Washington.

*August 3, 1953*—Today the nation said farewell to Senator Taft. The ceremony, in the Capitol, under the stately dome. He had won his fame in that building, the home of Congress—the Senate.

*August 4, 1953*—In Korea, "Operation Big Switch" gets under way. The transfer of prisoners from both sides. Right now American captives are pouring through the exchange points.

*August 5, 1953*—The returning American captives tell of hardships, malnutrition, long illness.

*August 10, 1953*—In Moscow the Supreme Soviet has okayed the downfall of Beria.
Malenkov said the Kremlin intends to improve the lot of the average Russian—give him better food, better clothing, better housing.

In Iran the nationwide voting is almost unanimous—supporting Premier Mossadegh against the Majlis, the Iranian parliament.

The figures from the Canadian election show a landslide for the Liberal party headed by Prime Minister St. Laurent.

*August 12, 1953*—The returning G.I.s continue to tell of Americans who accepted Red propaganda and became informers—tattling on their fellow prisoners. The Reds called them "progressives."

*August 13, 1953*—The entire American Sixth Fleet, based at Naples, has been placed at the disposal of the Greek Government for earthquake relief. The tremors continue, completing the utter devastation of three islands—Cephalonia, Zante, and Ithaca.

*August 17, 1953*—In Teheran today raging mobs were tearing down pictures and statues of the Shah, Riza Pahlevi. The Shah is in Baghdad, having fled from Iran after royalist military forces made a futile attempt to overthrow Premier Mossadegh.

*August 18, 1953*—Mossadegh is preparing to form a regency council to replace the Shah.

*August 19, 1953*—Mossadegh has been overthrown. The army is in control of Iran after a day of savage fighting and bloodshed.

*August 20, 1953*—Mossadegh is now under house arrest—waiting to stand trial as a traitor. The Shah cabled General Zahedi, the leader of the revolt, asking him to spare Mossadegh's life.

Tonight French Morocco has a new Sultan—Sidi Mohammed ben Moulay Arafa. He's a cousin of the man he replaces, Sidi Mohammed ben Youssef, who was deposed by French authorities. The ousted Sultan sympathized with Moroccan nationalists.

*August 25, 1953*—In Iran today the Communist party ordered a revolt against the new regime of the Shah. But Premier Zahedi says the Army has the country under firm control.

*August 26, 1953*—France rejects the right of the U.N. to take up the question of Morocco.

*September 3, 1953*—General Dean has been released. The hero of Taejon among ninety-five more Americans just brought through Panmunjom.

*September 7, 1953*—The landslide victory for Chancellor Adenauer in the West German election is an overwhelming endorsement for West German rearmament within the framework of the European army of NATO.

*September 10, 1953*—The Secretary of Labor resigns from the Cabinet! Union leader Martin Durkin is no longer a member of the Eisenhower team. He gives the reason for his resignation—the Taft-Hartley labor law.

*September 11, 1953*—Following the sudden resignation of Labor Secretary Durkin, union leaders are declaring open war on the Eisenhower administration. Charging domination by big business.

*September 14, 1953*—In West Berlin today the number came to four million. That many "Eisenhower food packages" handed out.

*September 16, 1953*—The police of Western Europe are on the lookout for Mrs. Donald MacLean and her three children. She's the American wife of one of Britain's "missing diplomats."
In Geneva, Switzerland, she told her mother she was going on a trip to a village about forty miles away. She never returned.

*September 21, 1953*—Today's news picture—one surprised American air base in Korea. A North Korean pilot landed in a Soviet-built MIG. He gets the hundred thousand dollars which General Mark Clark offered to the first Red pilot who would bring in a Communist plane.

*September 22, 1953*—The A.F. of L. expels the International Longshoremen. The action coming after many charges of "crime and corruption" in the union.

Twenty-three American prisoners want to stay behind the iron curtain. Prisoners who succumbed to the "brain washing" to which they were subjected in the prison camps.

*September 24, 1953*—Those twenty-three Americans who say they don't want to come home rode into Panmunjom today shouting Red slogans and singing Red songs—such as the "Internationale."

*September 29, 1953*—The Russians have killed all hope for a Big Four meeting on Germany and Austria. The Soviet note calls for a Big Five conference, with Red China participating, and a U.N. seat for Mao Tse-tung.

In the Kansas City kidnaping case six-year-old Bobby Greenlease was enticed away from his private school by a woman posing as his aunt.

*September 30, 1953*—The President announced the appointment of Governor Earl Warren of California as Chief Justice of the United States Supreme Court.

*October 7, 1953*—Detective Lieutenant Louis Shoulders of the St. Louis police force arrested Carl Austin Hall, who had two suitcases stuffed full of money.
He admitted his part in the Greenlease kidnaping, and said the six-year-old boy had been murdered.
He named Mrs. Bonnie Heady as the redheaded woman who enticed Bobby Greenlease from a convent school.

*October 12, 1953*—The FBI announces that the two prisoners in the Greenlease kidnaping have confessed the murder.

*October 14, 1953*—Senator McCarthy of Wisconsin declares there were thefts of military secrets from the army radar center, at Fort Monmouth, New Jersey, and says this may have been connected with the Rosenberg case.

President Eisenhower issued a new loyalty security order today—and it's a tough one. Authorizing government agencies to fire any employee who refuses to answer the $64 question about communism.

*October 15, 1953*—The Nobel Prize for Literature has been awarded to Sir Winston Churchill. Churchill gets the prize for his five-volume memoirs, *The Second World War*. Also for his oratory, those historic public speeches.

*October 20, 1953*—The United States withholds aid to Israel. Secretary Dulles told a news conference that funds may be held up as long as Israel rejects U.N. plans for maintaining peace in the Near East. This was in the Jordan dispute, Syria protesting that Israel was diverting water from the river.

*October 21, 1953*—One turncoat American prisoner of war has decided to come home. A Virginia mountaineer, Private Edward Dickenson of Big Stone Gap, changed his mind, and was handed over to the U.S. authorities.

*October 23, 1953*—In Palestine today the Armistice Commission of the U.N. condemned the Kingdom of Jordan for the blowing up of an Israeli freight train between Haifa and Tel Aviv.

*October 26, 1953*—On the prisoner-of-war front the Neutral Repatriation Commission is passing the deadlock on to the higher command, Communist and Allied. The chairman of the commission, Indian General Thimayya, says there's little chance that the program of "explanations" will ever be resumed. No way to make the 7,800 North Koreans face the Red "explainers."

*October 27, 1953*—The U.N. truce supervisor for Palestine condemns Israel for that raid on the town of Kibya in Jordan.

Today was the deadline for the Korean peace conference. According to the terms of the armistice, the conference was to start ninety days later. Now, because of the dispute about anti-Communist prisoners, the conference must be delayed. A dispatch from Panmunjom states that the delay may be indefinite.

*October 28, 1953*—American aid to Israel has been restored. Following Israel's agreement to suspend work on its Jordan River project, as required by the United Nations.

*October 30, 1953*—There's a new uproar at Panmunjom—with Korean prisoners of war facing the Red "explainers." There was shouting, howling, a raucous disturbance.

The Nobel Peace Prize for 1953 has been awarded to American General George Marshall. Actually, two Nobel Peace Prizes were granted. Last year the award was delayed until this year. The winner for last year—Albert Schweitzer, philosopher, musician, medical missionary, humanitarian.

*November 5, 1953*—The State Department has just announced that it has dismissed 306 American employees on grounds of security.

Senator McCarthy fires a blast at Harvard, saying: "I can't conceive of anyone sending children up there where they would be open to indoctrination by Communist professors."

The senator pointed at Professor Wendell Furry, who last spring refused to answer the $64 question. At that time the university decided to retain Dr. Furry on its teaching staff.

In the "explanation" business at Panmunjom the Indian guards allowed "rest periods" today. This followed complaints from our side that the anti-Communists were being put through mental torture.

*November 6, 1953*—Attorney General Brownell declared that in 1945 the FBI informed President Truman that Assistant Secretary of the Treasury Harry Dexter White was a spy for Soviet Russia. But the following month White was appointed to the International Monetary Fund.

The disclosure was taken to former President Truman, at Kansas City, who stated: "As soon as it was discovered that White was not loyal he was fired."

The White House declares: "Mr. White was not fired. He resigned."

*November 9, 1953*—Attorney General Brownell declares that the Truman administration had "full and adequate notice" that Assistant Secretary of the Treasury Harry Dexter White was a Soviet spy.

Governor Byrnes of South Carolina declares that he, as Secretary of

State, did receive a copy of the FBI report, and that he discussed it with President Truman.

Governor Byrnes says he urged the President to cancel the appointment of White to the Monetary Fund but nothing was done about it.

*November 10, 1953*—A newspaper correspondent asked: "Mr. President, do you feel that former President Truman knowingly appointed a Communist spy to high office?"

President Eisenhower replied—no, it was inconceivable.

Senator McCarthy said the President is just "being a gentleman." Whereupon he proceeded to call ex-President Truman a liar.

*November 12, 1953*—Former President Truman refuses to obey the subpoena from Congress in the Harry Dexter White affair. Mr. Truman thinks that if an ex-President could be compelled to testify, then the President would always have to worry about investigations after he left office.

Today Mr. Truman's former military aide testified before the Senate Internal Security Subcommittee. Harry Vaughan declared that he regularly carried FBI reports to the ex-President, but that he did not remember one on Harry Dexter White.

In the Filipino presidential election, an overwhelming victory for Ramón Magsaysay.

Rioting in Teheran. Touched off by the trial of Mossadegh.

*November 13, 1953*—The Army reports no evidence of espionage at Fort Monmouth, New Jersey. But Army Secretary Robert Stevens adds that, apparently, there were attempts at espionage during what he calls the "Rosenberg days."

*November 16, 1953*—Former President Truman tonight declared Harry Dexter White was assigned to the International Monetary Fund so that a watch might be kept on him.

H.S.T. had to take back what he said before—that he had never heard of the charges against Harry Dexter White.

He also admitted that he made a mistake when he said that Harry Dexter White had been fired when found to be disloyal. He resigned, a year later, for reasons of health.

Same noise at Panmunjom. Anti-Communist prisoners howling and raging at the Red "explainers."

*November 17, 1953*—According to J. Edgar Hoover, the appointment of White to that International Monetary Fund hampered the FBI in an attempt to keep an eye on him!

*November 24, 1953*—The United Nations Security Council expresses what it calls "the strongest censure" of Israel, because of the attack on the Jordan village of Kibya—where more than fifty persons were killed.

*December 4, 1953*—From Bermuda, a communiqué reading as follows: "President Eisenhower, Prime Minister Churchill, and Premier Laniel held their first meeting this afternoon at the Mid-Ocean Club. They embarked on a general review of the world situation which will be continued."

*December 7, 1953*—A dispatch from Tucker's Town, Bermuda, tells how America and France have come to an agreement on Indochina. President Eisenhower and Premier Laniel agreeing that an American military mission should be sent to train army units of Vietnam.

In Indochina, Red "suicide troops" have all but wiped out one loyalist garrison in a human sea attack on Gia Lok, about thirty-seven miles from Hanoi.

In Teheran, anti-government demonstrations following an announcement that Iran and Britain will resume diplomatic relations.

*December 8, 1953*—President Eisenhower proposes an international atomic agency. He made the dramatic suggestion in his address this afternoon before the U.N. General Assembly—an "atoms for peace" plan. This had been okayed.

*December 9, 1953*—The official Moscow radio tonight called the Eisenhower atomic peace plan "a threat to launch an atomic war." The Russian rebuff came as all Western Europe was hailing the Eisenhower declaration.

*December 10, 1953*—Here's a dispatch from Moscow, reading as follows: "Moscow, December 10. Soviet circles received President Eisenhower's atomic pool speech with deep interest—and consider that it requires careful study." This is in contrast to the radio propaganda line taken yesterday.

*December 15, 1953*—America offers to share our secret atomic information with the NATO countries. The offer was made today in Paris by Defense Secretary Wilson.

*December 16, 1953*—The Malenkov regime declared that Beria was a spy and a traitor all during the Soviet regime.

He tried to seize power by putting his own secret police at the top in Russia. He tried to sabotage Soviet agriculture and disrupt the government. He tried to grasp the dictatorship that Stalin had wielded. The Kremlin statement declares that Beria and his accomplices have confessed.

President Eisenhower backs up Secretary of State Dulles' statement in Paris that if that West European Army is not ratified soon the United States may reconsider its entire foreign aid policy.

*December 18, 1953*—Last night Carl Austin Hall and Mrs. Bonnie Heady, his woman accomplice, were executed in the lethal gas chamber for the Greenlease kidnap murder.

*December 21, 1953*—In Teheran a military tribunal sentenced Mossadegh to three years in solitary confinement. The former Premier of Iran found guilty of attempting to overthrow the monarchy.

*December 22, 1953*—Today at Panmunjom an American major spoke to the twenty-two G.I.s who have said they prefer communism. He gave them thirty minutes to choose freedom. Not a single one did so. Instead, the whole group broke into what is described as "a wild Communist demonstration."

*December 23, 1953*—The most significant bit of news about the trial and execution of Beria is in the make-up of the court which condemned the one-time boss of the dread secret police.

This is the first time in Soviet history that military commanders have sat in judgment over fallen top-ranking Red officials, and it's taken to signify that the Army overthrew Beria and his secret police.

Diplomatic relations were re-established formally today between Iran and Great Britain.

*December 31, 1953*—One of the Americans who refused repatriation has changed his mind. Corporal Claude Batchelor of Kermit, Texas, went to an Indian guard today and said he wanted to go home. He was turned over to the Americans.

# 1954

Another television extravaganza for Americans—the army-McCarthy hearings, when we hear about Private Schine and the favors that Roy Cohn tried to get for him. Later come the censure of McCarthy by the Senate and the senator's attack on President Eisenhower for expressing approval of it.

Abroad, West Germany gets the right to rearm. Disputes end in Trieste and the Suez Canal zone. A crypto-Communist regime is overthrown in Guatemala.

Against this is the tragic name of Dienbienphu in Indochina, where the French are overwhelmed by the Reds. In Paris, Mendes-France becomes Premier, and arranges a truce.

Two unusual stories come from Britain. Roger Bannister wins the four-minute mile. And a Roman sanctuary to the sun god Mithras is discovered.

---

*January 1, 1954*—Corporal Claude Batchelor, the G.I. who had refused repatriation and changed his mind suddenly, says he wanted to return to freedom a month ago but was afraid that other American prisoners would kill him.

*January 4, 1954*—Owners of the new Soviet encyclopedia are being urged to snip out the article on Beria. Rewriting history after the fall of a Communist leader.

*January 8, 1954*—President Truman denies that he ever called the Alger Hiss case a "red herring." But let's take a look at a transcript of what was said.

The newsmen asked Mr. Truman—could they quote him directly about the red herring? The unofficial transcript of the White House news conference gives the Truman reply as follows: "Yes, you can quote me. They are using this thing as a red herring to keep from doing what they ought to do!"

*January 19, 1954*—At Panmunjom it's freedom at last for the anti-Communist prisoners of war. Today the Indian command started releasing the Chinese and North Koreans who were captured by the Allies during the Korean War fighting.

The pro-Communist prisoners are still at Panmunjom. The Reds refusing to take them! Insisting they must be kept in detention until a peace conference has been held.

*January 21, 1954*—The Indian command will release the pro-Communist prisoners of war. General Thimayya declares that he will pull his men out of the neutral zone promptly at midnight.

America launches the world's first atomic submarine. At Groton, Connecticut, Mrs. Eisenhower christening the *Nautilus*.

*January 25, 1954*—At the Berlin Conference of Foreign Ministers today Molotov opened at once a proposal for a five-power meeting which would include Red China.

*January 26, 1954*—Secretary of State Dulles today rejected the Molotov-Soviet proposal for a Big Five meeting including Red China.

The Indian guards walked out at Panmunjom after handing over all remaining anti-Communist prisoners to the U.N. The Chinese and North Koreans now agree to accept the pro-Communist prisoners—including the twenty-one Americans.

In Indochina the French command declares that it is bracing to meet an all-out Red attack against the stronghold town of Dienbienphu.

*January 28, 1954*—Observers at the Big Four conference declare that Molotov seems changed—not quite so truculent as he has been in the past.

*February 2, 1954*—Today the Reds in Korea began making use of the twenty-one American soldiers who went over to communism. Three of the renegades—talking on the Communist radio—reeled off a line of Red propaganda.

*February 15, 1954*—A dispatch from Washington tells about General Charles A. Lindbergh. That's right—General! The Lone Eagle was famous for years as Colonel Lindbergh—and now President Eisenhower has named him brigadier general.

*February 17, 1954*—The news from Indochina tells of some of the wildest fighting to date. This is at the strong point of Dienbienphu—

where a French union garrison has been holding out against encircling Reds.

*February 18, 1954*—The Conference of the Foreign Ministers has agreed on a big-time parley concerning Korea and Indochina. Which will begin in Geneva, Switzerland, April 26.

*February 23, 1954*—Senator McCarthy charges that Secretary of the Army Stevens is "grossly misadvised and misinformed." The Army Secretary ordered General Zwicker not to appear before the McCarthy subcommittee again. Stevens calls the McCarthy treatment of General Zwicker "unwarranted abuse."

*February 24, 1954*—A surprise bulletin from Egypt tonight. Naguib is out, his place taken by his Vice-President, Abdel Nasser.

An "understanding" was concluded today between Senator Joe McCarthy and the U. S. Army. McCarthy is free to question high-ranking officers about communism in the Army. This includes General Zwicker. There's to be an army investigation in the case of the honorable discharge given former Major Peress, called a "Fifth Amendment Communist."
Secretary of the Army Stevens will not permit Senator McCarthy to humiliate army personnel. He said this in a formal statement after a two-hour conference at the White House. Secretary Stevens denied that he had "surrendered" to Senator McCarthy.

*February 26, 1954*—Tonight the Army issued a statement explaining the controversial affair of former Major Peress. They either had to court-martial Peress or give him that honorable discharge. They could find no legal grounds for court-martial—and the other alternative had to be followed.

*March 1, 1954*—In the shooting up of Congress this afternoon there were four Puerto Rican fanatics in the plot—three men and a woman. The leader was the woman Mrs. Lolita Lebron of New York City.
In the visitors' gallery they sat quietly until Mrs. Lebron jumped up, waved a Puerto Rican flag, and shouted: "Free Puerto Rico." Then started shooting.
Two of the men with her joined in a fusilade—firing their pistols. Congressman Bentley of Michigan was hit by two bullets. Representative Ben Jensen of Iowa was shot in the back. Five legislators in all were hit in the wild shooting.
This was the doing of the same fanatical outfit that attempted an assassination of President Truman several years ago. The bitter irony is that this country has repeatedly offered the Puerto Ricans full independence.

*March 2, 1954*—Four of the congressmen hit in the shooting yesterday are in good condition. But not so Representative Bentley of Michigan. The doctors give him a fifty-fifty chance.

*March 4, 1954*—Senator McCarthy reiterated that he is not fighting the Administration.

*March 8, 1954*—In Egypt, Naguib is at the top again—back in complete authority. President and Premier of Egypt, and head of the military junta.

*March 9, 1954*—Senator Flanders of Vermont made the first open attack against Joe McCarthy by a fellow Republican during this session.

*March 10, 1954*—Today the President stated that Senator Flanders was, in the President's words, "doing a service."

*March 12, 1954*—The army-McCarthy feud reached a thundering climax today. According to an army statement, Senator McCarthy tried to get an officer's commission for David Schine, an investigator for the McCarthy committee.

The Army refused, and Schine was drafted as a private. Whereupon attempts were made to get favored treatment of various kinds for Schine. There was even a plea to get Schine out of K.P. duty. Which the Army also rejected.

The army report pictures committee counsel Roy Cohn as trying to exert pressure in all this—making promises, making threats. Climaxing with menace—saying he'd "wreck the Army." He'd get Army Secretary Stevens fired!

This afternoon Senator McCarthy, with Roy Cohn sitting beside him, told a news conference that the army charges were "blackmail." He said the army people boasted they were holding Schine as a "hostage."

He says that Secretary of the Army Stevens suggested that the McCarthy subcommittee switch its investigation from the Army to the Air Force, the Navy, and the Defense Department. This is denied in the most positive terms by Army Secretary Stevens.

*March 15, 1954*—The Supreme Court upholds the constitutionality of the tidelands oil law.

Tokyo reports twenty-three Japanese fishermen suffering from atomic burns. They were tuna fishing in the Eniwetok area when they saw a giant atomic explosion in the distance. Later dust began to fall, and covered their clothing. They thought nothing of it until they noticed their skin began to turn black and blister.

Indochina reports the "biggest battle" in the war out there. A horde of Reds besieging the stronghold of Dienbienphu, which they've encircled.

*March 17, 1954*—President Eisenhower was emphatic today in stating that, in the army-McCarthy feud, he believes Army Secretary Stevens.

*March 19, 1954*—America will pay compensation to the Japanese fishermen injured by atomic radiation during our test explosion in the Marshall Islands early this month. So announced in Tokyo by Ambassador John Allison.

*March 31, 1954*—Here's the most astonishing piece of news in a long time. The dispatch: "Russia proposed today that she be admitted to the anti-Communist North Atlantic alliance."

The all-out Communist assault against the fortress of Dienbienphu has been driven back—temporarily at least.

The other day President Eisenhower spoke of Colonel de Castries—in command of the garrison at Dienbienphu. Saying if he had a colonel like De Castries he'd promote him to general right away.
Well, the promotion came today—a radio message flashing to the beleaguered fortress: De Castries—a general.

*April 1, 1954*—The Reds using human sea attacks—attempting to swamp the defenders of Dienbienphu.

President Eisenhower has signed the bill authorizing an air force academy. One hundred and twenty-six million dollars set aside for the "West Point of the Air."

*April 2, 1954*—A desperate crisis has come to the fortress of Dienbienphu, in Indochina. Forty thousand Reds assaulting the fortifications on the third day of an all-out offensive. The latest attack broke through the western side of the defenses and drove within a thousand yards of the heart of the fortress.

*April 5, 1954*—In Paris, Marshal Juin declared himself today. He's resigning as top French officer of the North Atlantic Treaty army, and will join General Charles de Gaulle in campaigning against the whole project of military forces for NATO.

*April 7, 1954*—They've picked a lawyer to direct that army-McCarthy investigation. Ray Jenkins, a Southern Republican. Prominent attorney at Knoxville, Tennessee. Who says he's not prejudiced in any way.

At the beleaguered fortress of Dienbienphu reinforcements were landed from the sky today.

*April 13, 1954*—French planes are fanning out over north Indochina to smash the supply routes leading down from the Chinese border. Returning pilots say that the roads are jammed up with convoys of Molotov trucks. Also coolie and mule trains—all carrying supplies to the Red siege army around Dienbienphu.

President Eisenhower personally ordered atomic secrets to be kept from Dr. Robert Oppenheimer.

*April 15, 1954*—Senator McCarthy and Roy Cohn face twenty-nine accusations by the Army. They run all the way from using abusive language to demanding special passes for Private David Schine when he was at Fort Dix, New Jersey.

*April 19, 1954*—Australia was the scene of a hair-raising real-life thriller today. The heroine—Madame Petrov, wife of the Russian diplomatic official, Vladimir Petrov, who has been granted political asylum. Today she was taken to an airplane at Sydney Airport. Observers say she began to struggle. She was forced into the plane by her companions.

The Australian Government flashed instructions to Darwin, where the plane would make a stop. Officials there ordered to see Madame Petrov and ask her if she really wanted to go home to Russia.

When the plane came down at Darwin, police went aboard. The two Soviet agents tried to resist, but were quickly overpowered.

Madame Petrov said she wanted to stay in Australia with her husband. She now will join him as a political refugee.

*April 20, 1954*—At Dienbienphu, General de Castries has tightened his defense perimeter—all set for the coming human sea attack.

Russia charges the Australian Government with kidnaping Madame Petrov.

*April 21, 1954*—Anti-Soviet demonstrations broke out in Sydney and Melbourne after newsreel pictures were shown of Madame Petrov being manhandled by Soviet agents.

*April 23, 1954*—The news from Indochina is bad. Today hordes of Reds overran a key outpost of Dienbienphu.

Soviet Russia today broke off diplomatic relations with Australia because of that Petrov case.

The McCarthy hearing in Washington is a television extravaganza. Army Secretary Stevens took the stand this morning and told about attempts to get an army commission and preferential treatment for David Schine, former member of the team of Cohn and Schine.

*April 28, 1954*—The independence of Vietnam was formally concluded today with the signing in Paris. The new independent state remains in association within the French union.

At the televised hearing today McCarthy charged that Army Secretary Stevens threatened to retaliate against General Lawton, commander at Fort Monmouth, because the general praised the investigation being made by the McCarthy committee.

*April 30, 1954*—The television audience witnessed an angry exchange between McCarthy and Senator Dworshak—whom the Wisconsin senator had named to take his place on the subcommittee during the hearings. McCarthy today indicating acidly he was sorry to have nominated the gentleman from Idaho.

*May 3, 1954*—The annual Pulitzer prizes were awarded today in New York. The most interesting—the award for biography. Which goes to Charles Lindbergh for his own story of the flight of years ago.

At Dienbienphu after savage fighting the Reds are less than five hundred yards from the command post of General de Castries.

*May 5, 1954*—The President made it clear during his news conference that he will stand with Stevens in the dispute with Senator McCarthy.

*May 6, 1954*—The greatest single exploit in contemporary athletics has been achieved—the four-minute mile! The place—Oxford. Roger Bannister running the mile in three minutes, fifty-nine and one quarter seconds.

The French request for an armistice at Dienbienphu has been rejected by the Communists at Geneva. The suggestion for a temporary cease-fire to permit evacuation of wounded from the fortress.

*May 7, 1954*—The fall of Dienbienphu was announced in the French Chamber of Deputies this morning by Premier Laniel. The Premier's voice shaking as he spoke.

When General de Castries' radiotelephone went dead, it was clear that the enemy had overwhelmed the garrison.

What of De Castries himself? We don't know whether he is a prisoner of the Reds or whether he, too, fell fighting. Also no information about the one woman who was there. Nurse Genevieve, the so-called "angel of Dienbienphu."

*May 10, 1954*—The Reds made it official today that General de Castries is a prisoner of war.

*May 11, 1954*—French officers in Hanoi estimate that the Reds now have a hundred thousand men inside the Red River delta.

At the McCarthy hearing today army counselor John Adams made the most striking and definite accusations thus far. He repeated in positive terms the charge that Roy Cohn threatened to "wreck the Army" and have Army Secretary Stevens ousted from his job if Schine was sent overseas.

*May 13, 1954*—Today President Eisenhower signed the St. Lawrence Seaway bill. The President authorizing this country to co-operate with Canada in cutting a great ship channel in the St. Lawrence River.

In the big television show army counselor Adams denied that he ever suggested that McCarthy should let the Army alone and investigate the Air Force and Navy.

*May 17, 1954*—Today the Supreme Court outlawed racial segregation in schools.
The reaction in the South is immediate—and angry. With new proposals to transform the public schools into a private school system.

The McCarthy hearings have been moving toward a clash between the subcommittee and the White House. President Eisenhower, in a signed letter, forbade further testimony about the meeting, in which White House aides participated, the meeting at which it was decided to bring army charges against McCarthy.

The State Department makes public a report that Soviet armament has been sent to Guatemala, in Central America.

In Indochina wounded prisoners released by the Reds give ugly accounts, now so familiar. After the fall of Dienbienphu they underwent ordeals of neglect, ill-treatment, and a brain washing of Red propaganda.

*May 18, 1954*—Today State Department spokesman Lincoln White told newsmen that the shipment of Communist arms to Guatemala is a threat to the Western Hemisphere.

*May 19, 1954*—The Indochinese Communists announced that they were setting free the "angel of Dienbienphu." But a later dispatch stated that Nurse Genevieve has refused. She won't be liberated. She'll remain behind as long as there are wounded to be evacuated.

*May 20, 1954*—In Dublin they're saying—the end of an epoch. Tonight a nearly final count in the Irish election shows a majority against Prime Minister de Valera.

The news from Indochina has a grim sound. Red columns pouring toward the Red River delta, the "rice bowl," and threatening Hanoi, the capital city of those parts.

*May 24, 1954*—A dispatch from Washington states that we are now flying arms to Honduras and Nicaragua to counteract the Communist weapons recently landed at Guatemala.

The "angel of Dienbienphu" returns. Nurse Genevieve flying into Hanoi along with a planeful of the wounded.

Today we heard more about Private Schine. General Cornelius Ryan, commanding general at Fort Dix, declared that Schine got no preferential treatment—except where committee work was concerned. Otherwise Schine did everything required of him—including guard duty and K.P.

*May 27, 1954*—Roy Cohn was a witness throughout most of the McCarthy proceedings today. He said little that was new. Communist infiltration of the Army, especially at Fort Monmouth, and the efforts of Army Secretary Stevens and his counselor, John Adams, to get the McCarthy hearings called off.

*May 28, 1954*—Today Charlie Chaplin said he is "very pleased." Yesterday he was awarded a Communist "peace prize."

A dispatch from Cairo states that at the Great Pyramid has been discovered a "solar boat of Cheops, the Pyramid builder." His funeral ship.

*June 1, 1954*—The Security Board of the Atomic Energy Commission finds that Dr. Robert Oppenheimer has done nothing that would make him disloyal. But Oppenheimer is not to be reinstated as consultant to the Atomic Energy Commission.

*June 2, 1954*—Soviet Russia has blocked all agreement on the Eisenhower program for a world atomic pool. So stated by the President today.

In Dublin tonight the Government of Ireland is headed by Prime Minister John Costello. Replacing De Valera.

*June 4, 1954*—Monitored phone calls became the storm center at the army-McCarthy hearing today—with dramatic emphasis on those of Senator Symington. Who was shown to have encouraged Stevens to defy McCarthy. Symington telling the Secretary to "forget the Marquis of Queensbury rules" in dealing with the Wisconsin senator.

A treaty was concluded at Athens today. Greece, Turkey, and Yugoslavia in a military alliance.

*June 7, 1954*—McCarthy today repeated his demand that Senator Stuart Symington withdraw from the subcommittee. He called him, Symington, "Sanctimonious Stu."

Senator Symington explained his conversations with Secretary Stevens by saying he was alarmed by the way charges were being made against the Army. Further—that McCarthy at the time knew of his conversations with Stevens.

Wisconsin reports the final failure of the "Joe Must Go" movement. Editor Leroy Gore, of Sauk City, says the petitions he collected for the recall of Senator McCarthy are being taken out of the state. Irregularities charged in the collection of signatures.

*June 9, 1954*—McCarthy objected to the way Welch, lawyer for the Army, was questioning Cohn, and that brought mention of Fred Fisher, a member of Welch's law firm. The senator said that Fisher had been a member of the National Lawyers Guild, which has been cited by the Attorney General as the "legal arm of the Communist party." In an emotional scene Welch accused McCarthy of trying to crucify a young lawyer. He said that Fisher had made "one mistake." In tense feeling Welch said to McCarthy: "Have you no sense of decency left, Senator?"

*June 11, 1954*—There were new dramatics in the hearing when this morning Senator Flanders of Vermont entered the committee room, walked up to Senator McCarthy, and handed him a note. Warning him that Flanders was about to attack McCarthy on the floor of the Senate.

Then the feuding was transferred to the Senate floor, where Flanders of Vermont offered a resolution to strip Senator McCarthy of his committee chairmanship.

*June 14, 1954*—One of the strangest of confessions was made public in Trenton, New Jersey, today. Former Governor Harold Hoffman, in a letter written shortly before his death, disclosing that he had embezzled three hundred thousand dollars from a bank. Never discovered.

Churchill today was made a knight. At Windsor Castle, Queen Elizabeth II invested Sir Winston with the Order of the Garter.

*June 15, 1954*–Secretary of State Dulles at his news conference today said there was a reign of terror in Guatemala.

We would have had the hydrogen bomb at least four years earlier if Dr. Robert Oppenheimer and other scientists had supported the project. So stated by Dr. Edward Teller, the man who is known as the "father of the H-bomb."

*June 17, 1954*–The final day of the Washington circus brought a loud political note. This is a congressional year, and the big TV show was too good an opportunity to miss for making political speeches. The positive results of the hearing in terms of statecraft may be dubious. But it sure was popular entertainment.

*June 18, 1954*–Guatemala is in the throes of revolution and invasion tonight. Anti-Communist Guatemalan exiles are striking from neighboring Central American republics. Striking by land, sea, and air.

*June 21, 1954*–Colonel Carlos Castillo Armas calls on the Guatemalan people to rally against the Communist-infiltrated government.

*June 22, 1954*–On the New York Stock Exchange tobacco stocks fell sharply. The reason—that report read at the convention of the American Medical Association. The one in which Drs. Hammond and Horn state that their research indicates a link between cigarettes and lung cancer and heart disease.

*June 23, 1954*–Today, in Switzerland, French Premier Mendes-France met the Premier of Red China, Chou En-lai. Subject—a settlement in Indochina.

*June 24, 1954*–In Paris today Premier Mendes-France told the National Assembly that Red China has agreed to work toward a quick cease-fire in Indochina.

Well, there's one question we can stop asking—where to locate our "West Point of the Air." Air Force Secretary Harold Talbott announced today that he has selected Colorado Springs, Colorado.

*June 28, 1954*—In Guatemala City the crisis produced a "palace revolution." Army leaders told President Arbenz he must get out. Arbenz quit—and the outlawing of the Communist party came less than twenty-four hours later.

*June 29, 1954*—The fighting in Guatemala has ended. The new government coming to an agreement with rebel leader Colonel Castillo Armas.

The Atomic Energy Commission denies security clearance to Dr. Robert Oppenheimer. The commission voting four to one against reinstating the famous atomic scientist in his job of consultant to the commission.

*July 1, 1954*—In Indochina the Reds take over a thousand square miles and two million people—almost without firing a shot. The French, making their biggest retreat of the war, abandoning the rich rice fields of the south Red River delta.

*July 2, 1954*—There's rejoicing in Britain over the final end of rationing.

*July 5, 1954*—Two thousand Communists arrested in Guatemala. A dispatch from Guatemala City tells of evidence piling up. Showing that the regime of deposed President Arbenz carried out a reign of terror before it collapsed.

*July 7, 1954*—In India, Prime Minister Nehru made a major statement of policy today. He repeated his former declaration of neutralism. India to stand neutral, as between the Communist and the free world.

*July 8, 1954*—The leader of the Guatemalan rebels becomes provisional President. Colonel Castillo Armas elected unanimously by the junta.

*July 20, 1954*—The armistice for Indochina signed at Geneva.
Under the terms Vietnam is divided—roughly along the 17th parallel. This will place twelve million Vietnamese under Communist rule. Elections to be held in all Vietnam by July of 1956.
The states of Laos and Cambodia are included in the cease-fire—remaining, apparently, immune from Communist domination.

*July 22, 1954*—In Paris the French Cabinet voted unanimously in approval of the armistice negotiated by Premier Mendes-France. He was received like a popular hero today.

*July 29, 1954*—In Washington it is being made clear that this country will not back Syngman Rhee in his demand for a renewal of war in Korea.

*July 30, 1954*—The exodus is on. A vast procession moving from the city of Hanoi to the port of Haiphong. Forty thousand people traveling day after day—in buses, in trucks. Vietnamese refugees from communism moving from their homes in the Red River delta as the time approaches for the Reds to take over.

*August 5, 1954*—Here's how the Iranian oil agreement works. The Western combine will operate the Abadan refinery, and will market the oil abroad. Iran will receive more than four hundred million dollars during the first three years. She will pay Anglo-Iranian sixty-four million over a ten-year period.

*August 6, 1954*—The committee to investigate censure charges against Senator McCarthy has elected Senator Watkins of Utah as chairman. The Senate had a debate for days on the censure resolution and then voted a committee hearing.

One of the Dionne quintuplets died today. Emilie—who was known to be in ill-health for some time.

*August 10, 1954*—Secretary of State Dulles told a news conference today that Russia has just about killed President Eisenhower's "atoms for peace" plan.

*August 17, 1954*—A Calvinist bishop from Communist Hungary told the World Council of Churches at Northwestern University that there is religious freedom in Red Hungary.

*August 20, 1954*—Representatives of the Hungarian National Council, an anti-Communist group, today said that all religious freedom in Hungary has been wiped out. They denounced Calvinist Bishop Janos Peter as a Communist agent.

*August 24, 1954*—President Eisenhower signed the Communist Control Act. The new law declares that the Party is not a genuine political organization—but is a conspiracy against the government.

*August 30, 1954*—In Paris today the European defense program went on to a showdown in the French National Assembly—and was killed. France rejects West German rearmament.

*August 31, 1954*—The hearing began in Washington on the proposal to censure McCarthy. The proceedings are being held in the same room where the big television show was staged. Otherwise there was little resemblance between these proceedings and the TV extravaganza. Two reports were presented on McCarthy versus the Army—Republican and Democrat.

The Republican version is that the testimony at the TV circus produced no proof that Senator McCarthy used improper influence in behalf of G. David Schine. But that he did fail to control the actions of his committee staff in pressuring the Army to give Schine special favors.

The Democrats say that Private Schine, as a committee investigator, contributed little that was useful and deserved no special treatment. Their verdict on Roy Cohn is that he "misused and abused the powers of his office."

Both Republicans and Democrats join in blaming Army Secretary Stevens and army counselor Adams—saying they were at fault in not protesting to the committee the minute they felt that improper influence was being brought to bear.

*September 2, 1954*—Senator McCarthy lashing out in protest. He's angry at Senator Watkins, chairman of the committee, because the senator said there was no reason to exclude committee member Senator Johnson, a Democrat, who is quoted as having said that the Democratic senators "loathed" McCarthy.

*September 3, 1954*—The "hero of Dienbienphu" returns to freedom. General de Castries liberated after almost four months in a Red prison camp.

*September 8, 1954*—Senator McCarthy was a witness in his own defense today, and he did not deny what he said to General Zwicker. McCarthy exploded and shouted: "I said he was not fit to wear the uniform of a general. I think he was not. I say it now, I will say it again." He termed General Zwicker arrogant and evasive on the subject of Major Peress.

*September 13, 1954*—General Zwicker testifies that Senator McCarthy had an army report on the Peress case before he questioned Zwicker at the stormy secret hearing. The general also denies that he was "evasive, arrogant, or irritating."

London reports the discovery of a Roman temple. A remarkable example of religious art and architecture back in the days when Britain was a Roman colony. The Roman temple dug up just four blocks away from where St. Paul's Cathedral now stands.

*September 16, 1954*—The Dalai Lama has given his approval to the

Red seizure of Tibet. One of those rubber stamp affairs favored by the Communists.

*September 22, 1954*—In London last night ten thousand people crowded at the scene where they've dug up that Roman temple. Today a queue half a mile long as multitudes came to gaze at the ruins of a shrine of the sun god Mithras.

*September 23, 1954*—The first victim of the hydrogen age died today in a Tokyo hospital. Aikichi Kuboyama, radio operator of the fishing boat *Fortunate Dragon*. The boat that was showered with radioactive ash during the H-bomb test last March.

We have already offered compensation—eighteen million dollars.

*September 27, 1954*—Here's the McCarthy decision. The committee report calls Senator McCarthy's conduct "contemptuous, contumacious and denunciatory." After these large words the verdict is—let him be censured.

*September 30, 1954*—Premier Mendes-France now agrees to West German rearmament. The nine-power conference in London issued a communiqué today. "Agreement was reached in principle on the modifications required in the Brussels Treaty—for the adherence of Italy, and the Federal German Republic." This means that France, after rejecting West German rearmament under E.D.C., agrees to it under the previous Brussels alliance.

The U.S.S. *Nautilus*, first of the world's atomic submarines, is ready for sea trials. The Navy formally accepted the *Nautilus* today, and it now joins the fleet.

*October 1, 1954*—The question of Trieste has been finally settled. The arrangement is for Italy to be given "Zone A," which includes Trieste and its important harbor. Yugoslavia getting "Zone B."

*October 4, 1954*—A new Undersecretary of State was sworn in today. Herbert Hoover, Jr., sworn in as his father, the former President, looked on.

*October 5, 1954*—Italy and Yugoslavia signed the treaty today ending the dispute over Trieste.

*October 7, 1954*—Today Molotov told the Germans that they must choose—choose between rearmament and unification. He was taking a swing at the London agreement to bring West Germany into the European defense alliance.

*October 11, 1954*—The Soviets announce that they are handing Port Arthur over to China. Today a Moscow broadcast emphasized the view that Red China is now a full-fledged partner of Soviet Russia.

*October 12, 1954*—The French National Assembly today voted an okay of the London accord. An overwhelming victory for Premier Mendes-France.

*October 14, 1954*—In Paris today Charlie Chaplin donated the "peace prize" he got from the Reds. He donated the Communist money to a Christian charity. Handing the check to a French priest, Abbé Pierre.

*October 19, 1954*—The dispute over the Suez Canal has been settled. British troops are to be withdrawn from the canal zone to Cyprus. British technicians are to remain. Britain has the right to return to the canal zone in case of war.

*October 26, 1954*—The Atomic Energy Commission announced tonight that Russia has been touching off atomic explosions since September.

*October 27, 1954*—The President today spoke vigorously in defense of the Dixon-Yates power contract. The arrangement for a private company to provide electrical power in the Tennessee Valley. The government atomic plants require so much that more is needed.

The headline marriage of the year came to a final end, with a divorce at Hollywood. Marilyn Monroe telling the court how Joe DiMaggio spurned her charms.

*October 28, 1954*—Ernest Hemingway becomes the fifth American to win the Nobel Prize for Literature. So Hemingway follows Sinclair Lewis, Eugene O'Neill, Pearl Buck, and William Faulkner.

*November 2, 1954*—A battalion of French paratroopers landed in Algeria today. To be followed by two other battalions for the suppression of the new wave of terrorism.

*November 3, 1954*—The congressional election results: the Democrats will control the House. They will probably control the Senate. California and the Republican party have a new major figure. Goodwin Knight, elected governor. New Jersey's controversial Republican, Clifford Case,

wins a seat in the Senate. In New York, Harriman has defeated Senator
Ives for governor. His running mate, F.D.R., Jr., was defeated for attorney
general. The star of Tammany's DeSapio has risen with Harriman.

President Eisenhower admits that he was surprised by Democratic victories in some areas. But he does not regard anything that happened as a
repudiation of his administration.

*November 8, 1954*—The Kansas City Athletics! That's the news in
baseball today. The American League voting to transfer the Philadelphia
Athletics to Kansas City.

*November 9, 1954*—In Indochina a second wave of refugees is streaming toward the sea. Victims of the Red tyranny now trying desperately to
get out of northern Vietnam.

The French have cracked down on the rebel movement in Algeria.
Authorities in Algiers say the roundup of nationalist leaders puts the top
men of the rebellion in jail.

*November 12, 1954*—Governor Allan Shivers of Texas calls for a
change in the leadership of the Democratic party. Declaring that an
"ultra-liberal" faction is trying to make the Democratic party a "labor
party."

*November 15, 1954*—The American delegate to the United Nations
today announced the first step in carrying out President Eisenhower's
"atoms for peace" plan. Cabot Lodge stating that we are ready to set up
atomic reactors throughout the world.

A passenger plane left Los Angeles today, the first of a regular schedule
of flights between Los Angeles and Copenhagen, Denmark, by way of
the North Pole.

*November 18, 1954*—The British House of Commons tonight approved the Paris agreements on German rearmament.

In Cairo, Premier Gamal Abdel Nasser today took over the duties of
President of Egypt. Naguib, who led in the overthrow of King Farouk, is
in eclipse.

Arrests of Roman Catholic priests continue in Argentina.

*November 19, 1954*—In Washington, Premier Mendes-France today
gave a promise of a quick French okay for the Paris accords on German

rearmament. Addressing the National Press Club, he said France will not be talked out of the agreements by any peace palaver from Soviet Russia.

The United States and Canada have agreed on plans for a billion-dollar radar chain across the Canadian Arctic.

*November 22, 1954*—At the United Nations today were glances of surprise. Where was Vishinsky? Shortly after Premier Mendes-France had addressed the General Assembly, the announcement was made. Vishinsky had died suddenly of a heart attack this morning.

*November 23, 1954*—The Chinese Red radio states that prison sentences have been imposed on thirteen American airmen shot down over Chinese territory since the Korean armistice. The charge against them—espionage.

*November 24, 1954*—Today President Eisenhower stated that we are doing everything we can to free those American airmen now in Red Chinese jails.

*November 29, 1954*—Dr. Enrico Fermi—who, more than anyone else, created the atomic bomb—victim of cancer at the age of only fifty-three. He performed the historic experiment which resulted in the A-bomb under the football stand in the stadium at the University of Chicago.

*December 3, 1954*—The first "Fermi Prize" was awarded today. The prize called after Enrico Fermi, who produced the first atomic chain reaction—which led to the atom bomb. The first winner—Enrico Fermi. Award accepted by his widow.

*December 7, 1954*—McCarthy today denounced President Eisenhower for congratulating Senators Flanders and Watkins—the leaders in pushing through the condemnation of McCarthy in the Senate. McCarthy censured.

Churchill says yes, he did want German arms kept ready for use against the Russians during the piecemeal Nazi surrenders of 1945. Meaning that at that time he felt the Germans should be rearmed at once if the Russian advance into Western Europe went too far.

*December 10, 1954*—The U.N. took action this afternoon in the case of the American airmen. Voting a resolution condemning Red China for sentencing the Americans to prison on espionage charges.

*December 14, 1954*—Governor-elect Averell Harriman today named a Secretary of State. The job going to Carmine deSapio, leader of Tammany Hall. Who masterminded the Harriman election campaign.

*December 23, 1954*—The Italian Chamber of Deputies has ratified the Paris accords on the rearmament of West Germany.

*December 30, 1954*—The ratification of rearmament for West Germany has been passed by the French Chamber of Deputies after long debate and hesitation. This means that Chancellor Adenauer's government in West Germany will have the right to raise an army of half a million men to work with the other Allies.

*December 31, 1954*—Three Soviet satellites made a pledge today to strengthen their armed forces and join with Soviet Russia in a common defense against a rearmed Germany. Which is quick reaction by the Communists to the French ratification of the Paris accords yesterday.

# 1955

*Khrushchev and Bulganin take over from Malenkov before the year is five weeks old. The Soviet "new look" startles the world, with apparent amiability replacing the old Stalinist scowl. The new Soviet leaders attract attention—first at the Big Four Geneva meeting, and then when they go to Yugoslavia to apologize to Tito.*

*There is trouble in Goa, Cyprus, North Africa, Indochina. There is a threat of war over the islands in the Formosa Strait. The nations of Asia and Africa meet at Bandung to discuss their problems. In Britain, Churchill retires. In Argentina, Perón falls. Austria becomes free.*

*At home the main concern is for President Eisenhower, who suffers a heart attack that leaves his political future in doubt. The nation is divided by controversy over the Dixon-Yates contract and the publication of the Yalta documents. Ford approves a guaranteed wage for its employees, and starts a trend. The Salk polio vaccine proves effective. President Eisenhower announces that we intend to put a man-made moon into the sky. Albert Einstein dies—the greatest mathematical physicist of his time.*

*January 3, 1955*—Panama tonight is quiet following the race track assassination of President José Remón, a fantastic crime.

The races were over, the track in darkness, the Presidential enclosure brightly lit. Out in the darkness three assassins with Tommy guns. There was a hail of bullets, killing Remón instantly.

*January 6, 1955*—The Secretary-General of the United Nations conferred with the Premier of Red China for more than three hours today in Peiping. Dag Hammarskjold and Chou En-lai considering the case of the American airmen now in Chinese prisons.

*January 13, 1955*—Dag Hammarskjold, the U.N. Secretary-General, landed in New York tonight, back from a mission halfway around the world in behalf of the American airmen jailed in Communist China. "The door has been opened," says he.

*January 27, 1955*—President Eisenhower today gave out a special statement—intended to reassure the Senate. He said that he alone will decide whether or not American forces based on Formosa are used along the China coast.

*February 1, 1955*—The chairman of the Atomic Energy Commission denied today that the dispute over the Dixon-Yates power contract has interfered with the production of atomic weapons.

*February 2, 1955*—Along the China coast indications are that the evacuation of the Tachen Islands is going on. Under American guidance and protection those offshore islands are being abandoned to the Reds.

President Eisenhower today stated he would not cancel the Dixon-Yates power contract.

*February 3, 1955*—The Moscow radio today announced that Soviet Russia has changed its economic policy. Shifting emphasis away from light industry, the manufacture of consumer goods. And going back to the former Stalin policy of concentrating on heavy industry.

*February 8, 1955*—Malenkov out as Premier of Russia. Marshal Bulganin goes in. All happening suddenly.

*February 9, 1955*—That shake-up in Moscow was completed today. A new Minister of Defense was named—chief of the Soviet armed forces. Marshal Zhukov, hero of the war against Nazi Germany. Deposed Premier Malenkov escapes the usual doom of fallen Red leaders. He becomes Minister of Electric Power.

The A.F. of L. and the C.I.O. have agreed to merge.

*February 16, 1955*—Secretary of State John Foster Dulles said tonight that we would intervene if the Chinese Reds should assail the coastal islands of Quemoy and Matsu as part of a campaign against Formosa.

*February 23, 1955*—Army Chief of Staff General Ridgway spoke in opposition to the army man power cuts recommended by the President for economy.

Today President Eisenhower said the income tax cut proposed by the Democrats in Congress is "the height of fiscal irresponsibility."

*February 24, 1955*—Fulgencio Batista inaugurated as President of Cuba again today. The third time the Cuban strong man has become President. Twice before through revolution. This time after an election.

*February 25, 1955*—Generalissimo Chiang Kai-shek has ordered a last-ditch defense of Quemoy and Matsu.

*March 2, 1955*—Rioting in Gaza today. Ten thousand Arab refugees from Palestine demonstrating against the United Nations and against the Egyptian administration. They claim that the refugees are not being protected against "Israeli raids."

*March 3, 1955*—Today returns were pouring in from the new Indian state of Andhra—where they had an election. The Congress party, headed by Prime Minister Nehru, piling up enormous majorities. Which represents a bitter defeat for the Communists.

*March 4, 1955*—Ten nations of the U.N. Security Council tonight denounced Israel for the Gaza battle in which forty-two Egyptians and ten Israelis were killed.

*March 10, 1955*—The world of exploration is the poorer tonight for the loss of one of its distinguished members, the Negro Matt Henson, who was with Peary at the North Pole.

*March 14, 1955*—Wall Street had the worst break of stock prices today since the collapse of 1929. Some blame it on the congressional investigation of the stock market.

*March 15, 1955*—An East German newspaper admits that the workers are protesting against food shortages.

In Casablanca, Morocco, army and police patrols are roaming the native quarter following an outbreak of terrorism.

*March 16, 1955*—The Yalta papers, now made public, will provide no end of discussion for a long time to come. In the matter of Manchuria, legally a part of China, F.D.R. suggested to Stalin that the Soviets might get Dairen under a lease. He added that he had not consulted the Chinese government of Chiang Kai-shek about this.

Stalin wanted the Manchurian railroads, and got them under a lease. F.D.R. said he hadn't consulted with Chiang Kai-shek about that either.

The Soviets, through the harbor and railroad arrangement, got control of Manchuria—which they turned over to the Chinese Reds as a base to build their power.

F.D.R. suggested to Stalin that Nationalist China might be compensated by getting British Hong Kong. F.D.R. made a remark to Stalin that Churchill would probably object. Well, he sure would.

Part of the information is based on memoranda made at Yalta, made by Alger Hiss, who, later on, was sent to prison, convicted of perjury in connection with Communist espionage.

President Eisenhower disagrees with Vice-President Nixon, who said the Republicans can't win in 1956 without an Eisenhower ticket.

*March 18, 1955*—The West German parliament today voted to accept the Paris agreements—which would rearm West Germany and make her a partner with the West.

The Yalta documents show that Ambassador Harriman, now Governor of New York, was against the concessions made to Stalin.

He opposed giving big areas of Poland to the Soviet Union.

He thought we should be very careful in accepting Stalin's promises because those promises could easily be broken.

*March 23, 1955*—General Douglas MacArthur spoke up today on the Yalta Conference. He said that several months before Yalta it was "clearly apparent" that Japan was about to collapse. So therefore it was unnecessary to make concessions to the Soviets to get them into the war in the Pacific.

*March 24, 1955*—Soviet Russia has invited the Chancellor of Austria to visit Moscow for the negotiation of an Austrian peace treaty. An Austrian treaty is one of the things President Eisenhower has named as a sign of Russian good faith.

*March 29, 1955*—Civil war broke out in Saigon, Indochina, today. The troops of a fanatical religious sect attacking army and police headquarters, and bombarding the palace of the Premier with mortar shells.

At last reports Premier Diem had the situation in hand.

The President of Panama has been convicted, implicated in the assassination of his predecessor. José Guizado, found guilty by the National Assembly of conspiring in the machine-gun murder of the President José Remón. He was Vice-President then, and succeeded to the top office. Now sentenced to six years in jail. The actual killer was a ruined gambler who expected financial favors from Guizado as President.

*March 30, 1955*—Aneurin Bevan will not be expelled from the British Labour party. Bevan, the stormy petrel, apologized humbly, protesting it was never his intention to challenge the leadership of Clement Attlee.

*March 31, 1955*–Moscow announces a huge plan to boost Russian agricultural production. Sounds like desperation–a scheme to send thousands of Communist party officials to collective farms.

The tension has eased in Indochina. One of the powerful religious-political sects now switching over to the side of Premier Diem.

"Cao Dai" the cult of the "all-seeing eye" is a strange mixture of Buddhism, Roman Catholicism, and mystical tendencies of one sort or another. Curiously, one of its semi-devine personalities is the French author Victor Hugo.

*April 1, 1955*–The death of Colonel Robert McCormick, of the Chicago *Tribune*, removes one of the most colorful newsmen in the history of American journalism. Colonel McCormick, leader of crusades for Americanism, as he saw it.

*April 5, 1955*–Winston Churchill has resigned. Surely one of the important moments in British history. The announcement reads: "The Right Honourable Sir Winston Churchill had an audience with the Queen this evening–and tendered his resignation as Prime Minister and First Lord of the Treasury–which Her Majesty was graciously pleased to accept."

After tomorrow he'll be just a back-bencher, with the government headed by the new Prime Minister, his long-time colleague and protégé Anthony Eden.

*April 7, 1955*–Back in 1945 General Ike accepted the unconditional surrender of Germany. Today he signed the Paris agreements, providing for the rearming of West Germany.

*April 11, 1955*–An Indian airliner carrying delegates from Red China has disappeared. The plane, American-built, left Hong Kong, bound for Indonesia.

*April 12, 1955*–At the University of Michigan everyone waiting to hear the answer to the question–Has the scourge of polio been conquered? The answer was given in three words of the official report by Dr. Thomas Francis–"The vaccine works."

The hero of the event was sitting on the platform. Dr. Jonas Salk, who discovered the vaccine.

The Peiping radio charges that agents of America and Nationalist China sabotaged the plane that crashed into the South China Sea yesterday with Communist officials aboard.

*April 13, 1955*—In Washington, Mrs. Oveta Culp Hobby, Secretary of Health, Education and Welfare, licensed the manufacture and sale of the new Salk polio vaccine.

*April 15, 1955*—The Soviet-Austrian terms, settled in Moscow, provide for the full independence of Austria, with the removal of all occupation troops.

Austria to have no alliances or military arrangements with other countries.

*April 18, 1955*—The Bandung Conference began today. The meeting of Asian-African countries.

The death of Professor Einstein was unexpected. Einstein, the creator of the theory of relativity, whose mathematics foreshadowed the atomic bomb.

*April 19, 1955*—At Bandung today Chou En-lai took an exceedingly hostile tone toward the United States. Saying that the Chinese Reds offered friendship to every country in the world. Except the U.S.A. Because the Americans were trying to overthrow the Red regime in China.

*April 21, 1955*—At Bandung today Sir John Kotelawala, Prime Minister of Ceylon, delivered a bitter attack on international communism.

He denounced "Soviet colonialism" and cited the cases of the Red satellites in Europe.

Chou En-lai grew angry, got up, and stalked out of the meeting.

*April 22, 1955*—President Eisenhower today presented a citation to Dr. Jonas Salk, creator of the anti-polio vaccine.

*April 25, 1955*—The Bandung Conference of Asian-African countries has ended. The most important result, it would seem, was the proposal made by Chou En-lai—that talks on Formosa be started.

*April 27, 1955*—The government has ordered the withdrawal of all the vaccine manufactured by the Cutter Laboratories of Berkeley, California. Six children stricken with polio after having been inoculated under the vaccine program. In every one of the six cases the drug used was made by the Cutter company.

*April 28, 1955*—The government announces it is setting up a nationwide "intelligence network." To keep a check on polio and the operation of the vaccine.

The city of Saigon, called "the Paris of the Orient," was a scene of flaming devastation today. A new outbreak of war between the government of Premier Diem and the forces of the religious-political sect called Binh Xuyen.

*April 29, 1955*—The government of Premier Diem seems to have won the battle of Saigon.

Word in Washington is that our government will continue to back Premier Diem.

*May 5, 1955*—West Germany became a sovereign, free nation today. Almost ten years to the day since the collapse of Hitler's Germany.

*May 6, 1955*—Dr. Leonard Scheele said the Salk vaccine would provide protection in a high percentage of cases.

The surgeon general repeated that some of those inoculated already may have been infected with polio virus before receiving the shots.

The government has stopped approving newly manufactured vaccine until there has been a review of safety standards.

*May 10, 1955*—The three Western powers have delivered identical notes to the Kremlin calling for a conference of the chiefs of state.

*May 11, 1955*—President Eisenhower today said he thought the Salk anti-polio vaccine may have been issued a little too soon. There had been powerful public pressure for a quick release of the vaccine. So the doctors may have taken a "short cut."

*May 12, 1955*—Singapore—a scene of daylong violence. That crossroads of southern Asia in the grip of a strike directed by a left-wing organization. U. P. correspondent Gene Symonds was fatally injured when rioters dragged him out of a taxicab and beat him savagely.

*May 16, 1955*—Vienna was celebrating today, following yesterday's signing of the treaty that ends the Soviet occupation.

*May 17, 1955*—Tonight French troops are fanning out through the mountains of northeastern Algeria. Their object, to capture the leader of the so-called "army of God," who is directing the terrorist campaign.

*May 18, 1955*—President Eisenhower today commended Mrs. Oveta Culp Hobby, saying that she, as Secretary of Health, Education and Welfare, has done a "magnificent job" in the handling of the polio vaccine program.

May 20, 1955—The Vatican newspaper L'Osservatore romano today issued a blast against the new Argentine legislation which disestablishes the Catholic Church.

May 25, 1955—The government set up a committee of scientists today to pass on each batch of polio vaccine before it is cleared for use. This the latest in a tightening of safety standards.

May 26, 1955—Some thirty million Britons went to the polls today.

Bulganin and Khrushchev, flying into Belgrade, were met at the airport by Marshal Tito.

What about that split between Tito and the Soviets in 1948? Khrushchev had an answer for that one. It was all the fault of Beria. A safe claim—because Beria was executed in 1953.

The Kremlin agrees to a Big Four conference.

The Indian airliner that crashed into the China Sea while enroute to the Bandung Conference was sabotaged. So stated by an official court of inquiry in New Delhi.

May 27, 1955—Today prominent people in the Tito regime expressed annoyance over the Bulganin-Khrushchev call for a restoration of the old ideological tie. They ridiculed the excuse that one man, Beria, had caused the Soviet condemnation of Yugoslavia in 1948.

The British Conservatives won the election, and have a majority in Parliament. The Labourites are blaming Aneurin Bevan, the anti-American insurgent who split the labor ranks.

May 31, 1955—Yugoslavia has agreed to resume friendly relations with the Soviet Union. However, Belgrade repeats that Tito has no intention of being drawn behind the iron curtain.

The Chinese Reds have released four of the U.S. airmen they charged with espionage. The airmen crossed the border a few miles from Hong Kong.

The Supreme Court clarifies its decision outlawing racial segregation in schools. All state and local laws requiring segregation in schools are nullified. But the ruling does not demand universal desegregation immediately. It gives the states the right to handle the problem each according to the local situation.

*June 2, 1955*—In Argentina obligatory religious instruction has been removed from the legal code. This is the latest in Perón's attacks on his ecclesiastical opponents.

*June 3, 1955*—The treaty providing home rule for Tunisia was signed today. According to the treaty, the Tunisians will control their own local affairs—foreign relations and defense to remain in the hands of the French.

*June 6, 1955*—The contract negotiated between the Ford Company and the C.I.O. is the first thing of this kind.

The company will set up a fifty-five-million-dollar trust fund; do this over a three-year period. The money to supplement workers' unemployment compensation during seasonal layoffs. This amounts to a guaranteed "semi-annual wage."

*June 7, 1955*—Parents can have complete confidence in the polio vaccine now being released by the government, declares Surgeon General Leonard Scheele. This is part of the Administration's campaign to restore confidence in the polio vaccine.

*June 8, 1955*—There were cheers in the British House of Commons today as a newly re-elected M.P. was sworn in. Sir Winston Churchill, taking his place as a back-bencher.

*June 13, 1955*—Today Moscow made it official. The Soviets will go into the Big Four "summit" conference at Geneva starting July 18.

The G.M. settlement with the auto workers follows the pattern of the contract signed by the Ford Motor Company last week. Another guaranteed wage.

*June 14, 1955*—Huge anti-church Perón demonstrations in Argentina.

*June 16, 1955*—Rebellion has broken out in Argentina. The revolt was staged by the Argentine Navy and Air Force. Planes bombed Perón's headquarters in Buenos Aires. This coincided with formal action as taken against Perón by the Roman Catholic Church—an ex-communication decree published at Vatican City.

*June 17, 1955*—The revolt against Perón has been suppressed. Buenos Aires is pockmarked by burned out Catholic churches. Seven of them put to the torch—along with the residence of the Cardinal Primate of Argentina.

*June 21, 1955*—On the island of Cyprus, in the eastern Mediterranean, a new wave of terrorism. More anti-British violence by nationalists demanding union with Greece.

*June 22, 1955*—Secretary of the Army Stevens is not forced out of office. Those army-McCarthy hearings created a nationwide sensation when they were televised last summer. But, under heavy fire, Robert Stevens stayed on until today. Now resigning for "personal reasons."

The President of General Motors, Harlow Curtice, announces that G.M. will soon put half a billion dollars into an expansion of the manufacture of automobiles.

Dr. Salk defends his vaccine. The inventor says it is both effective and safe.

*June 27, 1955*—Molotov was in Chicago today. The previously grim Soviet Foreign Minister still carrying on his campaign of trying to win friends and influence people. Refugees from the Baltic states again were booing him. But Molotov kept smiling and waving.

*June 28, 1955*—The Department of Justice has dropped its case against Owen Lattimore. That's the final—following rulings handed down by Judge Luther Youngdahl. Who twice dismissed two key charges against the Johns Hopkins University professor.

*June 29, 1955*—Molotov has left our shores—as genial as when he landed. You'd hardly recognize him as Old Stone-Face of the days of Stalin.

*June 30, 1955*—President Eisenhower tonight ordered a new investigation of the Dixon-Yates contract.

The figures on polio show a decline in this year of wholesale vaccinations.

Tonight Premier Diem is in unchallenged control of southern Vietnam, following the final victory of his troops over the rebels.

*July 6, 1955*—President Eisenhower says he'll cancel the Dixon-Yates power contract if Memphis, Tennessee, builds its own power plant.

*July 7, 1955*—Memphis, Tennessee, gives assurance that the city definitely will build its own power plant as a substitute for the Dixon-Yates proposal.

*July 8, 1955*—The University of Texas will adopt desegregation this fall.

*July 11, 1955*—Today President Eisenhower ordered immediate steps to terminate the Dixon-Yates contract. Mayor Frank Tobey gave the President personal assurance that Memphis will build its own power plant, and the Dixon-Yates contract is no longer necessary.

*July 13, 1955*—Mrs. Oveta Culp Hobby today quit her post as Secretary of Health, Education and Welfare. The President called her "the best man in the Cabinet."

*July 14, 1955*—In Washington today the Peress case came to an end. The Senate investigating subcommittee closed out the affair. Who promoted Peress, called a Fifth Amendment Communist? "Individual errors in judgment," says the report. "Lack of proper co-ordination. Ineffective administrative procedures. Inconsistent approach of existing regulations. And excessive delays."

*July 15, 1955*—There's optimism as the President takes off tonight on his transatlantic flight, bound for Geneva.

*July 18, 1955*—At Geneva today Khrushchev spoke up and stated that Marshal Zhukov had been so eager to renew his wartime acquaintance with General Ike that he passed up his daughter's wedding at Moscow. Tonight the President of the United States is entertaining the entire Soviet delegation at a dinner of state. The forbidding air of the cold war has thawed out until it's melting-warm.

In the land of tall corn there are a dozen Soviet farmers. The leader of the Russian delegation is Vladimir Matskevich. Today in Iowa they looked things over and made copious notes.

*July 19, 1955*—At the Geneva Conference, President Eisenhower argued that the Allies could not leave a vacuum in Germany—where nazism might revive. So NATO was the sensible way of dealing with the problem of German militarism.

The first reaction of the Russian delegation was given by Bulganin. He said that he was not questioning Mr. Eisenhower's word. But Bulganin went on to say that German unification is not proper at this time.

*July 20, 1955*—The Big Four "summit" meeting today, all four leaders said that no progress could be made on European security.

President Eisenhower made it clear that he is not pessimistic. He believes the Russians are as sincere in desiring peace as we are.

The President had a guest for lunch today—his old comrade in arms, Marshal Zhukov.

*July 21, 1955*—At Geneva, President Eisenhower today challenged the Russians to exchange complete military blueprints with the U.S. He called for aerial photography as a precaution against surprise attack by any nation.

*July 22, 1955*—President Eisenhower appears to have thrown the Russians off balance for the second day in a row—with a new plea to the Soviets to tear down their iron curtain against ideas, travel, and peaceful trade.

*July 25, 1955*—In Washington, President Eisenhower met leaders of Congress today, Democrats and Republicans, and gave them a report on the Geneva Conference.

He told them what, in his opinion, was the outstanding feature of that palaver at the "summit." "It is apparently the sincere desire, expressed by the Soviet delegation, to discuss world problems in an atmosphere of friendliness."

*July 27, 1955*—A state of Israel airliner with fifty-seven persons aboard has been shot down by Communist guns in Red Bulgaria.

*July 28, 1955*—Yesterday the House of Representatives defeated the bill presented by the President for multimillion-dollar highway construction. Today the President said he's deeply disappointed.

The Government of Israel has protested bitterly because of the shooting down of that airliner—fifty-eight lives lost. The Bulgarian Reds claim the airliner had violated Bulgarian air space.

*July 29, 1955*—The United States will put a satellite in the sky, an artificial planet that will rotate around this globe of ours. The project begins at once. The first of the man-made moons to be launched as early as next year. Today President Eisenhower signed the order to go ahead.

*August 1, 1955*—The Secretary of the Air Force has resigned. Harold Talbott stepping out after criticism of his connections with a business firm working for the government.

President Eisenhower today led the country in hailing the release of the eleven American flyers who have been imprisoned in Red China since January 1953. Mr. Eisenhower thanked everyone concerned with getting the men released—especially the Secretary-General of the U.N., Dag Hammarskjold.

*August 3, 1955*—Bulgaria promises to pay for the shooting down of the Israeli airliner. Nevertheless, the Bulgarian Reds say the pilot of the big passenger plane ignored signals ordering a landing at a Bulgarian airport.

*August 5, 1955*—Soviet Premier Bulganin states the following on the subject of President Eisenhower's proposal for aerial reconnaissance and photography: "The Soviet Government is studying it with all the attention and seriousness it deserves."

*August 11, 1955*—At the governors' conference in Chicago, Governor Shivers of Texas repeated his defiance. If Adlai Stevenson wins the Democratic presidential nomination, Shivers will bolt the party ticket.

*August 15, 1955*—The "non-violent" invasion of Goa today ended with violence—gunfire, sudden death. Twenty "passive resistance" marchers killed by the Portuguese border police.

*August 16, 1955*—The first order for an atomic reactor ever placed by a private business firm. The Fiat automobile works of Turin, Italy, placing the order with America's Westinghouse.

Tonight India is seething over that question of Goa, the Portuguese colony which the Indians want reunited with their country.

*August 24, 1955*—The federal government launched a mammoth flood-relief program today. To cost one hundred million dollars, or more.

*August 25, 1955*—Members of the American farm delegation, returning home from Russia, say soviet agriculture is twenty-five to one hundred years behind the United States.

*August 26, 1955*—Secretary of State Dulles said that we are ready to help establish permanent boundaries between Israel and the Arab states. We would promise to come to the aid of either side in case of aggression.

*August 31, 1955*—In Washington they wonder—is Perón's offer to resign sincere? Or is it a move to strengthen his power?
Here's the latest: Perón has withdrawn his offer to resign.

In Morocco a new French Resident General has arrived.

The next step is to oust the pro-French Sultan, Sidi ben Moulay Arafa, as a sop to the Moroccan nationalists. That's General la Tour's first assignment.

*September 1, 1955*—Turkey warns Greece to let Cyprus alone. If the British leave, Istanbul will demand that Cyprus revert to Turkey.

Mohammed ben Moulay Arafa still refuses to abdicate. He says he was made Sultan in accordance with the laws of the Koran.

*September 6, 1955*—Israel found guilty! Egypt found guilty!

First, the mixed armistice commission censured Israel for an attack on an Egyptian military post.

Second, the commission condemned Egypt for firing on a routine Israeli patrol.

Those clashes on August 22 set off retaliation by both sides along the Gaza strip.

The State Department says "no deals" were made in the release of nine American civilians. This action by the Chinese Reds is called "encouraging."

In Washington, Republican state chairmen won't even talk about 1956 on any other assumption than that President Eisenhower will run again.

*September 7, 1955*—Istanbul had the most savage riots in recent Turkish history. Anti-Greek riots over Cyprus, which Greece claims. The Turkish Government has apologized to Athens and promises to pay compensation.

*September 8, 1955*—Adenauer arrived in Moscow today. Chancellor Adenauer got the plush treatment—plush double-thick.

*September 13, 1955*—The Moscow palaver has ended in a success. Adenauer and Bulganin signing an agreement. Normal diplomatic relations will be established between West Germany and Soviet Russia. And the Soviets will set free German prisoners.

German reunification? Not mentioned.

*September 15, 1955*—In Washington our officials are also taking a second look at the Adenauer-Bulganin meeting. One thing leaves Washington a little uneasy. Will German reunification become a matter of bargaining between East and West Germany, with the Allies left out?

*September 16, 1955*—At least four provinces are in revolt against Perón. Army garrisons rising in rebellion.

Naval bases have joined the insurrection.

The rebel radio states that naval forces are now streaming to Buenos Aires against Perón.

There are reports in the capital that the army command is demanding the resignation of Perón.

*September 19, 1955*—Perón is out.

The Argentine fleet turned the trick. Sending an ultimatum that Buenos Aires would be bombarded unless the Perón regime yielded.

The Perón army forces far and wide were either defeated or went over to the anti-Perón insurgents.

Perón's generals have taken over, and are negotiating with the insurgents.

MacLean and Burgess had been Soviet spies all along. But that was kept a secret until forced into the open by the Petrov case, in Australia. Where Petrov, a Soviet Intelligence official, went over to the side of freedom.

The two diplomats were being investigated for espionage when they disappeared so mysteriously four years ago.

MacLean had access to top-secret American atomic information, and all the while was an espionage agent of Soviet Russia.

A twenty-year mutual aid pact between the Soviets and Finland. One clause—the return of the Porkkala military base on the Finnish coast. Which was taken by the Reds at the close of the Russo-Finnish War.

*September 20, 1955*—Perón is aboard a Paraguayan gunboat, which gives him the same protection as though he had taken refuge in a foreign embassy.

*September 21, 1955*—The Argentine civil war ended today with the unconditional surrender of Perón's generals. There's a new provisional government headed by General Eduardo Lonardi.

*September 23, 1955*—The Bulganin letter to President Eisenhower was made public tonight. Bulganin says that "in principle" he has no objection to President Eisenhower's plan for an exchange of military "blueprints." But he repeats the same old Moscow contention that nuclear weapons should be outlawed. On which subject we have always insisted that there must be all-out inspection for thorough safeguards.

Israel reports an oil strike in the Negeb, the burning, barren land in the south, next door to Egypt. Geologists have long suspected there might be oil in the Negeb.

We have British reaction to the latest revolution. Commercial TV, American style, which began last night. The response is favorable.

*September 26, 1955*—President Eisenhower was stricken with a heart attack over the weekend. In a Denver hospital he is in an oxygen tent, but they say he is recovering without complications. Will this take him out of the presidential campaign next year?

The doctor stated that, unless there are unexpected complications, there is no physical reason why President Eisenhower cannot run for a second term. But he wouldn't say it would be advisable.

Vice-President Nixon is assuming the role of acting president, carrying out routine duties.

*September 27, 1955*—The latest bulletin from Denver tells us that today the progress of the President was satisfactory.

Perón is still aboard that Paraguayan gunboat in Buenos Aires Harbor, waiting for a safe conduct from the new government.

*September 28, 1955*—President Eisenhower is out of the oxygen tent in the daytime.

Another sign that the patient is coming along fine.

A top official of the Cairo Ministry of War is leaving for Red Czechoslovakia, in connection with a deal for armament. The Czechoslovakian Communists have agreed to ship military supplies to Egypt in return for agricultural products.

French Premier Edgar Faure is facing a political crisis because of the compromise he proposed for peace in Morocco, which includes the removal of the Sultan.

14858

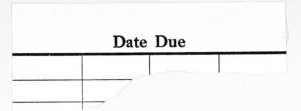

## Date Due